LAW AND AUTHORITY IN THE EARLY MIDDLE AGES

The barbarian law codes, compiled between the sixth and eighth centuries, were copied remarkably frequently in the Carolingian ninth century. They provide crucial evidence for early medieval society, including the settlement of disputes, the nature of political authority, literacy, and the construction of ethnic identities. Yet it has proved extremely difficult to establish why the codes were copied in the ninth century, how they were read, and how their rich evidence should be used. Thomas Faulkner tackles these questions more systematically than ever before, proposing new understandings of the relationship between the making of law and royal power, and the reading of law and the maintenance of ethnic identities. Faulkner suggests major reinterpretations of central texts, including the Carolingian law codes, the capitularies adding to the laws, and Carolingian revisions of earlier barbarian and Roman laws. He also provides detailed analysis of legal manuscripts, especially those associated with the *leges*-scriptorium.

THOMAS FAULKNER was awarded his PhD from the University of Cambridge in 2010. Since then he has continued his research independently alongside a career as an opera singer, principally in the UK and Germany. He has lectured on late antique and early medieval law, and published his first article, 'The Carolingian kings and the *leges barbarorum*' in 2013. Forthcoming publications include an edition of ordeal manuals found in Anglo-Saxon manuscripts for the Early English Laws project, and contributions to the *Oxford Dictionary of Late Antiquity* on legal texts, practices, and concepts.

The series *Cambridge Studies in Medieval Life and Thought* was inaugurated by G.G. Coulton in 1921; Professor Rosamond McKitterick now acts as General Editor of the Fourth Series, with Professor Christine Carpenter, Dr Magnus Ryan and Dr Len Scales as Advisory Editors. The series brings together outstanding work by medieval scholars over a wide range of human endeavour extending from political economy to the history of ideas.

This is book 104 in the series, and a full list of titles in the series can be found at:
www.cambridge.org/medievallifeandthought

LAW AND AUTHORITY IN THE EARLY MIDDLE AGES

The Frankish Leges in the Carolingian Period

THOMAS FAULKNER

CAMBRIDGE
UNIVERSITY PRESS

CAMBRIDGE
UNIVERSITY PRESS

University Printing House, Cambridge CB2 8BS, United Kingdom

Cambridge University Press is part of the University of Cambridge.

It furthers the University's mission by disseminating knowledge in the pursuit of education, learning and research at the highest international levels of excellence.

www.cambridge.org
Information on this title: www.cambridge.org/9781107084919

First published 2016

Printed in the United States of America by Sheridan Books, Inc.

A catalogue record for this publication is available from the British Library

Library of Congress Cataloguing in Publication data
Names: Faulkner, Thomas, 1983– author.
Title: Law and authority in the early middle ages : the Frankish leges in the Carolingian period / Thomas Faulkner.
Description: Cambridge, United Kingdom : Cambridge University Press, 2016. |
Series: Cambridge studies in medieval life and thought : fourth series |
Includes bibliographical references and index.
Identifiers: LCCN 2015040824| ISBN 9781107084919 (hardback) |
ISBN 9781107446892 (paperback)
Subjects: LCSH: Law, Frankish. | Carolingians.
Classification: LCC KJ320.F38 2016 | DDC 340.5/5–dc23
LC record available at http://lccn.loc.gov/2015040824

ISBN 978-1-107-08491-9 Hardback
ISBN 978-1-107-44689-2 Paperback

CONTENTS

List of illustrations — *page* ix
List of tables — x
Abbreviations — xii

INTRODUCTION — 1

1 THE MINOR *leges* PART 1. PROBLEMS, BACKGROUND, *Lex Ribuaria, Ewa ad Amorem* — 9
1.1 Introduction — 9
1.2 The Frankish background. History and ethnicity in the *Lex Salica* and *Lex Ribuaria* — 13
1.2.1 *Lex Salica* — 13
1.2.2 Ribuarian *Lex* and the Ribuarians in the Carolingian period — 16
1.2.3 Merovingian Ribuarians — 20
1.2.4 Summary — 22
1.3 The minor *leges* — 23
1.3.1 Einhard, the Lorsch annals, the link with Charlemagne — 24
1.3.2 General observations on the group: the use of earlier *leges* in their construction — 26
1.4 *Ewa ad Amorem* — 29
1.4.1 Dating and location — 29
1.4.2 Nature of the text. Themes — 31
1.4.3 The context for redaction. The charters — 36
1.5 Summary — 45

2 THE MINOR *leges* 2. SAXONY AND THE *Lex Saxonum* — 46
2.1 Introduction — 46
2.2 Law in Saxony in ninth-century descriptive sources — 47
2.2.1 Narrative accounts of the Stellinga rebellion — 47

2.2.2 Hagiography 52
2.2.3 Summary 62
2.3 Saxon law in practice: records of disputes 63
2.3.1 Charters 63
2.3.2 Gottschalk of Orbais 64
2.3.3 Marriage and The Council of Tribur 66
2.4 The legal texts 68
2.4.1 Fragments relating to Saxons in the capitularies 69
2.4.2 The *Lex Saxonum* 70
2.5 Summary 82

3 THE ADDITIONAL CAPITULARIES 84
3.1 Introduction, political theory 84
3.1.1 Political theory, mirrors of princes 89
3.1.2 Summary 96
3.2 Preliminaries to the additional capitularies 97
3.2.1 Historiography, classification 97
3.2.2 The texts 99
3.2.3 Catalogue of references in Frankish sources to capitularies adding to *leges*, with a brief commentary 100
3.3 The texts in detail. Construction and contents 105
3.3.1 No. 39 *Capitulare Legibus additum* 802 106
3.3.2 No. 139 *Capitula Legibus Addenda* 818–19 115
3.3.3 No. 68 *Capitula ad Legem Baiuwariorum Addita* 801–13 118
3.3.4 Summary 120
3.3.5 No. 41 *Capitulare Legi Ribuariae Additum* 803 121
3.3.6 No. 142 *Capitula Legi Salicae Addita* 819– 127
3.3.7 Nos. 134 and 135. *Capitula Legi Addita* 816. Drafts 133
3.3.8 Mordek's *Capitula Adhuc Conferenda* 134
3.3.9 Conclusion from the texts in detail 135
3.4 The manuscripts of the group 136
3.4.1 Patterns from a mass analysis 136
3.4.2 Particular groups of manuscripts 148
3.4.3 Summary: the contribution of the survey of manuscripts 152
3.5 Summary 152

4 THE READING OF NORMATIVE TEXTS: BENEDICTUS LEVITA AND REGINO 155
4.1 Clerical compensations 155

4.1.1 Texts and problems 155
4.1.2 Homicide of clerics in descriptive sources 159
4.1.3 Anxiety over status at low social levels 159
4.1.4 Ebbo and anxiety over status at high social levels 161
4.1.5 Benedictus Levita 163
4.1.6 Summary 168
4.2 Manumission *formulae* and *Regino of Prüm's Libri Duo* 168
4.2.1 Preliminaries 168
4.2.2 Regino 169
4.2.3 Distinctive terminology, and comparisons with other manumission *formulae* 180
4.2.4 The background of practice 186
4.3 Summary 192

5 THE MANUSCRIPTS OF THE *leges*-SCRIPTORIUM 193
5.1 Preliminaries 193
5.1.1 The importance of the material 193
5.1.2 The *leges*-scriptorium manuscripts considered 194
5.1.3 Other relevant manuscripts associated with Tours 198
5.1.4 Other legal manuscripts associated with the court 199
5.1.5 Script, physical appearance, the court link 199
5.2 The texts, their sources, and their influence. 1. The capitularies and barbarian *leges* in *leges*-scriptorium manuscripts 203
5.2.1 Capitularies 204
5.2.2 *Lex Visigothorum* and *Lex Burgundionum* 209
5.2.3 *Lex Ribuaria* 210
5.2.4 *Lex Salica* 212
5.2.5 Summary, and alternative channels of dissemination of the *Lex Ribuaria* and *Lex Salica* 216
5.2.6 *Lex Alemannorum* 217
5.2.7 *Lex Baiuwariorum* 218
5.2.8 Summary of connections between texts of *Leges Alemannorum* and *Baiuwarorium* 221
5.3 The texts, their sources, and their influence. 2. Roman law, *formulae, interpretative aids* 222
5.3.1 Roman law 222
5.3.2 *Formulae* 227
5.3.3 The legal compilations extracted from Isidore's *Etymologiae* 228
5.3.4 King lists 231
5.3.5 Summary of links 231

5.4 Sources of texts. Legal activity at Tours. The Warsaw manuscript, the *Formulae Turonenses*, and the *Epitome Aegidii* 231
5.4.1 The use of a 'W-B' Breviary manuscript in the *Epitome Aegidii* 231
5.4.2 The use of the *LRV* law in the *Formulae Turonenses* 233
5.4.3 The use of the *Epitome Aegidii* in the *Formulae Turonenses* 234
5.4.4 A fragment of *Formulae Turonenses* in Vat. Reg. Lat. 857 243
5.4.5 Contexts 243
5.5 Summary 246

CONCLUSION 248

Editions 253
Bibliography 269
General index 293
Index of legal texts 296
Index of manuscripts 298

ILLUSTRATIONS

3.1 Proposed relationship between the groups of manuscripts of Capitulary 39 *page* 113
3.2 Proposed stemma for Capitulary 142 132
3.3 Stemma of Ansegis text in Rheims group manuscripts 151
5.1 Stemma of Capitulary 143 205
5.2 Stemmata of Capitularies nos. 139 (left) and 140 (right) 206
5.3 Simplified stemma for *Lex Alemannorum* 218
5.4 Stemma of Novels of Majorian 227
5.5 Proposed relationship between the *Formulae Turonenses* and various texts of Roman law 235

TABLES

1.1 Chronological distribution of manuscripts of *leges Salica, Ribuaria, Baiuwarorium*, and *Alemannorum* *page* 17
1.2 Parallels between *Leges Ribuaria, Saxonum, and Thuringorum* 27
1.3 Parallels between *Ewa ad Amorem and Lex Baiuwariorum* 27
3.1 Information in titles to Capitulary no. 39 108
3.2 Manuscripts of Capitulary no. 39 before the twelfth century. Based on Mordek, *Bibliotheca* 110
3.3 Manuscripts of *Leges Salica, Baiuariorum*, and *Ribuaria*, with and without additional capitularies 126
3.4 Titles to Capitulary no. 41 in its manuscripts 126
3.5 Legal manuscripts by content and date, according to Wormald 138
3.6 Legal manuscripts by content and date, according to my new count 138
3.7 Changes in content of legal manuscripts over time, according to Wormald 138
3.8 Changes in content of legal manuscripts over time, according to my new count 138
3.9 Manuscripts of capitularies also containing *leges*, according to Wormald 139
3.10 Manuscripts of capitularies also containing *leges*, according to my new count 139
3.11 Manuscripts of additional capitularies and *leges* as a group 140
3.12 Manuscripts of each additional capitulary and particular *leges* 141
3.13 Transmission of popular capitularies 141
3.14 The manuscripts of the additional capitularies 143
3.15 Transmission of additional capitularies with each other 147
4.1 Summary (and simplification) of penalties for homicide of clerics in various legal texts 166

4.2 Sources and cross-references in Regino of Prüm's *Libri Duo* I, 400–19 177
4.3 Carolingian royal manumission charters 189
5.1 The manuscripts of the *leges*-scriptorium 1: the texts 195
5.2 The MS of the *leges*-scriptorium 2: more details 196
5.3 The manuscripts containing capitularies found in *leges*-scriptorium products 207
5.4 Comparison of Manuscripts BN Lat. 4632 and 4628 212
5.5 The quotations from Roman law in the *Formulae Turonenses* 1: text as it appears in the *Formulae* 236
5.6 The quotations from Roman law in the *Formulae Turonenses* 2: possible sources of each quotation and notes 237
5.7 Text of the unedited *formula* in Vat. Reg. Lat. 857, compared with its closest parallels in edited texts 239
5.8 Paul V, 39 in various compilations of Roman law 242

ABBREVIATIONS

Annales Bertiniani	*Annales Bertiniani* ed. G. Waitz (Hannover, 1883), MGH SRG V
Ansegis, Ans	*Der Kapitulariensammlung des Ansegis* ed. G. Schmitz (Hannover, 1996), MGH Capitularia regum Francorum, Nova series
Annales Xantenses	*Annales Xantenses* ed. B. von Simson (Hannover, 1909), MGH SRG XII
ARF	*Annales Regni Francorum* ed. F. Kurze (Hannover, 1895), MGH SRG VI
Ben Lev	Benedictus Levita's collection
BN Lat.	Blibliothèque Nationale de France, Paris, manuscrit Latin
Capit.	Capitulary
Capit.	*Capitularia Regum Francorum* ed. A. Boretius and V. Krause (Hannover, 1883–97), MGH Legum sectio II, 1–2
Chronicon	Freculf of Lisieux, *Historiarum Libri XII* ed. M. Allen (Turnhout, 2002), Frechulfi Lexoviensis episcopi opera omnia. Corpus Christianorum. Series Latina CLXIXA, pp. 9–724
Codex Laureshamenses	*Codex Laureshamensis* ed. K. Glöckner (Darmstadt, 1974)
CodTh	*Theodosiani libri XVI cum Constitutionibus Sirmondianis: et leges novellae ad Theodosianum pertinentes* ed. T. Mommsen and P. Meyer (Berlin, 1905)
Conc.	Concilia, Legum Sectio III

DA	*Deutsches Archiv für Erforschung des Mittelalters*
Diplomata Belgica	*Diplomata Belgica ante annum millesimum centesimum scripta* ed. M. Gysseling and A. C. F. Koch, Volume 1, (Brussels, 1950)
EHR	*English Historical Review*
EME	*Early Medieval Europe*
Epp.	Epistolae merowingici et karolini aevi (Hannover, 1892–1939)
Epit. Aegid., *EpA*	*Epitome Aegidii*, also edited in *Brevarium Alarici* ed. G. F. Haenel (Leipzig, 1848)
Form.	*Formulae Merowingici et Karolini Aevi* ed. K. Zeumer (Hannover, 1886), MGH Legum sectio V
Isid.	Extracts from Isidore of Seville's *Etymologiae* concerning law, edited in J. Tardif, 'Un abrégé juridique des Étymologies d'Isidore de Séville' in: *Mélanges Julien Havet. Receuil de travaux d'érudition dédiés à la mémoire de Julien Havet (1853–1983)* (Paris, 1895), pp. 673–81
Lex Alemannorum, *Al*	*Leges Alamannorum* ed. K. Lehmann 2nd edition (Hannover, 1966), MGH Leges nationum Germanicarum V, 1
Lex Bav, *Bav*	*Lex Baiuvariorum* ed. E. de Schwind (Hannover, 1926), MGH Leges nationum Germanicarum V, 2
Lex Burgundionum, *Burg*	*Liber Constitutionum*, in *Leges Burgundionum* ed. L. R. de Salis (Hannover, 1892), MGH Leges nationum Germanicarum II, 1
Lex Ribuaria, *Rib*	*Lex Ribuaria* ed. F. Beyerle and R. Buchner (Hannover, 1951), MGH Leges nationum Germanicarum III, 2
Lex Romana Burgundionum, *Rom. Burg.*	*Lex Romana Burgundionum* in *Leges Burgundionum* ed. L. R. de Salis (Hannover, 1892), MGH Leges nationum Germanicarum II, 1
Lex Salica, *Sal*	*Pactus Legis Salicae, Lex Salica* ed. K. A. Eckhardt (Hannover, 1962–9), MGH Leges nationum Germanicarum IV, 1–2

Libri Duo	Regino of Prüm, *Libri duo de synodalibus causis et disciplinis ecclesiasticis.* ed. F. Wasserschleben (Leipzig, 1840)
LRV	*Brevarium Alarici* ed. G. F. Haenel (Leipzig, 1848)
MGH	Monumenta Germaniae Historica
Oorkonden Werden	*De oudste partikuliere Oorkonden van het Klooster Werden* ed. D. P. Blok (Assen, 1960)
PL	*Patrologia cursus completus series Latina* ed. J.-P. Migne (Paris, 1841–64)
Prol.	Prologue
Settimane	Settimane di studio del Centro Italiano di Studi sull'Alto Medioevo
SRG	Scriptores rerum Germanicarum in usum scholarum separatim editi
SRM	Scriptores rerum Merovingicarum ed. B. Krusch and W. Levison
SS	Scriptores in folio
Thegan	Thegan, *Gesta Hludowici, Thegan: Die Taten Kaiser Ludwigs. Astronomus: das Leben Kaiser Ludwigs* ed. E. Tremp (Hannover, 1995), MGH SRG 64, pp. 167–279
TRHS	*Transactions of the Royal Historical Society*
Urbare Werden	*Die Urbare der Abtei Werden an der Ruhr* ed. R. Kötzschke (Bonn, 1906)
UrkLD	*Die Urkunden Ludwigs des Deutschen, Karlmanns und Ludwigs des Jüngeren* ed. P. Kehr (Berlin, 1934), MGH Diplomatum Karolinorum I
Urkundenbuch Niederrhein	*Urkundenbuch für die Geschichte des Niederrheins* ed. T. J. Lacomblet Volume 1, (Düsseldorf, 1840)
Vat. Reg. Lat.	Biblioteca Apostolica Vaticana, Codex Reginensis Latinus
ZRG GA	*Zeitschrift der Savigny-Stiftung für Rechtsgeschichte, Germanistische Abteilung*

INTRODUCTION

The *leges barbarorum* are among the richest of all sources for early medieval history. They potentially tell us about how disputes were settled, the forms of political authority, the extent and nature of literacy, the construction of ethnic communities and self-perception, economic and social organisation, the relationship between spoken and written language, and religious practice; in short, almost every subject of interest to historians. But tapping any of this potential has always proved very difficult indeed.

The texts were problematic first of all for generations of German scholars, from the very beginnings of professional history, often referred to as members of the *Historische Rechtsschule*. The approach underlying this German work was that, if the basic history of the composition of the laws could be established, and if an accurate *Urtext* of each could be produced, then the evolution of Germanic law could be traced, common principles deduced, and their rich evidence on social and political structures deployed in their proper context.[1] The historians therefore concentrated on establishing where and when the *leges* were produced, using which sources, whether they came together in layers over centuries, or were codified all at once, and so on. They then tried to deduce elements of a system from the diverse codes, and to place each one of them on a family tree of Germanic law, in much the same way as contemporary scholars of linguistics approached Germanic and other Indo-European languages.[2] But the raw difficulty of the texts and their manuscript traditions meant that the levels of consensus ever achieved on the very basics of the history of the texts were various.

1 The classic synthesis, still a useful reference work, is H. Brunner, *Deutsche Rechtsgeschichte* 2nd edition. (Leipzig, 1906). More specific examples of textual work are provided throughout this book.

2 Brunner (1906), *Deutsche Rechtsgeschichte*, pp. 1f.: 'Allerdings lässt sich ein mutmaßlicher Stammbaum der verschiedenen germanischen Rechte aufstellen, der auf ein germanisches Urrecht zurückführt.'

Since the later twentieth century, problems with the *leges* have been revealed also on a rather different level: the nature of the prescriptive legal texts' relationship with practice. It has been stressed that, even if one can date and locate them, one cannot read prescriptive texts at face value, as straightforward guides to practice in courts, or as direct evidence for social structure. This is true throughout the early middle ages, but especially so in the Carolingian period, in which texts of *lex* centuries old continued to be copied.

A new approach to studying disputing and law, pioneered in the *Settlement of Disputes* volume from 1986, turned away from the *leges* and other prescriptive sources altogether, and attempted to establish the 'norms' at play in disputing from the descriptive sources, mostly charters of various forms, as well as narratives.[3] This approach has been enormously influential in subsequent studies of disputing, and legal business.[4] One consequence has been the marginalisation of the complex system of the German school and the questioning of some of its central guiding assumptions, notably the capacity to distinguish between Roman and Germanic elements of legal practice, and their usefulness as concepts, and also the distinction between *Volksrecht* – ethnic law – and *Königsrecht* – royal law – as systematically different forms of law, with their own modes of production, senses of validity, and constitutive forces. Another consequence has been in social history, where the suspicion of the evidential value of the *leges* in their traditional sense has now gone so far that Wickham's recent, monumental social history of the period 400–800 scarcely employed them at all.[5]

But this new approach to studying disputes has thrown up a paradox. On the one hand it confirmed that there was little evidence for use and citation of normative texts: not a single citation of a Frankish *lex* has been identified in an early medieval charter. On the other, it uncovered as one of the most fundamental norms across sub-Roman societies the great respect for written documents in legal proceedings, at a striking variety of social levels. This appreciation has coincided with broader, wholesale re-evaluations of early medieval literacy.[6] If normative texts were not used, it was not because no one could read them, or that

3 W. Davies and P. Fouracre (eds.), *The settlement of disputes in early medieval Europe* (Cambridge, 1986).

4 Take, for example, W. Brown, *Unjust seizure: conflict, interest, and authority in an early medieval society* (Ithaca, NY, 2001), the essays in W. Brown (ed.), (ed.) *Conflict in medieval Europe* (Aldershot, 2003) and W. Davies and P. Fouracre (eds.), *Property and power in the early Middle Ages* (Cambridge, 1995).

5 C. Wickham, *Framing the early Middle Ages: Europe and the Mediterranean 400–800* (Oxford, 2005).

6 Most of all R. McKitterick, *The Carolingians and the written word* (Cambridge, 1989), but also, for example, I. Wood, 'Administration, law and culture in Merovingian Gaul' in: R. McKitterick (ed.), *The uses of literacy in early medieval Europe* (Cambridge, 1992), pp. 63–81; N. Everett, *Literacy in Lombard Italy, c.568–774* (Cambridge, 2003); N. Everett, 'Literacy and the law in Lombard

no one could, in theory, accept their utility as written documents, even if they themselves could not read or write well.

This paradox is at the heart of the prominent later twentieth-century debate over the 'effectiveness' and 'currency' of the *leges*, in both German and English.[7] The debate has involved the elaboration of stimulating theories about alternative uses the texts could have had. Patrick Wormald pointed in particular to the ways in which lawmaking and royal ideology interacted. The Frankish *leges* were written to relate Frankish kings to Roman emperors, whose function as lawgivers was kept in mind consciously. The *leges* could also be used by kings in the complex processes of ethnic engineering that followed the fall of the Roman empire in the West. Clovis's *Lex Salica* made a statement about a people, as well as their king, and offered various incentives to identify as Frankish.[8] Wormald argued that this Frankish use was different from that in the Visigothic, Lombard, and Burgundian entities, which retained a legal culture more clearly derived from the late Roman, founded on regular legislation from kings in response to petitions from subjects, the circulation of clear, usable codes, and courts that respected and cited the written law.[9]

These views may be powerful for explaining the patterns of evidence between the fall of the Roman empire and the rise of the Carolingians, even if they need some refinement. But this book focuses on the meaning of the same *leges* in the Carolingian period itself. And here there is a still more considerable disjunction in the evidence. We find not a single citation of Frankish *lex* in charters, but an explosion in the number of manuscripts containing *leges*. While there is some diversity in the context in which they are preserved, they are bundled overwhelmingly

government' *EME*, 9 (2000), pp. 93–127; J. L. Nelson, 'Literacy in Carolingian Government' in: J. L. Nelson, *The Frankish World* (London, 1996), pp. 1–36.

7 Among others, H. Nehlsen, 'Aktualität und Effektivität der ältesten germanischen Rechtsaufzeichnungen' in: P. Classen (ed.), *Recht und Schrift im Mittelalter* (Sigmaringen, 1977), Vorträge und Forschungen 23, pp. 449–502; P. Wormald, 'Lex Scripta and Verbum Regis: legislation and Germanic kingship from Euric to Cnut' in: P. Sawyer and I. Wood (eds.), *Early Medieval kingship* (Leeds, 1977), pp. 105–38; McKitterick (1989), *Written word*; the articles in H. Mordek (ed.), *Überlieferung und Geltung normativer Texte des frühen und hohen Mittelalters* (Sigmaringen, 1986).

8 P. Wormald, 'The Leges Barbarorum: law and ethnicity in the post-Roman West' in: H.-W. Goetz, J. Jarnut and W. Pohl (eds.), *Regna and gentes: the relationship between late antique and early medieval peoples and kingdoms in the transformation of the Roman world* (Leiden, 2003), The transformation of the Roman world 13, pp. 21–55.

9 Most clearly Wormald (2003), 'Leges Barbarorum', pp. 21–55. This is not the place to cover recent stimulating discussions of late Roman legal practice, taking on board similar concerns with the use of prescriptive texts, which potentially challenge Wormald's frame of reference. See esp. C. Humfress, 'Law and legal practice in the age of Justinian' in: M. Maas (ed.), *The Cambridge companion to the age of Justinian* (Cambridge, 2005), pp. 161–84; C. Humfress, 'A New Legal Cosmos: late Roman lawyers and the early medieval Church' in: P. Linehan and J. L. Nelson (eds.), *The Medieval world* (London, 2001), pp. 557–75; C. Humfress, 'Cracking the codex: Late roman law in practice' *Bulletin of the Institute of Classical Studies*, 49 (2006), pp. 251–64; C. Humfress, *Orthodoxy and the courts in the late antique world* (Oxford, 2007).

with other apparently 'legal' material, that is other *leges* and capitularies, texts on broadly legal subjects, some associated with Merovingian, but most with Carolingian rulers. A good number of these Carolingian legal manuscripts were convincingly argued by McKitterick from the 1980s onwards to have been owned and used by people involved in settling disputes.[10] But there was certainly no consensus on the function of these manuscripts in Wormald's lifetime. He preferred to see them as possessions of a learned, overwhelmingly clerical elite, for whom the texts continued to fulfil much the same role as he argued they did in the Merovingian period: they embodied a sense of Frankish history and identity, and made somewhat abstract claims about the power of Frankish kings.[11] In his view, although Carolingian kings vigorously tried to get the written *lex* observed in a practical sense in the localities, there was too much resistance, and only exceptionally did their efforts have any impact on how disputes were settled.

The effectiveness debate is currently rather frozen, and the nature and value of the *leges* as evidence remains ambiguous. This book attempts to contribute to the effort to make sense of the *leges* and their Carolingian manuscripts.

So how do we go further? One approach to the problem works on the survival patterns of documents. Extant charters overwhelmingly record cases in which a church gained some land. Churches had both the incentive, that is continued title, and the institutional continuity to preserve such records well. The *leges* treat the finer points of land law in far less detail than texts of Roman law, or even canons and capitularies, so were less likely to be cited in records of land transactions. A major new approach to this issue has been to focus more heavily on the formulary material, which preserves a wider range of legal documents, involving laymen and cases not related to land.[12] This approach has proved

10 Fundamental are McKitterick (1989), *Written word*, pp. 23–75; R. McKitterick, 'Some Carolingian law-books and their function' in: *Books, scribes and learning in the Frankish Kingdoms, 6th–9th centuries* (Aldershot, 1994), pp. 13–27.

11 A central conclusion of P. Wormald, *The making of English law: King Alfred to the twelfth century. Vol. 1, Legislation and its limits* (Oxford, 1999), pp. 29–92. Throughout, I use the term 'identity' in a relatively loose sense, as explained, for example, in M. de Jong et al., 'Introduction' in: R. Corradini et al. (eds.), *Texts and identities in the early Middle Ages* (Vienna, 2006) Österreichischen Akademie der Wissenschaften Philosophich-Historische Klasse Denkschriften 344, pp. 11–5. Alternative terms proposed in F. Cooper, 'Beyond Identity' *Theory and Society, 29* (2000), pp. 1–47 do not seem to me to be substantially clearer, or to carry fewer problematic associations.

12 See especially: W. Brown, 'When documents are destroyed or lost: lay people and archives in the early Middle Ages' *EME, 11* (2002), pp. 337–66; W. Brown, 'Conflict, letters, and personal relationships in the carolingian formula collections' *Law and History Review, 25* (2007), pp. 323–45; A. Rio, 'Freedom and unfreedom in early medieval Francia: the evidence of the legal formulae' *Past and Present, 193* (2006), pp. 7–40; A. Rio, 'Formulae, legal practice and the settlement of disputes in the Frankish kingdoms: the Formulary of Angers' in: P. Andersen, M. Münster-Swendsen and H. Vogt (eds.), *Law before Gratian: law in western Europe c.500–1100:*

extremely useful for this study, but the role of the *leges* themselves needs further work: only in one or two cases is it clear in what sense those compiling the *formulae*, or the charters with which they were related, knew texts of *lex*. I use charters and *formulae* extensively, but do not approach them head-on as possible straightforward reflections of rules from the *leges*. Rather, I approach them as giving evidence for the kinds of context in which the *leges* might have been useful, or as reflecting the concerns of *leges* in less obvious ways. A great deal of my work, however, bypasses charters, to reconsider the normative texts themselves, but with new questions and perspectives. Useful annotations and glosses to the *leges* can sometimes be found in manuscripts, although they are rare, but more fruitful have been variations between manuscripts, relationships between texts, the evidence of hagiographies and narratives, and the evidence of the form and palaeography of the manuscripts themselves. Many of my arguments involve digging deep, back into the technical debates of the German *Rechtsschule*, so as to deploy their historians' supreme knowledge of the texts, and undoubtedly subtle and thorough discussions, for new purposes.

My approach is to use these kinds of evidence to investigate the alternative suggestions proposed by Wormald a little further, and to investigate more closely what 'practical use' of *leges* in dispute settlements might actually mean.

We certainly cannot imagine practical use as a kind of end in itself, as somehow self-explanatory. This has been, in a sense, the assumption with which the effectiveness debate has operated. In the English historiography, it has been imagined that practical use of written law was a fundamental aim of the Carolingian kings, that it was imagined that there was a kind of law that could be followed, obeyed or not. And the debate has sometimes drawn its strength from relatively hard views on what literacy, conceived as a system opposed to orality does to societies. Thus effective use of written law is linked with a defined system of authority, contrasted with a more flexible, consensual decision making allied to a less hierarchical conception of political authority, typical of oral systems of law.[13] But it is increasingly clear that we

proceedings of the Third Carlsberg Academy Conference on Medieval Legal History 2006 (Copenhagen, 2007), pp. 21–35; A. Rio, *Legal practice and the written word in the early Middle Ages: Frankish Formulae, c. 500–1000* (Cambridge, 2009). Many thanks to Alice Rio for letting me see her book before it was published.

[13] This opposition is fundamental for a certain tradition of German scholars anchored in a slightly later period. See K. Heidecker, 'Communication by written texts in court cases: some charter evidence (ca. 800–ca. 1100)' in: M. Mostert (ed.), *New approaches to medieval communication* (Turnhout, 1999), pp. 101–26 and the essays in G. Dilcher (ed.), *Gewohnheitsrecht und Rechtsgewohnheiten im Mittelalter* (Berlin, 1992), Schriften zur Europäischen Rechts- und Verfassungsgeschichte 6 esp. J. Weitzel, 'Gewohnheitsrecht und fränkisch-deutsches Gerichtsverfahren' in: Dilcher (1992), *Gewohnheitsrecht*, pp. 67–87: p. 71 for Schriftrecht, 'das

need to move to a 'weak' thesis on the role of literacy: it could be integrated in different ways to different societies and coexist with oral practices in different ways.[14] It is clear that decisions made without reference to written texts, in which consensus is stressed, can be subject to pressures associated with social hierarchy, and I suggest equally that use of, and reference to written texts, can respond to the genuine need for consensus.[15]

It is certainly also now apparent that disputes in the early medieval period need to be understood primarily in the context of complex meshes of local social forces. Construction of at least a veneer of consensus by collective action was the central act in a dispute settlement.[16] Thus the power of even Carolingian office holders is seen increasingly in terms of their local connections and influence.[17] Into the Carolingian period the sanctions for enforcing the outcome of a legal process must also be sought in fundamentally local dynamics, and include the threat and reality of violence between the disputing parties.[18] The kind of custom employed in these societies has been considered, largely

Rechtsverständnis ist grundsätzlich authoritativ im Sinne von "obrigkeitlich vorgegebenen", "von außen kommend festgelegt"...' whereas 'das schriftlose Recht ist anti-obrigkeitlich'. See also the imposing J. Weitzel, *Dinggenossenschaft und Recht: Untersuchungen zum Rechtsverständnis im fränkisch-deutschen Mittelalter* (Cologne, 1985), Quellen und Forschungen zur höchsten Gerichtsbarkeit im Alten Reich 15. A recent application of such ideas to the earlier Carolingian material can be found in S. Patzold, 'Die Veränderung frühmittelalterlichen Rechts im Spiegel der Leges-Reformen Karls des Großen und Ludwigs des Frommen' in: S. Esders and C. Reinle (eds.), *Rechtsveränderung im politischen und sozialen Kontext mittelalterlicher Rechtsvielfalt* (Münster, 2005), pp. 63–99, and see also Patzold's comments in S. Patzold, 'Normen im Buch. Überlegungen zu Geltungsansprüchen so genannter "Kapitularien"' *Frühmittelalterliche Studien, 41* (2007), pp. 331–50 esp. pp. 348–9. See also Sellert, 'Aufzeichnung des Rechts und Gesetz' in W. Sellert (ed.), *Das Gesetz in Spätantike und frühem Mittelalter* (Göttingen, 1992), pp. 67–102.

14 On all aspects see McKitterick (1989), *Written word*, and also M. Innes, 'Memory, orality and literacy in an early medieval society' *Past and Present, 158* (1998), pp. 3–36 esp. pp. 3–5 for theory and historiography, and Rio (2009), *Frankish Formulae*, pp. 3–20.

15 Primarily C. Pössel, 'Symbolic communication and the negotiation of power at Carolingian regnal assemblies 814–840' (2004), unpublished PhD dissertation, University of Cambridge on assembly politics and 'imposed consensus' esp. at pp. 233f.

16 Another central theme of Davies and Fouracre (1986), *Settlement of disputes*. See also Pössel (2004), 'Symbolic communication', pp. 233f. for a sophisticated treatment of consensus, albeit one concentrating on its manufacture at regnal assemblies.

17 The clearest work is M. Innes, *State and society in the early Middle Ages: the Middle Rhine Valley, 400–1000* (Cambridge, 2000), but see also Brown (2001), *Unjust seizure*.

18 Still the fundamental article is J. M. Wallace-Hadrill, 'The bloodfeud of the Franks' in: *The Long-Haired Kings* (London, 1962), pp. 121–47. For the anthropology on which it was based see M. Gluckman, 'The peace in the feud' *Past and Present, 8* (1955), pp. 1–14, with a critique of his views and methodology in S. F. Moore, 'Certainties undone: fifty turbulent years of legal anthropology 1949–99' *Journal of the Royal Anthropological Institute, 7* (2001), pp. 95–116. For some problems with the term 'feud' see G. Halsall, 'Introductory survey' in: G. Halsall (ed.), *Violence and society in the early medieval West* (Woodbridge, 1998), pp. 16–28.

from comparison with anthropological work, as flexible and constantly evolving.[19]

With disputes following local logic, and with enforcement only from within society, there is little place for law 'as an abstract set of rules imposed in an impersonal manner by an external agency'.[20]

The approach that compares early medieval legal practice with that of the twelfth century should also be mentioned, briefly. While the debate on the rationality or irrationality of early medieval law has largely been swept aside, the more sophisticated concept of 'autonomy' is more fashionable.[21] It has been argued that the crucial feature of classical Roman law, picked up again in the twelfth century, but lacking from the early medieval record is a 'philosophic commitment to the independence of the legal system from the social and political context of which it formed a part'.[22] Radding argued further that the central new abstraction was the dissociation between law and the situation in which it was to be applied, that only in the twelfth century was it imaginable that one law might have implications for the interpretation of another, that juridical principles could be extracted from legal texts and applied in circumstances not explicitly covered by legislation.[23] While the evidence for Radding's views in full is debatable, and while we shall see cases in which abstractions were made from texts to situations that were not obviously relevant, we do need to consider in the ninth century the relationship between argument derived from legal texts and other

19 Cf. S. Reynolds, *Fiefs and vassals: the medieval evidence reinterpreted* (Oxford, 1994), p. 77. The clearest anthropological treatment still seems to be S. F. Moore, *Social facts and fabrications: 'customary' law on Kilimanjaro 1880–1908* (Cambridge, 1986).

20 As argued in Innes (2000), *State and society*, p. 134; S. Reynolds, *Kingdoms and communities in Western Europe 900–1300* (Oxford, 1984), pp. 1–20.

21 On rationality see esp. S. Reynolds, 'Rationality and collective judgement in the law of Western Europe before the twelfth century' *Quaestiones Medii Aevi Novae, 5* (2000), pp. 3–19. For autonomy, the most important collection is P. Coss (ed.), *Moral world of the law* (Cambridge, 2000), especially the sections by Chris Wickham.

22 A. Lewis, 'The autonomy of Roman law' in: Coss (2000), *Moral world*, pp. 46–7. But note Levy's view that already in the reign of Diocletian, law came to be governed by 'social and economic rather than legal considerations': E. Levy, *West Roman vulgar law: the law of property* (Philadelphia, PA, 1951), p. 7. But see M. Innes, 'Land, freedom and the making of the medieval west' *TRHS, 16* (2006), pp. 37–74 for an account of barbarian settlement in the fifth century, which very much stresses the intactness of sophisticated distinctions over property rights in Roman law in this period, albeit using indirect evidence.

23 C. M. Radding, *The origins of medieval jurisprudence: Pavia and Bologna, 850–1150* (New Haven, CT, 1988), p. 21: the laws were seen only as 'a set of more or less independent rules applying to a variety of concrete situations'. See also S. Reynolds (1984), *Kingdoms and Communities*, pp. 39–67. On professional law see S. Reynolds, 'The emergence of professional law in the long twelfth century' *Law and History Review, 21* (2003), pp. 347–66 and Radding's response, C. M. Radding, 'Legal theory and practice in eleventh-century Italy', *Law and History Review 21* (2003) available at http://web.archive.org/web/20081016055942/http://www.historycooperative.org/journals/lhr/21.2/comment_radding.html.

kinds of argument brought to bear on cases, especially those focused on Christian morality.

What then did, could, practical use of written *lex* mean in this context? The aim here is to excavate some possible answers for the Frankish case more exactly, from exclusively Frankish, and exclusively Carolingian evidence. Is there good evidence that *lex* was read for the statements it made about royal ideology, or ethnic identity? Is there a way of understanding the way in which *lex* was held to be normative, in a sense more closely aligned with the practical, 'legal', which would reconcile the conflict between the abundance of manuscripts and the lack of citation, while taking into account the insights of students of disputes?

In this work I offer five studies. A major theme of the first two is the relationship between certain *leges* texts and ethnic identity in the Carolingian period. This relationship in this period has received surprisingly little attention. Indeed, the question of ethnicity in general has remained strangely under-explored for the Carolingian period, where evidence is rather fuller than earlier. Having placed the colossal body of manuscript evidence firmly in the foreground, it might seem rather strange that, after examining briefly the history of the *Lex Ribuaria*, I turn my attention to two of the 'minor' *leges*, sources with a thin, patchy manuscript transmission. The point is that these texts, unlike the others considered, are actually products of the Carolingian period, so may shed light on the wider issues of the reading of *leges*. I suggest some contexts for the production of these texts, and investigate in detail how *lex* was written about, and why, in regions of recent Frankish domination.

The next three chapters grapple more with questions of the relationship between kings and the *leges*. One chapter considers the relationship between the Carolingian capitularies and the *leges*, through the 'additional capitularies'. The next chapter attempts to add some flesh to the arguments in the previous chapter by considering two cases in which there is indirect evidence for the use of *leges*. The last chapter considers the manuscripts of the *leges*-scriptorium group, often understood as evidence for the central royal dissemination of texts of *lex*, but not given a thorough treatment for some years.

In each case, the evidence is extremely difficult to interpret. It is hoped that the approach taken in attacking different texts from different angles shall allow more compelling common themes to emerge than would be possible from taking the chapters in isolation.

Chapter 1

THE MINOR *LEGES* PART 1. PROBLEMS, BACKGROUND, *LEX RIBUARIA*, *EWA AD AMOREM*

1.1 INTRODUCTION

The starting point and central theme of the next two chapters is the relationship between ethnic identity and the *leges*. The view that the possession of *leges* gave a sense of civilisation to *gentes* can be found in classical and late antique histories available to the Carolingians.[1] For Wormald, such a link was crucial also to understanding the *leges* in the early Middle Ages: the *leges* had a role in reinforcing feelings of ethnic identity, so 'The *lex* of the Franks was *more* than Frankish law. It was the Frankish past. It was Frankish identity'.[2] But ethnogenesis theorists have taught us to worry about what such statements might ever mean. We are constantly reminded that ethnic identity was malleable, and that we must be aware of the specific political context of each use of ethnic terminology. The production of each text encoded an argument, and each text might subsequently be used for different arguments in different contexts. As Pohl put it, texts 'can only be understood properly if we do not see them as evidence for the natural existence of ethnic communities, but as part of strategies to give shape to these communities'. Ethnic identity must also always be 'constituted through social contact', so the nature of that social contact needs to be central to any investigation of the meaning of the terminology.[3]

1 Take for example Ammianus Marcellinus, *Ammiani Marcellini Rerum gestarum libri qui supersunt* ed. W. Seyfarth (Leipzig, 1978) Vol. I pp. 8–9 and 12. Translations taken or adapted from Ammianus Marcellinus, *Rerum gestarum libri* ed. and trans. J. Rolfe (Cambridge, MA, 1963–4), Loeb Classical Library Vol. I pp. 26–7 and 36–7: XIV, 4, 1: The Saracens, whom 'we have never found ... desirable either as friends or as enemies' pointedly have no laws. XIV, 6, 5: laws are 'the everlasting foundations and moorings of liberty' that the Romans set up before entrusting the management of their inheritance to the Caesars.

2 Wormald (1999), *The making*, p. 49.

3 W. Pohl, 'Telling the difference: signs of ethnic identity' in: W. Pohl and H. Reimitz (eds.), *Strategies of distinction: the construction of ethnic communities, 300–800* (Leiden, 1998), The Transformation of the Roman World 2, p. 21. This approach is argued as useful for the *leges* directly in W. Pohl, 'Probleme einer Sinngeschichte ethnischer Gemeinschaften. Identität und Tradition' in: G. Dilcher (ed.), *Leges - Gentes - Regna* (Berlin, 2006), pp. 51–67.

Although we now have sophisticated accounts of the meaning and purpose of ethnic terminology in some of the earliest *leges barbarorum*, they have been geared towards the period in which the *leges* were composed.[4] In this period, the emergence of ethnic kingdoms and an ethnic discourse has been seen as a fundamental development in the transformation of the Roman world.[5] The possible use Wormald suggested, that *leges* continued in the Carolingian period to be relevant to questions of ethnicity, has not been considered in detail. Indeed, ethnicity, and ethnic processes in general, have been studied in less detail in the Carolingian period than in the previous period.

In the studies we have, the use of Frankish terminology in both Merovingian and Carolingian periods has emerged as uniquely slippery.[6] The term 'Frank' is apparently sometimes used as a term denoting free status, sometimes it is an ethnic term, and when it is, it overlaps with, is qualified by, or contrasts with a large variety of alternative identities or sub-identities, especially in connection with the division between East and West Franks. Sometimes it seems more to represent a sense of trans-ethnic political identity. One must be especially alert with the Franks to the possibility of very rapid shifts in the use of ethnic

4 Two of the most stimulating are on the rich Burgundian material: P. Amory, 'The meaning and purpose of ethnic terminology in the Burgundian laws' *EME*, *2* (1993), pp. 1–28 and Innes (2006), 'Land, freedom', pp. 37–74.

5 The bibliography is now colossal and ever-expanding. One might note the rarity of papers on ethnicity after 750 in such major collections as Pohl and Reimitz (1998), *Strategies of distinction*; A. Smyth (ed.), *Medieval Europeans. Studies in ethnic identity and national perspectives in medieval Europe* (London, 1998); A. Gillett (ed.), *On Barbarian Identity: Critical approaches to Ethnicity in the Early Middle Ages* (Turnhout, 2002); H. Wolfram and W. Pohl (eds.), *Typen der Ethnogenese unter besonderer Berücksichtigung der Bayern* (Vienna, 1990); F. Curta (ed.), *Borders, barriers, and ethnogenesis. Frontiers in late Antiquity and the Middle Ages* (Turnhout, 2006). A partial exception is the literature on Rhaetia, in which law indeed plays a role, but one that cannot be considered here. See H. Wolfram, 'Ethnogenesen im frühmittelalterlichen Donau- und Ostalpenraum (6.-10. Jahrhundert)' in: H. Beaumann and W. Schröder (eds.), *Frühmittelalterliche Ethnogenesen im Alpenraum* (Sigmaringen, 1985), Nationes: historische und philologische Untersuchungen zur Entstehung der europäischen Nationen im Mittelalter 5, pp. 97–151. More general exceptions are W. Pohl, 'Zur Bedeutung ethnischer Unterscheidungen in der frühen Karolingerzeit' in: H.-J. Hässler, J., Jarnut and M. Wemhoff (eds.), *Sachsen und Franken in Westfalen: zur Komplexität der ethnischen Deutung und Abgrenzung zweier frühmittelalterlicher Stämme* (Isensee, 1999), Studien zur Sachsenforschung 12, pp. 193–208; before that E. Ewig, 'Volkstum und Volksbewußtsein im Frankenreich des 7. Jahrhunderts' in: E. Ewig, *Spätantikes und Fränkisches Gallien: gesammelte Schriften 1952–73* Volume 1, (Munich, 1976), pp. 246–55.

6 For the Merovingian period see above all I. Wood, 'Defining the Franks' in: S. Forde, L. Johnson and A. Murray (eds.), *Concepts of nationality and national identity in the Middle Ages* (Leeds, 1995), pp. 47–57; Carolingians in J. L. Nelson, 'Frankish identity in Charlemagne's empire' in: P. Geary and Garipzanov, *Franks, Northmen, and Slavs* (Turnhout, 2008), pp. 71–83 as well as H. Reimitz, 'Omnes Franci: identification and identities of the Early Medieval Franks' in: Geary and Garipzanov (2008), *Franks, Northmen, and Slavs*, pp. 51–68. See also Pohl (1999), 'Bedeutung ethnischer Unterscheidungen', pp. 195f. and G. Halsall, *Settlement and social organization: the Merovingian region of Metz* (Cambridge, 1995), pp. 26–32.

terminology, and must look very hard at specific contexts to make a convincing argument about the link between *lex* and *gens*.[7]

The few published views on the relationship between ethnic identities and what I call the 'minor *leges*' – the group of ninth-century *leges* for Saxons, Thuringians, Frisians, and Chamavians – in the Carolingian period are too simple to swallow. Collins describes the *Lex Saxonum* as simply Charlemagne's will imposed on his new subjects, but given ethnic wrapping, whose purpose was the articulation of a characteristically Frankish obsession with defining the *gens* of all newly subjugated peoples, while simultaneously refining the sense of a Frankish *gens*.[8] But much more specific work is needed to make his suggestion convincing. Not only is the dating of the *Lex* problematic, but Collins's view of the role of ethnicity under the earlier Carolingians was somewhat narrow.[9] He placed great weight on his observation that *Aquitani* appear in Aquitaine as a symptom of 'ethnicisation' of territorial terminology. But he did not take account of a central result of Ewig's work in the 1960s, that the opposite tendency was most prevalent, that there was a widespread territorialisation of 'ethnic' terminology, and that this was a process with lasting significance.[10] Non-Frankish *gentes* in the ninth century can also be seen developing an internally focused self-awareness very much bound up with the history of the Franks, nowhere more clearly than in the Saxon case.[11] So several processes, the complexity of which we need to appreciate, were operating simultaneously in the same period. The history of the *lex* needs to be traced in all of this complexity.

Bound up in the connection between *gentes* and *leges* is the 'personality principle', under which each man was entitled to use and be judged under his own 'ethnic law'. This was considered a central feature of Germanic law by the scholars of the *Historische Rechtsschule*, and has since been the subject of some welcome revisionist attention. Amory most clearly suggested that the principle was not something imported

7 Brilliantly demonstrated in Reimitz (2008), 'Omnes Franci', pp. 51–68.

8 R. Collins, *Early medieval Europe (300–1000)* (Basingstoke, 1991), pp. 297f.: 'it does seem as if under Charles the Franks were trying to define their own identity against those of all surrounding groups, who were forced by their Frankish conquerors or political masters into accepting far more rigid and formal definitions of their customs, history and ethnicity, that were in many respects anachronistic. At the same time the older divisions within the Frankish body politic, notably the division between Neustrian and Austrasian kingdoms, virtually disappear'. For a conscious qualification of this view on the point of the Saxon *lex* see H. Mayr-Harting, 'Charlemagne, the Saxons and the imperial coronation of 800' *EHR*, *111* (1996), pp. 1129–30. See also R. Collins, 'Law and ethnic identity in the Western Kingdoms in the fifth and sixth centuries' in: Smyth (1998), *Medieval Europeans*, pp. 1–23.

9 For a discussion on dating, see Chapter 2, section 2.4.2

10 Ewig (1976), 'Volkstum und Volksbewußtsein', pp. 246–55; Pohl (1999), 'Bedeutung ethnischer Unterscheidungen', pp. 193–208.

11 See the work on *Selbstbewußtsein* esp. in M. Becher, *Rex, Dux und Gens* (Husum, 1996). This idea is used repeatedly in Chapter 2 below.

into Europe with the Germanic peoples, but developed as a consequence of the expansion of the Carolingian empire. He argued explicitly against Guterman, the author of the most recent studies focused on personality, and before him Stouff, who saw personal law being supplanted by territorial law only in the Carolingian period.[12] Amory suggested that the expansion of the Carolingian empire in fact led to a new, distinctive sense of ethnicity, in which 'law was not so much a result as a major determining factor'.[13]

It is difficult to find evidence in charters for the operation of personal law in the ninth century, and the majority of references in Carolingian legal texts to the need to preserve the *lex* of each individual can be read as guaranteeing to each individual a bundle of general rights, rather than the use of an ethnic *lex*.[14] Guterman's most recent work appeared in 1990, but he hardly cites a work more recent than 1900, and his perspective is that of a legal historian trying to uncover the system which is assumed to be there, not of an early medievalist who worries about system. In fact, clear *professiones iuris* – statements of the personal law of an individual – are restricted to Italy, and very occasionally Burgundy, in the Carolingian period, and do not reach their heyday anywhere until some time after.[15] Pohl-Resl even thought that the presence of a *professio*

[12] Amory (1993), 'Meaning and purpose', pp. 1–28; S. L. Guterman, *The principle of the personality of law in the Germanic kingdoms of western Europe from the fifth to the eleventh century* (New York, 1990); L. Stouff, 'Étude sur le principe de la personalité des lois depuis les invasions barbares jusqu'au XIIe siècle' *Revue bourguignonne* (1894), pp. 1–65, 273–310. For a conscious decision to ignore Amory's critique, and for bibliography on the Italian and Spanish territoriality-personality debates, see N. Everett, 'How territorial was Lombard Law?' in: W. Pohl and P. Erhart (eds.), *Die Langobarden* (Vienna, 2005), Forschungen zur Geschichte des Mittelalters 9, pp. 345–60.

[13] Amory (1993), 'Meaning and purpose', p. 23. Cf. Pohl and Reimitz (1998), 'Strategies of distinction', pp. 17–18.

[14] For this sense of 'law' see for example J. L. Nelson, 'Dispute settlement in Carolingian West Francia' in: Davies and Fouracre (1986), *Settlement of disputes*, p. 50, and J. L. Nelson, 'Kings with justice, kings without justice: an early medieval paradox' in: *La Giustizia nell'Alto Medioevo (secoli V–VIII)* (Spoleto, 1995), Settimane 42, p. 806. Capitularies: take for example MGH Capit. I p. 67 no. 25 c.5: *voluntas domni regis est, ut unusquisque homo suam legem pleniter habeat conservata*... A catalogue of such references in normative texts can be found in Guterman (1990), *Principle*, pp. 107f.; Wormald (1999), *The making*, p. 31: the principle is 'rather easier to find in textbooks than in evidence'. Amory (1993), 'Meaning and purpose', p. 21: 'These [tenth- and eleventh-century] examples are far-flung, but they show to what lengths scholars will go in pursuit of personality of the law'. Cf. anxiety about personality already in Nelson (1986), 'Dispute settlement', p. 60. Lupoi, working in a different tradition altogether, is also sceptical, although it is difficult to understand his arguments: M. Lupoi, *The origins of the European legal order* trans. A. Belton (Cambridge, 2000), pp. 388f. And see the heroic understatement in Guterman (1990), *Principle*, p. 113: 'Many documents, it is true, lack *professiones*'.

[15] Italian *professiones* can be found in *I placiti del "Regnum Italiae"* ed. C. Manaresi Volume 1, (Rome, 1955). See for a splendid example pp. 533–47 no. 142 from Regio in 944. Note the restriction of references to the *leges* as a possession to post-900 charters in the teaching volume, whose texts were selected specifically for their demonstration of territoriality and personality: *Textes relatifs aux institutions privées et publiques aux époques mérovingienne et carolingienne* ed. M. Thévenin (Paris, 1887). Wormald (1999), *The making*, pp. 78–9 for *Lex Salica* as a possession in documents from Autun; p. 81 for the only two non-Italian ninth-century explicit *professiones*.

iuris in Italian charters of the tenth century was a good sign that they had been forged in the eleventh century.[16]

A new, comprehensive study is needed tracing the personality principle through the Carolingian period and into the eleventh century, and I shall only offer some fragmentary suggestions arising from texts from my regions. But I shall suggest that, here, both territoriality and personality are concepts too rigid to fit much of the Carolingian evidence. We need to extend to our understanding of the use of the *leges* the emphasis on negotiation and consensus, which has informed so much recent work on society and disputing.

The minor *leges*, the *Leges Saxonum, Thuringorum, Frisionum*, and the enigmatic *Ewa ad Amorem* are obviously crucial sources for the reading of *lex* in the Carolingian period, because they are the only representatives of the genre actually composed in that period. The next two chapters investigate the production and use of two of them, the *Lex Saxonum* and the *Ewa ad Amorem*. The *Lex Salica* and especially *Lex Ribuaria* are first examined briefly, to provide some context.

1.2 THE FRANKISH BACKGROUND. HISTORY AND ETHNICITY IN THE *LEX SALICA* AND *LEX RIBUARIA*

1.2.1 Lex Salica

The *Lex Salica* is the most famous and most widely studied of all the *leges barbarorum*. It is reasonably confidently dated to before 511, and associated with King Clovis, so has naturally played a central role in discussions of all aspects of early Frankish society, government and culture. But its fifty-five extant Carolingian manuscripts suggest that it was also the most widely circulated legal text in the Carolingian period, which brings it to attention for these purposes.[17] Unfortunately, little can be said here about the link between the reading of the *Lex Salica* and the maintenance of ethnic identities in the Carolingian period, beyond what has already been printed, but a survey of some literature is worthwhile.

The first question is with what ethnic identity we should be concerned. The traditional view of the *Lex Salica* is that it represented the *Volksrecht* – the 'tribal law' – of the Western branch of the Franks, the 'Salian Franks', while the eastern Franks, the 'Ripuarian Franks' used the *Lex Ribuaria*. Already in the early twentieth century, however,

[16] B. Pohl-Resl, 'Ethnische Bezeichnungen und Rechtsbekentisse in langobardischen Urkunden' in: K. Brunner and B. Merta (eds.), *Ethnogenese und Überlieferung: angewandte Methoden der Frühmittelalterforschung* (Vienna, 1994), pp. 163–71; B. Pohl-Resl, 'Legal practice and ethnic identity in Lombard Italy' in: Pohl and Reimitz (1998), *Strategies of distinction*, pp. 205–19. The Burgundian context is important for reading Agobard's famous account *Adversum Gundobardum*, translated in Guterman (1990), *Principle*, pp. 242f.

[17] Fifty-five is the figure for complete manuscripts. There are also three fragments.

it was noticed that in almost all contexts, while the Alemannic and Bavarian laws tend to be styled in their manuscripts with a genitive plural, *leges Alemennorum* and *Baiuwariorum*, the *Salica* and *Ribuaria* are plain adjectives. It was already clear that the term *terra salica*, found in ninth-century charters and *formulae*, made little sense as 'land of the Salian Franks', so it was argued instead to relate to a particular kind of landholding, a *Herrenhof* administered directly by its lord.[18] Stein first suggested that the term *Salica* even in the context of the *Lex Salica* had nothing to do with a *gens*, and instead denoted something along the lines of the Latin term *dominica*, associated with lordship. More recently, it has also been argued that, in addition to the sense proposed by Stein, *Salica* is also possibly related to proto-Germanic **saljon*, whose clearest modern Germanic cognate is the term Ge-*selle*. The word implied something along the lines of 'common', 'communal', 'shared'. In Springer's most recent opinion, the term *Salica* shifted in meaning from 'common' to Stein's 'lordly' throughout the Merovingian period. Most radically, he argued that the 'Salian Franks' never existed at all.[19] The term *Salioi* and similar terms do appear in late antique texts, but there have been convoluted arguments as to its meaning and significance, revolving around Julian's use of the term, and other Latin sources' dependence on his work.[20] It seems that either 'Salians' never existed outside Julian's work and those who followed him, or a group identifying as 'Salians' was crushed by the Romans in the third century, never to appear again.

It is not possible here to treat the arguments concerning the migration period or the etymology in detail. It is, however, quite clear that there is no evidence that the *Lex Salica* was ever understood in the ninth century as 'law of the Salians' or 'law of the Salian Franks'. On the rare occasions in which a *Salicus* appears in a charter or a narrative, it is always in a narrowly legalistic context, as 'a user of *Lex Salica*'. There is no sense in our sources that there was ever a 'Salic' region.

The *gens* we should be concerned about in relation to the *Lex Salica* is, straightforwardly, the Franks. This is certainly the assumption of both of the extant prologues to the *Lex*. The first 'short' text, accompanying the

[18] For a concise account of attitudes to *terra salica* in the historiography see H. Tiefenbach, *Studien zu Wörtern volkssprachiger Herkunft in karolingischen Königsurkunden. Ein Beitrag zum Wortschatz der Diplome Lothars I. und Lothars II* (Munich, 1973), Münstersche Mittelalter-Schriften 15, pp. 105–8.

[19] M. Springer, 'Gab es ein Volk der Salier?' in: D. Geuenich, W., Haubrichs and J. Jarnut (eds.), *Nomen et gens: zur historischen Aussagekraft frümittelalterlicher Personennamen* (Berlin, 1997), pp. 58–83 and the shorter version M. Springer, 'Salier und salisches Recht – Beobachtungen zu den Worten Salii und Salicus' in: A. Wieczorek (ed.), *Die Franken, Wegbereiter Europas. Vor 1500 Jahren, König Chlodwig und seine Erben* (Mainz, 1996), pp. 485–7.

[20] The clearest account is in M. Becher, *Chlodwig I. Der Aufstieg der Merowinger und das Ende der antiken Welt* (Munich, 2011), pp. 55–60.

A redaction, is Merovingian, the 'long', attached to the D redaction, is likely a product of Pippin's chancery. Both do indeed tell a story about the Franks and their kings. The 'long' prologue in particular lauds Frankish achievements at length, displaying what has been described as 'anthemic arrogance'. This prologue offers the best evidence that the *lex* of the Franks was ever held up as an achievement, an attribute of a powerful, respectable people. Attempts to establish a role for the *Lex Salica* as a kind of ethnography, crystalising Frankish identity, have made much of this prologue, but otherwise have rested largely on negative arguments. Only because it is so difficult to see traces of the text in operation in a legal sense was it necessary or possible to forge an argument about alternative roles the text could fulfil. Once again, the central difficulties are that the *Lex Salica* was never directly cited, and that its revisions centred more on Latinity than substance. We do have reference to the *Lex Salica* in charters and *formulae*, but they never point explicitly to a passage in the text as we have it.[21] So if the written *lex* was not obviously and clearly cited or used as law, then the material in the prologues pointed to an alternative way of reading them.

What we lack is more direct evidence for the connections between the *Lex Salica* and feelings of ethnic identity. We get nowhere examining patterns in terminology in our sources, as we do with 'Ribuarians' and the *Lex Ribuaria*, and find very little helpful mention of Frankish law in historiography or hagiography, as we do for the Saxons.[22] Neither the 'long prologue' itself, nor other works on Frankish ethnography or history have left a considerable record in the surviving manuscripts of *Lex Salica*, while other texts of law are almost always copied with it. So the *Lex Salica* may well have been read in the context of Frankish ethnic identity, but the terminology surrounding the text is used too vaguely in other contexts for us to be able to see such a use clearly, and in any case such a use would not rule out other, more 'legal' uses. Later I advance an argument from a Carolingian text that the *Lex Salica* was at least sometimes read as law, in a certain, qualified sense. For the time being, however, to investigate further the connection between *lex* and *gens* in the Carolingian period, we must turn to other texts.

[21] See the examination of the term *lex salica* in the charters in G. Köbler, *Das Recht im frühen Mittelalter. Untersuchungen zu Herkunft und Inhalt frühmittelalterlicher Rechtsbegriffe im deutschen Sprachgebiet* (Cologne, 1971), Forschungen zur deutschen Rechtsgeschichte 7, pp. 96–8.

[22] A notable exception is the *Passio Leudegarii*, discussed in section 1.2.3 below. Another is the *Liber Historiae Francorum* on which see, for a recent discussion, R. McKitterick, *History and memory in the Carolingian world* (Cambridge, 2004), p. 12.

1.2.2 Ribuarian Lex *and the Ribuarians in the Carolingian period*

The *Lex Ribuaria* is generally understood in recent English historiography as a seventh-century text produced under a king in the eastern, Austrasian, Merovingian subkingdom.[23] The text has been associated with an early East Frankish group of 'Ripuarian Franks', sometimes referred to in German work as 'Rheinfranken'.[24] But almost every aspect of the text is problematic. There has been a vigorous German debate over its dating.[25] There were anxieties already in the nineteenth century about its status as *Volksrecht*, since extensive parts of the text were shown to consist of revised material from *Lex Salica*.[26] Thus the extant text was sometimes interpreted more as a species of *Königsrecht*, applicable nonetheless to *Ribuarii*, and incorporating material from older Ribuarian *Volksrecht*.[27] But there has been no German consensus on precisely what

23 Most clearly stated and influential is I. Wood, *The Merovingian Kingdoms 450–751* (Harlow, 1994), pp. 115–17. Also Wormald (1999), *The making*, p. 35; McKitterick (1989), *Written word*, p. 70. This was also Eckhardt's view of the text in its extant form: see *Lex Ribuaria. Austrasisches Recht in 7. Jahrhundert* ed. K. A. Eckhardt (Göttingen, 1959), Germanenrechte neue Folge. Westgermanisches Recht I, pp. 142–4 for his final conclusions. This section summarises and develops some of the conclusions of my Mphil thesis, T. Faulkner, 'Lex Ribuaria' (2005), unpublished M.phil dissertation, University of Cambridge. Although my views have changed, and the points have been developed further, more detail, and more exhaustive references than there is space for here can still, in some cases, be found there. The best edition is *Lex Ribuaria* ed. F. Beyerle and R. Buchner (Hannover, 1951), MGH Leges nationum Germanicarum III, 2, to which all references hereafter to *Lex Ribuaria* point. All numberings for chapters of the text are those used in this edition.

24 For the historiography in German see M. Springer, 'Riparii – Ribuarier – Rheinfranken nebst einigen Bemerkungen zum Geographen von Ravenna' in: *Die Franken und die Alemannen bis zur "Schlacht bei Zülpich"* (Berlin, 1998), pp. 200–3. See the introduction to *Laws of the Salian and Ripuarian Franks* trans. T. J. Rivers (New York, 1986) pp. 7–11. Even Ian Wood refers to a 'king of the Ripuarian Franks' in Wood (1994), *Merovingian Kingdoms*, p. 40. For some older, text-book examples in English work of projection of 'Ripuarian Franks', see for example J. M. Wallace-Hadrill, *The barbarian West, 400–1000* revised edition (Oxford, 1996), pp. 151–68. 'Ripuarian Franks' are sometimes supplied misleadingly in translations of Latin texts that do not mention them, for example in Gregory of Tours, *History of the Franks* trans. L. Thorpe (London, 1974), pp. 153, 209, 213. I have preferred a spelling with a 'b' rather than a 'p' because it represents more accurately the form found in the bulk of the manuscripts of the *lex*, and minimises any hint of continuity with the modern German Ripuarian dialect.

25 Arguments for an eighth-century dating include B. Krusch, *Neue Forschungen über die drei oberdeutschen Leges: Bajuvariorum, Alamannorum, Ribuariorum* (Berlin, 1927), Abhandlungen der Akademie der Wissenschaften in Göttingen. Philologisch-Historische Klasse XX, 1, pp. 147f.; arguments for a seventh-century dating include F. Beyerle, 'Zum Kleinreich Sigiberts III. und zur Datierung der Lex Ribuaria' *Rheinische Vierteljahrsblätter, 21* (1956), pp. 357–62, R. Buchner, *Die Rechtsquellen* (Weimar, 1953), Deutschlands Geschichtsquellen im Mittelalter: Vorzeit und Karolinger, pp. 21–5, but the debate was much more extensive.

26 See already Brunner (1906), *Deutsche Rechtsgeschichte*, pp. 303–8, and then F. Beyerle, 'Das Gesetzbuch Ribuariens. Volksrechtliche Studien III' *ZRG GA, 55* (1935), pp. 1–80; Beyerle (1956), 'Kleinreich Sigiberts', pp. 357–62; C. Schott, 'Der Stand der Leges-Forschung' *Frühmittelalterliche Studien, 13* (1979), p. 38.

27 So summarising the debate, R. Schmidt-Wiegand, 'Lex Ribuaria' in: J. Hoops and H. Jankuhn (eds.), *Reallexikon der germanischen Altertumskunde* Volume 18, (Berlin, 2001), p. 320 writes that '[*Lex Ribuaria*] mehr als die anderen Leges den Charakter eines Gesetzgebungswerkes hat'. On royal edicts in the text see also I. Wood, 'The Code in Merovingian Gaul' in: I. Wood and

Table 1.1 *Chronological distribution of manuscripts of* leges Salica, Ribuaria, Baiuwarorium, *and* Alemannorum

	Sal	*Bav*	*Rib*	*Al*
750–900	58 (66%)	13 (39%)	31 (83%)	39 (75%)
900–1100	15 (17%)	9 (27%)	4 (10%)	10 (19%)
1100–	14 (16%)	11 (33%)	2 (5%)	3 (5%)
	87	33	37	52

kind of kingdom, or region, the text referred to.[28] Springer's rejection of the notion of 'Salian Franks' involved a rejection of the notion of a division of the Franks into two groups. He pointed out that there was simply no evidence for 'Ripuarian Franks' in the Merovingian period.[29] So we cannot take Ribuarians or Ribuarian Franks for granted, and need to investigate what the use of Ribuarian terminology might mean wherever it appears.

The Carolingians were clearly very interested in the *Lex*. Some thirty-six manuscripts survive, of which thirty-one are from the Carolingian period. Table 1.1 shows the numbers of manuscripts of four *leges* by period.

Again, references to particular laws in Carolingian charters and other texts are notoriously rare, but such references as have been found do not give the impression that the *Lex Ribuaria* was restricted in applicability in the ninth century to any eastern Frankish region for which it is understood to have been written in the seventh or eighth century, nor restricted to use by those who held the law to be their own 'ethnic law'.

One of the few references is a passage from the Le Mans forgeries, composed in the 860s:

But what these monks say, that [the monastery of St Calais in the diocese of Le Mans] is your [Louis the Pious's] property, the aforementioned witnesses of Bishop Aldric affirm not to be. They also say that, if it were your property, the possessions of the same monastery would be defended according to *Lex Salica* or *Lex Ribuaria*, just as other

J. Harries (eds.), *The Theodosian Code: studies in the imperial law of late antiquity* (London, 1993), p. 169; Wood (1992), 'Administration, law and culture', p. 66. For the clearest summary of the various views about the origins of different layers of the text, see *Lex Ribuaria. Austrasisches Recht in 7. Jahrhundert* ed. K. A. Eckhardt (Göttingen, 1959), Germanenrechte neue Folge. Westgermanisches Recht I, pp. 34–8.

28 See section 1.2.3 below.

29 Springer (1998), 'Ribuarier', pp. 200–69; Springer (1997), 'Volk der Salier', pp. 58–83; Springer (1996), 'Salier und salisches Recht', pp. 485–7. For some early scepticism on the 'Salian Franks' as a people, see S. Stein, 'Lex und Capitula' *Mitteilungen des Instituts für Österreichische Geschichtsforschung, 41* (1926), pp. 296f., and for early anxiety about Ribuarians see Beyerle (1935), 'Gesetzbuch Ribuariens', pp. 2–3.

places and possessions do that are your property; and the slaves' [from different estates] children would not be divided [between those estates], as is the *consuetudo* to do in that region for other places and possessions that are your property.[30]

Although this was a forgery, it clearly shows that *Lex Ribuaria* could be argued broadly as attaching to land near Le Mans, on the other side of the Frankish kingdoms from Cologne. This attachment could conceivably be explained by some kind of use of a personality principle, but the explanation would need to be convoluted: the association here is strongly between royal property and two particular laws, not the law of a particular individual and his land.[31] It may be, instead, that the passage envisages the two *leges* as interchangeable alternatives. We shall see later a similar combination of *Lex Salica* and *Ribuaria* at the opposite end of the Frankish realm, in the Netherlands.[32]

It is also clear that the mainstream Carolingian idea of what and where 'Ribuaria' was was very far removed from an understanding of it having corresponded with a large Merovingian subkingdom in the east. The Ribuarians and Ribuaria are mentioned very rarely in Carolingian annals and histories, despite the popularity of the *Lex Ribuaria*, although we do sometimes find Ribuarian terminology in charters. In both historiographical sources and charters the formulation is usually *in pago Riboariense*, or something very similar.[33] Although there was clearly a great deal of variation in the use of the term, there were somewhere between two hundred and six hundred *pagi* in the ninth-century empire, and sixty-six in the Rhineland alone.[34] Certainly the term suggests a smaller territory than those used for other regions inhabited by *gentes*

30 Translation from W. Goffart, *The Le Mans forgeries: a chapter from the history of church property in the ninth century.* (Cambridge, MA, 1966), p. 144. *Concilia Aevi Karolini II* ed. A. Werminghoff (Hannover, 1908), MGH Concilia, Legum Sectio III, p. 838: *Sed et hoc, quod isti monachi dicunt, quod vestrum proprium sit, praedicti testes Aldrici episcopi per eorum auctoritates et per vestros vassallos et alios veridicos et bonos homines affirmant non esse. Dicunt etiam, quod, si vestrum proprium esset, res ipsius monasterii secundum legem Salicam aut Ribuariam tuerentur, sicut alia loca et res, quae de vestro sunt proprio, faciunt, et mancipia non partirentur, sicut de aliis locis et rebus, quae de vestro sunt proprio, in illa regione est consuetudo facere.*

31 So Goffart implies that some kind of law on personality was invoked by citing MGH Capit. I no. 145 p. 297: *ut ecclesiarum defensores res suas contra suos adpetitores eadem lege defendant, qua ipsi vixerunt qui easdem res ecclesiis condonaverunt...* but its precise relevance to royal lands is not clear. Goffart (1966), *Le Mans forgeries*, p. 144. Cf. brief consideration of the Church and Roman law in Chapter 5, section 5.3 below.

32 See section 1.4.3 below.

33 Although his attempt to find a system was perhaps unsuccessful, the most comprehensive list of references in print is in E. Ewig, 'Die Civitas Ubiorum, die Francia Rinensis und das Land Ribuarien' in: Ewig (1976), *Spätantikes und Fränkisches Gallien 1*, pp. 492f.

34 For *pagus*, see Innes (2000), *State and society*, p. 118 with comprehensive references; F. L. Ganshof; B. Lyon and M. Lyon (eds.), *Frankish institutions under Charlemagne* (Providence, RI, 1968), pp. 27–32; for the Rhineland *pagi* see T. Bauer, 'Die mittelalterlichen Gaue' in: F. Irsigler (ed.), *Geschichtlicher Atlas der Rheinlande* (Cologne, 1982–) map IV, 9.

with their own *leges*: Alaman and Bavarian territory in similar sources tends to be described as a *ducatus*.[35]

The place furthest from Cologne reckoned in any source as in the Ribuarian *pagus* is Werden, on the Ruhr, some sixty kilometres from Cologne.[36] But there is some noteworthy, and possibly revealing variation, especially clear but by no means restricted to the ninth-century *Divisio* documents, which divided the Carolingian kingdoms between members of the dynasty, from 831, 839, and 870, where we find *ducatum Ribuariorum, in Ribuarias comitatus quinque*, and simply *Ribuarias*, in lists of regions of greatly varying sizes.[37] There is no clear pattern in these variations, and they are best explained as expressions of a variety of perceptions of what Ribuaria was, which may correspond with a variety of understandings of who the Ribuarians were.

But there is one very major exception, the account of the Annals of Xanten. From 860 this text was written by a member of the cathedral chapter of Cologne, the epicentre of all views of where Ribuaria was.[38] In all other respects the compiler's terminology was deeply conventional, but he made prominent references to *Ripuaria* as a region in the same terms as Burgundy and Provence.[39] More strikingly still, *Ripuaria* is vastly upgraded in political significance, with Lothar I and II referred to as *rex Ripuariorum* and *rex Ripuariae*.[40]

How does this view fit in, and what was its influence? The Annals of Xanten, although considered essentially a product of the ninth century, survive in only one manuscript, London Cotton Tiberius c.xi., a highly complex compilation with hands from between the tenth and thirteenth centuries.[41] Although manuscripts have surely been lost, this may suggest that the text found limited distribution, that it was written perhaps with an audience of just the Cologne cathedral chapter in mind, and this would fit into a well-established Carolingian context for the writing of the institutional memory of a *familia*, a community.[42] Does the use of this

35 For the term *ducatus* see Becher (1996), *Rex, Dux und Gens*, pp. 122f. and his references. There is always the problem of the lack of differentiated articles in Latin, however.

36 The sources are the private charters from Werden examined in detail below, edited in *Urkundenbuch für die Geschichte des Niederrheins* ed. T. J. Lacomblet Volume 1, (Düsseldorf, 1840) [hereafter *Urkundenbuch Niederrheins*] and the less accessible *De oudste partikuliere Oorkonden van het Klooster Werden* ed. D. P. Blok (Assen, 1960) [hereafter *Oorkonden Werden*].

37 *Capitularia Regum Francorum* ed. A. Boretius and V. Krause (Hannover, 1883–97), MGH Legum sectio II, 1–2 Vol. II [hereafter MGH Capit. II] pp. 24, 58, 194 nos. 194, 200, 251.

38 H. Löwe, 'Studien zu den Annales Xantenses' *DA*, *8* (1950), pp. 59–99. See C. Carroll, 'The archbishops and church provinces of Mainz and Cologne during the Carolingian period, 751–911' (Cambridge, 1999), Unpublished PhD dissertation, University of Cambridge, pp. 8f.

39 *Annales Xantenses* ed. B. von Simson (Hannover, 1909), MGH SRG XII, pp. 13 and esp. 27 [Hereafter *Annales Xantenses*].

40 *Annales Xantenses* pp. 19 and 28.

41 See introduction to *Annales Xantenses* pp. V-VI.

42 See Innes, M. and McKitterick, R., 'The writing of history' in: R. McKitterick (ed.), *Carolingian culture: emulation and innovation* (Cambridge, 1994), pp. 193–220.

terminology suggest that Cologne had a very distinct, stable, historical consciousness, lost everywhere else in the Frankish kingdoms, that the Ribuarians had been an important people in their own right, with a kingdom? Or is this stress on the Ribuarians something substantially new, or at least newly packaged, in the mid-ninth century, and is there any way of relating this emphasis to the reading of the *Lex Ribuaria*?

We know there was a *Lex Ribuaria* at Cologne in the 830s, because its library catalogue from 833 lists it.[43] And there are also some high political concerns that would make Cologne a very interesting and plausible location for the construction or revival of historical claims for political ends. Charles Carroll has demonstrated that the Cologne chapter was in a tense position in the mid-ninth century because its suffragan sees were divided between the East Frankish kingdom of Louis the German and the middle kingdom of Lothar I and II. Cologne saw an unparalleled degree of interest from kings of both kingdoms in controlling episcopal appointments, and this is something to which our annalist was very hostile throughout his text.[44] In fact the only two ecclesiastics he portrayed positively are described as natives of Cologne. Liudbert is even described as *filius Ripuariae*.[45] So perhaps the use of Ribuarian terminology reflected, in part, a desire to express the Cologne region's historical independence, against outside interference.

1.2.3 Merovingian Ribuarians

The most notable impression from this Carolingian material is of disjunction. The Ribuarians are very prominent in Carolingian legal manuscripts, but in general not at all prominent in Carolingian historical writing. Apart from the Annals of Xanten, reference to Ribuarian *lex* can be far outside its East Frankish base, and when *Ribuaria* is referred to territorially, it is much smaller than a unit we might expect to have its own *lex* if we imagine *lex* being written for *regna* and *gentes*. Otherwise, no one quite agreed on how large Ribuarian territory was. How then does this fit understandings from the Merovingian era? It is worth reconsidering the evidence that the *Lex Ribuaria* was a king's law code for a substantial eastern Frankish kingdom.

There is no reference to a Ribuarian territory before the eighth century, and then only five references in eighth-century sources.[46] All locate Ribuarian territory in the immediate area of Cologne or within

43 See *Lex Ribuaria* p. 39. For library catalogues, see McKitterick (1989), *Written word*, pp. 191–2.

44 Carroll (1999), 'Mainz and Cologne', pp. 233f.

45 *Annales Xantenses* p. 30, Annal for 870: *Eodem anno V.Kal.Mai beatus episcopus Liudbertus Saxoniae et filius Ripuariae, de quo multa bona commemoravimus, de hac luce migravit ad Dominum.*

46 See Springer (1998), 'Ribuarier', pp. 200–69 as well as Springer (1996), 'Salier und salisches Recht', pp. 485–7 and Springer (1997), 'Volk der Salier', pp. 58–83.

a fifty kilometre radius of it. So they give no hints that it was ever considered a kingdom in its own right, nor that it was ever a very large place. The basis of Wood's view on the origins of the *Lex Ribuaria* boils down to the testimony of one squarely Merovingian text, the *Passio Leudegarii*, composed between 683 and 692, which states:

> All sought king Childeric, so that he might command throughout the three *regna* which he had obtained, that judges should preserve the *lex* or *consuetudo* of each *patria*, as used to be the case.[47]

Wood read this as a reference to three extant law codes, the *Lex Salica*, *Lex Ribuaria*, and the *Liber Constitutionum* of the Burgundians, for the Neustrian, Austrasian, and Burgundian kingdoms respectively. But it might be dangerous to assume that the *regna* and the *patriae* were the same: *patria* could refer to geographical regions of all sizes, as Eichenberger showed in his book-length study of the word in early medieval sources.[48] It is possible that the author of this text envisaged the *lex* and *consuetudo* to be a very much more local affair. Indeed, Beyerle argued that the kingdom for which the *lex* was written was very small, a tiny subkingdom granted to Sigibert III in 633.[49] Ewig found this view 'unthinkable' and suggested a far more extensive region.[50]

Even if we search inside the *Lex Ribuaria* itself, we find no clear answer to the question of who the Ribuarians were in relation to the Franks, despite the fact that the *lex* contains the most detailed treatment of different ethnic groups in any sub-Roman code. For example, c.40 lists penalties for a Ribuarian killing a 'foreign' Burgundian, Roman, Frisian, Alaman, Saxon, or critically an *advenam Francum*, but in c.61,1 a *Francus Ribuarius*, possibly interpreted as a 'Ribuarian Frank', appears.[51] So the text in its current state is confusing, describing Ribuarians opposed to

47 *Passio Leudegarii Episcopi Augustodunensis I* ed. R. Krusch and W. Levison (Hannover, 1910), MGH SRM V, p. 289 [hereafter MGH SRM V]: *Interea Childerico rege expetiunt universi, ut talia daret decreta per tria quam obtinuerat regna, ut uniusquisque patriae legem vel consuetudinem deberent, sicut antiquitus, iudices conservare.* See Wood (1994), *Merovingian Kingdoms*, pp. 113–14.

48 T. Eichenberger, *Patria. Studien zur Bedeutung des Wortes im Mittelalter (6.–12. Jahrhundert)* (Sigmaringen, 1991), Nationes: historische und philologische Untersuchungen zur Entstehung der europäischen Nationen im Mittelalter 9.

49 Beyerle (1956), 'Kleinreich Sigiberts', p. 24.

50 Ewig (1976), 'Spätantikes und Fränkisches Gallien 1', p. 497: '[Beyerle's view] ist jedoch undenkbar'. See also E. Ewig, 'Die Stellung Ribuariens in der Verfassungsgeschichte des Merowingerreiches' in: Ewig (1976), *Spätantikes und Fränkisches Gallien 1*, pp. 450–71.

51 *Lex Ribuaria* p. 92 c.40.1–4: *Si quis Ribuarius advenam Francum...advenam Burgundionem...Romanum, Alamannum seu Fresionem vel Bogium, Saxonem... [occiderit]...*; p. 108 c.61,1: *Hoc etiam iubemus, ut qualiscumque francus Ribuarius...* The term *Ribuarius* features in the literature as a 'Kennwort' for distinguishing different layers in the text: Schmidt-Wiegand (2001), 'Lex Ribuaria', p. 321, Buchner (1953), *Die Rechtsquellen*, p. 24.

Franks as well as Ribuarian Franks, and providing laws for all three of these groups.[52]

It seems that there was no clear consensus about who the Ribuarians were even at the time that the *Lex Ribuaria* was put together, and it could have been constructed over decades.

1.2.4 Summary

So in the case of the Annals of Xanten, where the interest in Ribuarian *lex* is exceptional, it seems possible that there was some interaction between the complex politics of the divided Carolingian kingdoms and a reappearance of, or perhaps just new emphasis on, Ribuarian terminology. This terminology could have carried a certain baggage, in this context, about Cologne once having been the focus of an independent and prestigious kingdom, and could have been derived from a reading of the *lex*. But really the evidence about the history of the Ribuarians is too murky to give more detail here, and it is this murkiness that may indeed be the most important feature of the evidence. It might be explained if we argue that the earlier Carolingians succeeded in promoting a view of the Franks that minimised any sense of division. Such an aim has been detected in the Royal Frankish Annals, which are insistent upon the action of the Franks as a unified body against their enemies, Lombards, Saxons, Saracens, and so on, a vision useful while the Carolingian kingdoms were at least nominally ruled by a single king, that is until 840 or so.[53]

So were the Ribuarians written out of history by the Carolingians? We should not discount the possibility out of hand. Helmut Reimitz in particular has shown that individual manuscripts could present very particular notions of who the Franks were. One compilation, assembled in the context of Charles the Bald's brief kingship over the middle kingdom, deleted all references to Franks in the East, presenting them as wholly western people.[54] But this was done by manipulating the history of the Franks and the associated terminology in just one manuscript. It is a different matter to delete references to Ribuarians systematically, wiping them out of almost all sixth- and seventh-century texts.

52 Cf. comments of lack of system in the Burgundian *lex* in Amory (1993), 'Meaning and purpose', pp. 1–28.

53 McKitterick (2004), *History and Memory* summarises many of her earlier arguments. Most relevant here is R. McKitterick, 'Constructing the past in the early Middle Ages: the case of the Royal Frankish Annals' *TRHS*, 7 (1997), pp. 100–30.

54 Reimitz (2008), 'Omnes Franci', pp. 63f.

An altogether more plausible view is that the *Lex Ribuaria* was indeed originally constructed for a rather small region. The prominence of the *Lex* in Carolingian manuscripts could then be explained by deliberate dissemination, or spontaneous increase in its use, with various possible motives, but not one grounded in history or identity. The Carolingians perhaps did not feel the need to rewrite Ribuarian history, and said only as little about Ribuarians in their histories as the Merovingian authors had themselves.

The central point is that, while *gens* and *lex* could be linked to form an argument, and might well have been on occasion, we lack any good evidence for the *Lex Salica*, and the link in the case of *Lex Ribuaria* is not at all conspicuous in most of the evidence. We need an explanation for the prominence of the *Lex Ribuaria* in Carolingian manuscripts that is not grounded in considerations of *gens*.

1.3 THE MINOR *LEGES*

This background is important for an approach to the construction of the minor *leges*. It is clear, at least, that we should approach our texts with no assumptions about the nature of the link between *lex* and *gens*.

The minor *leges* have been treated in two somewhat different kinds of work. The first are technical German analyses of their content.[55] While they are extremely valuable and will be used throughout, their narrow technical focus opens them up to the kinds of criticism conventionally levelled at the work of the *Historische Rechtsschule*: they provide only shallow contextualisation, and attempt only sporadically to link the history of the texts with considerations of application. The other group, more recent English synoptic accounts of Charlemagne's reign and of Frankish law, engage only very superficially with the texts, and are prone to making sweeping conclusions without explaining their bases.[56] All existing accounts, however, agree, explicitly or implicitly, that our *leges* were produced in the aftermath of Charlemagne's imperial coronation in 802, and many connect this with an ideological programme linked with expansion of the Frankish empire: they were codified by Charlemagne,

55 The most recent works are P. Landau, 'Die Lex Thuringorum – Karls des Großen Gesetz für die Thüringer' *ZRG GA*, *118* (2001), pp. 23–57; G. Theuerkauf, *Lex, Speculum, Compendium Iuris. Rechtsaufzeichnung und Rechtsbewußtsein in Norddeutschland vom 8. bis zum 16. Jahrhundert* (Cologne, 1968), Forschungen zur deutschen Rechtsgeschichte 6; H. Siems, *Studien zur Lex Frisionum* (Ebelsbach, 1980).

56 See esp. the discussion of Collins in section 1.1 above, and Wormald (1999), *The making*, p. 92 on *Lex Saxonum*.

with definite grand political purposes.[57] I shall argue that the evidence for such views is inadequate.

1.3.1 Einhard, the Lorsch annals, the link with Charlemagne

Arguments for dating the texts to 802 are based on two accounts of Charlemagne's legislative career. The first is from Einhard's *Vita Karoli*, describing the period immediately after Charlemagne's imperial coronation:

> He ordered the *iura* of all the *nationes* which were under his control, which were not written, to be written down in letters.[58]

The second is from the *Annales Laureshamenses* for 802:

> But the emperor, while that *synodum* was taking place, called together the dukes, counts and the rest of the Christian *populus* with *legislatores*, and he ordered that all the *leges* in his *regnum* be read, and that each man be given his *lex*, and emend it wherever it was necessary, and write down the emended *lex*...[59]

These accounts are conventionally linked, so that *omnes leges in regno suo* from the Lorsch Annals are taken to mean the *iura omnium nationum* from Einhard.[60] But in fact we are on very slippery ground terminologically: both *regnum* and *leges* are difficult. Did the Lorsch Annals refer, for example, only to *lex* within the Frankish *regnum* (or *a* Frankish *regnum*)? The *leges* might have been not just the *leges barbarorum* but also, and perhaps more importantly, the capitularies, with their shrill moral programme for lay officials. Charlemagne's further commands as described in the annal resonate closely with capitulary pronouncements: whatever Charlemagne did was accompanied by the declaration of their central *idées fixes*, that *iudices* 'should judge in accordance with what was written and not accept gifts, and that all men, *pauperes et divites* should

57 See, in addition to Wormald (1999), *The making* esp. pp. 47f., the view of F. L. Ganshof, 'Charlemagne's programme of imperial government' trans. J. Sondheimer in: F. L. Ganshof, *Carolingians and the Frankish monarchy* trans. J. Sondheimer (London, 1971), pp. 55–86 on the post-coronation phase, and W. Hartmann, 'Karl der Grosse und das Recht' in: P. L. Butzer, M. Kerner and W. Oberschelp (eds.), *Charlemagne and his heritage. 1200 Years of civilisation and science in Europe, 1 Scholarship, worldview and understanding* (Turnhout, 1997), pp. 173–92. But note the counterargument in R. McKitterick, 'Charlemagne's missi and their books' in: S. Baxter et al. (eds.), *Early medieval studies in memory of Patrick Wormald* (Farnham 2009), pp. 253–67.

58 Einhard, *Vita Karoli Magni* ed. O. Holder-Egger 6th edition (Hannover, 1911), MGH SRG 25, p. 33 [hereafter *Vita Karoli*] c.29: *Omnium tamen nationum, quae sub eius dominatu erant, iura quae scripta non erant describere ac litteris mandari fecit.*

59 *Annales Laureshamenses* ed. G. Pertz (Hannover, 1826), MGH Scriptores in folio I, p. 39 [hereafter MGH SS I]: *Sed et ipse imperator, interim quod ipsum synodum factum est, congregavit duces, comites et reliquo christiano populo cum legislatoribus, et fecit omnes leges in regno suo legi, et tradi unicuique homini legem suam, et emendare ubicumque necesse fuit, et emendatum legem scribere…*

60 E.g. Theuerkauf (1968), *Lex, Speculum*, pp. 54–67; Wormald (1999), *The making*, p. 46 with a note of caution.

have justice in his realm'.[61] In any case it may also be significant that the account refers to the relevant *leges* as *already* written, at least in a state in which they could be read out before being emended.

The context of the Lorsch Annal account, the holding of 'that *synodum*', is a discussion of religious lives, an attempt to encourage the Rule of Benedict to be followed more literally by monks, and the *canones* to be followed by all the clergy in general. The stress on the status of *omnes leges in regno sui* appear, in context, as the lay counterpart to this demand. The 'each man', in need of having his *lex* clarified, seems categorised not so much by *gens* as by *ordo*, by function and office in the Christian society Charlemagne was so intent on building.[62] The relevant people was the *populus christianus*, not the *gens francorum* and the central concern the ordering of society in a broad sense, not simply the relationship between *gentes*.[63]

Furthermore, while Einhard records Charlemagne's involvement in the laws as *post susceptum imperiale nomen*, in a way that hints at *some* level of ideological linkage between *lex* and imperial office, in the Lorsch Annal account such a sense is entirely lacking. Attention to the *leges* is presented in the context of a moral programme, but not one explicitly linked with the imperial Roman past. The problems were those involved in giving everyone access to *iustitia*, and an important stimulus was the urge to order ecclesiastical as well as lay society in a highly structured way mediated through written texts.

So taken on its own, without Einhard's account, the Lorsch Annal does not suggest primarily that new *leges* were codified from scratch for *gentes*. Einhard's claim about the *iura omnium nationum* may have meant something in more general terms, but one should not automatically base on Einhard a link between Charlemagne and the minor *leges as we have them*, and base on the Lorsch Annals the further link between the texts and the place, time, and process of the 802 assembly.[64]

A very particular reading of these two accounts has overshadowed discussion of the minor *leges*. I shall propose a slightly different way of approaching them, which, although it does not discount it totally, relativises the royal-imperial contribution, and brings the concerns of the

61 MGH SS I p. 38: *et ut iudices per scriptum iudicassent, et munera non accepissent; sed omnes homines, pauperes et divites, in regno suo iustitiam habuisset.*

62 On the notion of *ordo* and *populus christianus* under Charlemagne, see M. de Jong, 'Charlemagne's Church' in: J. Story (ed.), *Charlemagne: empire and society* (Manchester, 2005), pp. 103–35 esp. pp. 108–12. See also now for a stress on the ecclesiological scheme as background to some of the 802 texts M. Innes, 'Charlemagne, written law and justice' in: A. Rio (ed.), *Law, custom and justice in late antiquity and the early Middle Ages* (London, 2011), pp. 164–69.

63 Cf. the stress on Christian identity in Nelson (2008), 'Frankish identity', pp. 71–83.

64 Cf. rejection of an automatic link between assemblies and capitulary production discussed in section 3.2 below and in C. Pössel, 'Authors and recipients of Carolingian capitularies 779–829' in: Corradini et al. (2006), *Texts and identities*, pp. 255–9.

texts closer to the needs of those involved in dealing with recognisably 'legal' problems in the relevant territories.

1.3.2 General observations on the group: the use of earlier leges *in their construction*

It is clear that the dating of the minor *leges*, as well as their function and use, needs to be considered using different evidence. The manuscripts offer no direct help in dating: there is no extant manuscript of any of these texts from the ninth century, although I use manuscript variations to construct indirect arguments for the *Lex Saxonum* later. The manuscripts listed below are in general structural terms thoroughly representative of other ninth- and tenth-century manuscripts, containing other *leges* and capitularies, just as we would expect.

BN Lat. 9654	x/xi	Lotharingia	*Ewa ad Amorem*
BN Lat. 4628A	x/xi	N. France	*Ewa ad Amorem*
BN Lat. 4631	xv	France	*Ewa ad Amorem*
Mü msc. VII 5201	$x^{2/4}$	Corvey	*Lex Saxonum, Lex Thuringorum*
London Egerton 269	$x^{inc.}$	N. E. France	*Lex Saxonum*
No extant MS			*Lex Frisionum*

So what can we say about the texts as a group? A major theme is that the minor *leges* all betray the influence of earlier Frankish texts.[65] The *Lex Ribuaria* is clearest: it was a strong influence on the Saxon and Thuringian material, both in structure and in content. Table 1.2 shows the closest parallels. Numbers in the table represent chapter numbers as found in the MGH editions.

Lex Ribuaria has also been suggested as an influence on *Ewa Ad Amorem*.[66] Schmidt-Wiegand even maintained that only laws that diverged from what was written in the *Lex Ribuaria* were included in the text. However, she provided no detailed evidence for her suggestion, and it has proved difficult to find any parallels with *Lex Ribuaria* at all. Influence of the southern *Lex Alemannorum* has been detected in the *Lex*

[65] The most substantial treatment is in R. Schmidt-Wiegand, 'Stammesrecht und Volksprache in karolingischer Zeit' in: H. Beumann and W. Schröder (eds.), *Aspekte der Nationenbildung im Mittelalter* Volume 1, (Sigmaringen, 1978), pp. 192–6. See also Buchner (1953), *Die Rechtsquellen*, pp. 39–42.

[66] The first to propose influence on the *Ewa* was Pertz: G. Pertz, 'Über das Xantener Recht' *Abhandlungen der Königlichen Akademie der Wissenschaften zu Berlin*, (1846), pp. 417–21. Gaupp disagreed: E. T. Gaupp, *Lex Francorum Chamavorum oder das vermeintliche Xantener Gaurecht* (Breslau, 1855), pp. 35–6. See also J. F. Niermeyer, 'Het Midden-Nederlands rivierengebied in de Frankische tijd' *Tijdschrift voor Geschiedenis*, 66 (1953), pp. 164–5 as well as Schmidt-Wiegand (1978), 'Stammesrecht und Volksprache', pp. 192–6.

Table 1.2 *Parallels between* Leges Ribuaria, Saxonum, and Thuringorum

	Lex Ribuaria	*Lex Saxonum*	*Lex Thuringorum*
injuries	1	1	4, 5
	2	3	6, 7, (11)
	3	5	8, 9
	4	5, 10, (11)	
	5	11, 13	12–15, 19–21, 24, 25
	6	11	16, 17
homicides	7	14	1, 2
	8	16, 17	3
	...	...	...
	16 ...	?19	

Table 1.3 *Parallels between* Ewa ad Amorem and Lex Baiuwariorum

	Ewa ad Amorem		*Lex Baiuwariorum*
17	*Si quis hominem Francum sine culpa ligaverit, solidos 12 componat, et in fredo dominico solidos 4.*	IV, 7	*Si quis eum funibus ligaverit contra legem, 12 solid. conponat.*
19	*Si quis hominis Franci casam infregerit, solidos 12 componat, et in dominico solidos 4.*	XI, 1	*Si quis in curtem alterius per vi contra legem intraverit, cum 3 solid. conponat.*
20	*Si quis hominis Franci curtem infregerit, solidos 6 componat, in dominici solidos 4...*	XI, 2	*Si autem in domum per violentiam intraverit, et ibi suum nihil invenerit, cum 6 solid. conponat.*
24	*Quidquid involant, 9 geldos componere faciat, et de unoquoque latrocinio in dominico fredo solidos 4.*	IX, 1	*Si quis liber aliquid furaverit, qualemcumque rem niungeldo conponat, hoc est novem capita restituat.*

Frisionum, where it apparently played a similar role to *Lex Ribuaria* for the Saxon and Thuringian *leges*, at least in some parts of the text.[67]

Brunner also suggested that the *Lex Baiuwariorum* was used in the *Ewa ad Amorem*, and did provide some parallels, as shown in Table 1.3.[68]

67 Schmidt-Wiegand (1978), 'Stammesrecht und Volksprache', pp. 192–6. Tables of comparison appear in Siems (1980), *Studien zur Lex Frisionum*, pp. 356–9, and his reluctance to accept that the *Lex Alemannorum* was a *Fragebogen* for the whole text throughout, is summarised at pp. 370–1.

68 Brunner (1906), *Deutsche Rechtsgeschichte*, p. 474.

The quantities for fines are in places consistent, and the phraseology is similar. Although there are only so many ways of writing 'If someone shall have tied someone else up', the terms *niungeldo* and *9 geldos* may provide a more concrete and direct link, since the latter is apparently an expansion into Latin of some of the vernacular component of the former, and the term *geldos* is used elsewhere in the *Ewa* only for the same subject, theft.[69]

The use of different texts for the compilation of the various minor *leges* can be used to argue little in specific terms. Perhaps a single team was not responsible for the compilation of all the texts, or perhaps the production of the Saxon and Thuringian *leges* might be linked more closely with each other than with the others, but these are not terribly strong arguments. The very fact of their use itself, however, is significant, and points to an important role for the earlier *leges* in the Carolingian period. Seventh- and the eighth-century *leges* are being read here to inform the thinking about how a particular society might operate, in a loose, but important sense. They provided concepts and structures through which to assess the operation of society at a local level.

Such a use may have been more widespread than what is directly attested by our extant texts, since it is quite possible that more *lex* texts were produced than are extant. If, as I suggest below, the *Ewa ad Amorem* cannot be linked with a *gens*, and if the area to which it referred was fairly small, it could provide a context for similar compilations for other regions. After all, *Ewa ad Amorem* barely survived, and probably owes its survival to the peculiarities of the preservation of documents at Rheims.[70] No manuscript of the *Frisionum* has survived at all, although Rheims seems to have had a copy in the later ninth century.[71]

The use of the earlier texts as a structural and thematic guide harmonises well with the observations I make about the use of those texts in other contexts in later chapters. We might think of these texts as at one end of a spectrum of attention to older *leges*, on which we should also place modifications in manuscripts, revisions in compilations, and production of interpretative texts, all of which are discussed below.

69 C.26–7, dealing with theft, *in Amorem* and *in Mashau*. *Lex Baiuvariorum* ed. E. de Schwind (Hannover, 1926), MGH Leges nationum Germanicarum V, 2, p. 488 [hereafter, *Lex Bav* refers to this edition] explains *niungeldo* as 'neunfaches Wergeld'. See below also for some commentary on the heavier insistence than other *leges* on the *fredus*.

70 See Chapter 3, section 3.3 below, and for the 'Rheims group' manuscripts, section 3.4 below.

71 Siems (1980), *Studien zur Lex Frisionum*, pp. 368–9. The source is a library catalogue.

1.4 *EWA AD AMOREM*

This text is the most instructive of all the minor *leges* for our purposes, but remains thoroughly puzzling.[72] While Gaupp had already recognised its importance in the mid-nineteenth century, and while focused studies have concentrated on some of its most mysterious features, it has hardly played a role in wider discussions of Frankish *lex* since.[73] This is in part because there are so few manuscripts, only two, BN Lat. 4628 A and BN Lat. 9654. But in part it may be because it fits only problematically with the notion of the *leges* as *Stammesrecht* or *Volksrecht* that has directly or indirectly dominated most commentary. I suggest that the difficulty with this fit is important, and can be linked with my interpretation of the *Lex Ribuaria*, to downplay the significance of *gens* in the use and construction of the *leges* more generally.

1.4.1 *Dating and location*

Debates over dating and location have centred on how to decipher the place names in the text: Pertz first thought that references to procedures *in sanctis*, and *in loco qui dicitur sanctum* in fact referred to *Sanctum*, that is Xanten.[74] This form is certainly attested, but the use of the term in this context makes perfect sense as 'holy'.[75] More recent arguments have centred on identifying the *Amor* found in the text and title: for Gaupp, and most German commentators since, it could be equated with the German Hamaland; for Niermeyer it was a Dutch river Amor, reflected hazily in a handful of corrupted place names, and so the text was intended for the central Dutch river system.[76] In other words, German

[72] The edition used here is *Lex Francorum Chamavorum* ed. K. F. von Richthofen (Hannover, 1875), MGH Leges in folio V, pp. 271–6 [hereafter MGH Legum V], but see also *Lex Ribuaria et Lex Francorum Chamavorum* ed. R. Sohm (Hannover, 1883), MGH Fontes iuris Germanici antiqui in usum scholarum seperatim editi 6.

[73] Some classic studies are: Pertz (1846), 'Xantener Recht', pp. 411–23; Gaupp (1855), *Lex Francorum Chamavorum*; R. Schröder, 'Die Heimat der Lex Chamavorum' *Monatschrift für die Geschichte Westdeutschlands, VI* (1880), pp. 492–502; H. Froidevaux, *Études sur la "Lex dicta Francorum chamavorum" et sur les Francs du pays d'Amor* (Paris, 1891); N. Fustel de Coulanges, 'Quelques remarques sur la Loi dite des Francs Chamaves' in: *Nouvelles recherches sur quelques problèmes d'histoire* (Paris, 1891), pp. 399–415; Niermeyer (1953), 'Midden-Nederlands rivierengebied', pp. 145–69.

[74] MGH Legum V p. 272 c.10 and c.11.

[75] Fustel de Coulanges (1891), 'Nouvelles recherches', p. 403. Attested for example in *Annales Xantenses* p. 20 Annal for 864.

[76] Gaupp (1855), *Lex Francorum Chamavorum*, pp. 8f.; Niermeyer (1953), 'Midden-Nederlands rivierengebied', pp. 146–51. While A. Wirtz, 'Die Geschichte des Hamalandes' *Annalen des Historischen Vereins für den Niederrhein, 173* (1971), pp. 32–3 claims that the Dutch view was generally accepted even by the Germans, a more recent German acceptance of Gaupp's views can be found in R. Schmidt-Wiegand, 'Lex Francorum Chamavorum' in: Hoops and Jankuhn (2001), *Reallexikon der germanischen Altertumskunde*, pp. 317–18. For reservations with connecting *Amor* with any specific river see H. Heidinga, *Medieval settlement and economy north of*

scholars have claimed the land for Germany, Dutch scholars for the Netherlands.

These debates were needed, and were so vigorous, because the text provides no ethnic terminology for its subjects. The only extant title, in BN Lat. 9654 is *Notitia vel commemoratio de illa euua quae se ad Amorem habet.*[77] The familiar title *Lex Francorum Chamavorum,* enshrined in the MGH edition, is wholly fictitious, simply reflecting Gaupp's view that this was a text from the Hamaland, inhabited by 'Chamavian Franks'. But Gaupp's conception of the text as *Volksrecht* was already criticised in the nineteenth century. Froidevaux, for example, argued that the text could not be seen as 'loi populaire', but his only other possible category was a species of *Königsrecht* – royal law –, so he imagined it was an unfinished capitulary with an 'air of generality'.[78] I shall advance a rather different understanding of the text, as neither *Königsrecht* nor *Volksrecht.*

The approximate dating had proved far less problematic and controversial. It surely must be Carolingian, since it is so steeped in Carolingian vocabulary of office, with *comites* and *missi dominici* throughout, fulfiling functions strikingly resonant with what the capitularies prescribe: a count is described as responsible for dealing with thieves, summoning local assemblies, organising military duties, and work on dykes on the river.[79] But attempts to date it in any more detail have led nowhere. As argued above, links with the accounts of 802 are pure speculation, and Baluze's attempt to link it with the description in the Moissac chronicle of the redaction in 813 of forty-six *capitula* at Aachen was rightly exposed as absurd by Gaupp.[80]

I shall not engage any further with location and dating, but accept that the text referred to a society of the ninth century, located somewhere around where the north-eastern edge of the Frankish world had been in the period before the expansion into Saxony. Hamaland and 'Amor Land', taken, following Niermeyer, to be the central Dutch river system, are adjacent regions, which could even be seen as overlapping, and the

the lower Rhine: archaeology and history of Kootwijk and the Veluwe (the Netherlands) (Assen, 1987), p. 182.

77 For the term *Ewa*, see D. Green, *Language and history in the early Germanic world* (Cambridge, 1998), pp. 31–3 and Köbler (1971), *Recht im frühen Mittelalter*, pp. 181f. The term was glossed *Gezunfti*, meaning 'pact', 'contract' in BN Lat. 9654. See Gaupp (1855), *Lex Francorum Chamavorum*, p. 7; Froidevaux (1891), *Études*, p. 36.

78 Froidevaux (1891), *Études*, pp. 33f.

79 E.g. MGH Legum V p. 275 c.38: *Si quis sclusam dimiserit, quando suus comes ei commendat facere, in fredo solidos IV componere faciat. Quando rumpit et eam emendare noluerit, solidos IV in dominico componere faciat.*

80 Translated in P. D. King, *Charlemagne: translated sources* (Kendal, 1987), p. 148: 'And there came to the emperor bishops, abbots, counts and the magnates of the Franks, meeting together at Aachen; and he there laid down forty-six articles concerning matters of necessity to God's church and the Christian people'. See Gaupp (1855), *Lex Francorum Chamavorum*, pp. 1–2.

charters to which I refer below fit into either one or the other.[81] I now concentrate instead on characterising the text and investigating how it fits the concerns of our descriptive sources.

1.4.2 Nature of the text. Themes

If this is a piece of ethnography in any sense, it would be unique in not clearly identifying its *gens.* Instead, the subjects of the text appear in this way:

1. In the first chapter about ecclesiastical matters and about those *servi Dei* who serve there, we are to have it as other Franks do.[82]

2. We also have the *bannum dominicum,* just as other Franks have it.[83]

13. He who is *ingenuus* through a charter is to have this status in every way, like other Franks.[84]

This first-person style is unparalleled in *lex,* and rather rare in capitularies too (where the voice is not that of the king), so the text is unusually clearly presented as collectively developed for some kind of community.[85] But the content suggests very firmly that particular issues were at stake in this development: this is emphatically not simply a spontaneous act of writing of perceived customs to clarify and simplify the regulation of affairs internal to a local community. The whole reference to 'other Franks' suggests a context of some sort of contact, a situation in which practices and rights had to be specified *against* those of the 'other Franks'. While the phraseology can be approached with the same scepticism to which the rhetoric of consensus in the capitularies has been subjected, this is still striking and significant.[86] I shall suggest that this really does, in some sense, represent an agreement, almost a treaty, and I shall link this with attempts to gain control over the land.[87]

In comparison with other *leges,* the compensation list in the *Ewa* has a very firm emphasis on the payment of the *fredus,* the peace money generally imagined as paid to the king, as well as variously expressed

[81] The clearest map of the region can be found in A. Beekman, *Geschiedkundige atlas van Nederland* (The Hague, 1913–38) Vol. I map 15.

[82] MGH Legum V p. 271: *In primo capitulo de causis ecclesiae et de illis servis Dei, qui ibidem deserviunt, sic habemus, quomodo et alii Franci habent.*

[83] MGH Legum V p. 271: *De banno dominico similiter habemus, sicut alii Franci habent.*

[84] MGH Legum V p. 272: *Qui per cartam est ingenuus, sic debet in omnia pertinere sicut alii Franci.* The precise meaning is somewhat obscure.

[85] For first person *commands* in the *Lex Ribuaria* and their interpretation as edicts, however, see Wood (1993), 'Theodosian Code', p. 169; Wood (1992), 'Administration, law and culture', p. 66.

[86] Scepticism is to be found prominently in F. L. Ganshof, *Was waren die Kapitularien?* (Darmstadt, 1961) esp. pp. 54–62. For a brief overview of the debate see Pössel (2006), 'Authors and recipients', pp. 253–5.

[87] The gloss *gezunfti* is tenth or eleventh century. See note 77 above.

charges *in dominico* or similar.[88] The text is also focused quite heavily on the *bannum*, as its appearance already in chapter two suggests.[89] Eight more chapters, out of a total of forty-eight, concern the administration of the *bannum*, presumably the royal *bannum*, but also the *bannum* invoked by the *comes* or his *missus* to summon people to his *placitum*, as well as apparently for public duties such as guarding and fighting.[90] In contrast with the 'barely royal' *Lex Salica*, then, a strong theme in this text is outlining the rights of the king and his *comes*.[91]

The concentration on matters of freedom and unfreedom is also important. We have seen how it was worth emphasising that the status of someone manumitted by charter is to be the same as that of other Franks. We also learn of differences in manumission procedure: manumission by charter is established, but there is no mention of the penny-throw. Instead, the uniquely attested procedure is termed *hantrada*, to be performed with twelve witnesses.[92]

Inheritance is, surprisingly, not treated in any detail. Indeed the only time inheritance is mentioned is to describe the practices of the *Francus homo*, whose identification is deeply problematic, and deserves detailed treatment.

Franci homines

The *Franci homines* in the text are distinguished from *homines ingenui* by a *wergeld* three times higher. Their position is analogous to that of the *nobiles* in the Saxon and Thuringian material, and represents a departure from older *leges* that imagine the *ingenuus* or *liber* as the highest legally definable social rank.[93] The term *francus* is otherwise used only in those

88 Take for example 'He who kills a *homo Francus* is to pay 600 *solidi*. He is to pay 200 *solidi* for the work of the king as *fredus*'. MGH Legum V p. 271 c. 3: *Qui hominem Francum occiderit, solidus DC componat. Ad opus dominicum pro fredo solidos CC componat.* But note in this case the nineteenth-century conflict over the punctuation of the phrase, linked with the debate over whether the *franci homines* were a *Dienstadel* or a *Geschlechtsadel*, in e.g. E. von Moeller, 'Der Homo Francus der Ewa Chamavorum' *Mitteilungen des Instituts fur Österreichische Geschichtsforschung*, 23 (1902), pp. 219f. For the contrast with other *leges* see the examples in the comparison with *Lex Baiuwariorum* in Table 1.3 above.

89 Cf. MGH Capit. I no. 68 pp. 157–8 c.2–3 for Bavaria.

90 The most comprehensive account of the semantic field of the term *bannum* can now be found in C. West, *Reframing the feudal revolution. Political and social transformation between Marne and Moselle, c.800 to c.1100* (Cambridge, 2013), pp. 173–98.

91 In the most general terms found in the text: 'Anyone who has acted *contra rectum* is to make a compensation of four *solidi* as *fredum dominicum*.' MGH Legum V c.33 p. 275: *Quicquid contra rectum fecerit, cum solidis IV in fredo dominico componere faciat.* BN Lat. 9654 preserves the variant *Quicquid contra drictum fecerit, cum solidis 4 emendare faciat, in fredo solidos 4*. 'Barely royal' was Wormald's characterisation of the early *Lex Salica*: Wormald (1999), *The making*, p. 41.

92 The wording is somewhat obscure: MGH Legum V c.11 p. 272: *Qui per hantradam hominem ingenuum dimittere voluerit, sua manu duodecima ipsum ingenuum dimittere faciat.* BN Lat. 4628A adds *in loco que dicitur sanctum* before *sua manu*.

93 See H. Brunner, 'Nobiles und Gemeinfreie der Karolingischen Volksrechte' in: H. Brunner; K. Rauch (ed.), *Abhandlungen zur Rechtsgeschichte. Gesammelte Aufsätze* (Weimar, 1931), pp. 261–93.

passages of the text already quoted, in which someone freed by a charter to become *ingenuus* is envisaged as having the same rights as 'other Franks'. It seems, then, as if 'Frank' is used in two different senses in this text, a usage with parallels with at least the *Lex Ribuaria*.[94] But does this employment of terminology most often used in an ethnic context mean anything more here?

Niermeyer's most recent and influential assessment of the problem was produced before the seminal works of the ethnogenesis school were written. Thus these *homines franci* were Frankish settlers, 'real' Franks with royal protection, whose presence in the area could be traced back to the wars between Frisians and Franks at the end of the seventh century.[95] Niermeyer suggested certain individuals from charters who could be *homines franci*.[96] Some of these settlers and their descendants, then, he understood to have kept a distinct identity for more than a century, before the text was drawn up. The argument was enhanced by a reading of the structure of the text founded in the *Volksrecht–Königsrecht* distinction. The central evidence was the fact that, while the *wergeld* of the *homo Francus* was three times that of the *homo ingenuus*, the penalties for injuries were only one and a half times the value.[97] The hypothesis was essentially that an original codification of *Volksrecht* had been hijacked at some later stage to include the material on the *comites*, the *missi dominici*, and to increase the *wergeld* of the *homines Franci*, protected by the king. But this theory is not supported by any other strong arguments about the language and structure of the text. Fruin made much of the large difference in the levels of payments due apparently to the king, and related those to developments in coinage.[98] But these dues are described in different terms in the text, so he relied on an alleged, and problematic, conflation of the sense of *fredus* with *bannum*.[99] Essentially, arguments concerning the structure of text have

94 Wood (1995), 'Defining the Franks', pp. 48–9.

95 Niermeyer (1953), 'Midden-Nederlands rivierengebied', pp. 151–62. See also A. Bergengrün, *Adel und Grundherrschaft im Merowingerreich: siedlungs- und standesgeschichtliche Studie zu den Anfängen des fränkischen Adels in Nordfrankreich und Belgien* (Wiesbaden, 1958), Vierteljahrschrift für Sozial- und Wirtschaftsgeschichte. Beihefte 41, pp. 113–20.

96 See also the list of references to *Franci homines* in charters in A. Russchen, 'Sub lege Francorum. Ein Beitrag zur Abgrenzungen der Frisia Criterior' *It Beaken*, *26* (1964), p. 253: they are found throughout the Frankish kingdoms. The term is also in the *Formulae Senonenses*. See Rio (2009), *Frankish Formulae*, p. 178 and Brunner (1906), *Deutsche Rechtsgeschichte*, p. 351.

97 First noted in von Moeller (1902), 'Homo Francus', pp. 226–7.

98 R. Fruin, 'Opmerkingen over de Ewa quae se ad Amorem habet' *Verslagen en Mededeelingen van de vereniging tot uitgave der bronnen van het Oude Vaderlandsche Recht*, 7 (1924), pp. 571–96.

99 Fruin (1924), 'Opmerkingen', pp. 574–5. Schmidt-Wiegand's judgement, in contrast, was that the precision of Franco-Latin terminology was increasing in precisely these Carolingian-era texts. Schmidt-Wiegand (1978), 'Stammesrecht und Volksprache', pp. 156f.

rested purely on second guessing the intentions of the compilers, and how systematically they imagined scales of payments.[100]

There is, however, no reason to dismiss the view that there was 'Frankish' settlement out of hand: it makes some sense in the light of the charter evidence discussed below, and can be compared with well-attested importations of counts into Saxony in the ninth century.[101] But we now have reason to consider older views that the *homines Franci* were members of a local *Uradel* – an indigenous aristocracy.[102] We have a theoretical basis, since we can now envisage an indigenous aristocracy coming to identify as *Franci* in an ethnic sense, and at the same time we know that 'Frank' can have various layers of meaning. The text certainly provided incentives to identify as a *Francus homo* in just the same way Wormald observed for the *Franci* in *Lex Salica.* We also have a close parallel in Toxandria, immediately to the south, where Costambeys has established that an eighth-century aristocratic community was indigenous, but bought into the Frankish political order by supporting the Pippinids, and granting land to monasteries.[103]

But no attempt to decode this semi-ethnic terminology in terms of the actual origins of the group concerned can be wholly convincing. All we can say is that a distinction is being made, and that it was not strongly and explicitly drawn along ethnic lines. Groups that could be, and had been, distinguished in ethnic terms were present in the area: the text refers to thefts by Saxons and Frisians, and the whole region had been central in seventh- and eighth-century wars described in narratives as between Franks and Frisians. But in Costambeys's charters for eighth-century Toxandria, ethnicity was simply not an issue.[104] Equally Wood has reached beneath the Carolingian-era narratives, and suggested that 'tribal' boundaries in the later Merovingian period might not have been as important as previously thought, that there was cross-border landholding on some scale, and that the Saxons, Thuringians, and Frisians might have been both more deeply christianised and

100 Cf. treatment of the *Lex Saxonum* in section 2.4.2 below, where more sophisticated and convincing arguments are evaluated.

101 See Becher (1996), *Rex, Dux und Gens*, pp. 110f. The basic work is still S. Krüger, *Studien zur sächsischen Grafschaftsverfassung im 9. Jahrhundert* (Göttingen, 1950), Studien und Vorarbeiten zum historischen Atlas Niedersachsen 9.

102 Notably von Moeller (1902), 'Homo Francus', pp. 217–30. And cf. D. P. Blok, *De Franken in Nederland* 3rd edition (Haarlem, 1979), pp. 45–8 where it is suggested that they were an *Uradel* but one with a particular relationship with the Frankish king.

103 M. Costambeys, 'An aristocratic community on the northern Frankish frontier, 690–726' *EME*, *3* (1994), pp. 39–62.

104 Costambeys (1994), 'Aristocratic community', p. 62.

more deeply integrated into the Frankish political system than often imagined.[105] The most important change in the eighth century was, for Wood, less the importation of Frankish settlers or conversion to Christianity, than a deep reorganisation of landholding brought about by a monasticisation of the frontier zone. This is a process spread throughout western Europe in the eighth and ninth centuries: it has been estimated that between a quarter and a half of all land was transferred to the church in the period *c.*740–840.[106] The process had a profound effect on social structure, notably entrenching an elite. Could this be the kind of context in which to see the movement to identify as a *francus homo*?

A lowest common denominator view must be that the *homines Franci* were relatively high-status individuals, with some trans-local interests and connections. The only direct treatment of inheritance in the text becomes, then, very interesting, precisely because it concerns only these *homines Franci.*[107] It was perhaps just as important that the local, or lower status, inhabitants knew about the practices of more trans-regional 'high Frankish' individuals, their views about inheritance and assumptions about landholding, as vice versa. Although inheritance is treated only briefly, it still seems that the exchange of information provided might help lubricate a shift in landholding patterns in a way that was intended to minimise disputes. If landholders were remote, they faced problems of exactly how to tap the agrarian surplus, as I explore in more detail below. Understanding local issues of status, obligations, relationships, was crucial to their ability to exercise control. Equally, locally significant individuals might want to understand something of the traditions of remote parties before making agreements with them. In an important sense, what was crucial for both parties to a transaction was a result that land was held in a way that minimised the potential for disputes.

105 I. Wood, 'Before or after mission. Social relations across the middle and lower Rhine in the seventh and eighth centuries' in: I. L. Hansen and C. Wickham (eds.), *The long eighth century* (Leiden, 2000), pp. 149–66. And see already the view that there was no 'iron curtain' in the eighth century between Francia and pre-conquest Saxony in R. Wenskus, *Sächsischer Stammesadel und fränkischer Reichsadel* (Göttingen, 1976), Abhandlungen der Akademie der Wissenschaften in Göttingen. Philologisch-Historische Klasse, with the term at p. 474. The iron curtain did, of course, run through the historical Saxony. See also Chapter 2, note 8.

106 Innes (2000), *State and society*, pp. 42–7, and elsewhere on all aspects of the relationship between church land and the power of the elite.

107 MGH Legum V c.42 p. 275: *Si quis Francus homo habuerit filios, hereditatem suam de sylva et de terra eis dimittat et de mancipiis et de peculio. De materna hereditate similiter in filiam veniat.*

The hints in the text at collective decision, agreement, and exchange of information, then, suggest that it be seen neither as raw royal-imperial legislation complete with a debatably meaningful rhetoric of consensus, nor as independent local spontaneous codification, but as something falling between the two. It was a kind of treaty or agreement between sides who had not been enemies, nor were distinguished along straightforwardly ethnic lines, but that still reflected and expressed power relations, in the sense that it was clearly not an agreement between equal parties.

1.4.3 The context for redaction. The charters

Extant charters can add some depth to our understanding of the nature of this agreement. Before turning to them, we must first consider the need of those extracting resources by owning land to understand what a grant of land in these regions might mean. The problem of what landownership actually was, what any grant of land in early medieval society really meant, is already deep enough in regions that by the Carolingian period had long traditions of Frankish control or influence, or from which a rich documentary record survives.[108] Studies by Innes and Brown have shown just how 'fuzzy' property relations could be in the ninth century.[109] This is seen most spectacularly where different charters express parallel claims to ownership of the same piece of land, but even what seem to be unambiguous charters themselves granted land only within a very particular context of understandings of the rights of others. Notions of property were made up of complex bundles of interpersonal relations. Thus Innes writes of the 'asymmetry' of grants of land that carried a sense of appropriate use according to the wishes of previous owners.[110]

How then might a potentially even more complex situation be understood: how might property relations be negotiated in areas of more recent Frankish control, in contexts of new understandings of property, of duties and of status associated with social rank? Could our written

[108] A fine introduction to the theoretical problems and terminology can be found in F. Theuws, 'Landed property and manorial organisation in Northern Austrasia: some considerations and a case study' in: F. Theuws and N. Roymans (eds.), *Images of the past: studies on ancient societies in Northwestern Europe* (Amsterdam, 1991), pp. 299–397.

[109] Most recently M. Innes, 'Practices of property in the Carolingian Empire' in: J. R. Davis, and M. McCormick (eds.), *The Long Morning of Medieval Europe* (Aldershot, 2008), pp. 247–66; Brown (2001), *Unjust seizure*. See also C. West, 'Upper Lotharingia and Champagne c. 850–c. 1100' (2007), Unpublished PhD dissertation, University of Cambridge. A rather different notion of Frankish property conceptions seems to be held by Wickham, who talks of 'full landownership' as a Frankish export in Wickham (2005), *Framing*.

[110] Innes (2000), *State and society*, pp. 70–2.

leges be seen in part as by-products of negotiations to resolve these kinds of problem between old and new landholders?

Various charters for the region allow us to bring out some patterns.[111] Echternach's activity is very prominent in the record for the south of the region, and also *in Fresia* in the early eighth century.[112] Fulda owned much land in Frisia proper.[113] Lorsch had land scattered throughout the central Dutch river area.[114] Utrecht's cartulary also records several grants for the broad area, and Werden's property is treated in some detail below. So the charters show energetic land transfers in the region, a lot of them in the late eighth century, and a number in the earlier ninth.

Relating the charters explicitly to the process of elite formation, to contextualise the *homines franci* is harder. Size of grant in the Lorsch charters does not necessarily correlate well with the status of the donors. A grant from 800 by one bishop and one *vir illuster* grants only two *mansi*, one of them in *Betuwe*.[115] Tiny grants and large grants display no clear chronological patterning: already in 793 an individual gave a substantial grant of several scattered estates, complete with fifty-four *mancipia*.[116] Much more work than is possible here is needed to integrate some very fruitful archeological work on the Veluwe with the charters

111 The most convenient collections are *Oorkondenboek van Holland en Zeeland tot 1299* ed. A. C. F. Koch Volume 1, (La Haye, 1970), which lists 25 pre-900 charters or other records of land transaction, *Diplomata Belgica ante annum millesimum centesimum scripta* ed. M. Gysseling and A. C. F. Koch, Volume 1, (Brussels, 1950) [hereafter *Diplomata Belgica*], which lists 79, and *Oorkondenboek van het Sticht Utrecht tot 1301* ed. S. Muller and A. C. Bouman Volume 1, (Utrecht, 1920), which lists 91. Many of these are the same, since the catchment area of each collection overlaps, but does not coincide exactly. A list for Teisterband can be found in D. P. Blok, *Teisterband* (Amsterdam, 1963), Mededelingen der Koninklijke Nederlandse Akademie van Wetenschappen 12, p. 17. Only two ninth-century charters specify Hamaland, see Wirtz (1971), 'Geschichte des Hamalandes', pp. 7–84. Lists for the provinces of Holland and Westfriesland are in D. P. Blok, 'Holland und Westfriesland' *Frühmittelalterliche Studien, 3* (1969), p. 350.

112 About a third used in *Oorkondenboek Utrecht* are from Echternach. See C. Wampach, *Geschichte der Grundherrschaft Echternach im Frühmittelalter* Volume I, Textband (Luxemboug, 1930), which sadly lacks a map.

113 Most of the grants in *Oorkondenboek Holland en Zeeland* are from Fulda. For maps see F. Staab, 'Der Grundbesitz der Abtei Fulda bis zur Mitte des 9. Jahrhundert and seine Stifter' in: W. Böhne (ed.), *Hrabanus Maurus und seine Schule: Festschrift der Rabanus-Maurus-Schule 1980* (Fulda, 1980), pp. 48–63 with Frisia at p. 54. Abbreviated grants for Frisia and Saxony are recorded in the twelfth-century *Codex Eberhardi.* See E. E. Stengel, 'Über die karolingischen Cartulare des Klosters Fulda' in: *Abhandlungen und Untersuchungen zur Geschichte der Reichsabtei Fulda* (Fulda, 1960), Veröffentlichung des Fuldaer Geschichtsvereins 37, pp. 147–93 as well as E. Freise, 'Studien zur Einzugsbereich der Kloster von Fulda' in: K. Schmid and G. Althoff (eds.), *Die Klostergemeinschaft von Fulda im früheren Mittelalter* Volume 2,3 (Munich, 1978), pp. 1003–269.

114 See the maps attached to *Codex Laureshamensis* ed. K. Glöckner (Darmstadt, 1974) [hereafter *Codex Laureshamensis*].

115 *Codex Laureshamensis* Vol. 1 p. 381 Chr. 100.

116 *Codex Laureshamensis* Vol. 1 p. 381 Chr. 99.

in a thoughtful way.[117] We can, however, say more about the general pressures that might have led to the writing of a *lex*.

'International' cases in the Netherlands area

We start with a simple demonstration that land transactions at the old fringes of the Frankish sphere of influence could involve awareness of the need for care in taking into account conceptions of rights, described as different in terms of *gens*. A charter dated to 834 preserved in an eleventh-century manuscript records a grant of land in Oosterbeek to St Martin's Cathedral, Utrecht:

> ... So we, called by these names: Ouo, Addo, Hrodhard, Theodbald, Bern, Knut... give to the church of St Martin... for the care of the soul of Wihbreht, just as his son Waldbehrt himself gave to us in settlement (or: 'entrusted us to transact') [the property] which Wihbreht was seen to own in Oosterbeek and Praast, and all which was in their *dominium* according to *Lex Francorum*, with *mancipia*, ... and all neighbouring parts, which, lest they provoke a loathing of reading when all brought together - because they are of diverse kinds - we have avoided listing in this document...
>
> *Signum* of Theotans . *Signum* of Odbreht...
>
> AND OF THE SAXONS: Theodolf. Euerhard. Abbo...[118]

We can see something of the complexities of transferring land here, and of the problems St Martin's might face, trying to derive anything from the land after the transfer. The charter seems very concerned to make clear the different statuses of the parties to the transaction. Perhaps the abnormally heavy stress was a way of imposing some kind of system on a situation in which abnormally many interlocking relationships were at play. What was the relationship between the men making the grant, and their relationship with Waltbehrt? Even in this medium-range

[117] H. Hamerow, *Early medieval settlements: the archaeology of rural communities in Northwest Europe, 400–900* (Oxford, 2002), pp. 114–19; H. Heidinga, 'From Kootwijk to Rhenen: in search of the elite in the Central Netherlands in the Early Middle Ages' in: J. Besteman, J. Bos and H. Heidinga (eds.), *Medieval archaeology in the Netherlands: studies presented to H. H. van Regteren Altena* (Assen, 1990), pp. 9–40; Heidinga (1987), *Settlement and economy*.

[118] *Diplomata Belgica* pp. 317–8 no. 181: *...Idcirco nos his uocitati nominibus: Ouo, Addo, Hrodhard, Theodbald, Bern, Knut, ab ipso non despici sperantes allata, cui non nisi que dedit conferuntur, sed pro labentibus credentes dari mansura, tradimus ad ecclesiam sancti Martini que constructa est in castello Traiecto in pago Niftarlaca, pro remedio anime UUibrehti sicut nobis ipse hac filius eius Uualdbehrtus ad perficiendum legitime contradiderunt, quicquid in Ostarbac et in Prast isdem / Uuihbreht uidebantur possidere, omnique quod sub lege Francorum in eorum erat dominio, cum mancipiis, curtilibus....et cum omnibus adiacentibus, que ne congesta fastidium legenti generarent, quia in diuersis sunt speciebus, in presenti traditione numerare uitauimus. Hanc uero traditionem ... Signum Theotans. Signum Odbreht. ..... ITEM SAXONUM: Theodolf. Euerhard. Abbo. Alfheri...* The charter is also edited in *Scriptores rerum Sangallensium. Annales, chronica et historiae aevi Carolini* ed. G. Pertz (Hannover, 1829), MGH Scriptores in folio II, p. 217 [hereafter MGH SS II].

grant, these relationships spanned 'national' boundaries. Wihbreht and Waltbehrt were quite possibly high-status Saxons, the son and grandson of Widukind.[119] Oosterbeek is some sixty kilometres east of Utrecht, close to Deventer, yet we have a Knut, presumably someone connected in some way with Scandinavia, among the donors, and a list of Saxon witnesses clearly delimited. The mention of the fact that the possibly Saxon Wihbreht had held his land by *Lex Francorum* has been interpreted either as marking out these men as new, ninth-century kinds of *homines franci* in the sense of the term in the *Ewa ad Amorem* (whatever that really was), or as evidence for the *Geltungsbereich* of various *leges*, understood unusually early here as territorial rather than personal.[120] A simpler and more plausible interpretation is that the invocation of a particular *lex* was a response to these international interests: it may have expressed in compressed form an agreement or declaration of the rights that Wihbreht claimed to hold over the land. Critically here these would have been inheritance rights, or possibly the very right to alienate land to the church against the claims of family, which is so insistent a focus of various legal texts.[121] The relevant rights may also have been exactly those enumerated in the charter, over people and resources. The notion of agreement leading to the use of a particular *lex* is examined in more detail in the next chapter.[122] We cannot, however, see any more closely in this transaction how notions of *lex* related to the transaction and to the relationships, let alone relate the reference to any particular text. The issues at play, the complexities of the relationships, are, as usual, not revealed in the charter. It does, however, hint that the negotiations over the property were complex, that expressions of 'ethnic' status had some role, and that they could involve the packaging of bundles of rights into an ethnically designated *lex*. We might well imagine from the way this charter talks about relationships that written texts describing rights and traditions could have had a role in the negotiations, but we can go no further.

119 See K. Schmid, 'Die Nachfahren Widukinds' *DA*, *20* (1964), p. 3.

120 The former suggestion in Niermeyer (1953), 'Midden-Nederlands rivierengebied', pp. 159–60 and the latter in Russchen (1964), 'Sub lege Francorum', pp. 251–7 as well as A. Russchen, 'De akte van Folker (855)' *It Beaken*, *23* (1961), p. 96.

121 Prominently placed at the very beginning of both Bavarian and Alaman *leges*, though not *Lex Ribuaria* or *Salica*. MGH Capit. I no. 139 p. 282 c.6 on the practicalities of transferring land to a church when one is not physically present in the same *comitatus* as the land in question. But cf. MGH Capit. no. 138 pp. 276–7 c.7, concerning the protection of pauper children whose parents had given all their land to the church. This capitulary was wrongly ascribed to Charlemagne by Ansegis.

122 Chapter 2, section 2.2.1 below.

A second case is found in the Werden Polyptych, in a manuscript and hand of the late ninth century.[123] It records a grant to Werden of land in Hamaland and Betuwe by a certain Folcher in 855 of his inheritance:[124]

... my property, which is mine by *ius hereditarium*... according to *Lex Ribuaria* and *Lex Salica* as well as *Ewa Fresonum*... to the *ius* and *proprietas* of the aforementioned monastery [Werden] ... for the care of my soul and my parents' souls, I have given into permanent possession, and have transacted according to the aforementioned *leges*.[125]

Even if we do accept Kötzschke's suggestion that the reference to *Ewa Fresonum* was interpolated when two records of lands and transfers were spliced together, the text suggests that Folcher both held his land, and gave it, according to multiple *leges*.[126] Certainly this fits very problematically with a personality principle, so it has been interpreted as evidence for the territorial spheres of applicability of the relevant *leges* in the region.[127] The assumption has been that different lands were transacted according to different *leges*. But could we imagine instead that multiple procedures were used for the transaction of the same land? The *Lex Ribuaria*'s procedure involving charters could be imagined to be followed in the very writing up of the charter itself.[128] The *Lex Salica*'s ritual, involving a rod called the *festuca*, could be followed to give legitimacy on a different level to illiterate community members.[129] Again the text does not help us to go further.

All we can say for sure is that these grants display a sensitivity to issues of *lex*, of different *leges* and of *gens*. We can only further note that they show that the interaction of these notions was complex, and, as we have already seen in the case of *Lex Ribuaria*, cannot easily be reduced to a question of 'personality' or 'territoriality'. This complexity fits with the wider problems of imagining how 'legal personality' might have operated: that disputes occurred between individuals who might have different legal personalities, and that so much legal business related

123 According to the editor in *Die Urbare der Abtei Werden an der Ruhr* ed. R. Kötzschke (Bonn, 1906), p. CIX [hereafter *Urbare Werden*]. Düsseldorf St.-A Hs. A.88. Bischoff affirms this decision: B. Bischoff, *Katalog der festländischen Handschriften des neunten Jahrhunderts. Teil I.* (Wiesbaden, 1998), p. 227.

124 *Urbare Werden* pp. 8–11.

125 *Urbare Werden* pp. 8–11 at 10: *...ego quasdam proprietatis meae res, qui mihi iure hereditario in pago Hamulande, in comitatu Uuigmanni, nec non et in Batuue, in comitatu Ansfridi, cum edificis omnibus..., coram testibus et nobilium virorum presentia, secundum legem Ripuariam et Salicam necnon secundum ewa Fresonum, de iure et potestate mea, in ius et proprietatem predicti monasterii, in quo et laicalem habitum et secularem converationem Domino miserante dimisi, pro remedio anime mee et parentum meorum, perpetuo possidendas tradidi, et secundum predictas leges vestituram feci.*

126 *Urbare Werden* p. 9.

127 Russchen (1961), 'De akte van Folker', pp. 91–7, including also a discussion of interpolation.

128 For the importance of charters in *Lex Ribuaria* see McKitterick (1989), *Written word*, pp. 69–73.

129 See *Pactus Legis Salicae, Lex Salica* ed. K. A. Eckhardt (Hannover, 1962–9), MGH Leges nationum Germanicarum IV, 1–2 [Hereafter *Lex Salica*] Vol. 1 p. 177 *Lex Salica* K 48. For *festuca* in charters see Davies and Fouracre (1986), *Settlement of disputes*, p. 271.

to land that mediated relationships between people of different status. The central point then is that legal personality fits, in its basic sense, with only a certain subset of disputes, that in the kinds of case shown here, the sensitivity to different *leges* may well reveal extensive discussions and agreements over status and *lex*, rather than the application of rigid principle, and that these discussions might well have involved reference to texts in some form.

Later in this book I turn to a rather different set of Carolingian texts to suggest that a sensitivity to different laws, as well as a flexibility in approach to them, was more widespread in Carolingian society, certainly not restricted to the regions covered by these charters. The more specific argument here is that reference to existing bodies of law was not always enough for those making agreements, and that the need for clarity in those agreements could result in the compilation of new written texts, which look in some way normative. The next set of charters adds some flesh to this argument, by providing a deeper context for the compilation of the *Ewa*.

The Werden charters, Wichmond and Westphalia

These charters give more detail about the social interactions at play, but do not bring up particular *leges* or *gentes*. In this sense they fit with what we have seen from the *Ewa ad Amorem*, that ethnic terminology was not the only way to describe bundles of rights in written form. The central evidence is from Werden, from which survives not only an unusually rich collection of private charters from before 848, but also a polyptych from the 890s.[130] We can therefore see both something of Werden's understanding of its rights over land near the end of the century, and something of how it built up those rights in the preceding period.

Goetz's analysis of the polyptych has showed that Werden's holdings east of the Rhine differed from those on the Frankish side.[131] While its estate at Friemersheim was as close as one can find to an archetypal classical Frankish bipartite estate, the Westphalian holdings are better characterised even at the end of the century as *Streubesitz* – scattered holding. There exists a German debate over whether there was a characteristically Saxon form of pre-conquest holding, considered *Abgabengrundherrschaft* – lordship involving dues of some kind – rather

130 *Oorkonden Werden ed. D. P. Blok (Assen, 1960); Urbare Werden* ed. R. Kötzschke (Bonn, 1906). See also the discussion of the Werden cartulary in R. McKitterick, 'The uses of literacy in Carolingian and post-Carolingian Europe: literate conventions of memory' in: *Scrivere e leggere nel alto medioevo* (Spoleto, 2012), Settimane, pp. 189–98.

131 H.-W. Goetz, 'Herrschaft und Raum in der frühmittelalterlichen Grundherrschaft' *Annalen des historischen Vereins für den Niederrhein, 190* (1987), pp. 7–33 esp. pp. 14–15. Some of his specific conclusions on Werden were, however, already anticipated in G. Droege, 'Fränkische Siedlung in Westfalen' *Frühmittelalterliche Studien, 4* (1970), p. 286.

than the Frankish *Betriebsherrschaft* – lordship involving direct service –, which might explain this. Although the sources are deeply problematic and the methodologies used have been suspect, elements of this work are still salvageable.[132] It is quite possible that deportations of Saxons allowed, in some places, deep settlement by Franks, unimpeded by previous landholders, who were able to introduce more structured landholdings than were possible west of the Rhine, and it may be that, however infrequently we find actual examples of the classic bipartite estate in Francia, this form of organisation was held as an ideal.[133]

For Werden's lands, however, everything points away from such a process. However much Werden's monks may have wanted classic bipartite estates east of the Rhine and in the Netherlands, it is clear that they needed to build up their estates piece by piece, and negotiate hard with local landholders and wielders of power. We have for the Netherlands region a group of nine private charters granting land in and around Wichmond, some forty-five kilometres east of Oosterbeek, to Liudger and the relics of St Salvator from the period 793–806, when Liudger was attempting to found a church first in Wichmond, and then in Werden.[134] These show very clearly the 'fundamental fact' of fragmentation of property rights there.[135] Charter 200 grants the land that a single dependent man, *Landulfus litus meus*, has cultivated, and one field that Hildigerus *ingenuus homo* held in the *benefitium* of the donor. Charter 203 specifically retained the usufruct of the property while the donor and his wife lived, but agreed to pay one *solidus* per year as a contribution to the costs of lighting the church at Werden.[136]

Charter 204, a grant by a group of four *coheredes et conparticipes et consanguinei* of a single field, again specifically warns their heirs not to

[132] The classic article is Droege (1970), 'Fränkische Siedlung', pp. 271–88. Droege's methodology, which relied on place names and the eleventh-century Corvey polyptych, was taken to pieces by R. Rösener, 'Strukturformen der älteren Agrarverfassung in sächsischen Raum' *Niedersächsisches Jahrbuch für Landesgeschichte*, 52 (1980), pp. 107–43. See also W. Rösener, 'Zur Struktur und Entwicklung der Grundherrschaft in Sachsen in karolingisher und ottonischer Zeit' in: A. Verhulst (ed.), *Le grand domaine aux époques mérovingienne et carolingienne* (Ghent, 1985), pp. 173–207.

[133] See J.-P. Devroey, 'Les premiers polyptyches rémois VIIe–IXe siècles' in: Verhulst (1985), *Le grand domaine*, pp. 93f. This approach, which links an ideology of order with the actual practice of estate administration is important, and has some resonances with my arguments about hagiography in the next chapter. See also J. Devisse, *Hincmar, archevêque de Reims, 845–882* (Geneva, 1975), pp. 489f.; Theuws (1991), 'Landed property', p. 313. Innes (2000), *State and society*, pp. 77f. on how infrequently it comes up.

[134] *Diplomata Belgica* pp. 346–55 nos. 199–208. For Liudger's career, see B. Senger (ed.), *St. Liudger und die Abtei Werden* (Essen, 1962); B. Senger, *Liudger in seinem Zeit* (Münster, 1982); B. Senger, *Liudger, Leben und Werk* (Münster, 1984); A. Angenendt, *Liudger: Missionar, Abt, Bischof im frühen Mittelalter* (Münster, 2005) among others.

[135] Innes (2000), *State and society*, p. 77.

[136] For some insight onto the significance of church lighting see P. Fouracre, 'Eternal light and earthly needs: practical aspects of the development of Frankish immunities' in: Davies and Fouracre (1995), *Property and power in the early Middle Ages*, pp. 53–81.

try to recover the land. The charter shows awareness of a donation to Liudger by a count, and its sanction clause is interesting for specifying that a fine be paid *in dominicum* if any of their heirs go against the charter. Here we perhaps see one context for the stress on the role of the count in the *Ewa ad Amorem*: he might not have provided 'objective' justice in a recognisable sense, but the charters suggest that he did provide a certain conceptual nucleus for a forum in which land claims could be fixed. The clash between the feelings of rights of heirs and church really is of fundamental importance, and provides a very plausible context for the application of material written and confirmed in *leges* to disputes over asymmetrically understood property relations. Disputes along those lines are especially prominent in the Freising material; the *Lex Baiuwariorum* was clear on this question, and was cited in certain contexts.[137]

At Wichmond, then, grants to Liudger took a large variety of forms, and would involve negotiation with a range of individuals who thought they had relevant rights. Even these relatively terse charters show something of the complexity and interests behind local landholding patterns and practices in much the same way as for the Frankish heartlands. The church at Werden would in this case have a vital interest in understanding the heirs' conception of their rights, or what kind of relationship they could expect with a *litus.* These are precisely the kinds of subject covered by the minor *leges.* The texts of the minor *leges* by no means deliver a comprehensive guide to such matters, but at least provide some basic understanding, and a terminological framework for further investigation.

The compensation catalogues in the *leges* are also central to issues of landholding seen through the Werden charters. First they expressed hierarchies and explained terminology, such as *litus*. They also gave mechanisms for addressing the very real economic impact of the loss of labour a homicide would cause. In the Werden charters, in this case for territory in Westphalia, we find an unusually clear example of a homicide having another kind of impact, causing a realignment of property holding.

We wish it to be known to all *fideles*, how I Thangrinus and my two sons Hardgrimus and Atugrimus give, for the care of our souls and of the soul of the dead Bosco, a part of our inheritance, which came to us by just judgement from the grievous slaying of my son the same Bosco, in a *villa* called Hustene - that is the whole *patrimonium* which Brunricus and his sons, who carried through that killing at the incitement of the devil

[137] Wormald (1999), *The making*, p. 85. On the use of Bavarian *Lex* see above all C. Hammer, 'Lex scripta in early medieval Bavaria' in: B. King and S. Ridyard (eds.), *Law in mediaeval life and thought* (Sewanee, 1990), Sewanee mediaeval studies 5, pp. 185–95; C. Hammer, 'Land sales in eighth- and ninth-century Bavaria: legal, economic and social aspects' *EME, 6* (1997), pp. 47–76. Cf. Innes (2000), *State and society*, pp. 69–71. W. Brown, 'The use of norms in disputes in Early medieval Bavaria' *Viator*, *30* (1999), pp. 15–40; Brown (2001), *Unjust seizure.*

with malign hands, were seen to have in that *villa* by *leges*, and anything, wherever it is, that used to belong to them by *ius* - to the relics of St Salvator and into the hands of Liudger the abbot. For it was judged for me and my sons according to *leges seculi* into our power. Therefore we give... it all to Liudger: in land, in forest, and in every sense in which it provided by *leges* for Brunrico and his sons...[138]

We cannot read much on the surface into the recurrent stress on *lex* and *lex seculi*. Perhaps reference to written *lex* played some part in the conduct of the case that resulted in the transfer of the land to Thangrinus and his family, but yet again the terminology is not exact enough to know. It is, however, clear that, while the *formulae* of the Werden charters are fairly consistent over some fifty-five years, the stress on *lex* and *ius* is to be found much more frequently in the earlier charters, falling out of use in those later than this example. But again the charter exemplifies the kinds of problem faced by Liudger and Werden: they would have to find out somehow what rights Brunrico and his family had once claimed in this land, what holding it 'by *leges*' really meant, indeed where this land actually was. 'Hustene' seems to be in Neuheim, close to Arnsberg, also on the Ruhr, but some ninety-five kilometres away from Werden, more than half the way to Paderborn. Distance would have made Liudger's job harder.

These charters suggest, then, that the realities of control on the ground were rather complex in the regions to which *Ewa ad Amorem* referred (as well as in comparable regions), and that recipients of grants would want some insight into those realities beyond what could be conveyed in a charter because of constraints on space (explicitly invoked in the Oosterbeek example), ambiguities of terminology, or the formulaic veneer. Understanding how local hierarchies worked, what the terms might have meant, how individuals might, according to a certain view, legitimately claim a different status were therefore of prime importance. Equally important was instilling some kind of understanding of the traditions of those coming into possession of land. A text along the lines of the *Ewa ad Amorem* did not give detailed answers, but at least provided a framework for understanding a society, its social structure,

138 *Urkundenbuch Niederrheins* p. 13 no. 23: *Notum fieri desideramus omnibus fidelibus. qualiter ego Thangrinus et duo filii mei Hardgrimus et Atugrimus pro remedio animarum nostrarum et defuncti bosconis tradimus partem hereditas nostrae. quae nobis iusto iudicio ex lugubri occisione filii mei eiusdem bosconis aduenit in uilla quae dicitur hustene. id est omne patrimonium quod in eadem uilla brunrico et filii eius qui eandem occisionem instigante diabolo malignis manibus peregerunt legibus habere visi sunt. uel ubicunque aliquid iuste ad eos pertinebat ad reliquias s. saluatoris et in manus liudgeri abbatis. quia mihi et filiis meis secundum leges seculi potestati nostrae diiudicatum est. idcirco haec omnia in elemosinam nostram et filii mei bosconis cum omni integritate tradimus liudgero abbati. siue in terra siue in silua uel in omni conprehensione quae ad predictum brunriconem et filios eius legaliter respiciebat. traditaque in perpetuum esse uolumus et nullis umquam immutari temporibus.*

Acta est autem publice anno XXXIIII regni domni carli... in uilla quae dicitur hustene iuxta fluvium rura...

public duties, and the kind of ways disputes involving land, or anything else, could or should be resolved. While the text is perhaps best seen as an expression of a desire for clarity rather than as a binding normative resource, it might, in a certain sense have been envisaged, like a charter, as representing a firm agreement, as a potential resource in a dispute.

The range of the grants in the charters associated with the monasticisation of the frontier zone, and the complexity of the understanding of very localised societies needed to derive any good from the transactions they recorded, therefore, provide a context in that a *lex* might be written that, although it could invoke ethnic distinctions, conspicuously lacked an overriding ethnic message. Placing the text in this context also suggests that it was not aimed in the first instance at projecting Charlemagne's status as a lawgiver, although it upheld and clarified the rights and duties of counts. Later we add some depth to the notion of negotiation in legal business.

1.5 SUMMARY

I have suggested that the relationship between *lex* and *gens* varied substantially from situation to situation. *Lex Ribuaria* was barely associated with a *gens*, except in a particularly tense political situation, and the *Ewa ad Amorem* may never have been. *Leges* may sometimes have been read and compiled with questions concerning ethnicities in mind, but I have suggested that they could also be read and compiled for reasons related to real problems associated with land transactions, to help understand traditions of social rank and landholding. I have suggested also that the related issue of legal personality, and its counterpart, territoriality, are too narrow to make sense of the evidence, that we need to think instead about negotiation to establish the relevant *lex*, or negotiated codification to establish a new one.

Much of the treatment of these two cases has been quite speculative, because of a lack of sources and crippling ambiguities in the sources we do have, but is part of a wider cumulative argument. Our next case, the *Lex Saxonum*, is in some ways easier to study than either of these. The places and people referred to in the text are not controversial, and we also have complementary legal texts, some relevant accounts in narratives, and some records of disputes, all of which give a rich context to the production and possible use of the text. We are able to go further with the Saxon material for understanding themes sketched in this chapter, notably the notion of law by negotiation, legal personality, and wide participation in the drawing up of legal texts. So we turn now to Saxony.

Chapter 2

THE MINOR *LEGES* 2. SAXONY AND THE *LEX SAXONUM*

2.1 INTRODUCTION

The sources for Saxony allow us to observe *lex* from a completely different angle. They are unusually rich in references to *lex*, and often in contexts that tie it specifically to the Saxon *gens*. *Lex* clearly mattered to the Saxons, and to those wishing to write about Saxony, throughout the ninth century.

Very little positive information is known about the inhabitants of Saxony before the Carolingian conquest. We know only that they had no writing, no coin, probably had no centralised political organisation, and were not Christian.[1] But by the earlier tenth century the Saxons were sprouting the most powerful kings in Europe as the Carolingian political order was transformed. The ninth century was, then, a period of extraordinary social, political, and cultural change in Saxony. New forms of political organisation were established, writing and coin introduced, a new religion and network of churches and monasteries established, and an independent Saxon political identity developed.[2] I trace the role of *lex* in these processes of change in two kinds of source: narratives, including hagiographies, then various records of disputes and settlements. I shall then relate these observations to an analysis of the legal texts.

If we take our references as signifying written *lex*, the degree of interest found in Saxon texts and texts concerning Saxony is surprising.[3] Throughout the ninth century the Saxon church remained poor by comparison with the Frankish heartlands, royal lands were restricted

[1] On all aspects, in addition to works cited throughout, see the articles in D. Green and F. Siegmund (eds.), *The continental Saxons from the Migration period to the late ninth century* (Woodbridge, 2003), Studies in historical archaeoethnology 6. For the possibility that more Saxons were Christian than generally imagined, see Wood (2000), 'Before or after', pp. 149–66.

[2] Becher (1996), *Rex, Dux und Gens*.

[3] For an exhaustive account of the uses of the term *lex* see Köbler (1971), *Recht im frühen Mittelalter*, pp. 76f.; see also McKitterick (1989), *Written word*, p. 38 and Nehlsen (1977), 'Aktualität und Effektivität', pp. 863f.; Theuerkauf (1968), *Lex, Speculum*, p. 60.

in scope, and even royal visits were very infrequent.[4] Under Louis the German, it has been argued that Saxony was ruled far less 'intensively' than Franconia.[5] However we think of this difference, in quantitative or qualitative terms, it is clear that Saxony had a different relationship with royal power from that elsewhere in the Frankish kingdoms in the ninth century, and part of this may be connected with a reluctance of East Frankish kings to issue laws of any kind. We have capitularies from Charles the Bald, from the Lothars, but nothing from Louis the German.[6] Tenth-century Ottonian government in Saxony at least in certain senses went on to place less emphasis on written instruments than Carolingian, and just one text that looks like a capitulary survives from the tenth century, from 951.[7] So the ninth-century interest in *lex* seems strange both when one looks back from the tenth century, and when one looks at the activities of ninth-century kings. It needs to be explained.

My investigation of *lex* in Saxon society is organised by category of source. I start with narratives and hagiographies, then move to charters, treatises, and councils, and finally relate these analyses to an investigation of the written legal texts relevant to Saxony.

2.2 LAW IN SAXONY IN NINTH-CENTURY DESCRIPTIVE SOURCES

2.2.1 Narrative accounts of the Stellinga rebellion

The most striking references to *lex* of all are found in connection with the so-called Stellinga revolts. In their entries for 841–2, four near-contemporary narrative sources record a revolt among the Saxons. All the sources describe it as in some sense socially motivated, portraying members of lower social orders rising up against their masters. Accordingly, the revolt has been seen in the context of a worsening of the position of the peasantry, an intensification of their dependence, since

4 See C. Carroll, 'The bishoprics of Saxony in the first century after Christianization' *EME*, *8* (1999), pp. 219–45; S. MacLean, *Kingship and politics in the late ninth century. Charles the Fat and the end of the Carolingian Empire* (Cambridge, 2003), pp. 97f.

5 See for example T. Reuter, 'The Ottonians and Carolingian tradition' ed. J. L. Nelson in: T. Reuter, *Medieval polities and modern mentalities* ed. J. L. Nelson (Cambridge, 2006), pp. 279f. But see now the view that Louis the German radically intensified government in the East in E. J. Goldberg, *Struggle for Empire: Kingship and conflict under Louis the German 817–76* (Ithaca, NY, 2006), pp. 186f. Another recent work on Louis the German is W. Hartmann, *Ludwig der Deutscher* (Darmstadt, 2002).

6 See, however, for considerations of problems of survival and some assemblies that might have produced capitularies Goldberg (2006), *Struggle for Empire*, pp. 210f. and 228.

7 The basic article is K. Leyser, 'Ottonian government' in: *Medieval Germany and its neighbours 900–1250* (London, 1982), pp. 69–101. For the capitulary, see Leyser (1982), 'Ottonian government', p. 78; *Constitutiones et Acta Publica Imperatorum et Regum* ed. L. Weiland (Hannover, 1893), MGH Legum sectio IV I, p. 17 no. 8.

the Carolingian conquest.[8] The revolt's specific political context was also considered by Goldberg, who drew attention to the links between the revolt and the conflict between Lothar I and Louis the German.[9]

Two of the accounts suggest that issues involving *lex* were of central importance for the rebels:

Nithard records:

[Lothar promised...] that he would let them have the same *lex* in the future which their ancestors had observed when they were still worshipping idols. Since they desired this *lex* above all, they adopted a new name,'Stellinga', rallied to a large host, almost drove their lords from the kingdom, and each lived as their ancestors had done according to the *lex* of his choice.[10]

The *Annales Bertiniani* for 841 record:

Lothar, having turned tail, reached Aachen. To renew the struggle, he applied himself to winning over the Saxons and other frontier peoples. He went so far as to offer those Saxons called Stellinga - there is a very large number of them among that people - the choice between some kind of *lex* and the *consuetudo* of the ancient Saxons, whichever they preferred. Always prone to evil, they chose to imitate pagan usage rather than keep their oaths to the Christian faith.[11]

So what exactly was this *lex* that was such an emotive issue? The terms are certainly slippery. Nithard's account is phrased generally enough that

[8] Wickham (2005), *Framing*, pp. 585–88 at p. 585: 'nowhere in Europe did things change so fast for the worse for peasants as in Saxony'. The most comprehensive account of this process is R. Wenskus, 'Die ständische Entwicklung in Sachsen im Gefolge der fränkischen Eroberung' *Settimane*, *32* (1986), pp. 587–616, but the historiography is vast. For the relative lack of evidence of stratification in the Saxon archaeological record before the Carolingian conquest, see F. Siegmund, 'Social relations among the Old Saxons' in: Green and Siegmund (2003), *Continental Saxons*, pp. 85–91. Some recent accounts of social change, notably E. J. Goldberg, 'Popular revolt, dynastic politics, and aristocratic factionalism in the early middle ages: the Saxon Stellinga reconsidered' *Speculum*, *70* (1995), pp. 467–501 treat Marxist interpretations from the DDR. For a contextualisation of the approaches of historians in the former East Germany (DDR) see W. Zöllner, *Karl oder Widukind? Martin Lintzel und die NS- "Geschichtsdeutung" in den Anfangsjahren der faschistischen Diktatur* (Halle, 1975), Wissenschaftliche Beiträge der Martin-Luther-Universität Halle-Wittenberg 10/T9.

[9] Goldberg (1995), 'Popular revolt', pp. 467–501. Some earlier accounts of the revolt are: E. Müller-Mertens, 'Der Stellingaaufstand' *Zeitschrift für Geschichtswissenschaft*, *20* (1972), pp. 818–42; W. Eggert, 'Rebelliones servorum' *Zeitschrift für Geschichtswissenschaft*, *23* (1975), pp. 1147–64.

[10] *Carolingian Chronicles: Royal Frankish Annals and Nithard's Histories* trans. B. W. Scholz and B. Rogers (Michigan, 1970), p. 167; Nithard, *Historiarum libri IIII* ed. E. Müller (Hannover, 1907), MGH SRG XLIV, pp. 41–2: IV, 2: *...ut legem quam antecessores sui, tempore quo idolorum cultores erant, habuerant, eandem illis deinceps habendam concederet. Qua supra modum cupidi, nomen novum sibi, id est Stellinga, imposuerunt, et in unum conglobati, dominis e regno poene pulsis, more antiqo qua quisque volebat lege vivebat.*

[11] *The Annals of St Bertin* trans. J. L. Nelson (Manchester, 1991), p. 51; *Annales Bertiniani* ed. G. Waitz (Hannover, 1883), MGH SRG V, pp. 25–6 [hereafter *Annales Bertiniani*]: *Hlotharius terga vertens et Aquasgranii perveniens, Saxones ceterosque confines restaurandi praelii gratia sibi conciliare studet, in tantum ut Saxonibus qui Stellinga appellantur, quorum multiplicior numerus in eorum gente habetur, obtionem cuiscumque legis vel antiquorum Saxonum consuetudinis, utram earum mallent, concesserit.*

lex could refer only to a very vague sense of social relations, of the right ordering of society. Elsewhere, Nithard uses the term *lex* in a flexible, though instructively flexible sense: in the next chapter he describes the treaty made by the warring brothers as *leges,* in a way wholly familiar from late antique and classical usage.[12] Prudentius of Troyes, the author of this section of the *Annales Bertiniani*, on the other hand, draws a clearer contrast between *lex* and *consuetudo,* more clearly suggesting a contrast between written and unwritten law. If these sources had written *lex* in mind, they are perhaps the most explicit statements in the whole sphere of Frankish influence that written *lex* was directly relevant to the lives of at least some inhabitants.

But if it was written law, can we identify which written law it might be? Commentary that has noticed the invocation of *lex* has generally imagined *lex* to have consisted of the Saxon capitularies and the *Lex Saxonum.*[13] In these views, the peasants were revolting against the imposition of a Carolingian law that bolstered the position of landholders, while they had maintained or constructed a social memory of a valid *consuetudo* by which social relations were structured somewhat differently. This interpretation assumes implicitly that the texts were effective in practical application, and that they were read in a particular way still in the 830s and 840s. In fact the two capitulary texts were very different, products of very specific phases of Charlemagne's war.[14] Would the first Saxon capitulary, probably from the 780s, whose tone was heavily moderated in the second of 797, still be applied ruthlessly in the 840s?[15] Our manuscripts do not help us at all in establishing who might be reading what, and when: the capitularies survive in one and two manuscripts respectively. But in any case there is no hint in our narratives that the problematic *lex* was directed specifically at Saxons. It could be anything in the whole corpus of Frankish legal texts. Equally the *lex* in question could have been found in other royal capitularies: there survive puzzling capitulary chapters and fragments from Charlemagne's reign directed specifically at Saxons, which are analysed below.[16]

A problem yet more basic in understanding how the Stellinga's demands might have been related to *lex* is that we know so little about

[12] Nithard, *Historiarum* p. 43 IV, 3: *concederunt pacem et leges invicem sibi subiectis...*

[13] Eg. Goldberg (1995), 'Popular revolt', p. 842; Müller-Mertens (1972), 'Stellingaaufstand', p. 837. Note that they are edited together in MGH Legum V as *Leges Saxonum* although they have very different manuscript contexts.

[14] The most recent detailed and comprehensive treatment of these capitularies is still Theuerkauf (1968), *Lex, Speculum*, pp. 38–54. See also R. McKitterick, *Charlemagne: the formation of a European identity* (Cambridge, 2008), p. 253.

[15] The dating of the first capitulary is somewhat problematic. See literature in the previous note, as well as, for the suggestion that it be redated to the earlier 790s, Y. Hen, 'Charlemagne's Jihad' *Viator*, 37 (2006), pp. 33–51.

[16] See section 2.4.1.

Saxon society before the Frankish conquest of 772–804. We are forced to reconstruct it from fragmentary reports from outsiders, archaeological reports of only seventy to eighty cemeteries, and crucially also from our legal texts themselves.[17] Thus the texts have sometimes been stretched quite far. Goldberg, for example, used *Lex Saxonum* as evidence for social organisation 'by the eighth century', and argued that the Saxon *edhilingui* described by Nithard were descendents of a warrior elite who migrated to Saxony in the third century.[18] In this account, the *lex* was used both to reflect the basic social status of the Stellinga as accepted from at least the eighth century, *and* was an understandable object against which to revolt in favour of an older law. The basic problem is that the legal texts are both deeply implicated in our assessment of pre-conquest Saxon society, which is needed to provide a context for the Stellinga's demands, and are a possible object in themselves of the Stellinga's anger.

So it seems futile to probe the question of what specific elements of *lex* were the problem: perhaps it was something in written legal texts, but we simply do not have enough evidence to go further. We can, however, say a little more about the way our annalists wrote about the *lex*, and its associations, and compare this with the treatment of *lex* in other narrative sources, before returning to the legal texts themselves.

The choice of *lex*

Strikingly, both our accounts mention a choice of *lex* by which to live. There are fragmentary hints elsewhere also that the applicable law was subject to negotiation in contexts involving the king.

An important example is found a decade earlier in a letter of 830 drafted by Einhard for Louis the Pious to the political community of Merida, Spain, encouraging them to resist the demands of Abd ar-Rahman II, emir of Cordoba, principally in connection with unjust taxes and tribute. The letter adds:

> if you wish to abandon him and come over to us, we shall grant you your ancient rights ... and shall command you to follow no other *lex* than the one under which you wish to live[19]

[17] For a survey of the literary evidence see I. Wood, 'Beyond satraps and ostriches: political and social structures of the Saxons in the early Carolingian period' in: Green and Siegmund (2003), *Continental Saxons*, pp. 271–97. For the archaeology see Siegmund (2003), 'Social relations', p. 77. Wickham acknowledges the problem in understanding agricultural organisation, and proposes comparing Anglo-Saxon England: Wickham (2005), *Framing*, p. 585.

[18] Goldberg (1995), 'Popular revolt', pp. 471–2.

[19] Translated in P. E. Dutton, *Charlemagne's courtier: the complete Einhard* (Peterborough, 1998), pp. 148–9 Einhard, *Einhardi Epistolae* ed. K. Hampe (Berlin, 1899), MGH Epistolae V, pp. 115–16; [hereafter MGH Epp. V] no. 12: *antiqua libertate vestra plenissime... vobis uti [concedimus] et... non aliam legem, nisi qua ipsi vivere volueritis, vos tenere iubemus.*

The most convincing way of understanding *lex* here may be as already sketched, as a bundle of legal understandings, given shape by a kind of treaty, which established relationships between parties, in a way that went beyond, on the one hand, royal-imperial legislation (with some ideology of consensus attached) and on the other hand, beyond the notion of law as an immutable possession grounded in *gens*. The passage expresses at the same time the possibility that a particular law *could* be imposed, that people could be commanded to follow a particular law, in a way found in some other Carolingian accounts of the Romans, and thoroughly familiar from classical histories.[20]

But it also shows again that ideas could be flexible, that, perhaps especially in regions on the fringes of Frankish control, *lex* could be an important subject of negotiation between those with an interest in controlling the relationships it expressed.

A second important set of texts are the Saxon capitularies. They do not talk of a choice of law in quite the same terms as either of the previous two texts, but if we treat the language in the preamble as more than pure rhetoric, they appear to show a similar process of negotiation between kings and a group referred to as members of a particular *gens*.

In the 797th year..., there being assembled together in his service at the palace of Aachen on 28 October the venerable bishops and abbots and the illustrious counts, and there being gathered together at the same time Saxons from various districts, Westphalians and Angrarians as well as Eastfalians, all have with one accord agreed and determined that with regard to those provisions for which Franks, if they offend against the king's *bannum*, pay sixty *solidi* in composition Saxons shall pay likewise if they act in any respect against those *banna*.[21]

[20] So Freculf notes in two cases that Roman conquests involved a change of law. Mettelus after his conquest of Crete 'exchanged Minoan *leges* with Roman *leges*'. Freculf of Lisieux, *Historiarum Libri XII* ed. M. Allen (Turnhout, 2002), Frechulfi Lexoviensis episcopi opera omnia. Corpus Christianorum. Series Latina CLXIXA, p. 360 [Hereafter, *Chronicon*] I, 6, 17: *legesque Minois Romanis legibus permutavit.* Octavian Augustus also forced the peoples he conquered to 'serve' Roman laws, pp. 415–16 I, 7, 16: *Germanos videlicet, Gallos, Britones, Hispanos, Hyberes, Austeres, Cantabros, occiduo sub axe jacentes, per se Augustus, ad eos veniens, Romanis legibus servire coegit.* Cf. Hrabanus's attitude to the Saxons in his *De oblatione*, discussed in section 2.3.2 below, Hrabanus Maurus, *Liber de Oblatione Puerorum* ed. J.-P. Migne (Paris, 1864), PL Vol. 107 Col. 419–40: *Sed nunc a quibusdam primatibus de ipsa gente secundum carnem editis ingrate spernuntur, ac contra jus coeli contraque jus fori, ne testes esse veritatis valeant, indigne abjiciuntur: cum hoc nec ratio humana, neque divina id fieri de bere ullo modo dictet, nec talis ordo unquam in orbe triquadro fuerit. Narrant enim historiae totam Asiam, sub centum viginti satrapis constitutam, legibus Persarum obedisse. Sic etiam Romanorum dominationi omnes gentes censu ac sensu secundum sancita imperatorum per diversas provincias suis temporibus subjectas esse, civemque Romanum ascribi pro magna dignitate ac veneratione apud omnes nationes haberi. Sed non mirum quod isti, qui legibus divinis contraria sentiunt, foedera pacti humani rite non servent; errantes enim, et in errorem mittentes, apud Deum culpabiles et apud homines vituperabiles fiunt.*

[21] Translation from King (1987), *Charlemagne: translated sources*, p. 230. MGH Capit. I p. 71 no. 27: *Anno ab incarnatione domini nostri Iesu Christi DCCXCVII... convenientibus in unum Aquis palatii in eius obsequio venerabilis episcopis et abbatibus seu inlustris viris comitibus ... simulque congregatis Saxonibus de diversis pagis, tam de Westfalahis et Angariis quam et de Oostfalahis, omnes unanimiter consenserunt*

The very basic issue of the *bannum* is, then, very specifically presented as negotiated by a treaty. The thrust of the rest of the treaty is the protection of the king's *missi* and of priests, but more importantly the working out of how fines and fees are to be distributed, and how royal authority might be integrated into existing mechanisms for settling disputes, concentrated on local judicial assemblies.[22]

Law in these accounts is something negotiated between local groups of some sort and by kings and their representatives. One argument of these first two chapters is that we need to recognise the reality and depth of this negotiation: law was not laid down straightforwardly by kings, nor was it clung to straightforwardly as the ancestral possession of a *gens*. This sense of negotiation runs through our accounts of the Stellinga, but also through texts where kings are more remote. In the previous chapter we saw in the *Ewa ad Amorem* a kind of agreement with 'legal' content, negotiated at a lower social level, more removed from the actions of kings. In that case, royal interests were clearly at play, but in a rather more diffuse sense. We move now deeper into accounts of the operation of law within Saxon society, where we can see ideas about law still further removed from the court.

2.2.2 Hagiography

The hagiographical accounts play a large role in existing reconstructions of pre-conquest Saxon society, but I analyse them for what they reveal about the ninth century. Two historians have opened up this material to such an analysis. Beumann read Saxon hagiography of the ninth century in the context of attempts to legitimise the Saxons, to raise their profile with respect to the Franks, as part of a strategy of *Vergangenheitsbewältigung* – of coming to terms with the past.[23] Becher then extended an analysis into the tenth century, to construct a complementary picture of a growth in Saxon political self-determination

et aptificaverunt, ut de illis capitulis pro quibus Franci, si regis bannum transgressi sunt, solidos sexaginta conponunt, similiter Saxones solvent, si alicubi contra ipsos bannos fecerint.

22 Esp. MGH Capit. I p. 72 no. 27: *...condicto comune placito simuil ipsi pagenses veniant: et si unanimiter consenserint, pro districtione illius causa incendantur; tunc de ipso placito commune consilio facto secundum eorum ewa fiat peractum, et non pro qualibet iracundia aut malivola intentione, nisi pro districtione nostra.* Trans. as for previous note: 'Let a *placitum communum* be summoned and the *pagenses* come there together; and if they agree with one accord that his house should be burned in order to coerce him to judgement, then let the burning be carried out by virtue of the decision reached at the *placitum*, according to their *ewa*, and not by reason of any anger or malicious intent but solely for coercion to judgement on our behalf (*pro districtione nostra*)'.

23 H. Beumann, 'Die Hagiographie "bewältigt": Unterwerfung und Christianisierung der Sachsen durch Karl den Grossen' *Settimane, 28* (1982), pp. 129–63.

through the Carolingian into the Ottonian period.[24] Hagiography expressed, and was a tool in promoting, changing views of 'Saxonness', and we find that law comes up in this context, especially in Rudolph of Fulda's account, treated below.

But some of the missionary *Vitae* can also be read as bound up in a strategy of promoting and entrenching more concrete power relations at a local level, and so are relevant to our discussion of *Ewa ad Amorem*. Beumann showed that Altfrid's *Vita Liudgerii*, from the second quarter of the ninth century, still emphasised the Frankish achievement in conquering, something which derivative products such as the *Vita Lebuini Antiqua* (mid to late ninth century) already relativised.[25] And this text preserves a remarkable account of how the son of one of count Cobbo's *coloni* was possessed by an evil sprit, and saved by contact with Liudger's relics. Cobbo was perhaps the most powerful count in Saxony in the 840s, and enjoyed especially close relations with Louis the German.[26] The advice to seek out St Liudger came directly from Cobbo's wife: the decision by the victim's mother to take him is even described as *iuxta praeceptum dominae suae*.[27] This piece of hagiography then sent a simple, forceful message: one should do what one's lord says. References to *lex* in other relevant hagiographical work, of which we have several, must be seen in this context. The treatment of law in Saxon hagiography can be read as part of a commentary on the Saxon *gens* and political self-determination on the one hand, and power relations in a recently conquered society on the other.

24 Becher (1996), *Rex, Dux und Gens*. *Selbstbewußtsein* is the term used. See also, for a similar process working on a smaller scale K. Krüger, *Studien zur Corveyer Grundungsüberlieferung* (Münster, 2004).

25 Beumann (1982), 'Hagiographie', pp. 160f. I have accepted Ian Wood's datings of these texts. See I. Wood, 'Missionaries and the Christian frontier' in: I. Wood, The missionary life: saints and the evangelisation of Europe, 400–1050 (Harlow, 2001), p. 52.

26 See Goldberg (1995), 'Popular revolt', pp. 487f.; Krüger (1950), *Grafschaftsverfassung*, pp. 41–2 and 71–9 on Cobbo's Egbertiner family. See also J. Prinz, 'Das hohe Mittelalter vom Vertrag von Verdun (843) bis zur Schlacht von Worringen (1288)' in: W. Kohl (ed.), *Westfälische Geschichte* (Düsseldorf, 1983), Veröffentlichungen der Historischen Komission für Westfalen im Provinzialinstitut für westfälische Landes- und Volksforschung des Landschaftsverbandes Westfalen-Lippe 43, pp. 340f.

27 Altfrid, *Altfridi Vita Sancti Liudgerii* ed. G. Pertz (Hannover, 1829), MGH Scriptores in folio II, pp. 418–19 III, 21: *Cobbonis venerabilis comitis colonus quidam, adolescentem filium Warmundum nomine habuit, quem malignus spiritus invasit, et tam vehementer vexare coepit, ut ad desperationem vita eius perducta esset. Cuius mater haec dominae suae, vidilicet uxori Cobbonis, sollicite per nuntium indicare studuit. Illa vero confestim mandavit ei dicens: Si adhic filius vivit, fac eum celeriter efferri, et statue illum contra viam quae ducit ad sepulchrum sancti Liutgeri, atque ad sacrum sepulchrum eius te eum adducturam Deo favente promitte, et credo, quo pro eiusdem famuli Dei meritis sanandus sit. Cum ergo mater pro eodem semivivo puero iuxta praeceptum dominae suae vota perageret, continuo in eodem loco, et in eodem momento daemone expulso, plenam sanitatem accepit. Deinde secundum sponsionis votum ad memoratum viri Dei sepulchrum sanus a matre peructus est, sanusque rediit atque in ea, quam acceperat, sanitate, domino largiente, permansit.* See also the newer edition *Die vitae sancti Liudgeri* ed. W. Diekamp (Münster, 1881).

The literary background: Bede

Before turning to these texts we should first control for literary *topoi*. We can compare the accounts of the *origo gentis* with the only relevant earlier written source that mentions the internal business of Saxony and the Saxons, that is Bede's *Ecclesiastical History.* Bede writes nothing explicitly about law among the Saxons. He mentions *lex* only once in the *History*, where it was something given by kings, in Aethelbehrt's case given *iuxta exempla Romanorum,* whatever that might mean.[28] But he does provide an important account of Saxon political organisation, to which our authors had access:

> The Old Saxons have no king but only a number of Satraps who are set over the people and, when at any time war is about to break out, they cast lots impartially and all follow and obey the one on whom the lot falls, for the duration of the war. When the war is over they all become Satraps of equal rank again.[29]

I shall, then, attribute some importance to divergences from, and elaborations on, this account, and imagine that they related to some kind of experience, or presented some kind of argument.

The *Vita Lebuini Antiqua*

The mid or later ninth-century *Vita Lebuini Antiqua* records Lebuin's abortive attempt to evangelise the Saxons. The action is centred on the so-called 'Marklo council', for which this *Vita* is the only source. Lebuin's central message in his preaching at the council was that if the Saxons did not convert willingly, a 'certain prince' would come and convert them by force. Explaining the background of this council, the author writes:

> The Old Saxons had no king, but satraps established throughout the *pagi;* and it was their custom, that once a year they held a general council in the middle of Saxony next to the river Weser at a place which is called Marklo. Twelve *nobiles* chosen from the various *pagi,* and the same number of *liberi* and the same number of *lati* all used to convene in one satrapy. There they updated the *leges,* judged on particular matters, and established what was to be done that year both in war and in peace, by common counsel.[30]

[28] For the view that these 'Romans' were in fact 'sub-Romans' see Wormald (1999), *The making*, p. 29.

[29] Translation adapted from *The Ecclesiastical History of the English People* trans. by J. McClure and R. Collins (Oxford, 2008), p. 250 V, 10: Bede, *Historia ecclesiastica gentis Anglorum* ed. M. Lapidge (Paris, 2005), p. 58: *Non enim habent regem idem Antiqui Saxones, sed satrapas plurimos suae genti praepositos, qui ingruente belli articulo mittunt aequaliter sortes, et, quemcumque sors ostenderit, hunc tempore belli ducem omnes sequuntur, huic obtemperant; peracto autem bello, rursum aequalis potentiae omnes fiunt satrapae.*

[30] *Vita Lebuini Antiqua* ed. A. Hofmeister (Hannover, 1926), MGH Scriptores in folio XXX, 2, p. 793 [hereafter MGH SS XXX] p. 793: *Regem antiqui Saxones non habebant, sed per pagos satrapas constitutos; morisque erat, ut semel in anno generale consilium agerent in media Saxonia iuxta fluvium Wisuram ad locum qui dicitur Marklo. Solebant ibi omnes in unum satrapae convenire, ex pagis quoque*

The *Vita* as a whole is heavily dependent on earlier sources, especially Bede's *Historia,* Liudger's *Vita Gregorii* and Altfrid's *Vita Liudgeri*; this particular passage is very similar in phraseology and terminology to Bede's, especially in its use of the term 'Satrap'.[31] But this is also the single most independent passage of the work, and clearly diverges from Bede: there is far more interest in peace-time activities, wide social participation was explicitly invoked, and the issue of dispute settlement and the renovation of *lex* was added. Lintzel argued that this passage derived from an earlier text composed shortly after Charlemagne's conquest, with an Anglo-Saxon character.[32] There is no space here to evaluate Lintzel's work, but for our purposes we need to replace his concern about 'reliability' with one about the purpose of the passage in context: what was the compiler trying to achieve by including it, even if he did not write it himself?

The answer depends on the dating, location, and intended audience of the text. It is difficult to be precise on the dating: the only wholly convincing boundaries are the *terminus post quem* of the date of Altfrid's *Vita Liudgerii*, which must be before Altfrid's death in 849, and the *terminus ante quem* of its revision in the earlier tenth century.[33] So the text is certainly very plausibly mid ninth century, but could be later. Wood, in the most recent discussion, suggested a St Amand origin on the basis of the Romance form of Lebuin's name and the existence of an early tenth-century revision by Hucbald of St Amand.[34] Forms of names and vernacular words are, however, extremely flexible across manuscripts of better attested texts of almost all kinds: even the forms of 'Charles' and 'Louis' vary substantially between ninth-century manuscripts of

singulis duodecim electi nobilies totidemque liberi totidemque lati. Renovabant ibi leges, praecipuas causas adiudicabant et, quid per annum essent acturi sive in bello sive in pace, communi consilio statuebant. See also M. Becher, 'Non enim habent regem idem Antiqui Saxones... Verfassung und Ethnogenese in Sachsen während des 8. Jahrhunderts' in: Hässler, Jarnut, and Wemhoff (1999), *Sachsen und Franken in Westfalen*, pp. 13ff.

31 For much of this discussion, see I. Wood, *The missionary life: saints and the evangelisation of Europe, 400–1050* (Harlow, 2001), pp. 115–17.

32 M. Lintzel, 'Die Vita Lebuini Antiqua' *Sachsen und Anhalt*, *7* (1931), pp. 76–108. Pages in Lintzel's works refer hereafter to the versions in his collected papers: M. Lintzel, *Ausgewählte Schriften* 2 Volumes (Berlin, 1961). See also M. Springer, 'Was Lebuins Lebensbeschreibung über die Verfassung Sachsens wirklich sagt oder warum man sich mit einzelnen Wörtern beschäftigen muß' in: Hässler, Jarnut, and Wemhoff (1999), *Sachsen und Franken in Westfalen*, pp. 223–39 and A. Hofmeister, 'Über die älteste Vita Lebuini und die Stammesverfassung der Sachsen' in: W. Lammers (ed.), *Entstehung und Verfassung des Sachsenstammes* (Darmstadt, 1967), pp. 1–31.

33 See Wood (2001), *The missionary life*, pp. 54 and 115–17. More precise datings, among others: Beumann, using Löwe's work, preferred 840–64. See Beumann (1982), 'Hagiographie', p. 157. Lintzel preferred the later ninth century or early tenth. See Lintzel (1931), 'Vita Lebuini Antiqua', pp. 243–4.

34 See also J. Smith, 'The hagiography of Hucbald of Saint-Amand' *Studi Medievali*, *35* (1994), pp. 517–42. For parallel column presentation of the two lives, see Hofmeister (1967), 'Vita Lebuini', p. 12.

capitularies, so the fifteenth-century manuscripts in which this text is preserved could have undergone generations of reformulation. But Wood also noted that a Werden provenance might fit the attention paid to a certain Folcbraht as the most prominent of Lebuin's supporters, an argument already proposed in the nineteenth century, and supported by Hofmeister, among others.[35]

If the text were produced at Werden, it is possible to make a more complex argument. Werden's cartulary is the source for association between Folcbraht and the community.[36] The cartulary's last charter dates from 848, and although it survives in a tenth-century manuscript, it has seemed reasonable to date the collection itself to soon after that.[37] The cartulary and the *Vita Lebuini Antiqua* could therefore be placed in a similar geographical and historical context, and we might even relate their concerns to the pressures that led to the writing of the *Ewa ad Amorem*.

So the *Vita* might record views about the making of *lex* that reflected the needs of the community of Werden in some sense, at a time when Werden was consolidating its landholdings in Saxony and reorganising the records of that landholding. The text promotes a vision of harmony between social groups, with each order providing the same number of council delegates, so might have provided a kind of reassurance that the lower orders had had an important role. If the text were in some way directed at those very orders, it would provide a possible partial legitimation for a degree of continued self-reliance, a degree of collective action and decision making, which could be related to the kinds of agreement smallholders were indeed making with Werden right until the cartulary was compiled, as explored above. The text could be used to bolster Werden's claims to land against those of other landholders, supporting the rights of smallholders to make agreements on their own behalf, against attempts by greater landholders to bring them into closer dependence, to positions in which they had less control over the fate of land.[38] We could, alternatively, think of the *Vita* as a product of the

35 Wood (2001), *The missionary life*, p. 117. Hofmeister (1967), 'Vita Lebuini', pp. 1–31 and his references.

36 On cartularies and memory see above all P. Geary, *Phantoms of Remembrance: memory and oblivion at the end of the first millennium* (Princeton, NJ, 1994), esp. pp. 87–8 on administrative and memorial uses of the Carolingian examples. On the memorial function of the Werden cartulary itself see McKitterick (2012), 'Literate conventions', pp. 189–98.

37 Most recently and convincingly, see McKitterick (2012), 'Literate conventions', pp. 190–1.

38 An example of hagiography being written in connection with land claims can be found in the Le Mans forgeries: Goffart (1966), *Le Mans forgeries*, pp. 39–58. For some partial comparanda see A.-M. Helvétius, 'Les inventions de reliques en Gaule du Nord (IXe-XIIIe siècle)' in: E. Bozóky and A.-M. Helvétius (eds.), *Les Reliques. Objets, cultes, symboles. Actes du colloque international de l'Université du Littoral-Côte d'Opale (Boulogne-sur-Mer) 4–6 septembre 1997* (Turnhout, 1999), Hagiologia. Etudes sur la Sainteté en Occident / Studies on Western Sainthood 1, pp. 293–311.

years immediately after the Stellinga revolt, as necessarily conciliatory to smaller landholders.

We can have no clear understanding of circulation or audience of the text because its manuscripts are so late, so we cannot tell whether this might be an inward-facing account of how law was produced, or bound up with an attempt to spread such a view. We do, however, have some hints that Werden was a particular centre of interest in vernacular language, and translations. Fragments of an early ninth-century glossary have survived, providing some Latin – Old English translations as well as Latin – Latin explanations, and Bischoff attributed the Munich manuscript of the Old Saxon *Heliand* to Werden.[39] All we can say for sure, however, is that it is possible that the message was conveyed in the localities through preaching.[40] This interpretation may be far-fetched, but is a possible maximum view.

When we read the hagiography in this way, we come across a notable variety in the texts' views. We have already noted that Altfrid promoted a much more conspicuously hierarchical conception of authority in the *Vita Liudgerii*. The contrast with the view provided in our next, roughly contemporary, text is also conspicuous. But these differences are instructive. Visions of the ancient social organisation of the Saxons and its relationship with *lex* could be used for quite different purposes, dependent on context.

Rudolph of Fulda's *Translatio Alexandri* (*c.*865)

The second hagiographical text to mention *lex* explicitly in the Saxon context is Rudolph of Fulda's *Translatio Alexandri,* completed by Meginhard after Rudolph's death in 865.[41] The work was commissioned

39 B. Bischoff (ed.), *The Épinal, Erfurt, Werden, and Corpus glossaries* (Copenhagen, 1988); B. Bischoff, 'Die Schriftheimat der Münchner Heliand-Handschrift' in: B. Bischoff, *Mittelalterliche Studien* Volume 3, (Stuttgart, 1981), pp. 112–20. For a discussion of language at Werden, and a list of manuscripts associated with the house, see now R. McKitterick, 'Werden 8–9 Jht. im Spiegel seiner Handschriften' in: S. Patzold, A. Rathmann-Lutz and V. Scior (eds.), *Geschichtsvorstellungen. Bilder, Texte und Begriffe aus dem Mittelalter* (Vienna, Cologne Weimar, 2012).

40 A comprehensive guide to the stress on preaching in Carolingian texts, including consideration of language, is found in R. McKitterick, *The Frankish church and the Carolingian reforms 789–895* (London, 1977), pp. 80–114. See also for the importance of priests for Carolingian *correctio* see C. van Rhijn, 'Priests and the Carolingian reforms: the bottlenecks of local correctio' in: Corradini et al. (2006), *Texts and identities*, pp. 219–38 and also C. van Rhijn, *Shepherds of the Lord: priests and episcopal statutes in the Carolingian period* (Turnhout, 2007). For a suggestion that preaching could respond to the demands of the emperor in distant provinces, see the consideration of a newly edited Bavarian sermon collection in J. L. Nelson, 'Charlemagne and empire' in: Davis, and McCormick (2008), *The long morning*, p. 231. For concrete examples of non-clerical audiences for hagiography see also W. S. van Egmond, 'The audience of Early Medieval Hagiographical Texts: Some Questions Revisited' in: Mostert (1999), *Medieval communication*, pp. 41–67.

41 Rudolph of Fulda, *Translatio Sancti Alexandri auctoribus Rudolfo et Meginharto* ed. G. Pertz (Hannover, 1829), MGH Scriptores in folio II, pp. 673–81.

by Waltbehrt, count, and grandson of Widukind, so gives us a rare direct insight at least into the kind of account or argument that could have been acceptable to someone at the top of the social scale within Saxon society.[42] It records the translation of the relics of Alexander in 851 from Rome to Waltbehrt's foundation at Wildeshausen.

The work contains the first extant version of a Saxon *Origo Gentis*, modelled on Tacitus's *Germania*, and goes on to describe events that happened in the more recent past, probably 851. In describing Saxon society before conversion, Rudolph claims that it was 'established by *leges*', that the *gens* was divided into four *partes*, and that intermarriage between them was punishable by death.[43] Although he makes no specific judgement on this point, Rudolph's views on *leges* later in the text suggest that he approved, that he was legitimising a stark stratification in Saxon society by reference to a 'good old law'.[44] Immediately, then, the vision of the *Vita Lebuini Antiqua* is turned on its head: separation rather than cooperation between social groups is emphasised. Rudolph was also responsible for the Annals of Fulda entries in the 830s and 840s, where his silence on the question of law in the Stellinga revolt is of interest here.[45] Was Rudolph unwilling to consider even the possibility that the appropriate *lex* might have a different interpretation?

If the *Vita Lebuini Antiqua* provided a view of society that helped legitimate collective action and land grants at a relatively humble social level, did the *Translatio Alexandri* help legitimate grants by larger landowners, which possibly trampled on the perceived rights of humbler landholders, or were at least implicated in an unfavourable interpretation of those rights? It is certainly tempting to link Rudolph's view with the larger land grants sought by Fulda from high status individuals, and the *Vita Lebuini Antiqua* with the small grants to Werden. But while Fulda did, in general, attract larger gifts in this part of the world than Werden, the house continued to receive some tiny grants, and Werden, as in

[42] For Widukind's family, see Schmid (1964), 'Nachfahren', pp. 1–47.

[43] MGH SS II c.1 p. 675: The *gens* consisted of *nobilium scilicet et liberorum, libertorum atque servorum. Et id legibus firmatam, ut nulla pars in copulandis coniugiis propriae sortis terminos transferat, sed nobilis nobilem ducat uxorem, et liber liberam, libertus coniungatur libertae, et servus ancillae. Si vero quispiam horum sibi non congruentem et genere prestantiorem duxerit uxorem, cum vitae suae damno componat.* Cf. the references in P. L. Reynolds, *Marriage in the Western Church: the Christianization of marriage during the patristic and early medieval periods* (Leiden, 1994), p. 74 to restrictions between marriages between free and servile in Visigothic, Burgundian, and Lombard texts.

[44] Becher also argues that the stratification was in fact a consequence of the Frankish conquest, and that Rudolph was responsible for a 'Rechtfertigung der gesellschaftlichen Ungleichheit' in Becher (1999), 'Non enim habent regem', pp. 34–5. For the application of this term in a different context see M. Clanchy, 'Remembering the past and the Good Old Law' *History*, 55 (1970), pp. 166–72. For an examination of the concept see also F. Kern, *Kingship and law in the Middle Ages* (Oxford, 1948).

[45] See the introduction in *The Annals of Fulda* trans. T. Reuter (Manchester, 1992), pp. 5–9.

Folcher's charter, sometimes gained a great deal.[46] We need therefore to be careful about associating particular views too strongly with particular houses. But it is plausible in general that differences in views about social ordering might be related to different ambitions over land, and plausible also that different views might be invoked in different contexts for different purposes.

Certainly we should not dismiss the possibility that peasants could resist aristocratic incursions on their land or their conceptions of landholding or status. Although they are rare, there are enough examples extant of peasants challenging an interpretation of their status to suggest that such challenges were not hopeless, at least not everywhere.[47] Innes even brings out an instance of the careful recording of the consent of farmers on pieces of land exchanged between Wissembourg and Tours: their consent was clearly important.[48] Influencing views of social status and *lex* through hagiography might then have been a useful strategy, in a context in which such views were very much worth trying to influence.

Rudolph of Fulda 2: 'Saxonness', legislators

Rudolph's account can take us further still. It is especially rich in references to law, and his comments are relevant to more themes: the connection between law and a sense of 'Saxonness', and the responsibility for written texts of Saxon law.

In chapter two, covering the period before their conversion, Rudolph praises the *leges* of the Saxons, claiming that 'they used very good *leges* for punishing wrongdoers'.[49] Still more strikingly he adds immediately:

> And they made sure they had much which was useful and honest according to the *lex naturae* in the probity of their *mores*, which they would have been able to put into effect so as to earn true beatitude, if they had not been ignorant of the creator, and had not been apart from the truth of his worship.[50]

46 For small grants to Fulda see *Traditiones et antiquitates Fuldenses* ed. E. F. J. Dronke (Fulda, 1844), pp. 95–102. Folcher's charter is discussed in Chapter 1, section 1.4.3 above.

47 For examples see Nelson (1986), 'Dispute settlement', p. 50, J. L. Nelson, 'Peers in the early Middle Ages' in: P. Stafford, J. L. Nelson and J. Martindale (eds.), *Law, laity and solidarities* (Manchester, 2001), pp. 35–6.

48 Innes (2000), *State and society*, p. 111.

49 MGH SS II p. 675 c.2: *legibus etiam ad vindicatam malefactorum optimis utebantur.*

50 Ibid.: *Et multa utilia atque secundum legem naturae honesta in morum probitate habere studuerunt, quae eis ad veram beatitudinem promerendam proficere potuissent, si ignorantiam creatoris sui non haberent, et a veritate culturae illius non essent alieni.* Carolingian *lex naturae* should be studied further: see Alcuin in his *Commentariorum in Apocalipsin Libri Quinque* ed. Migne (Paris, 1863) PL Vol. 100 Col. 1087–1186 on the 'six *leges*', wholly religious in sense at Col. 1118: *Prima naturalis, secunda Moysi, tertia prophetarum, quarta gratiae, quinta apostolorum, sexta synodorum, quibus Ecclesia volat ad coelum.* cited in P. Boucard, 'Indices et sources d'une culture juridique romaine dans l'exégèse biblique carolingienne' in: M. Rouche and B. Dumézil (eds.), *Le Bréviaire d'Alaric. Aux origines du Code Civil.* (Paris, 2008), p. 334.

This emphasis on *lex* was clearly part of a strategy for *Vergangenheitsbewältigung,* for emphasising some basic good quality in a people who unfortunately had not yet been introduced to Christ. There is one hint that such a strategy was useful for other neighbouring *gentes*: Altfrid's *Vita Liudgerii*, again, insists that Wursingus, of the Frisian *gens,* was *in iudicio ... iustus* even before he came to know of Christ.[51] It is difficult to say, however, whether the pronounced emphasis on good law in the Saxon case is related to a sense of pride among the Saxons even before conversion, or a product of a later development, deriving once more from Frankish notions of a *gens* and infused into Saxon society through the Church. Certainly the account is interesting for its view that good *lex* and its application did not *need,* even in the eyes of the Abbot of Fulda, the kind of Christian moral underpinnings which were so deeply emphasised in the context of justice in Carolingian capitularies.

One further relevant anecdote can be found in what is largely a rather formulaic catalogue of miracles. Rudolph wrote that 'a certain man from the *pagus* of Tregwit', having been blinded by his enemies, 'who held the seat of the *legislatores*', had had his sight restored by Alexander's relics.[52] This was described in a recognisable place and a recognisable historical time and so possibly reflected or interacted with actual memory, or at least presented a picture that would have been believable. Indeed it may even be possible speculatively to identify this figure as Cobbo, encountered earlier in the *Vita Liudgerii,* who was a count in Tregwit, though not the only count in Tregwit, in the earlier ninth century. Although both Rudolph and Cobbo were politically aligned in the 840s as supporters of Louis the German, we might still read this as a kind of pointed coded criticism, showing something of the intricate and subtle channels through which political advice could flow.[53] Whether or not the *legislator* in question was Cobbo, he was admonished not to abuse his power, a power presented as legal in some sense.

It is tempting to make much of the term *legislator*, in its twelfth-century sense. But it is only possible that *legislator* was understood in the precise sense of 'one who makes written law'. The

[51] MGH SS II p. 405: *Fuit in diebus Radbodi, regis Fresonum, vir quidam nobilis in ea gente Wursingus nomine, cognomento Ado; qui quamvis fidem sanctae Trinitatis nondum sciret, erat tamen adiutor pauperum, defensor oppressorum, in iuditio quoque iustus...*

[52] MGH SS II p. 679: *Igitur quidam vir de pago Tregwiti, propter invidiam inimicorum suorum, qui sedem legislatorum possidebant, occulorum lumine iam 20 annis aut eo amplius privatus...*

[53] For the political alignments see Goldberg (1995), 'Popular revolt', pp. 484f. For other counts attested in Tregwit, Burchard, Waltbehrt, Albric, and Letti, see Krüger (1950), *Grafschaftsverfassung*, pp. 57f. For the role of historiography in a royal-political context as 'the discourse of constructive criticism' see J. L. Nelson, 'History writing at the courts of Louis the Pious and Charles the Bald' in: A. Scharer and G. Scheibelreiter (eds.), *Historiographie im frühen Mittelalter* (Vienna, 1994), Veröffentlichungen des Instituts für Österreichische Geschichtsforschung 32, p. 437.

term *iudex* is used of the same people later in the text. On the one hand, the terminology might be too fuzzy to make anything of, but on the other, the apparent equivalence of the terms in this case could be instructive: perhaps 'legislation' and 'justice' might not be so separable as is often imagined, and perhaps we should not rule out the possibility that men like Cobbo, local potentates and counts, could have issued written *leges* in some sense. Certainly the *legislatores* appear far removed from the context of the royal court. Rudolph in fact makes no reference whatsoever to Charlemagne's role in codifying Saxon law, a fact that seems strange when his *Translatio* presents Charlemagne in all other respects as the pivotal figure in the history of the Saxons, as Becher has argued.[54] The fact is stranger still when one considers that Rudolph had read Einhard's *Vita Karoli*. So he either interpreted its comments on the *iura omnium nationum* differently from modern historians, or sought to downplay the role he found in it for Charlemagne.[55] With this in mind, his determination on the one hand that the legal tradition of the Saxons had always been thoroughly positive, and on the other that there were independent *legislatores*, is very striking. Imagining contributions to written law in Saxony as not deriving directly from the royal court would provide a neat context for some of the observations about the text of the *Lex Saxonum* noted below.

This argument rests uncomfortably on the intepretation of a single work, but introduces a wider point, that surviving narratives fit awkwardly accepted understandings of Charlemagne's role in Saxon law. In fact, the first Saxon text, or even text about Saxony, that records Charlemagne as involved in any way with Saxon *lex*, as opposed to the development of the Saxon *gens* in general, is the work of the *Poeta Saxo*, working at Corvey around 880. The *Poeta Saxo* linked Charlemagne much more explicitly than did the hagiographies with a sort of grant of permission for Saxons to use their own *leges*:

> Then under the judges, which the king [Charlemagne] placed among them, and his legates, the Saxons were allowed to use their paternal *leges* and to have the honour of liberty, and at last became allies by a treaty with the Franks, so that there might be one people and *gens* in concord, always equally obeying one king.[56]

Leyser has traced the concepts of *lex patria* and *libertatis honor* in the tenth and eleventh centuries, showing that they had a great deal of currency,

[54] Becher (1996), *Rex, Dux und Gens*, pp. 31–40 and Beumann (1982), 'Hagiographie', p. 147.

[55] For modern views see Chapter 1, section 1.3.1 above.

[56] *Poeta Saxo* ed. P. Winterfeld (Hannover, 1899), MGH Poetae Latini aevi Carolini IV, 1, p. 48: *Tum sub iudicibus, quos rex inponerunt ipsis, / Legatisque suis permissi legibus uti / Saxones patriis et libertatis honore / Hoc sunt postremo sociati foedere Francis, / Ut gens et populus fieret concoditer unus / Ac semper regi parens aequaliter uni*. See B. Bischoff, 'Das Thema des Poeta Saxo' in: Bischoff (1981), *Mittelalterliche Studien*, pp. 253–9.

and suggested that the *Poeta Saxo* might be recording a genuine grant.[57] But there is a narrower context for this stress on Saxon *libertas* of Corvey's argument for full independence from its mother house Corbie in Neustria, which involved a concerted drive to rewrite its history, as well as the context of more general growth in Saxon political self-awareness through the ninth century.[58] So there is reason to be suspicious of the claim that this reflected an original grant. In any case, while law appears frequently in all manner of accounts concerning the ninth-century Saxons, for most of that century we have no clear evidence that anyone associated Charlemagne with a codification of Saxon law.

Quite what relevance Rudolph's remarks have for understanding more specifically the perceived *content* of ninth-century law is not clear. Certainly one should not assume, with several recent commentators, that Rudolph's comments on the application of the death penalty reflected actual practice accurately.[59] We can only identify more general themes. The text communicated to Waltbehrt something about the Saxons: their position is to be understood as directly dependent on Charlemagne, but the Saxons were a valid *gens* in their own right, whose good nature was shown especially and most clearly in their own pre-conquest *lex*. It also communicated something about social and political power within Saxony, that *legislatores* were an important presence in society, but were not to abuse their power, and that stark social stratification was legitimated by 'good old law'. In Rudolph's account, *lex* was used as an important medium for talking about some of the most important characteristics of the Saxon *gens*.

2.2.3 *Summary*

The central conclusion in this analysis is that *lex* was prominent in writing about Saxony, in a variety of contexts, with a variety of different purposes, tied to debates about the internal ordering of Saxon society, the status of the Saxon *gens*, and in the case of the Stellinga about its relationship with royal power. But Charlemagne's role, so prominent in the hagiography in general, was absent from discussions of *lex* until the *Poeta Saxo* in the 880s, and even in this text he only confirms existing Saxon practices. Could this perhaps be attributable precisely to the importance of *lex* in Saxon society? Perhaps it was in a sense only safe to attribute laws to Charlemagne when that attribution could no

57 K. Leyser, 'From Saxon freedoms to the freedom of Saxony: the crisis of the Eleventh century' in: T. Reuter (ed.), *Communications and power in medieval Europe: the Carolingian and Ottonian centuries* (London, 1994), pp. 51–67 at p. 53.

58 General theses of Krüger (2004), *Grundungsüberlieferung* and Becher (1996), *Rex, Dux und Gens.*

59 Eg. Goldberg (1995), 'Popular revolt', pp. 467–501 and Wenskus (1986), 'Die ständische Entwicklung', pp. 587–616.

longer reasonably be used to argue for direct Frankish imperial control in Saxon legal affairs?[60]

It must be stressed that the precise contours of the use of notions of *lex* cannot be understood in detail. It is so difficult to establish dating, location, and audience for many of our texts, and it is so difficult to disentangle how the arguments about historical *lex* related to attitudes about contemporary *lex*. An ideology of legislation that stressed wide participation in a primordial past could, perversely, be used to uphold a ruthlessly hierarchical social order, or could do quite the reverse. I have outlined some possible interpretations of the differences in views we find, but all we can say with any safety is that *lex*, whatever that term signified, was an unusually important part of the way social relations were described.

No source in this section explicitly mentions a *text* of Saxon law. Although the term *lex* could refer to such a law, the hagiography only used the term to refer to pre-Christian Saxon society. Only in the accounts of the Stellinga does written *lex* appear relevant in an immediate, political sense. Whether the authors of the other accounts ever imagined that the Saxons had written *lex* before the conquest, or even whether anyone in the ninth century kept an awareness that the Saxons had no writing before the conquest, is perhaps impossible to establish. We turn now to the written texts, to the textual history of the *Lex Saxonum* after a brief examination of records of Saxon law in practice.

2.3 SAXON LAW IN PRACTICE: RECORDS OF DISPUTES

2.3.1 Charters

Saxony provides no exception to the Frankish pattern, that establishing the nature of the use of law in charters is difficult. No ninth-century charters so far surveyed make explicit reference to *Lex Saxonum*. Hübner's still invaluable list of disputes has only five cases for Saxony and Westphalia, none of which is helpful here.[61] Most of the charters are royal, and there are some great lacunae in the record. There are private charters from Werden, summaries of grants from Fulda, and an extensive cartulary from Corvey, but only fourteen charters for bishoprics have survived from the century.[62] The only specific 'legal'

60 Such direct control was suggested in T. Reuter, 'Charlemagne and the world beyond the Rhine' in: J. Story (ed.), *Charlemagne: empire and society* (Manchester, 2005), p. 190: 'Alongside the disappearance of ethnic leaders went the Frankicisation of local institutions and at the same time the written codification of ethnic legal practice, itself a form of Frankicisation, since it meant that ethnic law was now defined and potentially modifiable by Frankish royal authority'.

61 R. Hübner, 'Gerichtsurkunden in fränkischer Zeit' *ZRG GA*, *12* (1891), pp. 1–118.

62 Royal charters are found in the MGH editions, except for some of Louis the Pious's, which can be found in *Regesta historiae Westfaliae: accedit codex diplomaticus* ed. H. A. Erhard (Münster,

appearance of Saxons occurs in the charter already quoted from 834 preserved in the cartulary of Utrecht cathedral, which contains a witness list divided by the words 'ITEM SAXONUM'.[63] We cannot go further here with charters than we have already gone, but there is evidence for legal business in Saxony in other kinds of source: treatises, letters, and councils.

2.3.2 Gottschalk of Orbais

Gottschalk of Orbais, son of a Saxon count named Berno, had been an oblate at Fulda but attempted to leave the monastery, claiming that his oblation and later tonsure had been invalid.[64] In 829 his case was discussed at the synod of Mainz, and he was later permitted to leave the monastery, although he had to remain a monk and leave his property behind. According to the treatise *De oblatione puerorum* written by Hrabanus Maurus, abbot of Fulda, as an appeal against this decision, Gottschalk claimed that his oblation had been invalid because it had been witnessed only by Franks. The witnesses should all have been Saxon for the oblation to be valid under Saxon *lex*. According to Hrabanus, Gottschalk and his associates claimed:

> that no-one from the *gens* of the Franks or the Romans, or from any other *gens*, noble born and honest in his way of life, may be had above a Saxon, unless he might be able to be a Saxon witness. For they say that the *lex* of his *gens* may not allow that a man of another *gens* be cited in witness to infringe the *lex* of his *libertas*.[65]

Hrabanus disagreed:

> Since they have it like this for themselves, what reason is there according to God or according to men, that those who are inferior by *virtus* and *dignitas* reject those who are better and more distinguished than them, and reject them and throw them out as if they were unworthy of any honour, to whom it is fitting that they be subject? For

1848). For the tradition of the Corvey charters see Krüger (2004), *Grundungsüberlieferung*, pp. 21f. For bishoprics, see Carroll (1999), 'Bishoprics of Saxony', pp. 221–4. The private charters from Werden are in *Oorkonden Werden* as well as *Urkundenbuch für die Geschichte des Niederrheins* ed. T. J. Lacomblet Volume 1, (Düsseldorf, 1840).

[63] *Diplomata Belgica* pp. 317–18 no. 181. The first manuscript of the cartulary dates from the end of the eleventh century, but I shall assume that this grant is original.

[64] This account is largely based on that in M. de Jong, *In Samuel's image: child oblation in the early medieval West* (Leiden, 1996), pp. 77–91. See also M. de Jong, 'Old Law and new-found power: Hrabanus Maurus and the Old Testament' in: J. Drijvers and A. MacDonald (eds.), *Centres of learning: learning and location in pre-modern Europe and the Near East* (Leiden, 1995), pp. 161–77 and R. Kottje, 'Hrabanus und das Recht' in: R. Kottje and Maurer H. (eds.), *Hrabanus Maurus: Lehrer, Abt und Bischof* (Wiesbaden, 1982), pp. 118–29.

[65] Hrabanus Maurus (1864), *Liber de Oblatione Puerorum*, Col. 431: *dicunt quod super Saxonem nullus de Francorum aut Romanorum, aut ex alia qualibet gente, licet inter suos nobilis natu atque honestus conversatione habeatur, nisi Saxo testis esse possit. Hoc enim, aiunt, legem gentis suae pati non posse, ut alterius gentis homo in testimonium citetur ad infringendum legem libertatis suae.* Note the double sense of the term *lex*, first as 'law', second as 'right'.

who, living in this misfortune of a world, can be unaware that the Franks were in the faith and religion of Christ before the Saxons, and then conquered them by arms to their domination, and when they had been made their superiors, they converted them to faith in Christ as they refrained from the cult of idols, by the rite of masters, but even more by paternal affection.[66]

We see here two very different approaches to the relationship between *lex* and *gens.* Certainly, Hrabanus's account appears to show something like a fully developed personality principle being invoked in the earlier ninth century: the *lex* appears as a kind of immutable possession, grounded in a strong sense of *gens*, carrying certain defined rights. Hrabanus's response invoked *gens* in a very different way, suggesting that *gens* be associated with law-worthiness, above and beyond any more specific rights. The picture is, however, more complicated. These views are represented only in Hrabanus's work. One problem is that Hrabanus may have been distorting, or simplifying Gottschalk's arguments, to set up a straw man for his own. The other is that the other extant sources for the dispute do not mention any arguments grounded in *gens* at all. The relevant texts, the letters of the monk Hatto and of Otgar, archbishop of Mainz, do not mention Gottschalk's argument explicitly, although they do use the language of secular law, *legibus componere*, for example, and invoke *lex humana.* They are, however not represented in their entirety in the quotations in sixteenth-century church history works, the only form in which they survive.[67] Instead, these letters stress the fact that Gottschalk's oblation had been *invitus*, against his will, which was explicitly forbidden at the council of Rome in 826, and also went against the spirit of certain capitulary chapters.[68] Perhaps Hrabanus did not mention this argument because it was rather more difficult to attack than something based on *gens.*

To the extent that the fragmentary evidence allows us any insight to the dispute, then, it seems that the arguments were multifaceted. What we see is a dispute, involving arguments couched in legalistic terms, drawing in further arguments about the relationship between *gens* and *lex.* A judgement based on Gottschalk's state of mind, his willingness or unwillingness, at the time of oblation might reasonably

66 PL Vol. 107 Col. 431–2: *Haec vero cum se ita habeant, quae ratio est secundum Deum, aut secundum homines, ut qui inferiores sunt virtute et dignitate, superiores sibi et eminentiores spernant, et quasi indignos omni honore respuentes abjiciant, quibus subjecti oportebat? Quis enim ignorat sub hac plaga mundi habitans, Francos ante Saxones in Christi fide atque religione fuisse, quos ipsi postmodum suae dominationi subegerunt armis, atque superiores effecti, dominorum ritu, imo magis paterno affectu, ab idolorum cultu abstehentes, ad fidem Christi converterunt?*

67 For the transmission, see de Jong (1996), *Samuel's image*, p. 79. MGH Epp. V 529f.

68 MGH Conc. II, 2 p. 580 c.32 ; Cf. MGH Capit. I no. 139, p. 285 c.21 on tonsure of a child with unwilling parents: *Si quis puerum invitis parentibus totonderit aut puellam velaverit, legem suam in triplo conponat* ... and MGH Capit. I no. 43 p. 122 c.14: *Ut infantulae artatis puellulae non velentur antequam illi elegere sciant quid velint, salva canonica auctoriate.*

be expected to involve the testimony of the witnesses involved in the oblation. The validity of their status as witnesses, and their possible ties and interests, could therefore have a real impact on the nature of their judgement or their behaviour in a court. In this sense, Hrabanus's views are helpful for understanding why the issue of the ethnicity of witnesses might have been considered important. However vigorous and successful hagiographical *Vergangenheitsbewältigung* may have been already by the 820s, the Saxons were still portrayed negatively in widely circulated historical accounts, not least the *Annales Regni Francorum* (*ARF*) and Einhard's *Vita Karoli*, in which Saxon perfidy was a major theme.[69] Hrabanus's views show that such conceptions of the Saxons might still be deployed, not just in narratives, but in real disputes in the 830s. The point may seem obvious and trite, but is worth stressing: control over the background of witnesses was important for clear practical reasons. This would be especially true in the case of purely oral transactions, where the content of the transaction might be more subject to dispute at a later stage than in a written transaction.

In other words, in this kind of case, what has been termed 'legal personality' really meant a right to have some influence over the choice of those who could be responsible for producing an interpretation of a transaction at a later stage, in a possible future dispute.[70] Seen from this angle, 'legal personality' looks less puzzling; it could consist less of a universally transmitted, and fundamentally abstract, legalistic rule, and more of a more or less normatised right, grounded in immediate practical needs, and always subject to criticism. Gottschalk's case may show us something of the practical origins, rooted in a characteristically Carolingian context of a newly expanded empire, of expectations and embryonic rights, which may or may not have coalesced by the end of the ninth century into something akin to a system, widely spread geographically and socially.

2.3.3 Marriage and The Council of Tribur

The records of the Council of Tribur of 895 preserve evidence of similar appeals at the end of the century. They describe a judgement on a case in which a noble Frank married a noble Saxon, kept her for many years and had children by her, then dismissed her and took another wife on the grounds that

69 For example *Vita Karoli* pp. 9–10 c.7.

70 For stress on the later interpretation of rituals in very different contexts, see, famously, P. Buc, *The dangers of ritual: between early medieval texts and social scientific theory* (Princeton, NJ, 2001).

he was betrothed to her, or accepted her in marriage or gave her dowry not by his *lex*, that is that of the Franks... for the Saxons and the Franks do not use the same *leges*.[71]

The noble Frank is judged as a 'transgressor of the evangelical law' and subjected to penance. Extracting the details of any legal argument used by the husband is unfortunately impossible from this terse record. Its principal concern seems to be the upholding of an Augustinian view of marriage as indissoluble under *lex divina* (or here *lex aevangelica*) as opposed to *lex humana*.[72] It seems that the argument for the dissolution of the marriage did not matter for those framing the canons of this council: dissolution was itself the problem.

The most obvious arguments the council could have faced might have been along the lines of Gottschalk's. For whatever reasons, a husband wished to divorce after many years, and invoked a technicality probably based on procedure, to argue that the marriage could not have been valid, ever. The council's specification of precise elements of the marriage procedure may even hint at a background of still more technical arguments. If we read *vel* and *aut* as meaning 'or' rather than 'and' we might imagine that the council had encountered a number of different arguments, perhaps focusing on particular elements of the marriage procedure. But beyond more restricted versions of Gottschalk's arguments, focusing for example on the precise procedure for the giving of the *dos*, are we able to identify any more possible technical arguments that might have more of a relationship with extant texts?

We would need to identify a feature of a married state distinct in Saxon *lex*, which might be felt most intensely after some years or after the birth of children, and lead either to a bitter dispute encouraging a divorce, or to a situation in which living married under Frankish *lex* was seen to be better. The only remotely possible point of contention to be derived from the *leges* is the arrangements for the possession of the *dos* originally given by the husband to the wife, after the wife has children. The *Lex Saxonum* treats this point; indeed the arrangement is different *apud Westfalos* from among the *Ostfalai et Angarii*.[73] *Lex Salica* does not

71 W. Hartmann, G., Schmitz and I. Schroder (eds.), *Die Konzilien Der Karolingischen Teilreiche 875–911* (Hannover, 2014), MGH Concilia V, p. 376: *De Francia nobilis quidam homo nobilem de Saxonia Saxonum lege duxit uxorem. Tenuit eam multis annis et ex ea filios procreavit. Verum quia non hisdem utuntur legibus Saxones et Franci, causatus est, quod eam non sua, id est Francorum, lege disponsaverit vel acceperit aut dotaverit, dimissaque illa duxit alteram. Definivit super hoc sancta synodus, ut ille transgressor aevangelice legis subigatur penitentie, a secunda coniuge separetur, priorem resumere cogatur.*

72 The distinction is argued as central in Augustine, and then Carolingian, thought in Reynolds (1994), *Marriage*, pp. 414f. Cf. 'mirrors of princes' literature I survey in Chapter 3 in section 3.1.1, especially the views of Jonas of Orléans on *lex humana* and *divina*.

73 *Lex Saxonum* ed. K. F. von Richthofen (Hannover, 1875), MGH Leges in folio V, pp. 47–84 pp. 73–4 c.47: *Dotis ratio duplex est: Ostfalai et Angarii volunt, si femina filios genuerit, habeat dotem, quam in nuptiis accepit, quamdiu vivit, filiisque dimittat; si vero filii matre superstite moriuntur, ipsaque*

treat the subject, although *Lex Ribuaria* does, and differs from the *Lex Saxonum*'s penalties (although the former apparently influenced the latter in the relevant clauses).[74] These differences in law if applied as read in the *leges* certainly would have very different impacts on family economics, since they relate to the rights of heirs in various scenarios. But there is no hint at all in the canons of Tribur that the man had this kind of distinction in mind. He was not claiming back his *dos*, or attempting to affect its distribution by his arguments.

This case shows yet again just how difficult it can be to pin down reference to a *lex* in a text. Essentially, if we imagine that the written *leges* did inform understandings about property relations inside families, the question of which *lex* to use *when marrying* would clearly have a real impact. It seems most likely however that in this case the Tribur council was treating a slightly different issue, something more technical. Here we may indeed see the presence of an argument based on a hardened personality principle, near the end of the ninth century.

These accounts get us no further in establishing the understood content of a specifically Saxon *lex* and its possible reference to texts, but they allow some observations on the development of the 'personality principle'. We now consider how the role of *lex* in narratives and the invocation of *lex* in disputes fit with the legal texts themselves.

2.4 THE LEGAL TEXTS

So far we have examined all of the evidence for attitudes to, and use of, *lex* in ninth-century descriptive sources relating to Saxony. We have seen how law and the choice of law was a major issue in high politics; we have seen how authors sought to tie the history of law in Saxony to very particular and divergent visions of social organisation; we have seen how the sense of law could have a role in integrating Saxons into the Frankish political order, in saying something positive about the Saxon *gens*. We have also seen how little evidence there is for Charlemagne's involvement in Saxon law, and seen hints that written texts might be

post obierit, dotem proximi eius in hereditatem accipiant; si autem filios non habuerit, dos ad dantem si vivit revertatur, si defunctus est ad proximos heredes eius. Apud Westfalos: postquam mulier filios genuerit, dotem amittat; si autem non genuerit, ad dies suos dotem possideat, post decessum eius dos ad dantem vel, si deest, ad proximos heredes eius revertatur. 48. ***De eo quod vir et mulier simul conquisierint mulier mediam porcionem accipiat; hoc apud Westfalaos;*** *apud Ostfalaos et Angarios nihil accipiat, sed contente sit dote sua.* References to *Lex Saxonum* are to this edition, but see also *Leges Saxonum et Lex Thuringorum* ed. C. von Schwerin (Hannover, 1918), MGH Fontes iuris Germanici antiqui in usum scholarum seperatim editi 3.

74 *Lex Ribuaria* c.41 pp. 95–6: 1. *Si quis mulierem disponsaverit, quicquid ei per tabularum seu cartarum instrumenta conscribserit, perpetualiter inconvulsum permaneat.* 2. *Sin autem per series scribturarum ei nihil contulerit, si mulier virum supervixerit, quinquaginta solidos in dude* [reading in the older A text; the Carolingian B text has *dote*] *recipiat,* ***et tertiam de omne re, quod simul conlaboraverint, sibi studeat evindicare;*** *vel quicquid ei in morgangaba traditum fuerit, similter faciat.*

issued at a very local level. We have also seen hints at how and why a personality principle might have developed over the course of the ninth century, in circumstances peculiar to the Frankish conquests.

What has been missing is the view from the legal texts themselves. Three full texts are extant from the ninth century that explicitly and exclusively concern the Saxons. Two are capitularies already examined. The other is known as *Lex Saxonum* or *Lex Saxonicum*. It is longer, and looks as if it was intended to codify a far wider range of customary practices, outside the immediate context of a violent war. It is normally dated to 802/3.

2.4.1 *Fragments relating to Saxons in the capitularies*

A number of other texts from late in Charlemagne's reign and early in Louis the Pious's, edited as Capitularies, refer to Saxons in some of their provisions. They may hint at a larger body of material than is now extant, but their interpretation is difficult. The most resistant to analysis are Capitulary no. 40, from 803, which contains a fragmentary chapter or a title (c.23) 'About those Saxons who do not have wives', and Capitulary no. 49, which refers very briefly to military levies from Saxony to fight in Spain or among the Avars.[75]

Most interestingly, two chapters in Ansegis's capitulary collection, with unknown sources, directly set out measures for *Saxones homines* about damage done to property.[76] The second of the chapters requires a triple compensation *secundum legem et secundum ewam*, the payment of the *bannum*, and the loss of a hand for the one who was 'disobedient to the *praeceptum* of the lord emperor'. What that *praeceptum* was is difficult to say: the problem seems to be interfering with the procedure for claiming that horses had damaged crops. How the Saxons fit in, specifically, is equally unclear.

The dates of these texts cannot be established with any certainty, but a *terminus ante quem* must be the compilation of Ansegis's collection in 827. They might be comparable with the *Capitula Legibus Addita,* discussed later, but Lintzel noted that they were more likely extracts from longer texts relating to various peoples, or else the designations of ethnicity would be superfluous.[77] Really, the intended and received understanding, or range of possible understandings, of these texts and their relationship with *leges* texts must remain unclear.

75 MGH Capit. I no. 40 c.23 p. 116: *de illis Saxonibus qui uxores non habent.* MGH Capit. I no. 49 p. 136.

76 These were edited as *Capitula Karoli apud Ansegisum Servata* as MGH Capit. I no. 70 p. 160.

77 M. Lintzel, 'Zur altsächsischen Rechtsgeschichte' *ZRG*, 52 (1932), in: *Augewählte Schriften*, p. 433.

Two further texts treat the Saxons, in a puzzling way: Capitularies no. 134 and no. 135, edited as 'additional capitularies' to other *leges*, produced in 816. They state that compensations listed in *Lex Salica* are to be paid at the rate of twelve *denarii* to a *solidus*, except for compensations paid by a Saxon or a Frisian to a *Salicus*, which are to be paid at the rate of forty *denarii* to the *solidus*.[78] Taken at face value, this looks like a punitive measure to give Franks or *Salici* a large advantage in their dealings with Saxons and Frisians. On the other hand, two standards for reckoning of the *solidus* are attested in Frankish texts: one of forty *denarii* found in all redactions of the *Lex Salica*, and one of twelve, found in most Frankish texts from the late Merovingian period, including the *Lex Ribuaria*.[79] Does this provision instead relate to the problems associated with introducing coin into Saxony?[80] The matter is complicated by an apparently contradictory provision in Capitulary no. 39 from 802/3, which implies that compensations as written in the *Lex Salica* were not, in normal cases, to be paid at the rate of twelve *solidi* to a *denarius*.[81] There may be no way to extract any system from any of these provisions, or the similar reckonings of coin we shall see in the *Lex Saxonum* and in the other 'additional capitularies': they are best used perhaps as evidence for a widespread perception of a problem in interpreting the fines.

These texts are singularly difficult to analyse, but have been mentioned for the sake of completeness.

2.4.2 The Lex Saxonum

The *Lex Saxonum* has been attributed to Charlemagne and dated to 802/3 as already discussed.[82] But again, the stress the ethnogenesists place on precise context makes a more thorough investigation worthwhile. While its unity as a single piece of legislation has been the subject of

[78] MGH Capit. I no. 134 p. 268 c.3: *Ut omnis solutio adque conpositio, que lege Salica continetur, in Francia per duodecum denariorum solidos conponatur, excepto ubi contentio inter Saxones et Frisiones exorta fuit: ibi volumus ut quadraginta denariorum quantitatem solidus habeat, quem vel Saxo vel Frisio ad partem Salici Franci cum eo litigantis solvere debet.* MGH Capit. I pp. 269–270 no. 135 c.2: *De omnibus debitis solvendis, sicut antiquitus fuit constitutum, per duodecim denarios solidus solvatur per totam Salicam legem, excepto leudes, si Saxo aut Frisio Salicum occiderit, per XL denarios solidi solvantur. Infra Salicos vero ex utraque parte de omnibus debitis sicut diximus XII dinarii per solidam salvantur, sive de homicidiis sive de omnibus rebus.* Some discussion in Brunner (1931c), 'Nobiles und Gemeinfreie', p. 267.

[79] M. Grierson and P. Blackburn, *Medieval European coinage* Volume I The early Middle Ages (5th–10th centuries) (Cambridge, 1986), pp. 102–7. See MGH Conc. I p. 257: petition to have the 40 *solidi denarius* officially abolished, since it led to perjury. The *solidus* is also rated much more cheaply in the *Lex Frisionum* to about 2–3 *denarii*.

[80] Grierson & Blackburn (1986), *Medieval European coinage*, pp. 225f.

[81] MGH Capit. I no. 39 c.9 p. 144 *Omnia debita quae ad partem regis solvere debent, solidis duodecim denariorum solvant, excepto freda quae in lege Salica scripta est; illa eodem solido quo caetere compositiones solvi debent componatur.*

[82] See Chapter 1, section 1.3.1 above.

vigorous debates since the mid-nineteenth century, it has always been assumed that the text as we have it was issued in some form at this time. I explore the possibilities that the text as we have it came together later than has been imagined, that it was subject to continued modification, and that the process of conglomeration responded to local forces and possibly to events in high politics.

The dating: received opinion and sources

In addition to the arguments for dating surveyed above, a parallel between the *Lex Saxonum* and the *Capitulare Legi Ribuariae Additum*, which is well dated, has also been used to help with dating.[83] The relevant passages are:

Capitulare Legi Ribuariae Additum	*Lex Saxonum*
5. XX cap. Nemini liceat servum suum propter damnum ab illo cuilibet inlatum dimittere;	*51. Si servus scelus quodlibet nesciente domino commiserit, ut puta homicidium, furtum,*
sed iuxta qualitatem damni dominus pro ipso respondeat vel eum in compositione aut ad poenam petitoris offerat.	***dominus eius pro illo iuxta qualitatem facti multam conponat***
Si autem servus perpetrato scelere fugerit, ita ut a domino penitus inveniri non possit, *sacramento se dominus eius excusare studeat, quod nec suae voluntatis nec conscientiae fuisset quod servus eius tale facinus commisit*	***Si servus perpetrato facinore fugerit, ita ut a domino ulterius inveniri non possit,*** *nihil solvat; si domino factum servi inputetur quasi consentiret, sua duodecima manu iurando se purificet*

There was some debate in the nineteenth and earlier twentieth century about the direction of the transfer of material, whether a common source was used, and so on.[84] Lintzel, for example, argued that the Capitulary was a source for the *lex*, but that the *lex* was still produced very soon after it. However, there seems to be no way to tell one way or the other, and certainly there is no reason to link the dates of the two. Perhaps the most elegant explanation would be if a manuscript similar to Vat. Pal. Lat. 773, which contained the *Lex Ribuaria*, used as described above, and its additional capitulary, was used for the compilation of the *Lex Saxonum*, at any point in the ninth century.[85] Another possible capitulary parallel, between *Lex Saxonum* and Capitulary no. 39 is far

83 See for example M. Lintzel, 'Die Entstehung der Lex Saxonum' *ZRG*, 47 (1927), in *Ausgewählte Schriften*, pp. 416–99.The parallel was first noted in R. Usinger, *Forschungen zur Lex Saxonum* (Berlin, 1867).

84 Described in detail in M. Lintzel, 'Die Entstehung der Lex Saxonum' *ZRG*, 47 (1927), pp. 416–19.

85 This manuscript is discussed in more detail in Chapter 3, section 3.3.5 below.

weaker, but in fact the capitulary is also found in this manuscript.[86] This is likely to be pure coincidence, but we must be aware how the influence of many texts could be transmitted through only one manuscript, and at any time. In any case, the weakness of such arguments for dating make an examination of the textual history from first principles worthwhile.

The dating according to the manuscripts

We have only two extant manuscripts. One, the 'Spannenburg' Codex, now divided between London and Paris, is from the very late ninth or early tenth century, and has been localised by Bischoff and Mordek to 'North-East France'.[87] The other, Münster msc. VII 5201 is a mid-tenth-century manuscript associated with Corvey, the most important monastery in Saxony in the ninth century in terms of political influence and landholding. This manuscript was probably described by Widukind of Corvey, whose views on *lex* and the *varietas legum* are of the greatest interest, but sadly cannot be treated here.[88] So no manuscripts of the *Lex Saxonum* are extant until nearly a century after its alleged redaction, and none is from Saxony itself.

Bischoff's incomplete catalogue of ninth-century manuscripts lists no shortage of codices for the regions 'Niederdeutschland', 'Nordwest Deutschland', and 'Niederrhein' and particular Saxon centres such as Corvey, Werden, and Herford. Among these are several manuscripts of canon law.[89] But only one extant manuscript containing secular law can be argued to have been in Saxony in the ninth century, that is Hamburg 141a in scrino.[90] The main hand wrote in a style close to that of Fulda, in the third third of the ninth century, but a second hand writing on pages 157–9 and 274–5 has been localised to Corvey. The codex also has an ownership mark from the fifteenth century linking it to Corvey, and late ninth-century glosses providing translations of certain words, according to Gallée in the same hand as the additions, and in Old Saxon dialect.[91] This manuscript contains Ansegis's capitulary collection,

86 MGH Capit. I no. 39. c.6. p. 114: *...et quae actenus in hoste factae sunt traditiones, de quibus nulla est quesitio, stabilis permaneant...*; MGH Legum V c.61 pp. 78–9: *traditiones et venditiones omnes legitime stabiles permaneant.*

87 The relevant part is London Egerton 269. See H. Mordek, *Bibliotheca capitularium regum Francorum manuscripta: Überlieferung und Traditionszusammenhang der fränkischen Herrschererlasse* (Munich, 1995), pp. 226–31.

88 *Quellen zur Geschichte der sächsischen Kaiserzeit: Widukinds Sachsengeschichte, Adalberts Fortsetzung der Chronik Reginos, Liudprands Werke* ed. and German trans. A. Bauer and R. Rau (Darmstadt, 1971), Ausgewählte Quellen zur deutschen Geschichte des Mittelalters 29, pp. 42–3: I, 14: *De legum vero varietate nostrum non est in hoc libello disserere, cum apud plures inveniatur lex Saxonica diligenter descripta.*

89 Bischoff (1998), *Katalog* Nos. 1071, 1072, 2747 2273, 1930.

90 Many thanks to the staff of the Hamburg Staats- und Universitätsbibliothek for lending me a microform of this manuscript.

91 R. Bergmann and S. Stricker (eds.), *Katalog der althochdeutschen und altsächsischen Glossenhandschriften* (Berlin, 2005), pp. 629–30; Mordek (1995), *Bibliotheca*, pp. 153–7 for Fulda association.

further capitularies, and *Lex Salica, Ribuaria*, and *Alemannorum*, but no *Lex Saxonum* . The glosses are to Ansegis's collection, but also, perhaps surprisingly, to the *Lex Alemannorum*. The glosses are not extensive enough to reveal in detail how the manuscript was read. It is, of course, possible that the *Lex Alemannorum* was read as ethnography, or that there were monks in Corvey who identified legally as Aleman.[92] But it is possible that these texts were read because they were useful for disputes and transactions more generally, regardless of ethnic attachment. We might wonder how this provision of legal manuscripts by Fulda for Saxony fits with what we have seen with Rudolph's, and before him Hrabanus's attitudes to *lex*, but it is difficult to make a clear case.

The central point is that, despite evidence that written law was an emotive issue, as far as we can tell, there is no evidence that even Corvey had a *Lex Saxonum* in the ninth century. Of course we might imagine that many codices of *Lex Saxonum* are now lost, but we have no evidence about them from library catalogues or any other source beyond two early printed editions, which used different texts from those now extant. The possible interpretations are various: that the controversy over written law connected with the Stellinga was so intense that manuscripts were destroyed, that the *Lex Saxonum* did not come together in its current form until later in the ninth century, or that the *Lex Saxonum* was marginal to the body of written law that caused the controversy. The question must, for now, remain open, until we have finished deeper textual work.

Layers in the construction of the *Urtext*

The issue of whether the *Lex* was constructed as a single whole, or whether it coalesced over a period of time, is important for our purposes, since it is an indication of how 'live' the process of legislation was.[93] A well-ordered *lex* is more likely to reflect a single attempt to set out what was perceived to have been the customs of a people, rather than reflecting an ongoing legislative process. Are we dealing with a set of provisions that responded to the actual problems of disputes, or the result of a single inquest, an attempt to set out what was seen as the customary practices of the Saxons? The question has implications not

Bischoff (1998), *Katalog*, p. 311 no. 1495 identifies it as 'nordwest Deutch, Corvey?' and $ix^{3/3}$. Commentary and transcription in J. H. Gallée, *Old-Saxon texts* (Leiden, 1894), pp. 210f.

92 See P. Erhart, 'Contentiones inter monachos - Ethnische und politische Identität in monastischen Germeinschaften des Frühmittelalters' in: Corradini et al. (2006), *Texts and identities*, pp. 373–87.

93 This is Wormald's term: see Wormald (2003), 'Leges Barbarorum', p. 33. See also the stimulating discussion of the ordering of chapters in the Burgundian material in P. Heather, 'Law and society in the Burgundian Kingdom' in: Rio (2011), *Law, custom and justice in late antiquity and the early Middle Ages*, pp. 115–54.

just for attitudes to written law within Saxony, but also for the nature of Saxon self-perception and of Charlemagne's legislative programme.

I shall evaluate four strands of argument for the existence of textual layers in our *Urtext*, based on ordering, vocabulary and style, content, and correspondence between the text and its index in the manuscripts. Layers derived from all methods have serious problems of interpretation, since it is not possible to determine how and when the layers were put together. Composition of a text at a single assembly could easily involve individuals or groups working in different styles, but we must certainly not assume that, so I reject Theuerkauf's argument that one must accept textual integrity in the absence of manuscript evidence to the contrary.[94] I shall then examine differences between the manuscripts, which produces much firmer results, albeit with problems of chronology.

Arguments by ordering:

At first glance, the *Lex Saxonum* does indeed appear to have a coherent structure. As set out in Theuerkauf's table, this is:[95]

1–20	Misdeeds, with penalties of fines
21–39	Misdeeds, with the death penalty
40–9	Family law including the law of property in marriages and inheritance
50–60	Liability for strange and accidental events
61–5	Alienations of property
66	The valuation of coin

The regularity of the length of the sections in terms of chapter numbers is very striking indeed; the text is better ordered than *any* other barbarian *lex*, suggesting that we are dealing with something of a unitary production. But there is no need to assume that all of the sections identified by content were put together at once: especially towards the end, thematically grouped material could have been tacked on at a later stage.

Arguments by vocabulary:

And it is indeed clear that c.61–66 as well as an addition to c.16 use a distinct set of vocabulary. Lintzel identified the core terms used in most of the text as *nobilis* rather than *nobilis homo, adalingus* or *nobilior*; *liber* rather than *ingenuus*; *litus* rather than *libertus*; *servus*, never *mancipium*; *occidere* rather than *interficere* or *interimere*; *vel* usually rather than *aut* or *sive*.[96] C.61–66 and c.16 diverge from this scheme, and are particularly significant because they regulate payment of compensations according to the *minor* and *maior solidus,* the former having two-thirds of the value

94 Theuerkauf (1968), *Lex, Speculum*, p. 47.
95 Theuerkauf (1968), *Lex, Speculum*, p. 50.
96 Lintzel (1927), 'Entstehung', pp. 414–16.

of the latter: homicides are to be paid for in *minores solidi*, but other fines are to be paid in *maiores*.[97]The relative dating of this section, therefore, matters very much, because if it was later than most of the text, it would be altering earlier penalties retrospectively. But again there is no obvious way to establish this relative dating.

Arguments by content:

Existing arguments by content focus on the position of the *litus*, some sort of half-freeman. Lintzel claimed that at some point in the tradition, the *wergeld* of a *litus* was upgraded from a twelfth that of a *nobilis*, to an eighth.[98] The claim rests on a particular reading of c.16, and the view that it was interpolated later than its surrounding text, as described above.

The text accepted as interpolated is marked in brackets:

A slain *litus* is to be compensated with 120 *solidi* [and the fine for his wounds is in all cases to be a twelfth of that of a *nobilis homo*, but is to be paid in *solidi maiores*] or if he denies it he is to swear with 12 hands.[99]

The interpolation into this chapter, in Lintzel's scheme, meant that the *wergeld* of a *litus*, uniquely among *wergelds*, was to be paid in *maiores solidi*. But the meaning of c.16 turns on the identity of the subject of *solvatur* in the phrase *multa vero vulnerum eius per omnia duodecima parte minor quam nobilis hominis, solvatur autem solido maiori*. Was it intended to refer to the *litus*, and thus to alter his *wergeld*, or just to the *multa vulnerum*, the fine for wounding him? Such arguments become very convoluted very quickly; there are no clear answers, and it is quite possible to argue contradictory cases. Thus Landwehr more recently argued quite the opposite, that a younger layer of text including c.18, 26, 65 portrayed the *litus* as far more servile than elsewhere in the text.[100] Lintzel's view was supported in part by considerations of language, so is plausible, but both arguments drew support from material in the hagiography and narratives about the *liti*, and imagined that the changes were in some way official, as responses or contributors to events in high politics, the Frankish conquest, and the Stellinga revolts. In fact, as we shall see, there are enough variations between manuscripts to give this

97 The relationship between *solidi* and *denarii* in the laws in general is extremely complex. See Grierson and Blackburn (1986), *Medieval European coinage*, pp. 102–7.

98 Lintzel (1932), 'Zur altsächsischen Rechtsgeschichte', pp. 420–5.

99 MGH Legum V pp. 54–5 c.16: *Litus occisus CXX solidis conponatur* ***multa vero vulnerum eius per omnia duodecima parte minor quam nobilis hominis, solvatur autem solido maiori****, vel si negat sua manu duodecima iuret.*

100 G. Landwehr, 'Die Liten in den altsächsischen Rechtsquellen. Ein Diskussionsbeitrag zur Textgeschichte der Lex Saxonum' in: G. Landwehr (ed.), *Studien zu den germanischen Volksrechten: Gedächtnisschrift für Wilhelm Ebel* (Frankfurt am Main, 1982), pp. 117–43. He connects this theory with an interpretation of the Stellinga.

kind of change a non-official context.

Arguments using the title lists:
Theuerkauf observed that the title headings in the London manuscript do not match the text described: they leave out c.7 and c.61–6.[101] He argued that the scribe was referring to two different versions of the text. This fits neatly with the view from the vocabulary of c.61–6, but requires that c.7 also be considered as from a different layer. C.7 does break the context of its surrounding chapters, but it is resistant to any further analysis: it has no parallel with *Lex Ribuaria* unlike some of its surrounding chapters, and none of the diagnostic vocabulary associated with c.61–6. But even if it was an interpolation, there is no evidence to assume, as Theuerkauf did, that the chapter is to be associated with the same textual layer as the addition to c.16 and c.61–6. In any case, hanging an argument on to c.7 is problematic because the omission of a single chapter heading genuinely is a very plausible and simple error.

The general conclusion is that the existence of a layer consisting of c.61–6, and the addition to c.16 is supported by more than one method, so is relatively safe. The other arguments should not be ruled out, but are too problematic to rely on. The basic point is that the base text, transmitted in all the manuscripts, had already been subject to modifications and additions, which cannot be dated more precisely than to some point in the ninth century. We can get no further, therefore, with the question of dating, but we can continue to trace a further set of modifications in text, using variations between manuscripts.

The three geographical legal groups in the *Lex Saxonum* and the problems

It is possible that the text as we have it anticipated further modifications. *Lex Saxonum* is unusually complex in the kind of applicability it claims. It is very unusual among Frankish *leges* texts, in that it records legal divisions between three regional groups of Saxons, the *Westfalie*, *Ostfaliae*, and *Angarii*.[102] These divisions are recorded around 800 in other sources connected with the Carolingian court, in the 797 *Capitulare Saxonicum*, the *ARF*, and the *Indiculus obsidum saxonum mogentium deducendorum*, which is well dated prosopographically to *c*.802.[103] The

[101] Theuerkauf (1968), *Lex, Speculum*, pp. 49f.

[102] Eg. MGH Legum V p. 74 c.48: *De eo quod vir et mulier simul conquisierint mulier mediam porcionem accipiat; hoc apud Westfalaos; apud Ostfalaos et Angarios nihil accipiat, sed contenta sit dote sua.*

[103] MGH Capit. I no. 115 p. 233. See A. Kosto, 'Hostages in the Carolingian world' *EME*, *11* (2002), pp. 123–47. The text is also translated in Nelson (2008); 'Charlemagne and Empire', pp. 233–4 in which a date of *c*.805 is preferred.

divisions immediately present a qualification to views such as those of Collins, placing great significance on the transfer of geographical terms to peoples.[104] The *lex* does not present the Saxon *gens* as a monolith.

The division in the law might point to a relatively conscientious level of inquisition or consultation. But strangely only one variation between the customs of these groups is actually recorded, and it has been argued to represent a borrowing into Westphalian law from *Lex Ribuaria.*[105] Why would a theoretical legal division be described, but not a significant practical division? It is possible that, as Saxon ethnogenesis and a sense of Saxon law progressed, references to the differences were deleted from the tradition.[106] Or perhaps the only difference worth noting at this stage *was* Westphalian practice, which had become significant through a web of intermarriage across the Saxon-Frankish frontier. It is precisely here that Wood's evidence for cross-border landholding in the eighth century is strongest, thanks to good evidence in the Werden charters and the *Vita Liudgerii.*[107]

However, the most convincing explanation is that the division was intended to provide a kind of structure, around which further law, written or unwritten, might coalesce. Thus the *Lex Saxonum* could act as a thematic guide for further codification, just as the *Lex Ribuaria* acted for the *Lex Saxonum.* The base text as we have it is at just one point of an evolution, and indeed the variations between manuscripts show something of the further directions that evolution might take.

Divergences between the texts and signs of local lawgiving

I have suggested that the core of the *Lex Saxonum* should be treated as a unitary text, the product of a single codification, but that the extant branch of the tradition absorbed some additions and perhaps envisaged scope for further modification. However, the arguments for later evolution of the text have been highly guarded, because they are methodologically unsound. They do not by themselves successfully counter the view that the texts of the *leges* were subject to modification only through mistakes, remaining fossilised to the extent of irrelevance.[108] But when we move to the more visible parts of the textual tradition, that of differences between the extant manuscripts of the *Lex*, we get some

104 See Chapter 1, section 1.1 above for Collins reference.
105 See the quotations from marriage law in note 72 above, with Wood (2003), 'Beyond satraps and ostriches', pp. 275f., and Becher (1999), 'Non enim habent regem', p. 25.
106 For a very clear example of deletion from a *Lex* in reception, see Regino of Prüm's treatment of *Lex Ribuaria* in his *De Synodalibus Causis* as described in Chapter 4, section 4.2.2 below.
107 See arguments in Chapter 1, section 1.4.2 above, as well as Wood (2001) 'Missionaries and the Christian frontier' p. 216, and Wood (2003), 'Beyond satraps and ostriches', pp. 271–97.
108 Wormald (1977), 'Lex Scripta', pp. 105–38 and his later works.

rather firmer evidence that the text continued to be treated flexibly, that it continued to evolve.

The London manuscript contains four chapters with apparently inserted provisions. In all cases the requirement for the death penalty is moderated, so that if the offence takes place outside the *patria*, it is allowed to be judged according to the *lex* of the relevant place. The manuscript is from the beginning of the tenth century, so surely represents changes made at some stage in the ninth.

Text found only in the London manuscript is marked in square brackets:

21/22. He who kills a man or steals something in a church, or breaks into one, [if it was done inside the *patria*] is to be punished by death, [but if he did not do it inside the *patria*, in whatever place he did it ⟨let it be settled⟩ according to their *lex*]...[109]

23. If someone hatches a plot and kills someone on a... feast day, he is to be punished by death [if he did it inside the *patria*; but if ⟨he did it⟩ in some other place, ⟨he is to be punished⟩ according to their *lex*]...[110]

35. He who steals something by day or night of a price of three *solidi*, is to be punished by death.[111]

36. If he takes away something worth less than 3 *solidi*, he to compensate for what he stole ninefold, and for the *fredus*... [On this point, what was said above about theft: he who steals something by which he ought to die inside the *patria*, if it was outside the *patria*, he is not to die, but ⟨it is to be settled⟩ according to the *lex* where it was done]...[112]

38. If someone burns the house of another by day or night, he is to be punished with death [in whatever place it is, according to their *lex*.][113]

Von Richthofen already noticed this in the mid-nineteenth century, but it puzzled him deeply: it was a worryingly early reference to territorially applied law in a world in which it was 'utterly foreign'.[114] He also argued on the basis of the garbling of the sense of c.36 that the insertions were copied into slightly the wrong place from marginal notes

109 MGH Legum V pp. 60–1: *Qui in ecclesia hominem occiderit vel aliquid furaverit, vel eam effregerit, vel sciens perjuraverit,* ***si infra patriam fuerit factum*** *capite puniatur,* ***sin autem infra patria non fuerit, in qualicumque loco fuerit, secundum illorum legem.*** *Et qui nesciens perjuraverit, manum suam redimat auctor sacramenti.*

110 MGH Legum V p. 61: *Qui homini ad ecclesiam vel de ecclesia die festo pergenti, id est dominica, pascha, pentecoste, natale, domini, sanctae Mariae, sancti Johannis baptisae, sancti Petri et sancti Martini, insidias posuerit eumque occiderit, capite puniatur, [si]* ***infra patria fuerit; sin autem in quali loco secundum illorum legem;*** *si non occiderit tamen insidias fecerit, bannum solvat de reliquis.*

111 MGH Legum V p. 67: *35. Qui in re qualicumque vel interdiu vel noctu trium solidorum precium furto abstulerit, capite puniatur.*

112 MGH Legum V p. 67: *36. Quicquid vel uno denario minus tribus solidis quislibet furto abstulerit, novies componat quod abstulit; et pro fredo, si nobilis fuerit, solidos 12, si liber 6,* ***De hac re, quod superius dictum est de furto: qui infra patriam furaverit aliquid unde morire debet, si foris patriae est, hoc fecerit, non moriatur, sed secundum illorum legem ubi factum fuerit,*** *si litus 4; et conscius similiter.*

113 MGH Legum V p. 68: *Qui domum alterius vel noctu vel interdiu suo tantum consilio volens incenderit, capite puniatur,* ***in qualicumque loco est, secundum legem illorum.***

114 K. F. von Richthofen, *Zur Lex Saxonum* (Berlin, 1868), p. 10: 'vóllig fremd'.

in an earlier exemplar. He suggested that the scribe was badly educated, and that the original marginalia were composed by someone who did not understand the basic principles of Carolingian law very well.[115]

But if we take the additions more seriously, it is clear that they express tendencies to respect very local law found throughout the Frankish material in a number of guises, which fit well with the stress this study has already placed on local practice, and flexible interpretation. And again, they point to a system in which territoriality and personality were entwined, if indeed they should be accepted as meaningful categories. Quite how local was the law referred to depends on our assessment of the meaning of the term *patria:* Eichenberger has argued that it could denote, in a legal context, a focus for identity of almost any size, from the level of *pagus* right up to what he saw as the *Geltungsbereich* – the region of validity – of Carolingian royal law.[116] Here, then, the term could very well refer to a very small area, but there is no way to tell what it was intended to signify, and what it was read to signify.

Hincmar, uneasiness about death penalty, choice of law

How, then, are we to understand such major modifications to the text, which clearly carried no 'official', royal force? The unavoidable answer is that interpretation of the legal texts could be very wide indeed, and that the membranes between normative text and interpretative, modificatory commentary were highly permeable. As we argue with the capitularies in the next chapter, the sense in which the apparent normativity of these texts was approached in the ninth century is rather foreign. In this particular case, uneasiness about the death penalty, we can add depth to our understanding of the sense of normativity, thanks to an intriguing parallel in a passage of Hincmar's *De Divortio*. It is always necessary to approach Hincmar's work with caution. In later chapters I argue quite specifically against holding some of his ideas up as representative of Carolingian thought more generally. At the same time, deployed sensitively, his work gives us unparalleled insights into possible attitudes. This particular passage is expressed in very obscure Latin:

> Let however the judges of the *leges* see if what is said about the woman should be found true... whether they decree her to be condemned to death, by *lex romana* or by their *leges* or by those to which that woman is subject, or through those they should want to judge her by. For as there are diverse *gentes*, so are there diverse *leges*, which the discerning holy

[115] von Richthofen (1868), *Zur Lex Saxonum*, p. 4: the scribe 'unleugbar eine sehr geringe Bildung besaß'.

[116] Cf. discussion in Chapter 1, section 1.2.1 above. Eichenberger (1991), *Patria*, pp. 89–100 at p. 89: 'Gerade als Rechtsbegriff war *patria* in diesem Zeitraum von einiger Bedeutung, ohne allerdings den Status eines wirklich exakt Rechtsterminus zu erlangen'. Of course *pagus* is also a very slippery term.

Church does not reject, if they are Christian in their commands, and these are just. But just as we know the offence of Bala and the punishment of the crime, and flee from the counsel given after the edict of the Lord, so we do not decree that anyone should die, but we want all to be saved, since we desire no-one to perish. Nor do we undertake to inflict any violence against the holy and just *leges* which until now the holy Church and episcopal religion at one time accepted, at another time sustained.[117]

This is one of the only clear references Hincmar makes to *leges barbarorum*.[118] Whether or not this suspicion of the death penalty can be considered part of a wider movement, or whether or not even the reviser of the *Lex Saxonum* was specifically influenced by Hincmarian views, this passage sheds important light on the reading of the *leges*.

The first point is that *gens* is linked to *lex*, but the applicability of particular *leges* to the case is treated with hesitation, as a matter on which there might be divergences in opinion. This is a reflection, from a very different angle, of the kind of discussions and arguments about the applicable *lex* that I suggested were behind some of the charter evidence in the previous chapter.

The second point is that, while much is made of respect for the *leges*, that respect operated only as one source of authority among others, notably the demands of the Bible. In this case, the 'notice of Bala' is obscure. Böhringer thought that it might possibly refer to Bilhah, Rachel's handmaid in Genesis 35: 22, who has sex, inappropriately, with Reuben. Another possibility is the extraordinary story of Balaam in Numbers 22–4.[119] While the Bilhah attribution fits well in the context of divorce and adultery, it is not clear at all how it fits with the death penalty theme.

117 Hincmar of Rheims, *De Divortio Lotharii Regi et Theutbergae Reginae* ed. L. Böhringer (Hannover, 1992), MGH Concilia IV Suppl. I, p. 183 [hereafter *De Divortio*]: *Viderint autem legum iudices, si verum inventum fuerit, quod de hac femina dicitur - scilicet ut ante desponsationem, quamdiu in sua vel eius, de quo denotatur, potestate extitit, indecens quid tale admisit et, postquam viro iuncta est, illi se soli servavit, utrum eam morte condemnari decernent sive per legem Romanam aut per illorum leges vel quibus illa femina est subiecta vel per quas illi eam voluerint iudicare. Sunt enim diverse ut gentes ita et earum leges, quas, si Christiane sunt in suis ordinibus, quae iusta sunt, decernentes ecclesia sancta non reicit. Nos autem sicuti Balae notam et criminis poenam nosse, qui de consilio post edictum domini dato refugimus, ita neminem mori decernimus, sed omnes salvos fieri volumus, qui neminem perire desideramus neque legibus sanctis et iustis, quas hactenus sancta ecclesia et episcopalis religio tum acceptavit tum sustinuit, violentiam ullam infere molimur.* The translation is adapted from R. Stone and C. West, *Hincmar of Rheims; On the Divorce of King Lothar and Queen Theutberga*, Manchester University Press, forthcoming. Thanks to Shane Bobrycki for his suggestions on what the *nota Balae* might be. The Latin is very obscure, and many problems remain: which *edictum* is this, by which *dominus*, and which *concilium*? This text deserves more exegesis than is possible here.

118 The other is in *De Divortio*, p. 145 *Responsio* 5: *Defendant se, quantum volunt, qui eiusmodi sunt sive per leges si ullae sunt, mundas sive per consuetudines humanas; tamen si Christiani sunt, sciant se in die iudicii nec Romanis nec Salicis nec Gundobadis, sed divinis et apostolicis legibus iudicandos....* The same passage is also found in Hincmar's *De raptu viduarum*.

119 This is Shane Bobrycki's suggestion.

It may be that some kind of convoluted exegesis is at play here, and although its contours are unclear to us, this fact is itself important. For Hincmar, the example of the Bible, and quite sophisticated exegesis, underlay the correct understanding of the applicability and nature of the *leges*. In Hincmar's case, if we turn to Roman law, we can go further even in *De Divortio*, and see a characteristically exegetical logic underlying his interpretation. In *Responsio* 12 he uses a Roman law found in the *Epitome Aegidii* on inheritance to argue one of his favourite points, that kings are bound by the laws of their Christian predecessors, in a passage introduced with terms lifted from Psalm 44.[120] Certainly, Hincmar was displaying a capacity for abstraction here, in a way foreign to the demands of Radding's 'concrete science'.[121] The third point, then, is that legal texts could be subjected to quite bizarre contortions, that legal argument happened alongside biblical argument, and that the nature of that argument, glimpsed all too rarely in our sources, could have a lot in common with biblical exegesis.

Further modifications

Whatever the underlying concerns of the modifications concerning the death penalty, and their relationship with Hincmar's thought, further differences between manuscripts, found at the end of the *lex* in c.66, show concerns directly connected with application. The Corvey manuscript and an early modern printed version by du Tillet contain some material in common not found in the other two manuscripts, as well as material not found in each other.[122] They relate to the value at which animals can be given instead of coin, a calculation we have seen in other texts, and the importance of which has already been mentioned.[123]

[120] Hincmar of Rheims (1992), *De Divortio*, p. 87: *Sed pro patre nati sunt filii, a quibus secundum legem Romanam, quam praedecessores eorum imperatores et reges condiderunt et sevaverunt et populos per eam feliciter rexerunt et correxerunt, actio, quae ab auctore inchoata est, ab heredicus peragenda est, quique ita praedecessorum suorum bene statuta debent in omnibus conservare, sicuti sua constituta a suis successoribus cupiunt conservari.* 'But "sons are born for the father", by whom, according to the Roman *lex* which their predecessor emperors and kings built and preserved and through which they ruled their peoples and corrected them happily, "an action begun by a progenitor should be completed by the heirs" and thus each of the statutes of their predecessors should be kept well in all ways, just as they desire that the things they constitute be preserved by their successors'. The law is I, 2, 7 of the *Epitome Aegidii*, edited in *Brevarium Alarici* ed. G. F. Haenel (Leipzig, 1848), p. 18, to which all further citations of *Epitome Aegidii*, as well as *LRV* refer.

[121] For Radding's 'concrete science' against 'interpretative science' see Radding (1988), *The origins of medieval jurisprudence: Pavia and Bologna, 850–1150* esp. p. 30. See also Introduction above for his views, and Chapter 3, section 3.1.1 below for more on Hincmar.

[122] The clearest tables here can be found in C. von Schwerin, 'Zu den Leges Saxonum' *ZRG GA*, *33* (1912), pp. 390–452.

[123] See section 2.4.1 above and Chapter 3, section 3.3.2 below, as well as H. Steuer, 'The beginnings of Urban economies among the Saxons' in: Green and Siegmund (2003), *Continental Saxons*, pp. 159–181.

The quantities for fines are also sometimes divergent between the manuscripts, to an extent and in a pattern that argues against treating them as simple mistakes.[124] In the *Lex Saxonum* the penalties in *solidi* or the number of oath helpers needed for a valid oath are altered, *only in the first eighteen chapters*, with just one exception: of these, nine chapters are altered in at least one manuscript, some in both the payments and the number of oath helpers. Although the largest concentration of figures in the text can be found in the first structural layer c.1–20, which therefore have the most scope for this kind of modification, there are still plenty of potentially modifiable figures in the rest of the text. This might indicate the independence of this part in the textual tradition: perhaps it was produced in writing earlier, giving more time for independent modifications, or perhaps more complex processes of interaction between memory and written preservation were at play. The penalty lists in some of the Anglo-Saxon material have been argued on linguistic grounds to have an earlier (presumably oral) composition than other parts of the text. Perhaps we can see a similar structure here, through very different means.[125]

These modifications are significant. In only four witnesses to the text, we have evidence for a great deal of modification and addition, and it may be that the compilers envisaged this when setting out the differences between the three groups of Saxons. This all suggests that there was not only one authority which could be seen legitimately to legislate, or at the very least that there was some fairly widespread usurpation of a perceived authority. So either the *lex* was not straightforwardly codified by Charlemagne to define and control local custom, or this intention was subverted throughout the course of the ninth century. We cannot establish precisely when any of these modifications were made, so we cannot go much further.

2.5 SUMMARY

The idea of *lex* has emerged in ninth-century Saxony as a political issue, a central point of contention in the Stellinga revolt, as a symbolic tool in the integration of Saxony into the Carolingian order, and as a resource to make very particular social and political arguments. This fits with a relatively rich history of construction and modification of the text of the *Lex Saxonum*. But it fits only in a general sense. There is simply not

124 See later, but for now see R. Schmidt-Wiegand, 'Die kritische Ausgabe der Lex Salica - noch immer ein Problem?' *ZRG GA*, *76* (1959), pp. 301–19.

125 See Wormald (1999), *The making*, p. 93 and esp. L. Oliver, *The beginnings of English law* (Toronto, 2002), pp. 25–34.

enough evidence to establish how the descriptive texts fit with the *Lex Saxonum*, or with the capitularies.

I have shown how *lex* could be used to say specific things about the Saxon *gens*, but that it was not imagined as *about* ethnic identity in a simple sense. It was used in writings about social differentiation *within* the Saxon *gens* to make arguments that suited the needs of the authors. I have also suggested that we need to resist making the *Lex Saxonum* all about Charlemagne. It was simply not seen as such as far as we can tell: only in the 880s is Saxon law linked with Charlemagne in any way.

The Saxon case, taken with the two in the previous chapter, combine to show quite some diversity in uses of and approaches to *leges*. We have seen the small-scale *Lex Ribuaria*, which became popular in the ninth century while remaining, in the vast majority of cases, untapped for its bearing on *gens*. We have seen the similarly small-scale *Ewa ad Amorem*, which may reflect elite formation and seems related to the monasticisation of the Netherlands area, and we have seen the Saxon *lex*, which was used in complex ways within Saxony, often associated with the notion of a Saxon *gens* but in various ways, to make particular claims about that *gens*, and which was subject to continued textual modification.

So the *leges* here did not simply reflect or generate ethnicities or notions of kingship. Each text needs to be read carefully, and may have had different roles from other *leges*, and different roles at different times. They may have found practical application in some sense, but they seem not to have found application according to definable principles of personality and territoriality.

We now move the investigation of the *leges* away from newly conquered territories towards the Frankish heartlands, to the world of the court and the capitularies, to consider the updating of the laws, where we may be able to get a firmer grip on the engagement with the *leges*.

Chapter 3

THE ADDITIONAL CAPITULARIES

3.1 INTRODUCTION, POLITICAL THEORY

I now turn away from the problems of law and ethnicity towards those of law and kingship. I examine the principal sources for early Carolingian kings' engagement with the *leges*, that is the capitularies that added to them (this chapter), the manuscripts that have been associated with their efforts to disseminate them (Chapter 4), and the revised texts of the *leges* that have been associated with their courts (Chapter 5). Arguments concerning the relationship between legal text and practice are also developed further in this chapter, and in Chapter 4. First I provide an extended introduction to the final three chapters, covering some central points in the historiography, and examining some Carolingian texts concerning rulership.

The relationship between the ideology of rulership and the making of law was already prominent in Ewig's work in the 1950s, before receiving the most thorough treatment in Nelson's and Wormald's work from the 1970s and 80s onwards.[1] A central message in this scholarship is that legislation, and other forms of engagement with legal texts, including revision and compilation, made a very deliberate statement about the power and authority of a king or emperor. The historical and cultural resonances of legislation need to be appreciated in the context of the symbolic display of power, and the underlying link was with the Christian Roman emperors.

The relationship between kingship and legislation in the Carolingian period has also been put on a more concrete level and linked with a

[1] Wormald (1977), 'Lex Scripta', pp. 105–38; E. Ewig, 'Das Bild Constantins des Großen in den ersten Jahrhunderten des abendländischen Mittelalters' *Historisches Jahrbuch*, *75* (1956), pp. 1–46 esp. pp. 20–1, 40–4; E. Ewig, 'Zum christlichen Königsgedanken im Frühmittelalter' *Vorträge und Forschungen*, *3* (1956), pp. 7–73; J. L. Nelson, 'Kingship, law and liturgy in the political thought of Hincmar of Rheims' *EHR*, *92* (1977), pp. 241–79; J. L. Nelson, 'Legislation and consensus in the reign of Charles the Bald' in: P. Wormald, D. Bullough and R. Collins (eds.), *Ideal and reality in Frankish and Anglo-Saxon Society: Studies presented to J. M. Wallace-Hadrill* (Oxford, 1983), pp. 202–22.

narrative of state building, often involving its eventual failure.[2] Thus Carolingian kings in their capitularies aspired to build a state founded on a defined, authoritative, literate, 'objective' legal system, controlled by royal authority, which turned out, after some moderate success under Charlemagne, to be ahead of its time, simply not manageable because of entrenched private aristocratic opposition. After Charlemagne's death, decadence set in, and with the disruption associated with the Viking invasions, private began to eclipse public, and public law was eclipsed by force. Wormald's view was subtle, but at its centre lay a careful reworking of such an argument.[3] The Carolingian kings tried hard, inspired by the Roman example, to build a working system of literate law, but simply could not persuade their aristocracy to apply it. Counter-arguments to Wormald have emphasised different evidence, but have tended to work within the same framework. So the debate has amounted to a question of whether the glass was half full or half empty.[4] For proponents of the 'half full' approach, the capitularies, the *leges*-scriptorium, and the revision of the *leges* deserve to be taken seriously as the means by which central control was exercised, and the production of manuscripts was testimony to the kings' success.

In the following chapters I suggest a rather different way of framing the problem of law. By taking a subtly different view of the relationship between king and society, I suggest that the legal texts may not be so problematic after all. First I shall explore some existing views in more detail.

In the background to the approach based on Carolingian state-building lurks a very particular view of what Carolingian kings were trying to achieve, and a very particular view of the place of kings

2 Notably Ganshof. See for example the articles translated in Ganshof (1971), *Carolingians and the Frankish monarchy*, especially 'Charlemagne's failure' pp. 256–60; 'The last period of Charlemagne's reign: a study of decomposition' pp. 240–55; 'Louis the Pious reconsidered' pp. 261–72. For all aspects of the historiography see W. Brown and P. Górecki, 'What conflict means: the making of medieval conflict studies in the United States, 1970–2000' in: Brown (2003), *Conflict in medieval Europe*, pp. 1–35. For Duby's Mâcon, where the Carolingian public order was argued to have remained in place until *c.*980, see S. D. White, 'Tenth-century courts at Mâcon and the perils of structuralist history: re-reading Burgundian judicial institutions' in: Brown (2003), *Conflict in medieval Europe*, pp. 37–68 and F. Cheyette, 'Georges Duby's Mâconnais after fifty years: reading it then and now' *Journal of Medieval History*, *28* (2002), pp. 291–317.

3 Wormald (1999), *The making*, p. 92: 'The earnestness of the [kings'] endeavour to hammer out a culture of written law befitting a Christian empire is an index of what might have been achieved under more malleable conditions.'

4 'Half full' approaches are clearest in McKitterick (1989), *Written word*, pp. 23–75; R. McKitterick, 'Perceptions of justice in western Europe in the ninth and tenth centuries' in: *La Giustizia nell'Alto Medioevo (secoli IX–XI)* (Spoleto, 1997), Settimane 44, pp. 1075–102. Mordek's view was complex and shifting. See H. Mordek, 'Kapitularien und Schriftlichkeit' in: H. Mordek, *Studien zur fränkischen Herrschergesetzgebung: Aufsätze über Kapitularien und Kapitulariensammlungen ausgewählt zum 60. Geburtstag* (Frankfurt, 2000), pp. 307–39; H. Mordek, 'Fränkische Kapitularien und Kapitulariensammlungen. Eine Einführung' in: Mordek (2000), *Studien*, pp. 1–55; H. Mordek, 'Leges und Kapitularien' in: Mordek (2000), *Studien*, pp. 341–53.

in society, rooted in a deeply ingrained perspective that the history of this period was played out in terms of the competition between king and aristocracy, and possibly king and clergy, with each party possessing distinct interests. Kings tried hard to get law done, in a recognisably modern way, with various degrees of success. Thus the production of a distinctive, systematically ordered, usable text of the *leges* in Lupus of Ferrières's *Liber Legum* was either an exceptional endeavour or not, but in either case demonstrated that Lupus was adopting the Carolingian kings' programme.[5] The ominous legal expert from the Gâtinais in the famous account of the *Ex Miraculis Sancti Benedicti*, to which we turn in more detail shortly, was either a good example of someone who knew 'the' royal law, or he was evidence that only exceptionally did anyone know it.[6] But few scholars of society and the court would still cling to a view of a serious opposition between king and secular aristocracy, (and between king and clergy,) for the purposes of understanding government.[7] Instead, we need to think about legal texts and the concerns they expressed as bound up in relationships between kings and quite an extensive aristocracy. My discussion of capitularies therefore pays great attention to the processes by which the texts were constructed, and the needs to which they responded.

The question of ideology and its importance is in a sense more complex and slippery. In Charles the Bald's psalter there is a picture of him with a lawbook in his hand, comparing him explicitly with Josiah on one side, and with Theodosius II on the other.[8] These two reference points, the Old Testament and the Roman past, were certainly fundamental to Carolingian understandings of kingship and of law. But they were also fundamental to Carolingian thought about everything else. We must ask what it really would have meant to compare oneself

[5] For the view that his effort was exceptional, see Wormald (1999), *The making*, pp. 30–6 and 53–70. A richer context for Lupus's engagement is given in H. Siems, 'Textbearbeitung und Umgang mit Rechtstexten im Frühmittelalter. Zur Umgestaltung der Leges im Liber legum des Lupus' in: H. Siems (ed.), *Recht im frühmittelalterlichen Gallien* (Cologne, 1995), pp. 29–72. A crucial context for this collection is the production of systematically and historically organised canon collections, on which see H. Mordek, *Kirchenrecht und Reform in Frankenreich: die collectio vetus Gallica: die älteste systematische Kanonenssammlung des fränkischen Gallien: Studien und Editio* (Berlin, 1975). See also O. Münsch, *Der liber legum des Lupus von Ferrières* Volume 14, Freiburger Beiträge zur Mittelalterlichen Geschichte (Frankfurt am Main, 2001).

[6] G. Schmitz, 'The capitulary legislation of Louis the Pious' in: P. Godman and R. Collins (eds.), *Charlemagne's heir: new perspectives on the reign of Louis the Pious* (Oxford, 1990), pp. 433–6. See section 3.1.1 below.

[7] This is most concisely put in S. Airlie, 'Charlemagne and the aristocracy: captains and kings' in: Story (2005), *Charlemagne*, pp. 91f., where he notes, however, Reuter's point that it is dangerous to allow too strong a reaction against a king-centred view of politics to become a rigid orthodoxy. For the sense of opposition to clergy and laity in the historiography see de Jong M. (2005), 'Charlemagne's Church', pp. 103–35 esp. pp. 103–7.

[8] This is BN Lat. 1152, fol. 3v, reproduced in McKitterick (1977), *Frankish church*, p. 3.

with, or to be compared with, Josiah and with Theodosius, rather than simply note the comparison.

The Old Testament model has featured less prominently than the Roman in the historiography for the simple reason that Old Testament kings do not make law.[9] While there are some early Carolingian comparisons of kings with Moses, the most commonly cited Old Testament kings, David, Solomon, and so on, were noted as successfully keeping the *existing* law of God: even Josiah himself, invoked in the prologue of the *Admonitio Generalis*, was responsible for a *reissue* of law.[10] What these kings did was described as justice, as McKitterick noted, not legislation as such.[11]

In legislation, we have been taught that the lawgiving of Roman emperors, especially the Christian Roman emperors, was the most fundamental inspiration to the Carolingians. As Wormald put it, legislation on the part of post-Roman kings 'replicated an archetypal function of Roman imperial sovereignty' and was understood to have done that, deliberately, by contemporaries.[12] But it is in fact quite difficult to find evidence that this link really was explicit, that there was conscious, politically motivated emulation of the Roman emperors. Is it not possible that kings and emperors saw themselves as acting in a tradition of legislation *shared* with Roman emperors, that giving written law was simply something kings did, and that certain Roman emperors were held as examples not because they made laws but because their laws were good?

The classical system of Roman law is justifiably seen as crucial, in some senses exceptional, and highly distinctive in the history of government, of the state, of western Europe.[13] However, it is necessary to be careful about attributing implicitly such a modern understanding to the Carolingians, and interpreting quite limited and ambiguous evidence with that implied assumption in mind.

Nelson pointed out some evidence that the lawgiving of Christian Roman emperors was held up as a model for Charles the Bald, and

9 But see R. Kottje, *Studien zum Einfluss des Alten Testaments auf Recht und Liturgie des frühen Mittelalters (6.–8. Jahrhundert)* (Bonn, 1964); Kottje (1982), 'Hrabanus und das Recht', pp. 118–29; R. Meens, 'The uses of the Old Testament in early medieval canon law' in: Y. Hen and M. Innes (eds.), *The uses of the past in the early Middle Ages* (Cambridge, 2000), pp. 67–77; de Jong (1995), 'Old Law', pp. 161–77.

10 Fundamental, with comprehensive references is M. Garrison, 'The Franks as the New Israel? Education for an identity from Pippin to Charlemagne' in: Hen and Innes (2000), *Uses of the past*, pp. 114–61. See also Ewig (1956), 'Christlichen Königsgedanken', pp. 7–73 on all aspects. The account of Josiah and the law is II Chronicles 34.

11 McKitterick (1997), 'Justice', pp. 1075–102, but see also other contributions to the *Giustizia* volumes.

12 Wormald (1999), *The making*, p. 64.

13 See eg. E. Levy, 'The vulgarisation of Roman law in the early Middle Ages' *Medievalia et Humanistica*, *1* (1943), p. 14: the works incorporated into the Digest were 'master pieces of expression and thought, never excelled and rarely equalled in legal history'.

that this model fundamentally informed Charles's legislative statements. But the significance of some of her evidence can be reconsidered. Nelson was, for example, interested in the passage of Freculf of Lisieux's *Chronicon,* written for the instruction of Charles the Bald, which briefly describes Theodosius attending to the laws.[14] But this is in fact the only substantial reference to lawmaking by the Christian Roman emperors in Freculf's extremely substantial work. The penance imposed on Theodosius I by Ambrose is the immediate context for the remark, and is far more prominent in the account. Freculf also apparently conflated Theodosius I and II, whose life is described at length in religious terms: he could, for example, recite scripture by heart, without a book; his campaigns are described, but not his laws.[15] Constantine was credited briefly with dissolving laws against Christians, but nothing further. Even the striking arrangement of Charles the Bald's Edict of Pîtres into thirty-seven chapters, one more than Valentinian III's thirty-six Novels, may be associated more with the divisions made in the modern edition than in ninth-century manuscripts.[16]

Ewig suggested that the Christian Roman emperors were especially remembered in the field of law.[17] But his examples of citations and references fit specifically with the broader elements of their reputations he identified, that is, by the ninth century, the awareness that they had first accepted the rights of the church in its own sphere, and even accepted its authority in certain respects over kings, notably in Theodosius's penance.[18] One of his examples was the introductory statement in *Formulae Imperiales* Additamenta, no. 2:

> As the statutes of our ancestors are reinforced even in our times, ecclesiastical authority is confirmed. We have learned that lord Louis most serene emperor has confirmed by healthy arrangement after the legislation of Augustuses Constantine and Theodosius,

[14] J. L. Nelson, 'Translating images of authority: the Christian Roman emperors in the Carolingian world' in: Nelson (1996), *The Frankish World,* p. 91. *Chronicon* p. 660 II, 2, 27: *Quo facto vinculum ejus solvit Ambrosius, quae lex hactenus observatur. His et aliis imperator sacratissimus a venerabili episcopo correptionibus illustratus, eum prae omnibus fatebatur in veritate se agnovisse episcopum. Theodosius enim, Valentiniano juvenculo in imperio restituto, Romam senior veniens, leges multas correxit, addidit, immutavit, et sub suo nomine conscripsit. Quae autem in civitate perniciosa adhuc supervacua ex consuetudine antiqua conspexit, auferre sancivit, et quae reipublicae supplemento necessaria addere curavit; his prope gestis pace composita, Valentinianum in Hesperia derelinquens, cum filio Honorio Constantinopolim remeavit.*

[15] *Chronicon* pp. 693–4 II, 5, 11.

[16] Nelson (1996), 'Images of authority', pp. 97–8. See S. Corcoran, 'Hincmar and his Roman legal sources' in: C. West and R. Stone (eds.), *Hincmar of Rheims: life and work* (Manchester, 2015) fn. 42: 'I am not sure that Nelsons ingenious suggestion can be correct that the 37 chapters of the Edict (stressed by Hincmar in his report in AB s.a. 864, p. 113 (trans. Nelson, p. 118)) were intended to go just one further than the 36 of Valentinians Novels. This numeration is that of the modern edition: the highest number recorded in the manuscripts being either 33 or 39, the latter only in a sequence including those of Theodosius II (Theodosiani Libri XVI, II, xvxvi)'.

[17] Ewig (1956), 'Bild Constantins', pp. 1–46 esp. pp. 20–1, 40–4.

[18] Ewig (1956), 'Bild Constantins', p. 40 for Theodosius.

that those who are to be promoted to sacred orders, but are detained by the bond of servitude, ought to gain the status of freedom from their masters, and are to attend to worship more freely, for which reason they shall remember that they are free from human service.[19]

The context here, the manumission of a slave about to be promoted to sacred orders, fits very specifically with the other elements of those emperors' reputations that Ewig identified. It was precisely the emperors' reputation as protectors of the church and establishers of the church as an autonomous institution, that made them suitable for attribution of such a law intended to further the church's autonomy. The *Formulae Imperiales* can no longer be seen as an 'official collection', and the two texts edited as *Additamenta* have, in any case, a very unclear relationship with the main group.[20] Moreover, this is a grant presided over by a bishop, not a king. So this introductory text was certainly not *about* Louis the Pious's kingship or empire; it was about making the charter's aim seem legitimate and necessary. Louis, whose relevant decree is extant, had confirmed the procedure, 'following legislation of Constantine and Theodosius': his role in the *formula* is to add a third pious king to the list associated with bolstering the rights of the church. So this attribution and the linking of Louis with these emperors was certainly highly conscious, but perhaps for slightly different reasons than sometimes imagined.[21]

3.1.1 *Political theory, mirrors of princes*

The most notable feature of Carolingian sources' treatment of law is their almost total lack of interest in it. Innes observed that certainly under Charlemagne, government was understood primarily in moral rather than institutional terms. Whether or not there was a notion of state, and whatever that meant, for the early Carolingians 'there was no real sense that their actions constituted a separate sphere of government over and above normal social action'.[22]

19 *Formulae Merowingici et Karolini Aevi* ed. K. Zeumer (Hannover, 1886), MGH Legum sectio V, p. 328 [hereafter MGH Form.]: *Auctoritas ecclesiastica confirmatur, dum nostris quoque temporibus maiorum statuta roborantur. Siquidem novimus, domnum Hludowicum serenissimum imperatorem post decretum augustorum Constantini atque Theodosii salubri institutione sanxisse, illos, qui ad sacros promovendi sunt ordines, quovis servitutis vinculo detineantur, a propriis dominis libertatis munus debere promereri, quo eo dignius, immo liberius dovinis famularentur cultibus, quo se meminerint ab humano famulatu esse liberos.*

20 All details in Rio (2009), *Frankish Formulae*, pp. 108–11.

21 See the further consideration of this text in Chapter 4, section 4.2.3 below.

22 M. Innes, 'Charlemagne's government' in: Story (2005), *Charlemagne*, p. 71. For old German debates on the state see H.-W. Goetz, 'The perception of "Power" and "State" in the Early Middle Ages: The case of the Astronomer's "Life of Louis the Pious"' in: B. Weiler and S. MacLean (eds.), *Perceptions of power in medieval Germany 800–1500* (Turnhout, 2006), pp. 15–36 and see also the articles in S. Airlie, H. Reimitz and W. Pohl (eds.), *Staat im frühen Mittelalter*

Carolingian historiography, much of which should be read as political ideology, barely treated law outside the examples already quoted in this book. And although late antique and classical works of history available to the Carolingians mentioned law much more frequently, they by no means presented a uniformly positive view of emperors' function as lawgivers. Tacitus wrote in his Annals that after the Twelve Tables, most lawmaking was corrupt, and Eutropius, whose *Breviarium* was used directly by Paul the Deacon in his *Historia Romana*, directly criticised much of even Constantine's lawgiving as 'superfluous' and 'harsh'.[23]

Carolingian works specifically and wholly devoted to the practice and ideology of rulership are also almost silent on law.[24] Smaragdus in his *Via Regia*, dedicated to Louis the Pious, mentions only the *lex dei*.[25] His treatment of justice and judgement is presented in wholly moral terms, and the frame of reference is the Old Testament, not the deeds of Roman emperors. Indeed, his treatment of *iustitia* is a straight quotation from Jeremiah 22: 1–3.[26] Sedulius Scottus's work, written *c.*855 for Lothar II, or for Charles the Bald according to Staubach, is similarly simply not interested in law in any sense, at all.[27] Cathwulf's eight columns of royal

(Vienna, 2006), Österreichischen Akademie der Wissenschaften Philosophich-Historische Klasse Denkschriften 334.

23 A list of such histories available to the Carolingians can be found at McKitterick (2004), *History and Memory*, p. 40. For Tacitus, the Twelve Tables were 'the last specimen of equitable legislation. For subsequent enactments, though occasionally directed against evildoers for some crime, were oftener carried by violence amid class dissensions, with a view to obtain honours not as yet conceded, or to banish distinguished citizens, or for other base ends... and laws were most numerous when the commonwealth was most corrupt'. Tacitus, *The annals and the histories* ed. A. Church and W. Brodribb (Chicago, 1990), p. 51. Tacitus, *Annales* ed. and trans. J. Jackson (London, 1937), Loeb Classical Library 312, pp. 564–5 III, 27: ... *duodecim tabulae, finis aequi iuris. nam secutae leges etsi aliquando in maleficos ex delicto, saepius tamen dissensione ordinum et apiscendi inlicitos honores aut pellendi claros viros aliaque ob prava per vim latae sunt... et corruptissima re publica plurimae leges.* For Eutropius, *[Constantine] Multas leges rogauit, quasdam ex bono et aequo, plerasque superfluas, nonnullas seueras...* Most recently edited in Eutropius, *Eutropii Breviarium ab urbe condita* ed. C. Santini (Leipzig, 1979), Bibliotheca scriptorum Graecorum et Romanorum Teubneriana, p. 67 X, 8. Trans. in *The Breviarium ab urbe condita of Eutropius* trans. H. Bird (Liverpool, 1993), Translated texts for historians 14, p. 66: 'He enacted many laws, some of them good and equitable, but most of them superfluous and a few severe'.

24 The essential guide to the genre is H. Anton, *Fürstenspiegel und Herrscherethos in der Karlolingerzeit* (Bonn, 1968).

25 See J. Scharf, 'Studien zu Smaragdus und Jonas' *DA, 17* (1961), pp. 333–84. See also J. Bovendeert, 'Royal or monastic identity? Smaragdus' Via Regia and Diadema monachorum reconsidered' in: Corradini et al. (2006), *Texts and identities*, pp. 239–51.

26 Smaragdus of St Mihiel, *Smaragdi Abbatis Via Regia* ed. J.-P. Migne (Paris, 1863), PL Vol. 102 Col. 931–970, Col. 947–8: *De justitia. Quod regale sit officium facere justitiam et judicium, Jeremias testatur, ubi: Et praecepit Dominus, dicens: Descende in domum regis Juda, et loqueris ibi verbum hoc, et dices: Audi verbum Domini, rex Juda, qui sedes super solium David: tu et servi tui, et populus tuus, qui ingredimini per portas istas. Haec dicit Dominus: Facite judicium et justitiam, et liberate vi oppressum de mana calumniatoris, et advenam, et pupillum, et viduam nolite contristari, neque opprimatis inique: et sanguinem innocentem ne effundatis in loco isto.*

27 For the Charles the Bald argument see N. Staubach, *Rex christianus. Hofkultur und Herrschaftspropaganda im Reich Karls des Kahlen* (Cologne, 1993), pp. 105–97.

iustitia do not include law, but represent a catalogue of general moral virtues associated with rulership.[28] One could go on.

So we can extend Innes's insight into views of government under Charlemagne and McKitterick's on perceptions of justice in the Carolingian period into even those texts most directly concerned with kingship in the reign of several Carolingians.[29] Emulation of Christian Roman emperors and of Roman law simply cannot be found.

Jonas of Orléans

So how did law fit with these moral attitudes to kingship? The case of Jonas of Orléans provides some help, because we can relate his works of advice to an admittedly problematic account of his behaviour in a dispute. He has little to say about secular law in his two relevant works *De Institutione Laicali* and *De Institutione Regia*, except to disparage it against God's law.[30] The clearest passage is in *De Institutione Laicali* c. XX:

> If men, on account of the business of public cases, busy themselves with learning most diligently and understanding most exactly the *iura* of the *leges mundanae*, which have been established by, and are to be dissolved by mortals, in order that, having noted those things well they may be able to know clearly what is true, what is false, what just, and what unjust in this world of mortals; how much more should be taught the heavenly *iura* promulgated and well collected by God, the highest workman and creator of men, by which it is taught how harm is to be guarded against, and good to be done; which indeed his followers among the living carry to earth, and which ought to be in mind for all *fideles* to learn and understand. And the *lex* of Christ, to be observed not only by clerics, but in general by all *fideles*, is attributed to God. Granted that in the gospels there are particular precepts, which are suited only to those who scorn the world and the followers of the apostles; but the others are to apply unambiguously to all *fideles*, and to each in whichever *ordo* he has devoted himself to God.[31]

[28] J. M. Wallace-Hadrill, 'The Via Regia of the Carolingian age' in: B. Smalley (ed.), *Trends in medieval political thought* (Oxford, 1965), p. 31. J. Story, 'Cathwulf, kingship and the royal abbey of Saint Denis' *Speculum*, 74 (1999), pp. 1–21; M. Garrison, 'Letters to a king and biblical exempla: the examples of Cathuulf and Clemens Peregrinus' *EME*, 7 (1998), pp. 305–28. Sedulius Scottus, *De Rectoribus Christianis* ed. S. Hellmann (Munich, 1906), *Sedulius Scottus*, Quellen und Untersuchungen zur lateinischen Philologie des Mittelalters 1, 1, pp. 19–91.

[29] McKitterick (1997), 'Justice', pp. 1075–102; Innes (2005), 'Charlemagne', pp. 71–89.

[30] The most recent edition of the former is *Le métier de roi = De institutione regia* ed. and French trans. A. Dubreucq (Paris, 1995), pp. 238–9.

[31] Jonas of Orléans, *Jonae de Institutione Laicali Libri Tres* ed. J.-P. Migne (Paris, 1864), PL Vol. 106 Col. 121–278, Col. 161: *Quod multi Christianam professionem verbis teneant, sed operibus negligant. Si mundanarum legum jura ob jurgiorum forensium negotia dirimenda a mortalibus edita, homines avidissime discere, et intelligere acutissime satagunt, ut his bene notis, quid verum, quid falsum, quid justum, quidve injustum sit in hac terra morientium liquido discernere queant; quanto magis jura coelestia a summo opice Deo omnium creatore hominibus promulgata, salubriterque collata, quibus cavendum malum, faciendumque bonum perdocetur; quae etiam sectatores suos ad terram provehunt viventium, cunctis fidelibus discere et intelligere intentioni esse debet. Lex itaque Christi non specialiter clericis, sed generaliter cunctis fidelibus observanda, est a Domino attributa. Licet in Evangelio quaedam sint praecepta specialia, quae solummodo*

Jonas's *De Institutione Regia* in fact repeats this passage verbatim in c.XI, so his treatment of law is in essence no different in his guide for royal life than in his guide for general-purpose lay life.[32] But this does not mean that law was alien to Jonas's conception of rule, and critically, the passage need not mean that he thought secular law unimportant at all.

Jonas's role in an actual judicial case is described in the famous passage in the text of Adalhard of Fleury's *Ex Miraculis Sancti Benedicti* concerning a dispute in the Loire valley over some unfree peasants.[33] Here he appears as a *missus a latere regis*, alongside legal experts from the disputing parties of Fleury and St Denis. His precise role cannot be determined from the narrative, but the narrator claims that it was at the instigation of the royal emissaries that the case was adjourned to Orléans, after it was decided that judges who knew Salic law could not judge according to Roman law. Legal experts from Orléans and the Gâtinais then joined in: it seems that it was imagined that there was a stronger tradition of Roman law scholarship at Orléans than wherever the dispute was initially discussed, or at least that was the pretext for moving the court, which could introduce new people to the dispute, and wholly new forces to the process by which consensus was constructed.

The detail of this narrative allows us only a speculative view into what Jonas's role and opinion might have been here, but it is worth considering in any case. We are told that it was agreed that a judicial battle was the right way to settle the dispute, but that then a legal specialist from the Gâtinais, plausibly Lupus of Ferrières, intervened, with the agreement of the *vicecomes* Genesius, arguing for a straight division of the peasants between the disputing parties. For the author, this argument was a grave affront to justice, and he invoked the stock charge of corruption by gift. It is likely, however, that the objection to battle settling a case between churches was derived from Louis the Pious's capitularies.[34]

Whatever we imagine the real reasons for the failure initially to achieve consensus, how important the technicality cited really was in the context of high power politics, it seems that Orléans could be chosen because of Jonas's high status and connections, and that Jonas presented Orléans as a place where Roman Law was well known, or at least allowed it to be understood as such a place. So Jonas's views expressed in his work

contemptoribus mundi et apostolorum sectatoribus conveniant; caetera tamen cunctis fidelibus, unicuique scilicet in ordine quo se Deo deservire devovit, indissimulanter observanda censentur.

32 *Le métier de roi* pp. 238–9.

33 A translation can be found in Wormald (1999), *The making*, pp. 30–1. Text in Adrevald of Fleury, *Ex miraculis Sancti Benedicti* ed. O. Holder-Egger (Hannover, 1887), MGH Scriptores in folio XV, pp. 474–500.

34 Argued convincingly in Schmitz (1990), 'Capitulary legislation', pp. 433–5.

were not incompatible with at least the reputation of serious knowledge and practice of law at his see.

The passage can help us further in an indirect way, because the author's attitude resonates with Jonas's view on the place of secular law, and may show what such views really meant applied to cases. It is very striking that the only argument against Lupus the narrator was willing to use was that of moral corruption, and he concedes that everyone at the meeting was convinced by his argument. He also gives a precise legalistic reason for the move to Orléans, treating it as reasonable. This was not, then, someone who objected to legal distinctions in general, nor someone with a very narrow view of the gulf between *lex mundana* and *lex dei*. The narrator's attitude in fact neatly demonstrates how the moral and the legal interacted: there was nothing wrong with legal arguments, no sense of an *opposition* between *lex mundana* and *lex dei*.[35] It was rather that in this particular case the very fact that a strong argument from a legal text was able to convince the listeners happened to have led to an injustice. Only someone acting against *lex dei*, and thereby not properly respecting the property of the church, would in this case have brought out a particular law from *lex mundana*, the only possible consequence of its application being a reduction in the rights of the original legitimate owners. Laws, even recent laws associated with the ruling emperor, could be used unjustly, dependent on the context.

This kind of reasoning is in line with what we have seen in Hrabanus's attitudes to Gottschalk of Orbais, where a moral case derived from exegesis took precedence over other arguments.[36] We also have a more explicit comparison in Paschasius Radbertus's *Epitaphium Arsenii*, in which Arsenius intervenes in the case of a widow having been cheated out of her inheritance by a certain *iudiciario vir*:

> Those who did not fear to violate justice were the ones who set forth the law... Now with laws, now with witnesses, now with many persuasive arguments, all the nobles of the palace were acting so that he [Arsenius] might dismiss the culprit as an innocent man... Ultimately, perceiving his [Arsenius's] constancy, they decided that unless he came to a judgement about it, they would do nothing further in this dispute even though the law was manifestly on their side. The people applauded as though Christ's soldier would not wish to come to judgement.[37]

35 A very recent face-value account of the reasons for transferral of the court to Orléans in terms of well-established principles, and a reading of the passage of *De Institutione Laicali* as simply upholding the difference between the ecclesiastical and secular spheres of law can be found in Boucard (2008), 'Indices', pp. 330–1. However, Boucard ends his quote from Jonas at *intentioni esse debet*, missing the crucial next sentence about the application of *lex divina* to everyone.

36 See Chapter 2, section 2.3.2 above.

37 Text in Paschasius Radbertus, 'Radberts Epitaphium Arsenii' ed. E. Dümmler *Abhandlungen der königlichen Akademie der Wissenschaften zu Berlin, phil.-hist. Klasse*, (1900), p. 56: *Legem igitur proponebant, qui justitiam non metuebant infringere: sed sanguis innoxius de terra clamabat: etiam et perempti, quod eum injuste fudissent, jam apud inferos recepti publicabant. Quid plura? etiam omnes*

Arsenius, however, by prayer, compelled the *iudiciario vir* to confess his many crimes, settling the matter. The precise meaning of the sentence in which the *proceres* percieved Arsenius's contancy is somewhat obscure, but the point is that the *leges* themselves are held out quite specifically as a possible source of unjust argument, and Arsenius was compelled to cause a legal judgement to be bypassed completely, through prayer. This is likely the way we should read Hincmar's more famous complaint that bad judges 'when they hope for profit of some kind, invoke the *lex*, but when they reckon there's no advantage to be had there, they seek refuge in the capitularies: thus it comes about that neither capitularies nor *lex* are properly observed'.[38]

So it is plausible that Jonas himself knew various laws quite well, and certainly his work assumed that use of *lex mundana* was commonplace in day-to-day business. He was not in any way against the use of *lex mundana*, but rather sought to guide the way it was interpreted, and the contexts in which it was invoked.

Exceptions: Alcuin and Hincmar

So kingship and law were not generally linked in the texts already surveyed, at least not strongly and explicitly. Law was rather an accepted presence in society and users of law were subject to moral exhortation. But there are two exceptions, where kingship and law seem, at least on the surface, to be linked more closely. Alcuin's *Disputatio de Rhetorica et de Virtutibus*, composed probably around 794, has been described as 'the closest Alcuin got to political theory', and also characterised as his *Via Regia*.[39] The duties of a ruler sketched by Alcuin are thoroughly familiar:

proceres palatii nunc legibus, nunc testibus, nunc vero multis argumentorum ingeniis agebant, ut eumdem reum quasi innocentem dimitteret: interdum autem precibus eum fatigabant... Tunc ad ultimum videntes eius constantiam, decrevere, quod nisi iudicium de eo acciperet, nihil amplius, licet lex pro parte manifesta esset, in hac controversia facerent. Adpaludebat autem populus, quasi miles Christi nec iudicium vellet recipere. Translation in *Charlemagne's cousins: contemporary lives of Adalard and Wala* trans. A. Cabaniss (Syracuse, 1967), pp. 138–42 esp. 140–1. This remarkable account deserves much more attention than is possible here. McKitterick (1997), 'Justice', pp. 1087–8; D. Ganz, 'The Epitaphium Arsenii and opposition to Louis the Pious' in: Godman and Collins (1990), *Charlemagne's heir*, pp. 537–50..

38 Hincmar of Rheims, *Ad episcopos regni admonitio altera* ed. J.-P. Migne (Paris, 1879), PL Vol. 125 Col. 1007–18, Col. 1016: *Quando enim sperant aliquid lucrari, ad legem se convertunt: quando vero per legem non aestimant acquirere, ad capitula confugiunt: sicque interdum fit, ut nec capitula pleniter conserventur, sed pro nihilo habeantur, nec lex.* See also Hincmar's views on the death penalty in Chapter 2, section 2.3.2 above.

39 Wallace-Hadrill (1965), 'The Via Regia', p. 30. See L. Wallach, *Alcuin and Charlemagne: studies in Carolingian history and literature* (New York, 1959). Text is conveniently edited and translated in Alcuin, *The rhetoric of Alcuin and Charlemagne: a translation* trans. W. Howell (Princeton, NJ, 1941). The base text is that in Alcuin, *Disputatio de rhetorica et de virtutibus* ed. K. Halm (Leipzig, 1863), Rhetores Latini Minores, ex codicibus maximam partem primum adhibitis, pp. 523–50. Many thanks to Richard Pollard for discussing this text with me and bringing my attention back to it. See also M. S. Kempshall, 'The virtues of rhetoric: Alcuin's Disputatio de rhetorica et de uirtutibus' *Anglo-Saxon England*, *37* (2008), pp. 7–30.

he is to correct, defend, judge, not to oppress, not to rule through terror, but to conquer following David, to keep his people free from heresy and to convert the heathen. But the work starts with an extremely full discussion of rhetoric and its employment in legal argument, including quite a sophisticated treatment of conflict of laws, the letter and spirit of the law, and the possibility of a wide interpretation of texts, derived to a great extent from Cicero's *De inventione*, directly, or through Julius Victor's *Ars Rhetorica*.[40] However, the law is treated from the point of view of someone making a legal argument: law and kingship are in fact not linked explicitly, and there is no talk of legislation, even though one of the fictional participants in the dialogue was Charlemagne himself.

Hincmar of Rheims's work is saturated with references to laws, mostly Roman law and canons, but also Carolingian capitularies. He returns most often to the argument that kings, as much as anyone else, are bound by the laws of their Christian predecessors, and this involves placing Carolingian capitularies in much the same context as Roman laws.[41] Capitularies in Hincmar's work, then, are treated as quite specifically technically binding, even though, according to Nelson, Hincmar claimed jurisdiction over kings for bishops.[42] Certainly earlier Carolingian texts had argued that capitularies were to be taken seriously: Ansegis's prologue specified that they should be held as *lex*.[43] But in Hincmar, we get a clear sense of what that might actually mean. Equally, Ansegis had organised his material by ruler, and made it clear that the capitularies were to be understood as the rulers' work. But it is only in Hincmar's work that the capitularies and Roman laws are specifically put into the same framework. In Hincmar's work the criteria for their validity were defined, with special emphasis on the fact that they were issued by Christians, and their sense of authority – universal, fully binding – was explicitly examined.

I would suggest, then, that Hincmar was responsible for an intensification of the link between kings and capitularies, and the treatment of the capitularies as the universally binding legislation of kings. It is

40 *Rhetoric of Alcuin* c.9 pp. 76–9. For sources see pp. 24f. This text deserves more treatment than is possible here.

41 See Chapter 2, section 2.4.2 above for the view in *De Divortio*. It is found prominently in *De Ordine Palatii*, where it has been identified as the most unique argument: see Wallace-Hadrill (1965), 'The Via Regia', p. 35: the text is 'fresh and interesting in its preoccupation with the king as the servant and creator of law, and his conviction that the king is the source of all law made for the proper purpose of fulfilling or complementing divine law'. It is also scattered through Hincmar's other work, and used specifically to argue against kings: see J. Devisse, *Hincmar et la loi* (Dakar, 1962), pp. 74f.

42 T. Reuter, 'Regemque, quem in Francia pene perditi, in patria manifice recepit: Ottonian ruler representation in synchronic and diachronic comparison' ed. J. L. Nelson in: Reuter (2006), *Medieval polities*, pp. 127–47. And see the view that there was a 'new edge' in Hincmar's thought in Nelson (1995), 'Kings with Justice', p. 802.

43 See section 3.2.3 below for the text.

tempting to extrapolate attitudes from Hincmar to Carolingian society more generally, but ultimately misleading. His work was singular, and although it did continue developments we can see already in Ansegis, it was caught up in the very specific context of Charles the Bald's court. Devisse noted that citations of Roman law dry up very suddenly in Hincmar's work after Charles the Bald's death, and this may be significant.[44] Goldberg showed how circumstances and history led to the development of a particularly militarised style of kingship under Louis the German, and noted Charles the Bald's preference for lavish ceremony and display as a way of compensating for his youth.[45] Was the stress on law and Roman law in particular in Hincmar's work also related to Charles's strategy for distinguishing his rule from that of his brothers?

3.1.2 Summary

So it seems that in general the Christian Roman emperors were remembered clearly in the sphere of law, because they quite clearly contributed a great deal to it: the law concerning the church in the Theodosian code, and the compilation of the code itself, were undeniable and fundamental facts confronting any reader of the many Carolingian manuscripts of Roman law. For those engaging with kingship, and for historians, these facts were *sometimes* noted, but law was much less important than questions of morality, orthodoxy, and military might. It is perhaps only in Hincmar's work that both perspectives were combined, that the legislative efforts of the Christian emperors were worked into a theory that incorporated the moral perspectives, and the correct attitude to their work, the laws, was expounded.

The consequences of this are twofold. Firstly, we need to be very careful about laying too much stress on the symbolic role for law and lawmaking in relating kings to the Christian Romans. We should investigate further evidence for the role of kings in law with caution. Secondly, we need to question how widespread in Carolingian society was the notion that a single law produced or upheld by kings had binding, official status. We should replace the question of effectiveness in practice of enacted, official law with a deeper investigation of the relationships between the reading and production of legal texts, practice, and ideology. The next chapters treat texts and manuscripts with this in mind.

44 Devisse (1962), *Hincmar et la loi*, pp. 91f.

45 E. J. Goldberg, '"More devoted to the equipment of battle than the splendor of banquets": frontier kingship, martial ritual and early knighthood at the court of Louis the German' *Viator*, 30 (1999), pp. 41–78.

3.2 PRELIMINARIES TO THE ADDITIONAL CAPITULARIES

We can find in the capitularies adding to the *leges* direct as well as indirect engagement with the specific provisions of the *leges* themselves, something to be found almost nowhere else in the ninth century. This chapter attempts to use the material as fully as possible. But the capitularies are notoriously slippery sources, and much work needs to be done to establish their perspective, their processes of construction, the sense in which they were intended to be understood, and how they actually were understood. First I examine the historiography, and try to unpick the assumptions upon which previous work on the texts has relied, before returning to first principles, and assembling ninth-century references to 'additional capitularies' in a catalogue. I then examine each text and its manuscripts in detail, asking what each can tell us about the nature of kings' engagement with the *leges*, and how the *leges* were read and used. I then consider the manuscripts of the additional capitularies as a group, with a view to understanding how they were transmitted, what their associations are in the manuscripts, and what that can tell us about how they were read.

3.2.1 Historiography, classification

The texts considered here were interpreted by Boretius, their MGH editor, as a distinct class of capitularies, which were constructed with a uniquely wide consensus, and enjoyed a more pressing and longer-lasting sense of authority than other capitularies. Their significance was indeed that they were a channel by which *Königsrecht* could be added directly into the *Volksrecht* of the *leges*.[46] Boretius's typology has endured into this century: Mordek and Wormald, among others, although they rejected or qualified notions of *Volksrecht* and *Königsrecht* in theory, continued to think of capitularies substantially in Boretius's terms.[47] So these texts have been seen as royal attempts to alter the law, and their content has been assessed as prime evidence for how successfully Carolingian kings kept the law up to date.[48] The texts composed under Charlemagne have been set alongside the revision of the major *leges* and the codification of

[46] A. Boretius, *Beiträge zur Capitularienkritik* (Leipzig, 1874) esp. clearly formulated at pp. 3f.

[47] For example Wormald (1999), *The making*, pp. 47–50. Although Mordek commented little on typology in his published work, its acceptance, at least in part, is implicit in his discussions. See for example Mordek (2000), 'Kapitularien und Schriftlichkeit', pp. 307–39, and his categorisations of the new texts he discovered, discussed in section 3.3.8 below. Ganshof also accepted these basic categories: Ganshof (1961), *Was waren die Kapitularien?*, pp. 117–19.

[48] See Wormald (1999), *The making*, pp. 47–8, where he sees in them evidence of Charlemagne's 'reticence' compared with Lombard and Visigothic kings. A related approach is taken in a sophisticated and thoughtful way in Patzold (2005), 'Veränderung', pp. 63–99.

the minor *leges* as some of his most important engagement with the *leges*, his 'reforms'.[49]

Yet some of the assumptions Boretius used in the construction of his scheme were already successfully challenged in the nineteenth century. Seeliger argued that the evidence for a substantive difference in attitude to Boretius's different classes, the *capitula legibus addita, capitula missorum*, and *capitula per se scribenda*, was severely limited, and that there is no direct evidence that the promulgation of *capitula legibus addenda* required more consensus than other forms of capitulary, nor that they had a longer period of validity.[50] He also showed that the scheme did not correspond very well with the messy reality of the texts, even in the sense in which Boretius's structure was best rooted in the evidence, that is, in the clear differences between their concerns. Most capitularies, as Ganshof put it, could be seen as *capitula mixta*.[51] Seeliger's work indeed went further, questioning the whole notion of *Königsrecht* and *Volksrecht* in a way that reminds us that the work of nineteenth-century German legal historians was far from monolithic, either in its results or in its guiding assumptions.[52]

Only very recently have the threads of this work been picked up.[53] A suspicion of typology permeates Pokorny's work on a letter fragment from the 810s, which suggested that responses to questions put by individuals associated with the court could find their way into texts edited as, or analogous to, capitularies.[54] Pössel developed this line further, and suggested that capitulary production in general be seen as divorced from any single formal procedure or set of procedures. Capitularies might well not always have been the product of assemblies in a straightforward sense, and differences in their concerns can sometimes be explained in terms of their intended recipients rather than their membership of a tightly defined class. The extant form of at least some capitulary texts, which had been conceptualised as relating to a different 'type', a distinct, controlled, and defined means of production

49 For example Schmidt-Wiegand (1978), 'Stammesrecht und Volksprache', pp. 166–7; Theuerkauf (1968), *Lex, Speculum*, pp. 54–67.

50 G. Seeliger, *Die Kapitularien der Karolinger* (Munich, 1893), pp. 36–56. Stein's work is also sometimes important and insightful, if one can ignore his attempts to make almost every text a forgery: Stein (1926), 'Lex und Capitula', pp. 289–301.

51 Ganshof (1961), *Was waren die Kapitularien?*, pp. 28–31. See also Pössel (2006), 'Authors and recipients', p. 260.

52 G. Seeliger, 'Volksrecht und Königsrecht? Untersuchungen zur fränkischen Verfassungs- und Rechtsgeschichte' *Historische Vierteljahrschrift*, *1* (1898), pp. 1–40.

53 See for example Mordek (2000), 'Leges und Kapitularien', pp. 341–53 and H. Mordek, 'Recently discovered Capitulary texts belonging to the legislation of Louis the Pious' in: Godman and Collins (1990), *Charlemagne's heir*, pp. 437–55.

54 R. Pokorny, 'Eine Brief-Instruktion aus dem Hofkreis Karls des Großen an einen geistlichen Missus' *DA*, *52* (1996), pp. 59–83.

and intended sphere of validity, can be seen as reflecting the chains of communication which linked the royal court to the provinces.[55]

So it is now quite clear that the 'additional capitularies' cannot be analysed straightforwardly as products of a particular, defined process for adding new material to the *leges*, with a clear legalistic function in relation to other legal texts, at least not without a great deal of further justification. Still, I shall concentrate on the very same texts Boretius classified as 'additional capitularies', for the simple reason that they really do provide the richest evidence for the reading of the *leges*. Boretius did not base his work on no evidence at all, but the texts do need to be reread with updated assumptions.

3.2.2 The texts

Boretius identified seven 'additional' capitularies from the Carolingian period, named them, and dated them as follows:

39.	*Capitulare Legibus Additum*	803
41.	*Capitulare Legi Ribuariae Additum*	803
68.	*Capitula ad Legem Baiuwariorum Addita*	801–13
134.	*Capitula Legi Addita*	816
135.	*Item Capitula Legi Addita*	816
139.	*Capitula Legibus Addenda*	818–19
142.	*Capitula Legi Salicae Addita*	819 *vel paullo post*

These titles, like so many others, were the work of the MGH editors. They bear some relation to the titles in the manuscripts, but those relationships are hardly close. Boretius was more interested in giving a sense of what he thought the legalistic function of the text was than accurately reproducing their presentation in the manuscripts. For example, he gave Capitulary no. 144 the title *Capitula de iustitiis faciendis* even though both of its manuscripts give *Capitula legis salicae addenda*, because he found it not to be related closely enough to the text of *Lex Salica* or of any extant *lex* to fit into his scheme.[56] Equally the most common title for Capitulary no. 39, to be found in sixteen manuscripts, is *Capitula que in lege salica mittenda sunt*, whereas Boretius preferred *Capitulare legibus additum*, dropping the association with *Lex Salica*, because he could find no specific point of contact between the texts of the capitulary and the *Lex Salica*.

I shall take their titles in the manuscripts more seriously than Boretius, and investigate how their variation from manuscript to manuscript might relate to variations in the understandings of the relationship between the

[55] Pössel (2006), 'Authors and recipients', pp. 253–74.

[56] See Mordek (1995), *Bibliotheca*, pp. 427 and 622.

capitularies, the *lex* in general and specific *leges.*[57] The critical issues are how specific a sense of *lex* is invoked, both in the sense of whether *lex* was used as a wholly general term denoting 'law' or whether it signified a specific genre of texts, and also, if it did denote a specific genre of text, which particular *lex* was invoked. This matters for understanding how kings expected *lex* to be read and whether there was any sense of addition by which the *lex* could be controlled by royal authority.

The first, most obvious point is that these texts are all from the first quarter of the ninth century, but most of our manuscripts are from later in the century, so we must distinguish quite clearly between, on the one hand, how the texts were constructed and how they were *intended* to be read, and, on the other hand, how they were *imagined* to have been constructed by readers, and how those readers did read them. This is especially important considering the possible differences I outlined above between Charles the Bald's approach and those of his predecessors.

3.2.3 Catalogue of references in Frankish sources to capitularies adding to leges, *with a brief commentary*

First of all, I provide a list of possible references to capitularies adding to *leges*. Most of the references here have been noted before, by Boretius, Seeliger, Stein, and others, but are worth listing systematically, both to give a single, clear picture of what the evidence for the understanding of these texts really is, and because the quotations are examined repeatedly in the following chapters. I also provide a brief commentary to some of the texts as I go along, principally to identify any specific references to extant texts, and to examine the sense of the term *lex*, which, as we have already seen, can have a very wide sphere of meaning.[58]

Texts associated with Frankish emperors

A. Capitulary no. 40, dated to 803:

> That the *populus* is to be asked about the *capitula* which were recently added into the *lex*; and after all shall have consented, they are to make their subscriptions and professions in those *capitula*.[59]

B. The text edited by Boretius as Capitulary no. 103, which is in fact a letter from Charlemagne to his son Pippin king in Italy, dated to 806–10. After admonishing him for some disorder in his kingdom, it warns:

[57] This approach is suggested as useful already in R. Schneider, 'Schriftlichkeit und Mündlichkeit im Bereich der Kapitularien' in: Classen (1977), *Recht und Schrift*, pp. 265–6.

[58] See for example comments about identifying the *lex* in accounts of the Stellinga rebellions in Chapter 2, section 2.2.1 above.

[59] MGH Capit. I no. 40 c.19 p. 116: *ut populus interrogetur de capitulis quae in lege noviter addita sunt; et postquam omnes consenserint, subscriptiones et manufirmationes suas in ipsis capitulis faciant.*

We have also heard, that those *capitula* which we ordered to be written into the *lex*, in some places in your land and mine, they say that... they do not want to obey them nor consent to them nor to hold them as *lex*...[60]

C. Louis the Pious's Capitulary no. 143, c.5 (821) relates:

In general we warn, that the *capitula* which we decreed in a past year should be added to the *Lex Salica* by the consent of all should now no longer be spoken of as *capitula*, but as *lex*, and be held as *lex*.[61]

Boretius thought that this was a direct reference to Capitulary no. 142, but as I argue below, at least one scribe in the 820s or 830s seems to have identified it as Capitulary no. 139.[62]

D. Capitulary no. 142, c.12 gives :

the truth of the matter should be investigated according to the *capitula* of the lord emperor, which he previously established for holding the *lex*...[63] no. 137 'Proemium generale ad capitularia' at p. 275: *quid etiam in legibus mundanis addenda, quid quoque in capitulis inserenda forent.*

The context makes it very likely that this refers to a chapter of Capitulary no. 139, but it refers to it as 'for holding the *lex*' rather than 'adding to the *lex*'.[64]

So Charlemagne and Louis the Pious cared about having certain *capitula* held as *lex*. But none of these references need mean more than that certain *capitula* should be taken seriously as a normative force. Not keeping *capitula* as *lex* might mean no more than not observing the *capitula*.[65] Equally, we might imagine that capitularies and *leges* were copied into the same manuscripts as a result of this pressure: the *lex*, into which the capitularies were to be added, might even be read as a *book of lex*.

Direct references elsewhere

E(a). The library catalogue of Reichenau 821–2 contains an entry for a book containing

60 *Ibid.* no. 103 p. 212: *audivimus etiam, quod quedam capitula quae in lege scribi iussimus, per aliqua loca aliqui ex nostris ac vestris dicunt, quod nos nequamquam illis hanc causam ad notitiam per nosmetipsos condictam habeamus, et ideo nolunt ea oboedire nec consentire neque pro lege tenere. Tu autem nosti, quomodo vel qualiter tecum locuti fuimus de ipsis capitulis, et ideo monemus tuam amabilem dilectionem, ut per universum regnum... ea nota facias et oboedire atque inplere praecipias.*

61 MGH Capit. I no. 143 c.5 p. 295: *Generaliter omnes admonemus, ut capitula que praeterito anno legis Salicae per omnium consensum addenda esse censuimus iam non ulterius capitula sed tantum lex dicantur, immo pro lege teneantur.* This text does not translate easily. Especially the sense of *dico* is not clear.

62 See section 3.3.2 below.

63 MGH Capit. I no. 142 c.12 p. 293: *...secundum capitula domni imperatoris, quae prius pro lege tenenda constituit, rei veritas conprobetur.*

64 For the reference, see section 3.3.6 below.

65 Cf. Stein (1926), 'Lex und Capitula', pp. 289–301.

leges and *capitula* of lord Charles and Louis to be added to the *leges* as well as others of his *capitula* for the raising of animals and for the care of working in domestic agriculture.[66]

Exactly what this means is difficult to establish because we have no extant manuscripts containing capitularies from Reichenau at all, except for *Capitulare Monasticum* III, no. 130.[67] But from the context here, it could be that the *capitula* '*legibus addenda*' were any capitularies on any vaguely legal matters not involving agriculture and animals. There is really no way to tell.

E(b). The mid-ninth-century catalogue from St Gallen contains a volume of *capitula que legibus addenda sunt*, as well as volumes of Roman laws, Frankish and Alemannic *leges*, one of *capitula ludouuici imperatoris* alone, and one containing *capitula caroli imperatoris* alongside biblical glosses. Note also how the *leges* are separated from the capitularies, in the context of the Theodosian code, but that the *Institutiones* of Roman emperors are grouped with the capitularies.[68]

F. The *ARF* for 819 relates:

An assembly was held at Aachen after Christmas at which many matters regarding the condition of the churches and monasteries were brought up and settled. Some greatly needed *capitula*, as yet still lacking, were drawn up and added to the *leges*.[69]

The *capitula* which were lacking in the *leges*, then, are contrasted only with the business of churches and monasteries. The *leges* that were deficient could have included capitularies, or Roman law.

G. Einhard too may be referring to additional capitularies in the famous passage so often, perhaps unfortunately, used as the cornerstone for discussion of early Carolingian legislation:

After he had received the imperial title, he noticed that the *leges* of his people had many defects – for the Franks have two *leges*, differing greatly in many details. So he planned to add what was lacking, to reconcile discrepancies, and to correct what was badly or

[66] J. Duft, *Die Abtei St. Gallen Band I: Beiträge zur Erforschung ihrer Manuskripte* (Sigmaringen, 1990), pp. 178–81: *leges et capitula domni Karoli et domni Hludowici imperatorum addenda legibus necnon et alia capitula eius de nutriendis animalibus et laborandi cura in domestica agricultura.*

[67] St Gallen Stiftsbibliothek 914. See Mordek (1995), *Bibliotheca*, pp. 680–3.

[68] St Gallen 728 p. 17. An image can be found on the website *Codices Electronici Sangallenses (CESG)* www.e-codices.unifr.ch/en/csg/0728 last viewed on August 26 2014.

[69] *Carolingian Chronicles: Royal Frankish Annals and Nithard's Histories* trans. B. W. Scholz and B. Rogers (Michigan, 1970), p. 105; *Annales Regni Francorum* ed. F. Kurze (Hannover, 1895), MGH SRG VI, p. 150: *Conventus Aquisgrani post natalem Domini habitus, in quo multa de statu ecclesiarum et monasteriorum tractata atque ordinata sunt, legibus etiam capitula quaedam pernecessaria, quia deerant, conscripta atque addita sunt.*

falsely stated. Yet little of this was done by him, except that he added to the *leges* a few *capitula*, themselves unfinished.[70]

As explained earlier, this passage is often taken at face value, to illustrate the lack of interest contemporaries had in legislation, and the unimpressive legislative record of Charlemagne himself.[71] But what were these *capitula* adding to the *leges*? Is there any reason to think of these as anything other than *capitula* concerned with broadly secular matters? Wormald thought that they must be just the 'additional capitularies' because Einhard described them as 'few', but this is hardly convincing.[72] Certainly his reference in the sentence before to the two *leges* makes it clear he was dealing with texts of *lex*, but we have seen how quickly the sense of *lex* could shift, even in a single text.

Whether or not Einhard had something more specific in mind, it may be possible to link his comments about *lex* and *capitula* with the general aims of his work. If Innes's and McKitterick's dating of the *Vita Karoli* to *c.*817 is accepted, this passage was written only the year before a period of very major legislative activity of 818–19, in which two capitularies classified as additional, assessed in detail below, as well as several others, were composed.[73] Einhard was perhaps drawing attention to his own patron's activity by denigrating that of his predecessor. And if the 'additional' vocabulary means anything specific, it may also be that the terms in which Charlemagne's activity was criticised were quite new, and even alien to Charlemagne. Adding to the *leges* in quantity and with thoroughness could have been a particular concern of Louis's, one he attempted to remedy in 818–19.

We can go further, if we accept Mordek's argument that Einhard was involved in some way in the production of a text he discovered, edited, and named *Capitula adhuc Conferenda*.[74] The text, which appears to be an agenda for discussion, treats themes addressed already in the *leges*, especially in the *Lex Ribuaria*, leading Mordek to characterise it as a plan for the compilation of another additional capitulary. If this attribution is correct, we have a rare insight into the attitudes of a legislator, and of

70 The translation is in Wormald (1999), *The making*, p. 45. The text is from *Vita Karoli* p. 33: *Post susceptum imperiale nomen, cum adverteret multa legibus populi sui deesse - nam Franci duas habent leges, in plurimis locis valde diversas - cogitavit quae deerant addere et discrepantia unire, prave quoque ac perperam prolata corrigere, sed de his nihil aliud ab eo factum est, nisi quod pauca capitula, et ea inperfecta, legibus addidit. Omnium tamen nationum, quae sub eius dominatu erant, iura quae scripta non erant describere ac litteris mandari fecit.*

71 Wormald (1999), *The making*, pp. 45–7. Also, see Chapter 1, section 1.3.1 above.

72 Wormald (1999), *The making*, p. 47.

73 Innes, M. and McKitterick (1994), 'The writing of history', pp. 193–220. See also the discussion in McKitterick (2008), *Charlemagne*, pp. 11–14 where a date even before 817 is suggested.

74 Mordek (1990), 'Recently discovered capitulary texts', pp. 437–55.

his output. This text is treated in more detail below.[75]

H. A text preserved in Benedictus Levita's collection, Mordek's so-called *Capitula a Benedicto Levita singillatim tradita*:

If someone shall have killed or wounded a priest or a deacon or a monk [he is to compensate] according to the *statuta priorum capitulorum quae legi Salicae sunt addita*, and in addition our *bannum*, that is sixty *solidi*.[76]

The status of this text is very problematic, and its transmission history complex.[77] But it very probably does refer to an extant text, Capitulary no. 39, and perhaps also no. 139, both of which are labelled as adding to *Lex Salica* in many of their manuscripts, and do exactly what this text says they should.

I. The Astronomer wrote:

Meanwhile, to the *leges* in which public matters seemed to be defective, he [Louis the Pious] added certain *capitula*, which to this day are retained as indispensable.[78]

Possible indirect references and citations

So it is difficult to pin down the precise meaning of most of the direct references to capitularies adding to *lex*. Such indirect references as we can find also suggest that, often, no distinction was felt between additional capitularies and other capitularies. First and foremost, we have the texts' presentation in Ansegis's collection, as well as Benedictus's.[79] Here, there is no direct indication that they are different from the other texts in any way. In fact, in the prologue to Ansegis's collection, all of the capitularies 'are to be held as *lex*, because they are for the benefit of the church,' and the capitularies of book three are all described as 'pertaining to *lex mundana*'.[80] Hincmar of Rheims did cite additional capitularies, but through Ansegis, and there is no evidence that he ever thought of them

75 See section 3.3.8 below.

76 Edited in Mordek (1995), *Bibliotheca*, p. 1023: *Si quis sacerdotem vel levitam aut monachum interfecerit vel debilitaverit, iuxta statuta priorum capitulorum quae legi Salicae sunt addita; et insuper bannum nostrum, id est, sexaginta solidos...*

77 See more treatment in Chapter 4, section 4.1.5 below.

78 *Son of Charlemagne; a contemporary life of Louis the Pious* trans. A. Cabaniss (Syracuse, 1961), p. 68; *Thegan: Die Taten Kaiser Ludwigs. Astronomus: das Leben Kaiser Ludwigs* ed. E. Tremp (Hannover, 1995), MGH SRG 64, p. 392 [Hereafter *Thegan / Astronomus*] c.32: *Interea capitula quedam legibus superaddidit, in quibus cause forenses claudicare videbantur, que actenus veluti pernecessaria servantur.*

79 For this point, and its treatment by Boretius, see Stein (1926), 'Lex und Capitula', pp. 291f.

80 *Der Kapitulariensammlung des Ansegis* ed. G. Schmitz (Hannover, 1996), MGH Capitularia regum Francorum, Nova series, pp. 432–3 [Hereafter *Ansegis*]: *...quia ad sanctae ecclesiae profectum facta sunt, pro utili firmiter tenenda sunt lege.* Also: *...Illa autem, quae domnus Karolus in diversis fecit temporibus ad mundanam pertinentia legem, in tertio adunavi.* Cf. Benedictus Levita's Prologue www.benedictus.mgh.de/edition/aktuell/praef.pdf p. 3: *...pro lege tam ecclesiastica quam et seculari iure firmissimo sunt tenenda.* Last viewed 26 August 2014.

as having a special status.[81] There is a lot of interest in the texts specifically in the 'Rheims group' of manuscripts, which may be linked to him, however.[82] Similarly, the tenth-century Old High German translation of Capitulary no. 139 used a base text from Ansegis's collection, according to its inscription, so there is no direct evidence that it received attention because of its particular status.[83]

Schmitz has argued that the procedure for the famous Fleury dispute in the 830s and 40s was settled by law based on Louis the Pious's additional capitularies, specifically Capitulary no. 139.[84] The problem is that the hagiographer thought that the case was due to be settled by Roman law, so the use of capitularies, whatever the sense of their attachment to *Lex Salica*, makes an underlying system still harder to identify. The essential conclusion concerning the use of Capitulary no. 139 here, then, is that its attachment to *lex* generally or to *Lex Salica* in particular was either not significant to anyone involved in the dispute, or its significance is not recoverable because of the nature of the account.

Summary: evidence outside the texts themselves and their manuscripts

The evidence surveyed here is every, or at least nearly every, direct and specific reference to a capitulary adding to a *lex* in Carolingian sources outside Italy, a rather special case that cannot be investigated here.[85] With two exceptions, Benedictus's text (**H**) and the reference in Capitulary no. 142 (**D**), we cannot be sure that the texts they describe as *capitula* adding to the *leges* are specifically those Boretius identified. In our other passages, 'adding to the *lex*' was most probably meant in a broad sense, as 'adding to the law', which might be thought of as the whole variety of texts found in Carolingian legal manuscripts: in a sense 'adding to the *lex*' could be understood as 'writing into the book of *lex*'.

3.3 THE TEXTS IN DETAIL. CONSTRUCTION AND CONTENTS

So far we know very little about the 'additional capitularies', except that we need to read each carefully, and assume nothing about them in advance based on the titles given to them by nineteenth-century German scholars. We now turn to their texts, to investigate what they

81 See the tables in Devisse (1962), *Hincmar et la loi*, pp. 11–13.

82 See section 3.4.2 below.

83 For this text see Schmidt-Wiegand (1978), 'Stammesrecht und Volkssprache', pp. 174f.

84 Schmitz (1990), 'Capitulary legislation', pp. 433–5. This case is discussed in another context below. It is translated in Wormald (1999), *The making*, pp. 30–1, and discussed in Nelson (1986), 'Dispute settlement', pp. 45–65.

85 The best introduction to Italy is F. Bougard, *La justice dans le royaume d'Italie: de la fin du VIIIe siècle au début du XIe siècle* (Rome, 1995). Detailed consideration of the Italian context should be a priority for future work.

are from first principles. The central questions concern how they were constructed, what they were intended to achieve, and how they were read. What sort of attachment to the *leges* do they envisage? What do they tell us about royal authority on the one hand, and the reading of *leges* for practical purposes on the other?

3.3.1 No. 39 Capitulare Legibus additum *802*

We start with a text that has been seen as a prime product of Charlemagne's legal 'reforms'. This text is short, with only eleven chapters. It provides no direct quotation from a *lex* text, nor can anything from it be considered an addition to, or interpretation of, any particular passage of any *lex*. It makes just one reference to the *freda quae in lege Saliga scripta est*, providing a special rate at which it is to be paid.[86] Because of this lack of direct engagement, Boretius removed a link with *Lex Salica*, which is found in the titles given in most of its manuscripts. He did not feel it added to the *Lex Salica* text in the same way as nos. 41, 68, and 142 did to their *leges*.

The subjects covered, however, are very much in line with what is found in the *leges*: *wergelds* for different grades of clerics, procedures for doing justice inside an immunity, sanctuary in church, court procedure, disputes over social status, land transactions to the church, and the payment of compensations. The material on sanctuary inside an immunity has been linked convincingly with a conflict between Theodulf of Orléans and Alcuin, shortly before the construction of this capitulary.[87] And the capitulary adds treatments of subjects involving the church and written documents that would have seemed conspicuously absent in the *Lex Salica* by the ninth century, especially compensations for clerics, land transactions to churches and *servi* freed by charter. In quite a crude but important and direct sense, then, this text could be seen as updating the text of *Lex Salica*.

An investigation into the process of construction of the text is hindered by the bareness of its style. Still, it is striking that it is not phrased at all as a strong expression of an imperial will. Indeed it uses the term *rex* or even *princeps* rather than *imperator*, strange in a document which is so often read as part of a conscious programme of advancing Romanising imperial ideology.[88] *Rex* is also only used with third-person verbs.[89] The use of *rex* rather than *imperator* could suggest an earlier dating, to the period before Charlemagne's imperial coronation, but

86 MGH Capit. I no. 39 c.9 p. 114.

87 R. Meens, 'Sanctuary, penance, and dispute settlement under Charlemagne: the conflict between Alcuin and Theodulf of Orléans over a sinful cleric' *Speculum*, *82* (2007), p. 292.

88 Literature as for Chapter 1, note 67.

89 Cf. Pokorny (1996), 'Eine Brief-Instruktion', pp. 77f.

it might also say something about the relationship of the process of construction with the emperor. In fact, all of our evidence for dating, for the imperial context of its promulgation, and for its intended sense of authority comes from the titles gven in the manuscripts. These titles are various, and a pattern can be identified.

Titles

The most common title for this capitulary, which I have labelled (1), is also the most simple:

capitula que in lege salica mittenda sunt.

This reveals nothing about the process of construction, does not attribute it a date, or even a king or emperor. Indeed it does not even mention that *any* king was involved in its production.

The next most common title, which I have labelled (2), gives both an emperor and a date:

incipiunt capitula que in lege Salica domnus Augustus Karolus ann ab incarnatione domini nostri Iesu Christi DCCCIII. imperii vero sui anno tertio praeponendo addere iussit.

A few titles, which I have labelled (1.5), provide a level of detail falling between these, giving Charlemagne's name, but not a date, and a few accounts add further information: Montpellier H 136, close to a chancery, provided:

Haec sunt capitula quae a gloriosissimo imperatore Karolus in legem Salicam mittere precepit[90]

and Lupus's redaction provided something similar.[91]

I class as **(3)** the prologue in BN Lat. 4995 from tenth-century North France, described in more detail below, and this title from BN Lat. 4613:

Hec sunt capitula que domnus karolus magnus imperator iussit scribere in consilio suo et iussit eas ponere inter alias leges. INPRimis de homicidiis clericorum.

This was printed misleadingly by Boretius as part of the main text, even though it is found only in this tenth-century manuscript. The reference to *alias leges* can be explained by the fact that this is overwhelmingly a manuscript of Lombard *leges* and Carolingian capitularies relating explicitly to Italy.[92] So the title fits the contents of the manuscripts.

A broad, simplified presentation of the quantity of information provided in the title, by period, is shown in Table 3.1.

[90] This is Boretius's text, at MGH Capit. I p. 112, but Mordek gives *HEC SUNT CAPL. QUE GLORIOSISSIMO INPERATOR CAROLUS IN LEGE SALICA METTERE PRAECEPIT*, Mordek (1995), *Bibliotheca*, p. 278. Either way the grammar is strange.

[91] Gotha Memb. I 84 gives: *Incipiunt capitula legi salicae quos constituit dom. karolus imperator de homicidiis clericorum.*

[92] Mordek (1995), *Bibliotheca*, pp. 469–76.

Table 3.1 *Information in titles to Capitulary no. 39*

		750–900	900–1100	1100–	Total
(0)	None / *De hom clericorum*	3 (11%)	3 (19%)	2 (29%)	8
(1)	*Salica* association only	18 (64%)	4 (25%)	2 (29%)	24
(1.5)	*Salica* and Charlemagne	1 (4%)	2 (12%)	0	3
(2)	*Salica*, Charlemagne, date	6 (21%)	4 (25%)	3 (43%)	13
(3)	Other / particular info	0	2 (12%)	0	2
	Totals	28	15	7	50

At first glance, these differences may seem trivial, but I suggest that they relate to important differences in the ways the texts were presented and read, and what kind of authority was held to lie behind them. After all, *the most common* title hardly expresses any difference between its nature and that of the *Lex Salica* itself, while in some manuscripts, the text looks far more like self-conscious imperial legislation. The clear pattern in the figures is that later manuscripts, in proportion to their numbers, give most detail on the background of the construction of the text. Indeed, our very earliest manuscripts, such as BN Lat. 4404, produced at some stage shortly after 804, and BN Lat. 4629 from *c.*805, probably only a few years after the construction of the capitulary, preserve title **(1)**. And with one exception, title **(2)** appears only from the second half of the ninth century. The language of the titles in a sense fit with the dating of the manuscripts in which they are found. The gerundive form *mittenda* – 'to be sent' – in **(1)** might well reflect a text of an actual command, whereas the straight perfect of the fuller text, found mostly in later manusripts, could show a later, secondary attempt to give the capitulary some context. If so, exactly why was extra context felt to be needed?

We can trace the incorporation of longer titles into the tradition in more detail, because the transmission of Capitulary no. 39 is diverse. Although Boretius's edition does not preserve enough clear divergences in the text to propose a stemma, the text is, in all but six of its manuscripts, transmitted with Capitulary no. 40, usually directly before it, and often the two texts are numbered through as if one. Capitulary no. 40 has a remarkably varied textual history, much more so than no. 39, so the transmission of the latter can be studied through that of the former. I have identified four clear groups of manuscripts of these two capitularies, as well as a fifth group of unclassifiables. The differences are in the order in which the chapters are presented, and in what is omitted, as shown in Table 3.2 below.

The following are the earliest manuscripts to preserve the title **(2)**. 'Group' refers to the presentation of Capitulary no. 40 in the manuscript.

Wolfenbüttel Aug. 4 50.2	$\text{ix}^{1/2}$	N. E. France	Group 0 (No Capit. 40)
BN Lat. 10754	$\text{ix}^{2/3}$	E. France	Group 0
St Gallen 728	$\text{ix}^{2/2}$	E. France	Group 0
BN Lat. 10758	$\text{ix}^{4/4}$	Rheims	Group 5a
Cambrai 625	$\text{ix}^{\text{ex.}}$	Brittany	Group 2
Wolfenbüttel Gud. Lat. 299	$\text{ix}^{3/4}$	N. E. France	Group 5
And the later manuscripts:			
BN Lat. 4760	x	Lyons	Group 5a
BN Lat. 3182	$\text{x}^{2/2}$	Brittany	Group 2
BN Lat. 4626	x/xi	Burgundy?	Group 5
BN Lat. 4628 A	x/xi	France	Group 2

We can see that title **(2)** is found in manuscripts of Group 0, Group 2, and Group 5. Group 3 manuscripts preserve **(1)**. Most Group 2 manuscripts, some of which are dated to the earlier ninth century, preserve title **(1)**. The exception in the ninth century carrying title **(2)**, Cambrai 625, is from Brittany, as is the later exception BN Lat. 3182. It seems that already in the ninth century the compiler of the Cambrai manuscript (or one on which it was directly dependent) took his text from one source, and his prologue from another. So the transmission of prologue **(2)** is independent of the transmission of the text of Capitulary no. 39/40 itself. I suggest that this is because there was a real movement on the part of compilers to understand the origins and the dates of the texts, both in order to know how to interpret them, and to fit them into a historicised codex.

That the earliest codices with title **(2)** do not contain Capitulary no. 40 may be significant, because the other five manuscripts of no. 39 without no. 40 preserve no title at all: so title **(1)** is found only in the joined tradition of Capitularies nos. 39 and 40. A possible hypothetical transmission of no. 39, then, could be that there was an 'original', early distribution of nos. 39 and 40, with title **(1)**, so in the form roughly of our Group 4. This group then fragmented quite early into the other groups we can identify. This hypothetical relationship is sketched in Figure 3.1. There might also have been a separate strand of tradition of no. 39 alone with no title at all, resembling our Group 1. The compilers of St Gallen 728 and BN Lat. 10754, or some scribes earlier in their transmission, could have brought the fuller title **(2)** into their manuscripts, so might then be thought also as having an interest in the origins of the capitulary, already in the mid to late ninth century.

Strikingly, all our evidence for the deliberate bringing of prologue **(2)** into the text of Capitularies nos. 39/40 can be associated with the kingdom of Charles the Bald, or perhaps also West Francia in the slightly

Table 3.2 *Manuscripts of Capitulary no. 39 before the twelfth century. Based on Mordek,* Bibliotheca

MS (Boretius's number)		Text of Capit. no. 40	Prol.	Capits. 39 and 40 pres.	*Sal*
Group 0		No Capit. no. 40			
BN Lat. 10754	$ix^{2/3}$		2		K-39
St Gallen 728	$ix^{2/2}$		2		K
St Paul im Lavanttal 4/1	817–23				39-K
Wolfenbüttel Aug. 4 50.2	$x^{1/2}$		2		K-39
BN Lat. 3851	x				No *Sal*
Group 1		1–20 and 29 (or nearly)			
Ivrea XXXIII (23)	$ix^{med.}$	1–20, 29	1	Not numbered through.	K
Ivrea XXXIV (24)	c.830	1–20, 29	1	Not numbered through.	No *Sal*
München Lat. 19416 (33)	$ix^{ex.}$	1–20, 29	1	Not numbered through.	No *Sal*
BN Lat. 4404 (1)	c.805	1–6, 8–20, 29	1	Not numbered through.	A
Group 2		23 and 24 behind 28			
Cambrai 625 (42)	$ix^{ex.}$	1–22, 25–28, 23, 24, 29	2	Numbered through.	39-40-K
München Lat. 19415 (22)	ix	1–22, 25–28, 23, 24	1	Numbered through	No *Sal*
BN Lat. 4758 (15)	$ix^{1/3}$	1–22, 25–28, 23, 24, 29	1	39 is numbered, 40 is not.	39-40-K
London Add. 22398 (x)	ix/x	1–22, 25–28, 23, 24, 29	1	Not numbered through.	K-39-40
Nürnberg Cent. V, App. 96 (5)	$ix^{1/2}$	1–22, 25–28, 23, 24, 29	1	Not numbered through	K
Gotha Memb. I 84	x/xi	1–22, 25–28, 23, 24, 29	1.5	Numbered through.	S
Modena O. I. 2	x	1–22, 25–28, 23, 24, 29	1.5	Numbered through.	S
BN Lat. 4628A	x/xi	1–22, 25–28, 23, 24, 29	2	Not numbered through.	39-40-K
BN Lat. 3182	$x^{2/2}$	1–22, 25–28, 23, 24, 29	2	Numbered through.	39-40-K

Group 3		8 and 7 swapped			
BN Lat. 10753 (27)	ix$^{med.}$	1–6, 8, 7, 9–22, 25–8, 24, 29	1	Not numbered through.	K-39-40
BN Lat. 4628 (28)	ix$^{2/3}$	1–6, 8, 7, 9–22, 25–8, 24, 29		Similar presentation to 4632.	K-39-40
BN Lat. 4632 (29)	ix$^{3/4}$	1–6, 8, 7, 9–22, 25–8, 24	1	Not numbered through. 40 has chapter numberings in red (39 has none), and its text is indented compared with that of 39.	K-39-40
Group 4		Complete, in order, or nearly so			
Montpellier H 136 (20)	c.818	Complete, but repeats beginning of Capit. no. 39.	1.5	Not numbered through.	D
BN Lat. 4788 (16)	ix$^{2/3}$	Complete, but repeats beginning of c.29 at end.	1	Not numbered through.	K-39-40
Sélestat 14 (104) (x)	ix$^{3/3}$	Complete.	1	Not numbered through. Note different from other Rheims group MSs.	No *Sal*
Vat. Reg. Lat. 1050 (18)	ix$^{med.}$	Almost complete, but a little shaved off the end.	1	Not numbered through.	39-40-K
BN Lat. 4629 (3)	c.805	No c.16. Otherwise complete.	1	Not numbered through.	E
Berlin Phil. 1736	x$^{2/2}$	No c.16. Otherwise complete.	1	Not numbered through.	E
Vat. Pal. Lat. 773 (30)	ix$^{1/2}$	No c.10. Ends fragmentarily.	1	Not numbered through.	No *Sal*
London Eg. 2832	x$^{inc.}$	Complete.	1	Not numbered through.	K
BN Lat. 4995	x	No c.29, otherwise complete.	3	Not numbered through.	K
BN Lat. 9654	x/xi	Complete.	1	Not numbered through.	K
Leiden Voss. Lat. Q. 119	ix$^{4/4}$	No c.21, 27, 28. Otherwise complete			K

(cont.)

Table 3.2 (*cont.*)

MS (Boretius's number)		Text of Capit. no. 40	Prol.	Capits. 39 and 40 pres.	*Sal*
Group 5		No clear pattern			
Cologny Bodmer 107 (x)	$ix^{ex.}$	1–2, 6, 3–5, 7–13, 15–9, 14, 20–22, 25–28, 23, 24	1	Not joined with no. 39.	K
St Petersburg Q. v. II. 11 (21)	$ix^{inc.}$	1, 2, 6, 3–5, 6–22, 25–8, 23–4	1	Not joined with no. 40.	K
Wolf. Blank. 130 (34)	$ix^{3/4}$	1–9, 11, 10, 12–20. Capit no. 39 c.9 added after c.12	1	Numbered through.	K
Cava dei Tirreni 4	c.1005	4–5		Split up.	No *Sal*
München Lat. 3853	$x^{2.2}$	c.18 and 19 only.		Split up.	No *Sal*
BN Lat. 4613	x	1–7, 9–22, 28, 24, 29	3	Numbered through.	No *Sal*
BN Lat. 4626	x/xi	1, 10–11, 15, 16, 13, 9, 20	2	Numbered through.	K-39-40
Wolf. Gud. Lat. 299 (7)	$ix^{3/4}$	10–12, 15, 16, 20	2	Numbered through.	K-39-40
Group 5a					
BN Lat. 10758 (12)	$ix^{4/4}$	11–13, 15, 16, 20	2	Not numbered through.	39-40-K
BN Lat. 4760	x	11–13, 15, 16, 20	2	Not numbered through.	39-40-K

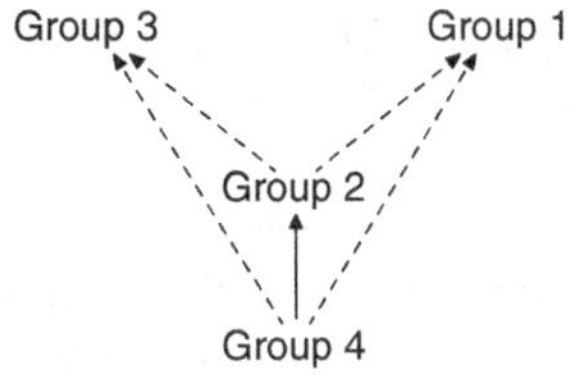

Fig. 3.1 Proposed relationship between the groups of manuscripts of Capitulary 39

later period. We have the Breton strain (Group 2), and the East France strain (Group 0). With this pattern in mind we return to the prologue of BN Lat. 4995:

In the name of Christ begin the recently discovered[93] *capitula legis* of emperor Charles in the third year of our most merciful lord emperor Charles. In this year these *capitula* were made and authenticated by count Stephen, to make them known in the city of Paris in the *mallum publicum* and to have them read in the presence of *scabini*... And everyone consented as one, that they wanted to observe for all time in posterity, and all *scabini*, bishops, abbots, and counts affirmed below with their own hand.[94]

This remarkable text has received attention, and has been used to support a particular view of the adoption of Charlemagne's capitularies. But it is found only in a tenth-century manuscript.[95] It is quite possible instead that this is a back projection of what a later compiler felt count Stephen ought to have done. This was after all a northern French manuscript, the compiler of which might have had an interest in Parisian history.

There is nothing in the language of the prologue that restricts it to the ninth century. *Scabini* are found in tenth-century charters, and the *mallum publicum* if anything becomes more prominent in sources of the tenth century, as Charles West has argued.[96] The prologue also fits very neatly with other texts in the manuscript, and can be seen in part as a logical extension of their themes. This manuscript's version of

93 The sense of *inventa* is not clear. Cf. *inventa* in the prologue to Benedictus Levita's collection at www.benedictus.mgh.de/edition/aktuell/praef.pdf. Last viewed 26 August 2014.

94 MGH Capit I no. 39 p. 112: *In Christi nomine incipiunt capitula legis imperatoris Karoli nuper inventa anno tertio clementissimi domni nostri Karoli augusti. Sub ipso anno haec capitula facta sunt et consignata Stephano comiti, ut haec manifesta fecisset in civitate Parisius mallo pubplico et ipsa legere fecisset coram illis scabineis; quod ita et fecit. Et omnes in uno consenserunt, quod ipsi voluissent omni tempore observare usque in posterum etiam omnes scabinei, episcopi, abbatis, comitis manu propria subter firmaverunt. Capitula que in lege Salica mittenda sunt.*

95 For the view that its use may have reflected practice under Charlemagne, see for example K.-F. Werner, 'Missus-marchio-comes: entre l'administration centrale et l'administration locale de l'empire carolingien' in: W. Paravicini and K.-F. Werner (eds.), *Histoire comparée de l'administration (IVe–XVIIIe siècles)* (Munich, 1980), pp. 99–100, A. Krah, 'Zur Kapitulariengesetzgebung in und für Neustrien' in: H. Atsma (ed.), *La Neustrie. Les pays au nord de la Loire de 650 à 850. Colloque historique internationale 1* (Sigmaringen, 1989), Beihefte der Francia 16/1, p. 569, and in part McKitterick (2008), *Charlemagne*, p. 230. It is often related to text A discussed at section 3.2.3 above.

96 West (2013), *Reframing the Feudal Revolution*, pp. 145–7.

Capitulary no. 34, the *Capitulare Missorum Specialia* of 802, mentions count Stephen specifically as a *missus dominicus*, a recipient of the capitulary.[97] It also preserves interpolated extracts of Isidore of Seville's *Etymologiae*, concerning what *lex* is, which stresses the role of the *populus* and *maiores natu*, perhaps precisely men like Stephen, in establishing the *lex*.

As found in the *Etymologiae*, the passage reads:

Lex est constitutio populi, quam maiores natu cum plebibus sancierunt. Nam quod rex uel imperator edicit, constitutio uel edictum uocatur.[98]

But this manuscript preserves:

Lex quid est?

Responsio. Lex est constitutio populi quam majores natu cum plebibus sanxerunt, ***id est statuerunt vel dijudicaverunt seu stabilierunt ad decernendum rectum****; nam quod rex vel imperator edidit,* ***hoc est facit****, constitutio uel edictum vocatur...*[99]

Not a great deal more is known about Count Stephen than his role in these two texts, but it seems fairly clear that he was remembered after his death as some sort of significant political figure.[100] His death was recorded in various necrologies, including that constructed around 860 at Saint-Germain-des-Prés. Einhard also recorded him as a witness of Charlemagne's 'will'. Perhaps most revealingly of all, a Parisian sacramentary from the later ninth century in Vat. Ottob. 313 f. 111 preserves a list of figures to be commemorated, with Stephen strikingly high, just below *Lotharius imperator*.[101] A charter in count Stephen's name, purportedly from 811, may also be a forgery of the tenth century and so shows the continued memory of count Stephen from a different angle.[102]

Thus Stephen's high profile could have been projected back as justification for the powers of counts, possibly in the period of

97 Consideration of the text, and a better presentation of the variations than in Boretius can be found in W. A. Eckhardt, 'Die Capitularia Missorum Specialia von 802' *DA*, *12* (1956), pp. 498–516.

98 Isidore of Seville, *Etymologiarum sive Originum Libri XX* ed. W. M. Lindsay (Oxford, 1911) II, 10 (unpaginated edition).

99 The bold words are the additions found in BN Lat. 4626, 4628, 4631, 4760, 4995, 10758. For full references and some commentary see Chapter 5, section 5.3.3 below.

100 For what follows see L. Levillain 'Les comtes de Paris á l'èpoque franque', *Le Moyen Age*, *50*, (1941), pp. 137–205 and R. Louis, *De l'histoire à la légende. Girart, comte de Vienne et ses fondations monastiques* (Auxerre, 1946), pp. 10f.

101 Transcribed in Louis (1946), *Girart, comte de Vienne*, p. 10: *Carolus imperator Hludowicus imperator Pippinus rex Lotharius imperator Stephanus comes Amaltrudis Deutfredus Beringarius Benjamin...*

102 The charter is in *Cartulaire générale de Paris* ed. R. de Lasteyrie (Paris, 1887), pp. 37–40 no. 29. It is full of anachronistic terms, especially the *comitessa* and the count's *cancellarius*, so it is at least interpolated, as argued in L. Levillain, 'Note critique sur la charte du comte Etienne et de la comtesse Amaltrude de 811' *Revue d'Histoire de L'Eglise de France*, *116* (1943), pp. 54–74.

fragmentation of the Carolingian political order. A context could even be the establishment of the Capetians in the Île de France, or, more interestingly for our purposes, it could be a projection onto an earlier period of how Charles the Bald might have gone about legislating and gaining consensus. In fact, even the date could be a projection, based on a reading of the annalistic material, through a newly intense understanding of the link between imperial status and legislation. Thus a text that in a sense was not even especially associated with a king, but was in some way intended to add to *Lex Salica*, became understood as imperial legislation.

This capitulary and its transmission, therefore, are quite rich for consideration of our themes. Some of its provisions can be understood as additions to a *Lex Salica* text that had so many conspicuous omissions, and others certainly resonated with the kinds of subject covered, perhaps adding to the *Lex Salica* in a looser, less textual sense. But the form of the text, and the tradition of its prologues hardly suggest that this 'addition' was intended to express anything about Charlemagne's power, even if it was produced in the period immediately following his imperial coronation. The text has a perfunctory feel if compared to, say the *Admonitio Generalis*, and this is something to bear in mind when reading the other additional capitularies, which preserve further clues about the processes of construction. It is mostly later in the ninth century and into the tenth that the text's presentation demonstrates in any way that it was read directly in connection with ideas about kingship and comital office.

3.3.2 No. 139 Capitula Legibus Addenda *818–19*

This text is far more intricate in style than its roughly equivalent text from Charlemagne's reign, no. 39. It is, at least as a complete text, phrased unambiguously as an expression of Louis's will, full of references to *bannum nostrum*, *ad quantum tempus nobis placuerit*, and so on, and is far longer than any of the additional capitularies from Charlemagne's reign. It can also be linked with a very elaborate prologue, attached to the series of Capitularies nos. 138–40 in two earlier ninth-century manuscripts.[103] This text sets out the responsibility of kings for cultivating justice, piety, and humility in their kingdoms, in language stuffed full of quotations from and allusions to the Bible, especially the Old Testament, and circles around the theme of *emendatio*, both 'in ecclesiastical matters' and 'in the state of the *res publica*', proposing to achieve this *emendatio* through consultation with each *ordo*, 'so that we might record exactly what, in

[103] Edited by Boretius as *Hludowici proemium generale ad capitularia tam ecclesiastica quam mundana*. MGH Capit. I no. 137 pp. 273–5. It is found in BN Lat. 2718 and Kopenhagen Gl. Kgl. Saml. 1943.

these matters, canons or monks must observe, and what must be added to the *leges mundanae*, and also what must be put down under *capitula*'.[104] The three capitularies that follow were clearly highly self-conscious royal pronouncements, although it is biblical, not Roman underpinnings that are most prominent.[105]

The text covers a similar, but extended, range of subjects to no. 39. Penalties for injuries of clerics are covered, as well as violence in church, the payment of *wergelds*, alienation to the church, false witnesses, oaths, feuds, tolls, and those favourite subjects for capitularies, the protection of widows, *pupilli*, and *pauperes.* Only one chapter makes an identifiable reference to a text of *lex*, and this is in fact to the *Lex Ribuaria*: c.8 concerns the rates at which various commodities can be given instead of coin, upholding penalties *quae in lege continentur*, except for hawks and swords 'because perjury is sometimes committed for the sake of those two things, when they are sworn to be of greater price than they are'.[106] This text certainly envisages the *Lex Ribuaria* being read as a practical reference work, but offers no more detailed help on how the *leges* were read.

Titles

The titles of this text are not as revealing as those of no. 39, but worth describing in any case. The most common title, found in fifteen manuscripts of Capitulary no. 139 is:

Incipiunt capitula quae legibus addenda sunt, quae et missi et comites habere et ceteris nota facere debent[107]

Titles in other manuscripts are less full, but no pattern such as was found for no. 39 can be established. The only remarkable prologue that provides any more information is that found in BN nouv. acq. Lat. 204:

Here begin the *capitula* which the most serene Lord emperor Louis in the fifth year of his reign promulgated with a universal gathering of the people brought together by God,

[104] MGH Capit. I pp. 274–5, *ita ut quid canonicis proprie de his, quidve monachis observanda, quid etiam in legibus mundanis addenda, quid quoque in capitulis inserenda forent, adnotaverimus et singulis singula observanda contraderemus...* Thanks again to Shane Bobrycki for applying his expert eye for biblical allusions to this text.

[105] The ideology expressed here has been most carefully investigated by Mayke de Jong. See, in addition to references for Charlemagne as for Chapter 1, note 72 above, her comments on others of Louis's capitularies in M. de Jong, *The penitential state: authority and atonement in the age of Louis the Pious, 814–840* (Cambridge, 2009), pp. 131–4.

[106] MGH Capit. I no. 139 c.8 p. 282: *In conpositione wirgildi volumus ut ea dentur quae in lege continentur, excepto accipitre et spata, quia propter illa duo aliquoties periurium conmittitur, quando maioris pretii quam illa sint esse iurantur.* Cf. *Lex Ribuaria* pp. 94–5 c.40,11: *Spatam cum scoligilo pro septem solidi.... Auceptorem mutatum pro 12 solid. tribuat.*

[107] MGH Capit. I no. 139 p. 281. Ganshof thought that this was the title given in the manuscript in Louis's palace archive, though it is not quite clear why he thought this. Ganshof (1961), *Was waren die Kapitularien?*, pp. 64 and 94.

that is with the venerable bishops and abbots and counts and the rest of the *populus*, at Aachen, and ordered all superior and inferior orders in his *imperium* to hold firmly and to add to *Lex Salica*, and afterwards, when he had a general *conventum* in the villa Thionville, he prohibited them from being called *capitula* any longer, but, rather with the counsel of all of his *optimates* he ordered it to be spoken of as *lex* and to be held most firmly as *lex* by everyone.[108]

This is from a *leges*-scriptorium manuscript, very closely related in its texts to BN Lat. 2718, another *leges*-scriptorium product, which provides only the most common, simpler, title. I suggest later that BN nouv. acq. Lat. 204 was most probably derived, directly or indirectly, from BN Lat. 2718, not the other way around.

Capitulary no. 143, our text (**C**), which seems to refer to additional capitularies, is found in both the relevant Paris *leges*-scriptorium manuscripts.[109] This seems to be more than coincidence when one notes remarkable similarities between the capitulary and the prologue in BN nouv. acq. Lat. 204. Both insist that the *capitula* be held as *lex*, whatever that might actually mean. BN nouv. acq. Lat. 204 presents them as follows:

fol. 20v (prologue to Capit. no. 139):	fol. 23v (Capit. no. 143):
capitula appellandum esse prohibuit, ***sed tantum lex dicenda immoque*** *firmissime ab omnibus* ***pro lege tenenda*** *cum totius optimatum suorum consilio precepit.*	*ut capitula ... per omnium consensum addenda esse censuimus iam non ulterius capitula* ***sed tantum lex dicantur, immo pro lege teneantur***

It seems, then, that this prologue was composed partially with the text of Capitulary no. 143 in mind, that the scribe looked through the capitularies available, and constructed the prologue according to what he understood of the emperor's wishes expressed there.[110] Here we can see quite clearly something of the scribal initiative we proposed in the case of the titles for no. 39, although in this case we can derive no further arguments from it.

[108] MGH Capit. I no. 139 p. 280: *incipiunt capitula quae domnus hludowicus serenissimus imperator imperii sui Vto cum universo coetu populi a Deo sibi commissi, id est cum venerabilibus episcopis et abbatibus atque comitibus vel cum reliquo populo in Aquisgrani palatio promulgavit atque legis Salicae addere et universis ordinibus superioris videlicet inferiorisque gradus populi imperii sui firmiter tenere praecepit ipsaque postea, cum in Theodone villa generale conventum habuisset, ulterius capitula appellandum esse prohibuit, sed tantum lex dicenda immoque firmissime ab omnibus pro lege tenenda cum totius optimatum suorum consilio precepit.*

[109] Text C in the catalogue as set out in 3.3.1 above. Otherwise the text is found only in Wolfenbüttel Blank. 130.

[110] Stein noted the similarity here, but thought the use was in the other direction, that Capit. no. 143 used the 'long prologue' to no. 139. See Stein (1926), 'Lex und Capitula', p. 294.

3.3.3 No. 68 Capitula ad Legem Baiuwariorum Addita *801–13*

This text is short, only seven chapters long, restricted to making a terse statement of some principles, in sharp contrast with the other additional capitularies from Charlemagne's reign, which are longer and more discursive. There is no engagement with the text of the *Lex Baiuwariorum*. Rather, the central concern is the promotion of royal power, as well as the promotion of the central moral concerns of Carolingian capitularies, the protection of widows, orphans, and the *pauperes*, and, in one chapter, the authority of bishops.

The form of the capitulary is clearly tailored to the form of the *Lex* to which it is explicitly attached in every manuscript. The *Lex* provided a very distinctive, ambiguous, view of political authority in pre-Carolingian Bavaria. Although the authority of Frankish kings was conspicuous, four families had particular legal status and rights, and the hereditary authority of the Agilolfing dukes was stressed.[111] In the context of early Carolingian politics, the hereditary claim was clearly potentially explosive.[112] This capitulary can therefore be understood as a way of writing the Carolingian kings directly into this text, in its function as a treatise on status and authority, of emphasising the Frankish kings' authority in the context of a tension present in the *Lex*.

The transmission of the text is significantly later than the average for capitularies, and later than the other texts surveyed here. Only four of the eleven manuscripts are from the ninth century, and in two of those, Vat. Reg. Lat. 991, and München Lat. 19415, the capitulary was added later, in the tenth and eleventh centuries respectively, leaving us with only two fully ninth-century witnesses. Neither of these is from Bavaria, and although this correlates with the surprisingly meagre haul of ninth-century Bavarian manuscripts of the *Lex*, it seems possible that there was some particular reluctance to copy the capitulary in Bavaria in the ninth century, and this could well be bound up with views concerning the Carolingian takeover. Manuscripts of Bavarian *Lex* from the twelfth century onwards that incorporate this capitulary often also copy the councils associated with Tassilo, which have a direct relationship with the *Lex*, and present them all next to each other, after the *Lex*.[113] By this time Charlemagne's involvement in Bavarian history

[111] Wood (1994), *Merovingian Kingdoms*, pp. 116–17. The *Lex* mentions a king in these chapters: I, 1, 2, 10, 11; II, 1, 4, 8, 9, 14; III 1, 2; X, 19. See also the prologue and the unusual reference to the 'Merovingian kingdom' in the first chapter.

[112] See S. Airlie, 'Narratives of triumph and rituals of submission: charlemagne's mastering of Bavaria' *TRHS*, *9* (1999), pp. 93–119 esp. p. 97 on the law.

[113] Manuscripts such as München Lat. 3519, 4639, 5260. See entries in Mordek (1995), *Bibliotheca*. The texts are: *Concilia Aevi Karolini I* ed. A. Werminghoff (Hannover, 1906), MGH Concilia, Legum Sectio III II, pp. 56–8 no. 10 e.g. c.12: *De reliquo promiscuo vulgo, ut in lege Baiovariorum*

had been more thoroughly digested, and was no longer controversial.[114] But this was not the case in the earlier ninth century. The manuscript Wolfenbüttel Helmst. 532, from earlier ninth-century Salzburg, does not contain Charlemagne's capitulary, although it preserves a few excerpts of the councils of Tassilo.[115] These excerpts do not mention Tassilo by name, and are numbered through from the *Lex* as if part of the same text. This particular arrangement is unique: one wonders whether it was intended deliberately to hide the origin of Tassilo's texts.

There is some reason to think, therefore, that Charlemagne's capitulary was most significant for its writing of Charlemagne into Bavarian history, judging both from its contents, and from the way it was received in the manuscripts.

Titles

The basic title is:

Capitula quae [ad legem Baiuwariorum] domnus Karolus serenissimus imperator addere iussit, ut banum (pannum) ipsius quislibet inruperit conponere debeat.[116]

It is noteworthy again that the lavish imperial language of this title is not matched in the capitulary itself, which mentions only the *rex*. It might be that the title was an addition into the tradition after 800, and that the text itself should be redated, to some time between Charlemagne's takeover in 788 and his imperial coronation in 800. However, for this capitulary, each and every manuscript does preserve the title. The principal variation is that in five manuscripts, the text *ad legem Baiuwariorum* is omitted, and *bannum* is spelt *pannum*.[117] All of these manuscripts are of South German or Bavarian origin, from the late tenth century onwards, and contain the *Lex Baiuwariorum* itself. The specification of the *lex* into which the capitulary was to be added, therefore, might have seemed redundant. The spelling *pannum* reflects South German dialect.[118]

consistere debeat, ut de eorum hereditate, exceptis capitalis criminibus, non alienentur... and pp. 93–7 no. 15 (hereafter MGH Conc. II,1). For the association of royal capitularies and church councils in the Merovingian period see Wood (1994), *Merovingian Kingdoms*, pp. 104–8.

114 For consideration of accommodation to Carolingian rule and its complexity see Airlie (1999), 'Narratives of Triumph', pp. 102f. For Tassilo and political thought in comparison with Charlemagne, see Garrison (1998), 'Letters to a king', pp. 305–28.

115 Mordek (1995), *Bibliotheca*, pp. 952–7.

116 MGH Capit. I no. 68 p. 157.

117 München Lat. 19415, 4460, 3853, 5260, and 3519.

118 A basic guide to the dialects of Old High German can be found in S. Sonderegger, *Althochdeutsche Sprache und Literatur: eine Einführung in das älteste Deutsch: Darstellung und Grammatik* 3rd edition (Berlin, 2003). b → p was a product of a supercharged second consonant shift in South Germany. My thanks to Sheila Watts for allowing me to take part in her undergraduate Old High German class.

3.3.4 Summary

These first three texts considered are phrased as royal will, and seem to be finished, deliberately constructed texts, which really might be termed legislation, and which did in various ways add to their respective *leges*. The sense of addition might be considered 'soft': they hardly modified or updated the old *lex*, but rather provided material that might usefully be read in the same context. There is certainly no sense in their manuscripts that the *leges*, accompanied by the additional capitularies, were held to represent an up-to-date, complete statement of the law. The texts might well have been identified by compilers of catalogues as adding to the *leges*, and they were certainly grouped with the *leges* in manuscripts, as I explore more fully in a later section, but there is no reason to see these particular texts as the only ones so identified, and so imagine that our texts represent the sum total of legislation considered relevant to the concerns of the *leges*.

There is also no sense in these texts that the 'additional capitularies' were ever *intended* to function as more or less comprehensive 'updates'. This is perhaps the point Wormald misses by understanding the Carolingian kings' desire to have cases settled by *lex scripta* in overly narrow terms. Carolingian statements contrasted the use of what was written with arbitrary judgement, not explicitly with just judgement relying on unwritten norms.[119] Use of texts could facilitate the doing of justice, but it did not constitute it entirely, and as pointed out earlier, written laws could be used to do injustice.[120] So although the Carolingian kings did not control the versions of the *leges* in circulation, as perhaps did the Visigoths, there is no evidence that they ever claimed, expected, or aspired to such control.

And this fits with the variation in the rhetoric accompanying the texts. For Capitulary no. 39, it may be that the text hardened into something seen as a grand piece of imperial legislation only later in the century; for Capitulary no. 139, the rhetoric is found in the prologue attached to a string of capitularies, only one of which claimed to be adding to the *leges*, and is about every man's *ordo* within the *imperium*, in very distinctively Carolingian terms, and inspired more by the Old Testament than the knowledge of the Roman past. The Bavarian text, on the other hand, really is about Charlemagne. So the meaning of additions to *lex*

119 A thorough consideration of Charlemagne's instruction to judge in accordance with what was written can be found in Innes (2011), 'Charlemagne, written law and justice', pp. 155–204. See MGH Capit. I p. 96 no. 33 c.26: *Ut iudices secundum scriptam legem iuste iudicent, non secundum arbitrium suum.* See also the Lorsch Annal for 802, Chapter 1, section 1.3.1 above. This has been pointed out already in Innes (2005), 'Charlemagne', p. 82. A list of relevant capitularies is provided in Schneider (1977), 'Schriftlichkeit und Mündlichkeit', pp. 259f.

120 See section 3.1.1 above.

depended on the particular *lex* and the particular context, not on the simple fact that a king or emperor was engaging with *lex*.

The next texts discussed provide a rather different perspective. I shall suggest that they take us closer to the contexts in which the *leges* might be applied to cases.

3.3.5 No. 41 Capitulare Legi Ribuariae Additum *803*

Capitularies nos. 41 and 142 reveal how *leges* were engaged with in the most detail, because they quote directly from the *leges*, or at least refer to them by chapter number. We are certainly able to continue our arguments concerning the notion of updating the law, and the connection between royal symbolism and lawmaking, but we can also start to argue much more directly about how the existing *leges* were read, tackling especially the question of their practical, 'legal' use.

Capitulary no. 41 provides not only additions in the sense explored for no. 39, but also, and perhaps more importantly, provides *interpretations*, by which apparently outdated vocabulary and clearly inapplicable conditions were updated. C.2 reiterates the provisions of *Lex Ribuaria* c.9 and c.10, on the *wergeld* for a *homo regius,* and conserves the penalty, adding only an explanation that this *homo regius* is equivalent to the *fiscalinus*, a group not found elsewhere in *Lex Ribuaria.*[121] Its purpose is identical with that of a gloss.

C.8 allows for some erosion of the royal role in confirming someone's designation of an heir if he dies without sons. The original *lex* requires a designation in the presence of the king, but this allows it also *coram comite et scabineis vel missis dominicis.*[122] C.11 specifies that all oaths must be sworn in a church or on relics, overriding the reference to their performance at the perhaps archaic *harahus* or *stafflus regis* in *Lex Ribuaria* c.69,5 and c.75.[123] New terminology is supplied, and burdensome requirements are moderated, fitted to the now vast Carolingian kingdoms.

Where penalties and procedures are changed more substantially they appear to respond to clear oddities in the original text. For example, c.4

121 MGH Capit. I no. 41 c.2 p. 117: *X. cap. Homo regius, id est fiscalinus, et aeclesiasticus vel litus interfectus centum solidis conponatur.* Cf. *Lex Ribuaria* p. 77 c.9: *Si quis regium hominem interfecerit, 100 solid. culpabilis iudicetur aut cum 12 iuret.*

122 MGH Capit. I no. 41 c.8 p. 118: *VLVIII. cap. Qui filios non habuerit et alium quemlibet haeredem sibi facere voluerit, coram rege vel coram comite et scabineis vel missis dominicis, qui tunc ad iustitias faciendas in provincia fuerint ordinati, traditionem faciat.* Cf. *Lex Ribuaria* p. 101 c.50: *Si quis procreatione filiorum vel filiarum non habuerit, omnem facultatem suam in presentia regis... cuicumlibet de proximis vel extraneis adoptare in hereditate... licentiam habeat.*

123 MGH Capit. I no. 41 c.1 p. 118: *LXVII. cap. Omne sacramentum in ecclesia aut supra reliquias iuretur.*

slashed the requirement for numbers of oath helpers for those accused of stealing a flock from the unusually high seventy-two, to just twelve.[124]

The subjects covered are homicide, practicalities of giving compensation when someone cannot afford to pay it, responsibility for damage caused by slaves, summons to the *mallum*, property transactions, the designation of an heir, inheritance of freedmen, oaths, and theft. So the way the *Lex* was used in the construction of the capitulary, and the pressures that made the capitulary desirable, make immediate, intuitive sense, if we imagine that the *Lex Ribuaria* was being read in a fundamentally 'practical' way.

Construction

Can we go any further in establishing the pressures that led to this modification and interpretation, and can we see how the resulting text was read? Did the text continue to be read together with the *Lex Ribuaria*?

The *Urtext* is not especially revealing about its process of construction. The style does not betray anything about the underlying discussion, as it does for no. 142, described in a moment, although it may be significant, again, that the king is referred to only in the third person. A more powerful point about the construction of the text can be made from manuscript variations. A chapter, or partial chapter, is extant in two manuscripts, in the earliest manuscript of all, BN Lat. 4629, compiled only a few years after the text was constructed, and in Berlin Phil. 1736. The addition is also found in Benedictus Levita's collection, where the text was apparently copied from an existing collection of Charlemagne's capitularies.[125] It reads:

> The lord emperor consented, just as they asked.[126]

It is not quite clear to what this refers in the manuscripts of the capitulary, since it is preceded by the numerals XXX, but supplies no other content. In Benedictus Levita's compilation there is no extra numeral XXX, and so the passage is presented associated with the previous chapter of the capitulary, that is, c.5. This c.5 refers to c.20 of *Lex Ribuaria*, and allows landholders to excuse themselves from responsibility for the payment of a fine if one of their *servi* had committed a crime and then disappeared utterly.[127] It is, in fact, quite possible

[124] MGH Capit. I no. 41 c.4 p. 117: …*De soniste aut sexcentos solidos conponat aut cum duodecim iuret…*

[125] *Ben Lev* II, 210. See the online edition at www.benedictus.mgh.de/edition/ aktuell/libII.pdf p. 36. Last viewed August 24 2014.

[126] MGH Capit. I no. 41 p. 118: *Sicut petierunt, ita dominus imperator consensit.*

[127] MGH Capit. I no. 41 c.5 pp. 117–18: *XX. cap. Nemini liceat servum suum propter damnum ab illo cuilibet inlatum dimittere; sed iuxta qualitatem damni dominus pro ipso respondeat vel eum in compositione aut ad poenam petitoris offerat. Si autem servus perpetrato scelere fugerit, ita ut a dominus penitus inveniri*

that the numeral XXX in the manuscripts was intended to draw a link between cs.20 and 30 of the *Lex Ribuaria*, which are very similar in theme, and to connect the capitulary provision with both. But whatever the addition refers to, we find here a reason to turn on its head the whole way consensus has been treated in the literature: here it is the emperor whose consent was sought.

The two manuscripts containing this extra text have otherwise very closely related content, including very related texts of the E *Lex Salica*.[128] One other reading in the relevant chapter of Benedictus Levita, the omission of an *eius* after *dominus*, possibly links the citation in Benedictus to BN Lat. 4629.[129] The additional phrase was therefore present in just one, fairly small, but very early, strand of the tradition. Indeed it is possible that it was deleted at some stage from a manuscript crucial to the rest of the tradition, and that its presence or absence relates to differences in how compilers felt that capitularies ought to have been constructed. This might provide a neat parallel with the transmission of the titles of Capitulary no. 39, and, as I suggest below, of the titles of this capitulary itself.

So what does this phrase reveal? The precise content of c.5 of Capitulary no. 41 deserves some attention, because it is in fact the only chapter of the text in which royal rights are directly, and significantly, affected. Excusing landholders from the liability of a fine would, depending on how the case was handled, have deprived the king of revenue, or whatever social pressure that revenue could be converted into.[130] It may be, then, that this was the *only* point in the text for which royal assent was felt to be needed. But this issue was also such that a royal judgement between disputing landowners might have been seen as useful. Besides allowing landowners to excuse themselves from responsibility, the chapter introduced the notion that payment of fines for damage done by *servi* be *iuxta qualitatem damni*, whereas the *lex* had required a flat fine of thirty-six *solidi*, no trifling sum, in any case in which a *servus* did some damage, and in some cases, compensation for the damage too.[131] If we forget any preconceptions about the origins of the texts we have come to think of as capitularies, we might see this text as the work of landowners, seeking to regulate disputes between each other with reference to a text, and invoking the king, both because

non possit, sacramento se dominus eius excusare studeat, quod nec suae voluntatis nec conscientiae fuisset quod servus eius tale facinus commisit. Cf. MGH Capit. no. 142 c.7.

128 See Chapter 5, section 5.2.5 below.

129 This is a reading not shown in Boretius's edition of the capitularies, but only in the new edition of Benedictus Levita. Reference as for note 126.

130 For such a conversion, see Chapter 4, section 4.1.2 below for the case of a homicide of a priest.

131 *Lex Ribuaria* p. 84 c.29–31. This part of the *Lex* can also be characterised as a point of 'textual stress' in the sense explored in Chapter 4, section 4.1.1 below, but is a milder case than those explored there.

their dispute might affect his rights, and because he was a useful figure of authority.

A chance survival of another text adds some depth. A short text very close to Capitulary no. 41 c.5 has survived in a collection found in the twin tenth-century manuscripts BN Lat. 9654 and Vat. Pal. Lat. 582, and was edited by Boretius as c.1 of Capitulary no. 56.[132] Boretius imagined that this was from a single capitulary he called *Capitula Karoli Magni*, but it is found in both manuscripts as chapters XII–XV of a list headed *Al. Cap. addenda sunt ea que nuper audita et comperta habemus*. The sense of *addenda* must surely be 'to be added to the collection': the texts include some material apparently derived from direct royal instructions, but also the *Recapitulatio solidorum*, which simply summarises some of the penalties of the *Lex Salica*.[133] No. 56 c.1 does not specify that the owners may excuse themselves, but it does provide that the judgement of the king is needed if the owner is required to pay more than the *leudes* of a *liber homo*. The problem this text seeks to solve, then, is that of disputes between landowners over damage done by *servi*, and it does not specifically treat royal rights to income in such situations as does Capit. no. 41. The status of this text and its relationship with c.5 of no. 41 is very uncertain, and there is no way of telling which might be derived from which. Its two manuscripts are tenth- and eleventh-century, and in fact contain both Capitularies nos. 41 and 56. If Capitulary no. 41 were later than no. 56, however, we might imagine that the king's consent in no. 41 was sought only on the new material in no. 41, that is the matter of landholders excusing themselves from fines altogether.

Whatever the relationship between these two texts, we might wonder who 'they' were who sought the king's consent, and in what context they were working. The concerns of Capitulary no. 41 as a whole seem related to the problems of application of the *lex* to changed conditions, in terms of language, of conceptions of office, and in terms of the geographical range of politics, so those who framed the text might have been counts or anyone else who sought to apply the text to their business. The significance of the addition is that it strengthens this impression that the text was a response to real, rather than hypothetical, problems applying the *lex*, and strengthens the view that the text is not *about* royal power, as the Bavarian additional capitulary undoubtedly is. Indeed there is no reason to connect the king with its contents at all, except in the case in which royal rights are directly affected. Even then, the king did not take the initiative.

[132] MGH Capit. I no. 56 p. 143 c.1: *Nemini liceat servum suum propter dampnum a se dimittere, sed iuxta qualitatem culpae dominus eius pro ipso respondeat aut componat quicquid ille fecit usque ad super plenam leudem liberi hominis; quicquid super hoc fuerit, in regis iuditio esse videtur.*

[133] For the full list see Mordek (1995), *Bibliotheca*, pp. 566–7.

So the text might be interpreted as, in origin, more a reflection of the strategies employed by counts and others who might have wanted to put the *lex* to use, than a grandly conceived, but flawed, piece of royal legislation adding to the *lex*.

Reception, titles

A smaller proportion of manuscripts of this capitulary contain the *Lex Ribuaria*, the 'right' *lex*, than in the case of the other additional capitularies.[134] Table 3.3 illustrates the proportions in more detail for the three relevant *leges*. These bald statistics in fact overstate the linkage both in the case of *Lex Baiuwariorum* (see immediately above) and in the case of *Lex Ribuaria*, because in St Paul im Lavanttal 4/1 we find only two chapters of Capitulary no. 41, and in München Lat. 19416, just one chapter of *Lex Ribuaria*. Not many manuscripts of *Lex Ribuaria*, then, were 'updated'. A fairly small proportion of manuscripts, only five of fourteen, of Capitulary no. 41 even identify it in their titles as relating to *Lex Ribuaria* at all, as shown in Table 3.4.

The sample size is of course much smaller than with Capitulary no. 39, making conclusions difficult to draw, but it is still striking that only the ninth-century manuscripts make the link with *Lex Ribuaria*. This mirrors the very rapid disappearance of the *Lex Ribuaria* itself from manuscripts after 900. It is also suggestive that only one ninth-century manuscript mentions Charlemagne at all. So in the titles we have a general shift from a 'Ribuarian' context to a 'Charlemagne' context over time. We also see that all the evidence for the dating of the text is derived from post-Carolingian manuscripts. It is, once again, possible that this dating was a projection based on later ideas about what Charlemagne was doing in the years immediately following his imperial coronation.

Four of the seven manuscripts that contain both *Lex Ribuaria* and the capitulary identify the capitulary as attaching to the *Lex*, although one of these has only a single chapter of the *Lex*. The numberings show that the *Urtext* of the capitulary used a B text of *Lex Ribuaria* for reference, but one that probably contained already some notable divergences from the B *Urtext*. Take, for example, the reference in c.4 of the capitulary to c.12 of *Lex Ribuaria*, whereas it really fits with c.19.[135] But in the manuscripts, the numberings of titles and cross-references vary greatly, and none of them has fully and systematically adjusted the title numbers to facilitate cross-referencing. In other words, in each manuscript of *lex*

134 Table 3.4 shows which manuscripts of the relevant capitularies also include the relevant *leges*.

135 See the tables in Buchner's introduction in *Lex Ribuaria* pp. 11–13.

Table 3.3 *Manuscripts of* Leges Salica, Baiuariorum, *and* Ribuaria, *with and without additional capitularies*

		Sal	*Bav*	*Rib*
Total	750–900	58	13	31
	900–1100	15	9	4
	1100–	14	11	2
Of which	'updated'	(+ Capit. 39)	(+ Capit. 68)	(+ Capit. 41)
	750–900	23 (43%)	4 (31%)	6 (19%)
	900–1100	11	0	1
	1100–	3	3	0

Table 3.4 *Titles to Capitulary no. 41 in its manuscripts*

Title to Capit. no. 41	750–900	900–1100	1100–	Total
No title or e.g. *Item alios cap.*	2	2	3	7
Lex Rib association only	4			4
Charlemagne and *Lex Rib*	1			1
Charlemagne, date, place (no *Rib*)		2		2
	7	4	3	14

and capitulary, the capitulary points to the wrong chapter of the *Lex* in at least some cases.[136]

We can see some hints of cross-referencing, however, in Vat. Pal. Lat. 773. This manuscript contains only the *Lex Ribuaria* and Capitularies nos. 39, 40, and 41. Here the edition is responsible for some confusion. The edition suggests that c.5 of the additional capitulary in the *Urtext* provided an error in linking its provisions with c.20 of *Lex Ribuaria*, and that it really fits with c.30. But c.31 as represented in the edition is very close thematically to c.30, concerning the responsibility of masters for crimes committed by their *servi*. Yet its place in the edition follows that of only one manuscript, A5, that is Wien ÖNB 502. Otherwise this chapter is found after Buchner's c.18 (in position of 'c.19'). So it is in fact perfectly possible that the redactors of the capitulary itself cross-referenced their work with a manuscript with only minor differences in title division from most others extant, and that the link with *Lex Ribuaria* c.20 was in fact quite accurate in their manuscript. In Vat. Pal. Lat. 773, the reference in the capitulary's c.5 is to c.18, not

[136] Patzold describes some similar features of other manuscripts including Wolf. Blank. 130: Patzold (2005), 'Veränderung', pp. 88–9.

the c.20 of the *Urtext,* and c.18 of this manuscript's *Lex Ribuaria,* on fol. 8v, indeed contains a passage about the responsibility for masters for fire damage caused by their *servi.* The cross-reference is quite exact, but the edition makes this difficult to see.

So although the capitulary was constructed with very close engagement with the *Lex Ribuaria,* this link between the two texts is, with notable exceptions, often lost in the manuscripts, and was lost increasingly throughout the ninth and into the tenth centuries, as *Lex Ribuaria* itself fell out of use. The perception of the capitulary shifted from an aid to interpretation of another text to a more autonomous piece of legislation produced by Charlemagne.

3.3.6 No. 142 Capitula Legi Salicae Addita *819–*

This is perhaps the single richest text of all for understanding attitudes to *leges* texts, even more so than no. 41, because it directly quotes from the *Lex Salica,* and comments on it. Like no. 41, this text offers relatively minor clarifications and interpretations to its *lex.* It deals in c.4, for example, with the question of to whom compensation of a sum laid out in the *Lex Salica* is due, in the case of a man taking someone's wife in marriage, while her old husband was still alive.[137] It also offers in c.5 some kind of clarification of what kind of liability a child younger than twelve years old should have for compensations, since the *Lex Salica* is rather confusing on the subject.[138] Like Capitulary no. 41, the text envisages a common-sense approach to the *lex*: the provisions have the air of responding to problems actually encountered when trying to use it to settle a dispute.

C.8, however, is quite dramatic: it specifically advocates ignoring 'what is written in the *Lex Salica*' concerning someone wishing to marry a widow, which is a complicated procedure. It suggests instead simply securing the consent of the widow's parents 'just as their predecessors did'.[139] Only one other Frankish text directly advocates such an extreme approach: the famous passage concerning the *impia inter nos consuetudo* in Marculf's formulary.[140] It is possible that something similar is implied

137 MGH Capit. I no. 142 c.4 p. 292: *4. Item de eodo capitulo 'Si quis uxorem alienam vivo marito tulerit, octo milia denarios...culpabilis iudicetur'. De hoc capitulo iudicatum est, ut vivo marito cui eadem uxor contra legem subtracta fuerat ab illo qui eam iuste tulerat cum lege suprascripta, id est CC solidis, reddita fiat.*

138 MGH Capit. I no. 142 c.5 p. 293: *'Si quis puer infra duodecum annos aliquam culpam commiserit, fredus ei non requiratur.' De hoc capitulo iudicatum est...*

139 MGH Capit. I no. 142 c.8 p. 293: *...iudicaverunt omnes, ut non ita sicut in lege Salica scriptum est eam accipiat, sed cum parentorum consensu et voluntate, velut usque nunc antecessores eorum fecerunt, in coniugium sibi eam sumat.* This is also pointed out in Patzold (2005), 'Veränderung', p. 77.

140 MGH Form. p. 83 *Form. Marc.* II, 12. See most recently Rio (2009), *Frankish Formulae*, p. 165.

also in c.10 for *affatomie*, a ritual for transfer of property, but the text is not clear, and only states that 'as their ancestors have done through long custom, so also are all who live by *Lex Salica* to have it and do it as before'.[141]

The last two chapters treat similar themes, but break the pattern of quoting and interpreting the *Lex Salica*, to treat the validity of charters of freedom, and a point of procedure for summoning witnesses. In the latter case the text suggests explicitly in c.12 that *capitula domni imperatoris, quae prius pro lege tenenda constituit* be observed. Boretius suggested that this was a reference to Capitulary no. 139 c.10, which is very plausible considering the context of procedures for summoning witnesses. C.11 may also offer a further commentary on c.7 of Capitulary no. 39, which stressed that charters of freedom were to be valid. Capitulary no. 142, then, offers good evidence that the two most widely disseminated additional capitularies, explicitly linked with *Lex Salica* in their most common prologues, really were read specifically in the same context as the *Lex Salica* at some stage. It does not, of course, show that these were the only two texts read in such a context.

The nature of the modifications to the *Lex Salica* proposed by this text, therefore, seems inconsistent: on the one hand there was a concerted attempt to clarify and interpret the text of *Lex Salica*, but on the other a willingness to disregard it completely when it did not seem reasonable. The significance of this depends a great deal on what the text really was, and how it was constructed.

Construction

The first point concerning the construction of the text is that its dating may be less solid than conventionally accepted. The standard dating is based on the reference to Capitulary no. 139 already quoted, but *prius* was interpreted as 'a short while ago' rather than the equally possible 'some time ago'. The passage does refer to the emperor as if he were still reigning, but it may well be that we should date this text only to 818–40 rather than the more precise '819 or shortly after' proposed by Boretius. If the text were dated towards the end of this range, it might make a little more sense of the manuscript transmission discussed below.

The text is otherwise uniquely rich in evidence for its process of construction. It appears to be the result of a discussion: phrases such as *iudicaverunt omnes* run throughout. Although most capitularies were surely the result of discussions, in other texts of Louis the Pious, the

[141] MGH Capit. I no. 142 p. 293 c.10: *De affatomie dixerunt quod traditio fuisset. De hoc capitulo iudicatum est, ut, sicut per longam consuetudinem antecessores eorum facientes habuerunt, ita et omnes qui lege Salica vivunt inantea habeant et faciant.*

phraseology tends to run along the lines of *statutum est* or *decrevi*, stressing the force of the emperor's will.

But the really critical passage concerning construction is found in c.7:

[On the question of] whether *ecclesiastici* or *beneficiarii servi* are able to be handed over or dismissed like those of free men, they wanted to wait until they could ask the lord emperor, because the *lex* makes no distinction between an *ecclesiasticus servus* and a *beneficarius servus* and a *servus* of another person.[142]

If we imagine at least that the text records a snapshot of discussions at a particular stage, that it was not a later rearrangement of material from several earlier texts, it looks as if the emperor was not involved in the discussions up to this point at all.[143] The apparent confidence earlier in the text with which the decision was made to ignore the *lex*, as well as the other modifications, is then particularly extraordinary.

I am by no means the first to draw attention to this passage, and it has played a role in discussions of the nature of consensus involved in making capitularies in general, and altering the *Volksrecht* in particular. For Buchner, for example, the text was the result of some sort of popular council – he talked of a *Volksbeschluß* –, whose work was approved and officially given the force of *lex* in the following year, by Capitulary no. 143.[144] Ganshof, who did not believe that consensus was anything more than rhetoric, cut elements of this view down to size: there was no indication that those involved in drawing up the text were the representatives of a *Stamm* or *Volk*; the work derived from a 'technical collaboration of people with specific knowledge, no more'.[145]

These views all imagine that this is a draft text, which had not yet come before the emperor, so that the text is evidence for how the king's legislation relating to *leges* could have been constructed: in some cases his own input could have been only secondary; he had an active group of advisors who knew the text of their *leges* well. But perhaps this text was not intended to come before the emperor at all. Could it perhaps record a more local discussion about how to interpret the *leges* between those involved in holding courts and settling disputes? The reference to the emperor certainly suggests that he was seen as an important authority in interpreting the *leges*, but perhaps the need to refer to him on just one

142 MGH Capit. I no. 142 c.7 p. 293: *Quia nullum de ecclesiastico aut beneficario vel alterius personae servo discretionem lex facit, si ita ecclesiastici aut beneficarii servi sicut liberorum tradi aut dimitti possunt, ad interrogationem domni imperatoris reservare voluerunt.*

143 Seeliger suggested that the common themes in the capitularies of various typologies might be explained by such a process. Seeliger (1893), *Kapitularien*, p. 56. I consider it unlikely considering the considerable stylistic unity of each text.

144 Buchner (1953), *Die Rechtsquellen*, pp. 45–6. For the text see text C in section 3.2.3 above.

145 Ganshof (1961), *Was waren die Kapitularien?*, pp. 58–9: 'technische Mitarbeit von Personen mit besonderer Sachkenntniss, nicht mehr.'

matter relates only to a failure among those involved in the discussion to achieve an easy consensus on that matter.

In fact, the context of the deferral of judgement to the emperor is, again, one in which imperial rights were especially affected, and indeed broadly the same as that in which the consent of the emperor was sought in Capitulary no. 41, that is, the responsibility of a master for the misdeeds of his *servi*. The passage in question is:

Concerning the thirty-seventh chapter. 'If a *servus* shall have killed a free man, the killer is to be handed over to the parents of the killed man for half the composition, and the master of the *servus* is to accept that he pay the other half; or if he understands the *lex*, he can *obmaler* that he not pay the *leodis*.'

The issue seems to have been that *beneficarii servi* were attached to benefices granted by the king, which were theoretically revocable, but that the holder of the benefice was at the same time the master of the *servus*, and responsible for his behaviour.[146] The loss of labour attached to a benefice, caused by a master handing a *servus* over for perhaps grisly punishment, would therefore affect future royal rights. The status of the groups of *servi* mentioned here was a continuing problem, already flagged as a concern in Capitulary no. 139 in the context of homicide.[147]

In general, citations in the text seem to have been taken from the K text, but the state of the edition makes it impossible to pin down a particular manuscript or family.[148] Remarkably, however, the citation in c.4 is far closer to the E text.[149] If different texts were used, the possibility emerges that it was worked on by correspondence, with each contributor using whichever version he had to hand, although it is perfectly possible that a single session involved the use of several texts.

Whatever the precise status of this text, the way it interprets the *Lex Salica* seems to derive from real problems encountered when seeking to apply the *Lex Salica* to Carolingian society. A study of the manuscripts may be able to refine our picture of the nature of the text.

Manuscripts

The text survives in five manuscripts. In all of them it is presented among other capitularies and legal material. Notably lacking, however, is any inscription in any manuscript describing its circumstances of production.

146 On the benefice, see F. Lot, 'Origine et nature du benefice' in: *Recueil des travaux historiques de Ferdinand Lot* Volume 2, (Geneva, 1970), pp. 331–41; B. Kasten, 'Beneficium zwischen Landleihe und Lehen - eine alte Frage, neu gestellt' in: D. Bauer (ed.), *Mönchtum, Kirche, Herrschaft, 750–1000* (Sigmaringen, 1998), pp. 243–61.

147 MGH Capit. I no. 139 c.1 p. 281. The text was then quoted again in MGH Capit. II no. 193 c.1 p. 18.

148 An edition of samples, and a list of manuscripts not used by Eckhardt, can be found in Editions at the back of this book.

149 *Lex Salica* Vol. 2 p. 55.

It is not ascribed to a king or emperor or even dated according to an emperor or king's reign. The other 'additional capitularies' do carry such an attribution in at least some of their manuscripts.

Of the five extant manuscripts, three are from the ninth century, one from the tenth or eleventh century, and one from the fifteenth:

BN Lat. 4632	(Autr)	$ix^{3/4}$	St Stephen, Templeuve	*Sal* K, *Rib* B, *Al*, Capits. nos. 39, 40, 134, 139, 142. Written by *Autramnus indignus advocatus laicus*.
Sélestat 14 (104)	(Sel)	$ix^{3/3}$	W. France	*Ans* with 'Rheims group' insertions, Capits. incl. nos. 39, 139. 142.
BN Lat. 10758	(Par)	$ix^{4/4}$	Rheims	*Ans* with 'Rheims group' insertions, Capits. incl. no. 39, *Sal* K.
BN Lat. 4628A		x/xi	France	Largely a copy of BN Lat. 10758.
BN Lat. 4631		xv	France	Largely a copy of BN Lat. 4628A.

The early modern codex is largely a copy of the post-Carolingian, which in turn is largely a copy of the late ninth-century BN Lat. 10758, written at Rheims, and a member of the 'Rheims group' of distinctive capitulary manuscripts.[150] Of the other two ninth-century manuscripts, Sélestat 14 (104) is also from the Rheims group. The circulation of the text, then, is restricted to two Rheims group manuscripts from a family of about ten. Many other rare capitularies seem to owe their preservation to a Rheims connection, many found in the large, related, tenth-century codices BN Lat. 9654 and Vat. Pal. Lat. 582. Palaeographically, the latter is likely to come from near Rheims, while BN Lat. 9654 is probably from near Metz, but its collection refers uniquely to the circuit of the Archbishop of Sens, which led Wormald to the conclusion that some of its contents were derived from the archive at Sens.[151]

It may be significant for the circulation of Capitulary no. 142 that it is found in the Sélestat manuscript in a small quire inserted into the main collection, in which blank sheets surround the capitulary on either side.[152] The script of the additional quire, not the same as that of the

[150] On the Rheims group, see section 3.4.2 below.

[151] Wormald (1999), *The making*, p. 61; Mordek (1995), *Bibliotheca*, pp. 562 and 780; C. West, 'The significance of the Carolingian advocate' *EME*, *17* (2009), p. 197.

[152] Compare the discussion of the role of *libelli* in the construction of the Bobbio Missal in R. McKitterick, 'The scripts of the Bobbio Missal' in: Y. Hen and R. Meens (eds.), *The Bobbio missal: liturgy and religious culture in Merovingian Gaul* (Cambridge, 2004), pp. 19–52.

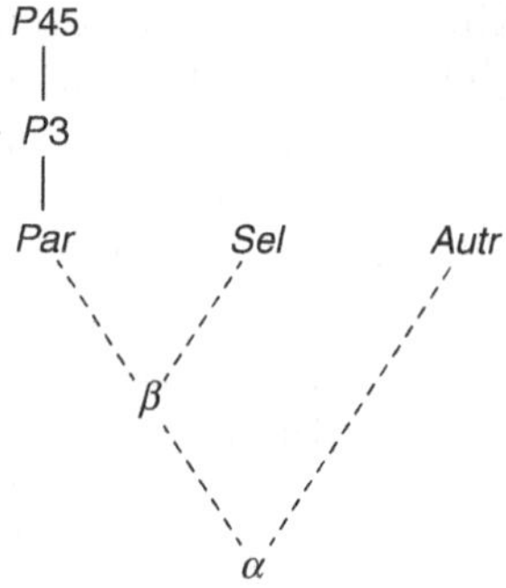

Fig. 3.2 Proposed stemma for Capitulary 142

main manuscript, is from s. ix$^{3/3}$, so some time after the construction of the text, even if we extend its *terminus ante quem* to 840.

Boretius did not edit the Sélestat manuscript, but I established that its text of Capitulary no. 142 is closely related to that of BN Lat. 10758.[153] The most probable stemma is as shown in Figure 3.2. So no. 142 cannot have entered BN Lat. 10758 (*Par*) through direct contact with the Sélestat manuscript because of the relationship between the texts. Its localisation to West France would not, however, rule out contact through perhaps a single intermediary manuscript.

The final manuscript, and the earliest, BN Lat. 4632 (ix$^{\text{med.-}2/2}$) is a collection of *Lex Salica*, a fragment of *Lex Ribuaria* and *Lex Alemannorum*, with a few capitularies, among them nos. 39, and parts of 134, 139, and 142. Indeed the only capitulary presented in full not classed as 'additional' in this manuscript is no. 40. It was written by a certain *Autramnus indignus advocatus laicus*. As Charles West has pointed out, this manuscript has textual links with some Rheims manuscripts.[154]

Of course, loss of manuscripts makes it impossible to make firm conclusions about how the text would have circulated, or how it came to be included in manuscripts. But the extant manuscripts suggest that the text only circulated within the reach of Rheims, and its context in the Sélestat manuscript and absence from others of the Rheims Group perhaps indicate that it had circulated separately from, and was sometimes in the later ninth century at least identified as different from, a more recognised corpus of royal capitularies. One might imagine that the text was subject to the same process by which Capitularies nos. 39

153 This was already Mordek's view on the relationship between the texts. See H. Mordek, 'Weltliches Recht im Kloster Weißsenburg/Elsaß. Hinkmar von Rheims und die Kapitulariensammlung des Cod. Sélestat, Bibliothèque Humaniste, 14 (104)' in: Mordek (2000), *Studien*, pp. 274–5. See the edition in Editions at the end of this book below.

154 West (2009), 'Carolingian advocate', pp. 197–8. And see Chapter 5, section 5.2.3 below.

and 41 came to be presented ever more as royal legislation, but that the process never advanced as far in this case.

3.3.7 Nos. 134 and 135. Capitula Legi Addita *816. Drafts*

Capitularies nos. 134 and 135 are both described as 'additional', dated by inscriptions in manuscripts to 816, and attributed to Louis the Pious. They both seem to originate in some form from the same discussions: no. 134 covers all the ground covered by no. 135, draws the same conclusions in different language, while also adding some unique material. But one is not simply an interpolated or expanded version of the other: the basic language is quite different, suggesting a thorough revision. The fuller text, no. 134, is extant in thirteen manuscripts, against only five for no. 135.[155]

A significant peculiarity is that, of the manuscripts containing both texts as edited, they are presented in all but one as intertwined with each other, with some or all of the chapters numbered through in sequence. This frequently results in repetition of material in different words. The mid ninth-century sister codices from Ivrea, which are the earliest in which either of these texts is included, present the following as a single text:[156]

In nomine domini nostri iesu christi hludovvicus diuino nuto coronatus romanum regens imperium serenissimus augustus omnibus episcopis abbatibus ducibus comitibus seu cunctis fidelibus nostris capl. que nobis addere placuit

Cap I	134,1	Disagreements between witnesses
Cap II	134,2	Charges in a foreign *patria*
Cap III	134,3	*Solidi* and *Denarii* in cases involving Saxons and Frisians
Cap IV	135,1	Disagreements between witnesses
Cap V	135,2	*Solidi* and *Denarii* in cases involving Saxons and Frisians
Cap VI	135,3	*mannire*

A similar presentation and inscription can be found in the related Italian manuscripts of *c.*1000, Cava dei Tirreni 4, and Vat. Chigi F. IV. 75. Only in the later ninth-century Wolfenbüttel Gud. Lat. 299 is the text of no. 135, as edited by Boretius, presented independently, without no. 134. The implications of two versions of the records of a set of

155 These manuscripts contain nos. 134 and 135: Cava dei Tirreni 4 (c.1005, S. Italy), Ivrea XXXIII (ix$^{med.}$, N. Italy), Ivrea XXXIV (c.830, Pavia), Vat. Chigi F. IV. 75 (c.1000, Central Italy). These contain no. 134 only: Gotha Memb. I 84 (x/xi), Heligenkreuz 217 (x$^{ex.}$), Leiden Voss. Lat. Q. 119 (ix$^{4/4}$, France), London Egerton 269/2832/BN Lat. 4633 (x$^{1/4}$, N.E. France), München Lat. 3853 (x$^{2/2}$, S. Germany), München Lat. 4460 (xi$^{2/2}$, S. Germany?), BN Lat. 4632 (ix$^{3/4}$, St Stephen, Templeuve), Sélestat 14 (104) (ix$^{3/3}$, W. France), St Paul im Lavanttal 4/1 (817–23, N. Italy/Aquliea). This contains no. 135 only: Wolfenbüttel Gud. Lat. 299 (ix$^{3/4}$, N. E. France).

156 Again, this is something noticed in Patzold (2005), 'Veränderung', p. 86.

discussions circulating interdependently as well as independently are not clear.

Perhaps it shows most clearly that more and less mature versions of discussions, identified at least by a compiler from the 830s as 'official' *could* leak in a form in which manuscript compilers would take an interest, presumably during the process of discussion itself. Perhaps the versions are in fact drafts which circulated over distance in writing, for the purposes of consultation, and were included by compilers in legal manuscripts who were unaware of, or perhaps more likely unconcerned about their status as 'finished' legislation or otherwise.

3.3.8 Mordek's Capitula Adhuc Conferenda

The text recently discovered on a single sheet of parchment by Mordek should be studied alongside these texts.[157] This is very certainly an agenda for discussion, often treating subjects covered in the *Lex Ribuaria*; the manuscript is dated on palaeographical grounds to Louis the Pious's reign.

Striking is its reference to St Bavo in a context that suggests that the author was a member of the community there:

> Concerning property (or revenues)[158] of churches, which cannot be maintained over the years, which we have in Cologne, and was handed over to St Bavo at the time of king Pippin.[159]

Mordek imagined that this text was a draft for a royal capitulary, so found this passage puzzling.[160] He suggested Einhard as a figure who could fit into the context both of the court and of St Bavo. But the text in fact makes no reference to the royal court at all. The bareness of the text, that it is simply a set of matters to be discussed, makes it very difficult to infer what kind of aims the discussions would have. C.16 for example concerns the problem of infringement of charters

[157] Edited in Mordek (1995), *Bibliotheca*, pp. 1009–11 and with commentary in Mordek (1990), 'Recently discovered capitulary texts', pp. 437–55.

[158] For translation as the latter see H. Mordek, 'Ein exemplarische Rechtsstreit' in: Mordek (2000), *Studien*, p. 280.

[159] Mordek (1995), *Bibliotheca*, p. 1010 c.17: *De longa vestitura ecclesiarum, quae per annos defendi non potest, sicut est, quod nos in Colonia habemus et traditum fuit ad sanctum Bavonem tempore Pippini regis.* For an interpretation of this passage for understanding St Bavo's landholding see G. de Clercq, 'De Capitula adhuc conferenda van Lodewijk de Vrome en de domeinen van de Gentse Sint-Baafsabij in Noord-Frankrijk' in: J-M. Duvorsquel and E. Thoen (eds.), *Peasants and townsmen in medieval europe: Studia in honorem Adriaan Verhulst* (Ghent, 1995), pp. 325–45 esp. 335f.

[160] Mordek (1990), 'Recently discovered capitulary texts', p. 443: 'The renewal of interest in legal questions already dealt with in the national laws could have only one aim: to amend and modify the older laws and customs through royal decree.' See also de Clercq (1995), 'Capitula adhuc conferenda', pp. 325–45 with a basic acceptance, but refinement of Mordek's views at esp. pp. 334–5.

of manumission, but this is a problem that could be tackled on very many levels: the chapter could envisage discussion leading to a royal decree to establish a new principle, but there is no reason to read it as anything other than a local discussion about how courts should handle these cases, what legal texts were relevant, and how they should be interpreted. Certainly some subjects hint that intercession with the king might have been imagined, for example c.12 on problems with *servi dominici* and c.14 on safeguarding property sent into presumably royal *bannum*. But the first few chapters, concerning minimum and maximum permissible fines, surely do not demand any royal input at all. Indeed, texts summarising these fines have survived for both *Lex Salica* and *Lex Ribuaria*, and nothing substantial in their content or manuscripts suggests that they need to be seen as royal legislation.[161]

Mordek's text, then, might well be most convincing as an agenda for a discussion among local *potentes*, perhaps including counts (see c.18), connected with St Bavo involved in settling disputes and holding courts. The discussion would have touched on matters of interpretation of *lex* texts, envisaged some royal involvement and intervention, but perhaps would have reached its own conclusions.

The context of survival does not help any further with the nature of the discussion. The text is preserved on a single leaf of parchment, but Mordek's description, which he in turn derived only from the Sotheby's catalogue, gives no information on whether the sheet had ever been, or was ever intended to be, inserted into a codex. We do know that the verso side is a palimpsest, which perhaps points to a rather ephemeral conception of the value of the text. The recto side has the last chapter of another text, numbered as XV, which also seems to connect with the *Lex Ribuaria*, so material with similar concerns was written in the same place.

3.3.9 Conclusion from the texts in detail

We have seen in this section just how diverse the texts edited as additional capitularies are in their concerns, relationships with *leges* texts, in how they were constructed, and in how they were received in the manuscripts. At one extreme we have the Baviarian capitulary, the central purpose of which was the symbolic insertion of Charlemagne into Bavarian law, and the manuscripts of which hint at some controversy over the role of the text in that tradition. At the other extreme we have Capitulary no. 142, which is a detailed consideration of technical, legal points made in the *Lex Salica*, and seems not to have involved a

161 See most recently Siems (1995), 'Textbearbeitung', pp. 43–7. But see section 3.3.5 above for a hint that in later manuscripts the *Recapitulatio* of *Lex Salica* might be treated as a royal capitulary.

king at all in its production. We have also seen how the texts could be reinterpreted down the generations, how the capitulary to *Lex Ribuaria* was reinterpreted from a gloss to the relevant *Lex*, towards an autonomous piece of legislation by Charlemagne, and how even Capitulary no. 39, unambiguously a royal-imperial product, took on ever more lavish imperial baggage as the ninth century progressed.

We now zoom back out, to look at the manuscripts of the additional capitularies as a group, and to study their connection with the *leges* themselves in the manuscripts in greater depth. The aim is to move away from considerations of construction and intent, and to get an ever clearer view of how the texts were understood by compilers and readers of manuscipts.

3.4 THE MANUSCRIPTS OF THE GROUP

This section investigates whether there are features of the manuscript transmission of additional capitularies that have significance for how we understand them to have been read and used. I ask whether they have a different manuscript context to the body of capitularies as a whole, and what their relationship is with the *leges* and with each other. I hope to find out whether there is a special sense of connection with the *leges*, if so why and how, and whether there is any hint that the additional capitularies were transmitted as a group.

Although, again, a full study of the post-Carolingian period is not possible here, I shall at each stage treat the ninth-century evidence in comparison with that of later periods, because comparison also discloses particular features of the ninth-century transmission. It is important in future work to investigate the later manuscripts fully, because some features of the later transmission have had an effect on the tradition of understanding the texts embodied in the MGH editions.

The analysis starts from broad groups of manuscripts, and treats progressively smaller subsets, investigating the transmission of our texts from several angles, with several points of comparison. It has been impossible to avoid something of a deluge of figures, charts, and tables in this section, but the patterns make it worthwhile.

3.4.1 Patterns from a mass analysis

Manuscripts of all *leges* and capitularies

At first a general presentation of the relationship between capitularies and *leges* in the manuscripts is needed to give the broadest context to our additional capitularies. How difficult it can be to take a holistic approach to the corpus of manuscripts is apparent already in the difference in the number of manuscripts considered by different historians. The last full survey of the corpus was Wormald's.[162] In his reckoning there are 238 extant manuscripts, excluding fragments, containing Frankish (including Lombard) law from the period 750–*c.*1500.[163] According to my count, there are 339, more than a hundred more. While we have both tried to ignore fragments, it can be very difficult to establish clear criteria for classification as a fragment, and we have presumably differed. But the reasons for the disparity relate principally to more or less arbitrary choices. I have included every, or nearly every manuscript in Mordek's work; counted a manuscript as containing a capitulary even if it contains only a few chapters of the text; have included texts that Wormald specifically discounted, such as the so-called 'monastic capitularies', as well as manuscripts of English origin. Wormald counted the Merovingian capitularies that accompany the *Lex Salica* in certain manuscripts as part of *Lex Salica*, whereas I treat them as capitularies. I clearly include more later copies than did Wormald, in a world in which manuscript shades into early printed edition. In any case, the differences are such that it is worth presenting two sets of figures: one Wormald's minimal figures, and the other my maximal figures.

According to Wormald's figures, 120 manuscripts contain capitularies only, 53 manuscripts contain *leges* only, and 65 contain both *leges* and capitularies. The numbers can be broken down by period as shown in Table 3.5. According to my figures, the picture is as shown in Table 3.6. Table 3.7 gives the same figures from Wormald, but with different proportions calculated, those of the number of manuscripts of a particular class in each period against the total number for each period, to help see the significance of changes over time. Table 3.8 gives the same, according to my figures.

The differences between the proportions calculated in the two sets are significant mostly in the '*leges* only' category. The dominant reason seems to be that I have taken a wider view of which capitularies to include than did Wormald. Taking a wider view of capitularies moves manuscripts of *leges* and Merovingian capitularies into the 'both' class, and moves us into completely new manuscript contexts and distributions for certain Carolingian texts. A very clear case in point is Capitulary no. 170, included in my figures, but excluded in Wormald's, which is

162 Wormald (1999), *The making*, p. 57.

163 His total is 299, from which I have subtracted the 'Only Roman' and 'Only Visigothic' manuscripts, and those written before 750. Around 2008 I compiled a searchable electronic database, linked with a program capable of providing figures and calculations. Since then the Bibliotheca Legum project directed by K. Ubl at Cologne (www.leges.uni-koeln.de) has emerged as an excellent resource. My thanks to Charles Collicutt for helping me with problems I encountered when teaching myself to write software in Python. I have included manuscripts the dating of which is on the border between categories as in the earlier category.

Table 3.5 *Legal manuscripts by content and date, according to Wormald*

	Capitularies only	*Leges* only	Both	Totals
750–900	65	38	30	133 (55.9%)
900–1100	38	4	26	68 (28.6%)
1100–	17	11	9	37 (15.5%)
Totals	120 (50.4%)	53 (22.3%)	65 (27.3%)	238

Table 3.6 *Legal manuscripts by content and date, according to my new count*

	Capitularies only	*Leges* only	Both	Totals
750–900	84	25	44	153 (45.1%)
900–1100	77	6	19	102 (30.1%)
1100–	61	11	12	84 (24.8%)
Totals	222 (65.5%)	42 (12.4%)	75 (22.1%)	339

Table 3.7 *Changes in content of legal manuscripts over time, according to Wormald*

	Capitularies only	*Leges* only	Both	Totals
750–900	65 (48.9%)	38 (28.6%)	30 (22.5%)	133
900–1100	38 (55.9%)	4 (5.9%)	26 (38.2%)	68
1100–	17 (45.9%)	11 (29.7%)	9 (24.4%)	37
Totals	120	53	65	238

Table 3.8 *Changes in content of legal manuscripts over time, according to my new count*

	Capitularies only	*Leges* only	Both	Totals
750–900	84 (54.9%)	25 (16.3%)	44 (28.8%)	153
900–1100	77 (75.5%)	6 (5.9%)	19 (18.6%)	102
1100–	61 (72.6%)	11 (13.1%)	12 (14.3%)	84
Totals	222	42	75	339

Table 3.9 *Manuscripts of capitularies also containing* leges, *according to Wormald*

	Capitularies only	*Leges* and Capits	Totals
750–900	65 (68.4%)	30 (31.6%)	95 (51.4%)
900–1100	38 (59.4%)	26 (40.6%)	64 (34.6%)
1100–	17 (65.4%)	9 (34.6%)	26 (14.1%)
Totals	120 (64.9%)	65 (35.1%)	185

Table 3.10 *Manuscripts of capitularies also containing* leges, *according to my new count*

	Capitularies only	*Leges* and Capits	Totals
750–900	84 (65.6%)	44 (34.4%)	128 (43.1%)
900–1100	77 (80.2%)	19 (19.8%)	96 (32.3%)
1100–	61 (83.6%)	12 (16.4%)	73 (24.6%)
Totals	222 (74.7%)	75 (15.3%)	297

explored below. However we calculate it, around half of Carolingian manuscripts containing legal texts contain capitularies only.

In Table 3.9 we home in one level closer to the additional capitularies using Wormald's figures, and ask, of those manuscripts containing captularies, which also contain *leges*? Table 3.10 uses my figures for the same purposes. We now have some idea about the relationship between *leges* and capitularies in the manuscripts, with which we can compare the manuscripts of additional capitularies.

Manuscripts of additional capitularies

The central question is how well manuscripts containing additional capitularies correlate with these averages. In total there are 69, broken down by period as shown in Table 3.11.[164] So the basic distribution of manuscripts containing additional capitularies across time is broadly consistent with the results shown above for legal manuscripts in general. Around half are from the Carolingian period, around a third from the tenth and eleventh centuries, and around a sixth from later (right hand total columns with percentages). So additional capitularies do not seem to have a markedly different rate of reproduction over time than Frankish

164 My figures are based on Mordek (1995), *Bibliotheca*, although I have discounted the lost volume Cluny 443, and I have counted London Egerton 269 and 2832 as a single manuscript. See Mordek (1995), *Bibliotheca*, pp. 1029 and 1041.

Table 3.11 *Manuscripts of additional capitularies and* leges *as a group*

	Capitularies only	*Leges* and Capitularies	Totals
750–900	4 (10.5%)	34 (89.5%)	38 (55.1%)
900–1100	3 (14.3%)	18 (85.7%)	21 (30.4%)
1100–	4 (40%)	6 (60%)	10 (14.5%)
Totals	11 (15.9%)	58 (84.1%)	69

legal texts in general. The striking difference is how great a proportion of additional capitulary manuscripts contain *leges*: 84.1 per cent across the whole range. Of the manuscripts containing capitularies in general, depending on the set of figures used, only 15–35 per cent contain *leges*. This is a very significant discrepancy.

It is not clear whether the sample size is large enough here to formulate convincing conclusions on points of detail. Can anything be made of the relative tendency of the post-1100 manuscripts containing additional capitularies to exclude *leges*? Was the bond between additional capitularies and *leges* dissolving, or is our sample of only ten manuscripts simply not good enough to determine anything further? Specific regional patterns would need to be taken into account in a way that is not possible here. The *Lex Baiuwariorum*, for example, seems to have remained in use far later than other *leges*, according to the manuscripts, and to have a rather different manuscript context. Peter Landau has even argued that the *Lex* was used heavily in the construction of King Stephen of Hungary's laws in the eleventh century.[165] For now the pattern must remain unanalysed.

But after obtaining the general result that additional capitularies were copied frequently with *leges*, we can analyse the transmissions of the additional capitularies in more detail. These are illustrated in Table 3.12. These figures show three patterns, to be treated in turn. The first is that each and every additional capitulary has a very strong association with *leges* in the manuscripts. The second is that there is a very great variety in the scale of their transmission: nos. 39 and 139 tower above the others.[166] The third is that there is some discrepancy between the extent to which

165 P. Landau, 'The legislation of Stephan I and Bavarian Law', paper delivered at the International Medieval Congress, Leeds, July 2007. On the manuscripts of the *Lex Baiuwariorum*, and its later transmission, see R. Kottje, 'Die Lex Baiuvariorum - das Recht der Bayern' in: Mordek (1986), *Überlieferung und Geltung*, pp. 9–23. For the chronology of the distribution of the *leges* see above p. 17.

166 Note discrepancies between my figures and Mordek's: I have only included extant codices, not those lost.

Table 3.12 *Manuscripts of each additional capitulary and particular* leges

		No. of MS	Incl. a *lex*	Incl. 'right' *lex*
39.	*Cap. Legibus Add.* (803)	51	44 (86.3%)	n/a / 37 (72.5%)
41.	*Cap. Legi Rib. Add.* (803)	14	11 (78.6%)	7 (50%)
68.	*Cap. Leg. Bai. Add.* (801–13)	11	9 (81.8%)	7 (64.6%)
134.	*Cap. Legi Add.* (816)	13	10 (76.9%)	n/a
135.	*Item Cap. Legi Add.* (816)	5	4 (80%)	n/a
139.	*Cap. Legibus Add.* (818–9)	32	27 (84.4%)	n/a
142.	*Cap. Legi Sal. Add.* (819 –)	5	4 (80%)	4 (80%)

Table 3.13 *Transmission of popular capitularies*

		No. of MS	Incl. *leges*
20a.	*Capitulare Haristallense* (779)	32	23 (71.9%)
22.	*Admonitio generalis* (789)	39	15 (38.5%)
39.	*Capitulare legibus additum* (803)	51	43 (**84.3%**)
40.	*Capitulare missorum* (803)	49	44 (**89.8%**)
44.	*Capit. miss in Theod. villa dat. 2ndum* (805)	30	26 (**86.7%**)
139.	*Capitulare legibus addenda* (818–9)	32	27 (**84.4%**)
170.	*Capitulare Monasticum* III (818–9?)	38	2 (5.3%)
191.	*Capitulare Wormatiense* (829)	31	16 (51.6%)
192.	*Capitulare missorum Wormatiense* (829)	26	13 (50%)
193.	*Capit. pro lege habendum Wormatiense* (829)	25	13 (52%)

the capitularies are combined with the *leges* to which they are imagined to have been attached specifically, the 'right' *lex*.

The transmission of popular capitularies in general with respect to *leges*

Firstly, before rushing to conclusions about the reasons for the very close association between additional capitularies and *leges* in the manuscripts, we should compare the transmissions of some other texts individually. The less popular members of the group could owe their association to coincidence, such is our small sample size. However, Capitularies nos. 39 and 139 are among the most widely copied Frankish capitularies of all. In fact, no. 39 is *the* most popular of all. With such popular texts, we can take associations seriously, but should compare other popular capitularies to see their transmission in context. Only seven survive in more than twenty-five manuscripts:

Table 3.13 shows again, from a different angle, just how various the transmission of the capitularies is in its relationship with the *leges*. The additional capitularies are indeed the most closely associated with the *leges*, but they are not the only ones. Can the patterns be related to their content?

No. 40, as discussed above, is found almost exclusively with no. 39, usually immediately following it, so owes its connection with the *leges* to this stronger connection.[167] Equally, there is a nearly universal coincidence of no. 39 with no. 44. Only one manuscript of no. 44 does not also contain no. 39, that is Vat. Reg. Lat. 263, a tenth-century compilation, probably from Italy. The capitulary contains much material of relevance to holding courts and doing justice, such as provisions for upholding the decisions of *scabini*, what to do with bad advocates, the access of ecclesiastics to public courts, and perjury. Certainly the text also covered a range of other subjects, including the equipment of the army, and the regulation of merchants, but the strong association of this text with the *leges* is readily comprehensible.

At the other extreme, no. 170 only ever shares a manuscript with other capitulary material on six occasions. It is generally found with canonical material, and has a very singular transmission, with an important group of English manuscripts, now in London and Cambridge.[168] The tendency to exclude this text from consideration of Louis the Pious's capitularies seems justified in a certain sense, because it is so singular, and does distort the figures.[169] On the other hand, its singularity is important, and its transmission should perhaps be placed at one end of a spectrum, firmly in the context of other capitularies.

In the middle of the range, with moderate connection with the *leges*, are the Worms texts from 829. The Worms group forms a supplement to Ansegis, as some of the earliest texts to cite it directly, in the 'Rheims group' of Ansegis manuscripts, which have a clear association with the work of Hincmar of Rheims.[170] No. 191 largely concerns problems of church property, the division of churches between heirs, tithes, churches destroyed, and so on. No. 192 takes up problems related more to the operation of courts and the doing of justice: what to do with bad *scabini*, how *missi* and counts and the *populus* are to cooperate to do justice, what to do with criminal *fiscalini*, and so on. No. 193 is about yet more 'legal' concerns: homicide committed in church, or to gain property, taking a second wife, unjust usurpation of property, local officials holding burdensome numbers of assemblies, the status of poor freemen, and feuds.

[167] A point made in Pössel (2006), 'Authors and recipients', p. 259.

[168] See the list in Mordek (1995), *Bibliotheca*, pp. 1098–9. For the transmission of this text see J. Semmler, 'Zur Überlieferung der monastischen Gesetzgebung Ludwigs der Frommen' *DA*, *16* (1960), pp. 309–89 with Mordek (1995), *Bibliotheca*, pp. 999–1008.

[169] Wormald excludes it from consideration: Wormald (1999), *The making*, p. 57.

[170] See Mordek (2000), 'Recht im Kloster Weißenburg', pp. 261–79 and Schmitz's introduction in *Ansegis* pp. 269f.

Table 3.14 *The manuscripts of the additional capitularies*

Manuscript	Date	Additional Capitularies							Other contents, in order (**bold** denotes no *lex*)
Avranches 145	$xii^{2/2}$	39						1	***Ans*, Capits.**
Berlin Lat. Fol. 626	$xii^{1/2}$	39	41					2	***Ans*, Capits, Canons (Ghaerbald's collection).**
Berlin Phil. 1736	$x^{2/2}$	39	41					2	*Sal*(E), 8 Capits.
Berlin Phil. 1737	$x^{2/2}$						139	1	***Ans*, Capits.**
Cambrai 625	$ix^{ex.}$	39						1	Canons, Penitentials, 2 Capits, fragment of *Sal*.
Cava dei Tirreni 4	c.1005	39			134	135	139	4	Lombard *Origo Gentis*, *Ed. Roth.*, Glosses, Beneventan law, 39 Capits.
Cologny Bodmer 107	$ix^{ex.}$	39						1	*Isid.*, Roman Law, Rule of Benedict, *Sal*, *Rib*, *Al*, *Bav*, 6 Capits incl. Recap. Sol.
Gotha Memb. I 84	x/xi	39			134		139	3	*Ans*, Ben Lev, Burchard, King List, *Bav* Prologue, *Sal*, *Rib*, *Lang*, *Al*.
Heligenkreuz 217	$x^{ex.}$			68	134			2	**Penitentials, Canons, *Ans*, some 35 Capits.**
Ivrea XXXIII	$ix^{med.}$	39	41	68	134	135	139	6	*Rib*, *Sal*, *Al*, *Burg*, *Bav*, about 19 Capits.
Ivrea XXXIV	830	39	41		134	135	139	5	**About 34 Capits.**
Kopenhagen Gl. Kgl. Saml. 1943	$ix^{ex.}$						139	1	*Sal*, *Rib*, *Al*, Homilies, *formulae*, Alcuin, 4 Capits.
Leiden Voss. Lat. Q. 119	$ix^{4/4}$	39			134			2	*Isid.*, Roman law, OT Excerpt, *Epit. Aegid.*, *Sal*, 17 Capits.
London Add. 22398	ix/x	39						1	NT excerpt, *Ans*, *Sal*, 3 Capits, Alcuin, *Rib*.
London Egerton 269/2832	$x^{1/4}$	39			134		139	3	*Sal*, *Rib*, Sax, 8 Capits, *Al*, *Bav*, *LRV*, *Burg*.

(*cont.*)

Table 3.14 (*cont.*)

Manuscript	Date	Additional Capitularies						Other contents, in order (**bold** denotes no *lex*)
Modena O. I. 2	990	39					1	*Isid.*, Lombard *Origo Gentis*, King list, *Bav*, *Sal*, 25 Capits.
Montpellier H 136	ix$^{1/2}$	39				139	2	*LRV*, *Rom. Burg.* frag, *Sal*(D), 12 Capits.
München Lat. 3519	xii	39	41	68			3	*Bav*, 9 Capits, *Ed. Roth.* fragment.
München Lat. 3853	x$^{2/2}$			68	134		2	Penitentials, large Capit, Canon collection, *Bav*, *Al*, 28 Capits, Tribur, 17 Capits.
München Lat. 4460	xi$^{2/2}$			68	134	139	3	*Bav*, *Al*, 7 Capits, excerpts of *Epit. Aegid.*
München Lat. 5260	xii	39	41	68			3	*Bav*, 9 Capits, *Ed. Roth.* fragment, Chronicle.
München Lat. 19415	ix (xi)	39		68			2	*Bav*, Capits, Junilius Africanus, *Al.*
München Lat. 19416	ix$^{ex.}$	39	41				2	8 Capits, *Rib*, 15 Capits, Letters.
Münster msc. VII 5201	x$^{2/4}$					139	1	*Sax*, *Thur*, 4 Capits, Astr/Comp texts, Penitentials, Canons, Letters.
Nürnberg Cent. V, App. 96	ix$^{1/2}$	39					1	*Sal*, Capits.
Nürnberg 110 447b/47	xiii/xiv			68			1	**4 Capits.**
BN Baluze 94	xvii	39					1	**16 Capits, *Ans***
BN Lat. 2718	c.830					139	1	**King list, Augustine, *formulae*, 11 Capits, Cyprian, Sermons.**
BN Lat. 3182	x$^{2/2}$	39					1	Bible excerpts, Patristics, Penitentials, Canons, 2 Capits, *Sal.*
BN Lat. 3851	x	39					1	**Epitome of *Ans* and *Ben Lev*, 4 Capits, Prayers, Augustine.**
BN Lat. 4280 A	ix$^{ex.}$					139	1	**Orosius, Canons, 4 Capits, Misc.**

BN Lat. 4404	ix$^{inc.}$	39						1	*LRV*, *Sal*(A), Capits, *Al*, *Rib*, 6 Capits.
BN Lat. 4417	ix$^{ex.}$			68				1	*Epit. Aegid.*, *Rib*, *Sal*, *Al*, *Bav*, Capit, *Burg*, *Ans*, 7 Capits.
BN Lat. 4613	x	39						1	Lombard material, 21 Capits.
BN Lat. 4626	x/xi	39				139		2	*Sal*, 14 Capits, *Isid.*, Recap. Sol., *Epit. Aegid.*, *Burg*.
BN Lat. 4628	ix$^{2/3}$	39				139		2	*Sal*, 10 Capits, *Rib*, *Al*.
BN Lat. 4628 A	x/xi	39				139	142	3	Council, King list, *Sal*, 6 Capits, *Ewa ad Amorem*, 6 Capits, Paulinus.
BN Lat. 4629	c. 805	39	41					2	*Isid.*, *Epit. Aegid.*, *formulae*, *Sal*(E) frags, 8 Capits, *Rib*, Recap. Sol., Theology.
BN Lat. 4631	xv	39				139	142	3	King list, *Sal*.
BN Lat. 4632	ix$^{3/4}$	39			134	139	142	4	*Rib* frag, *Sal*, 6 Capits, *Al*.
BN Lat. 4758	ix$^{1/3}$	39						1	2 Capits, *Sal*, *Burg*.
BN Lat. 4760	x	39				139		2	*Summula de Bannis*, *Isid.*, Capits, *Sal*, Hrabanus.
BN Lat. 4788	ix$^{2/3}$	39				139		2	*Sal*, 8 Capits.
BN Lat. 4995	x	39				139		2	*Annales Petaviani*, *Isid.*, 4 Capits, *Al* and *Bav* fragment, 12 Capits, Recap. Sol.
BN Lat. 9653	ix$^{1/2}$					139		1	Rom frag, *Burg*, *Sal*(A), Capits, *Isid.*, *LRV*.
BN Lat. 9654	x/xi	39	41					2	Many Capits, *Sal*, *Ewa ad Amorem*, *Rib*, *Al*, *Bav*.
BN Lat. 10753	ix$^{med.}$	39				139		2	*LRV*, *Rom. Burg.*, *Burg*, 2 Capits, *Sal*, 3 Capits, *Rib*, *Al*.
BN Lat. 10754	ix$^{2/3}$	39						1	*Sal*, 4 Capits, Bible excerpts.
BN Lat. 10758	ix$^{4/4}$	39					142	2	Paulinus, *Sal*.
BN Lat. 18237	ix$^{2/4}$					139		1	2 Capits, *Ans*, *Sal*(C), 2 Capits, *Isid.*, *Al*.
BN Lat. 18238	ix$^{1/2}$					139		1	4 Capits, *Ans*, *Sal*.
BN nouv. acq. Lat. 204	ix$^{2/4}$					139		1	*Sal*, 6 Capits, *Al*, *Bav* fragment, *Burg* fragment, *formulae*, *LRV* fragment.

(*cont.*)

Table 3.14 *(cont.)*

Manuscript	Date	Additional Capitularies								Other contents, in order (**bold** denotes no *lex*)
St Gallen 728	$ix^{2/2}$	39							1	Library catalogue, *Ans*, Recap. Solid, *Isid.*, Capits, *Sal*, *Rib*.
St Paul im Lavanttal 4/1	$ix^{1/4}$	39	41		134		139		3	2 Capits, *Rib*, *Sal*, *Bav*, *Al*, *Epit. Aegid.*, *Burg*, many Capits.
St Petersburg Q. v. II. 11	$ix^{inc.}$	39							1	*Sal* fragment, 6 Capits, Recap. Sol.
Sélestat 14 (104)	$ix^{3/3}$	39			134		139	142	4	**(1st part) *Ans*, 21 Capits.**
Stuttgart Jur. Q. 134	x/xi						139		1	Just 2 chapters of 139. *Al*, *Ans*
Vatikan Chigi F. IV. 75	c.1000	39	41		134	135	139		4	Chronicle, *Sal*, many Capits.
Vatikan Pal. Lat. 582	$x^{1/2}$	39	41						2	**Vita, 38 Capits, Recap. Sol, *Ans*, many more Capits.**
Vatikan Pal. Lat. 773	$ix^{1/2}$	39	41						2	*Rib*, 3 Capits.
Vatikan Reg. Lat. 338	$ix^{med.}$ (x)						139		1	*Rib*, *Sal*, Capit, Recap. Sol.
Vatikan Reg. Lat. 991	$ix^{2/4}$			68					1	*Rib*, Alcuin, *Sal*, *Al*, *Bav*, Capits, *Epit. Aegid.*
Vatikan Reg. Lat. 1036	xv	39							1	Frankish *Origo Gentis*, 6 Capits, *Sal*, 4 Capits, *Ans*.
Vatikan Reg. Lat. 1050	$ix^{med.}$	39							1	*Isid.*, *LRV*, *Rom. Burg.*, Capits, *Sal*, *Rib*, *Al*, *formulae*.
Vatikan Reg. Lat. 1728	xv	39							1	Frankish *Origo Gentis*, 11 Capits, (*Sal* is lost).
Wien ÖNB 406	xii			68					1	*Bav*, 3 Capits, *Historia Langobardorum*.
Wolfenbüttel Aug. 4 50.2	$ix^{1/2}$	39					139		2	*Sal*, 4 Capits.
Wolfenbüttel Blank. 130	$ix^{3/4}$	39	41				139		2	*Lang*, Capits, *Rib* chapter, many Capits, *Sal*, *Burg*, *Rib*.
Wolfenbüttel Gud. Lat.299	$ix^{3/4}$	39				135			2	*Sal*, 5 Capits, *Rib*.

Table 3.15 *Transmission of additional capitularies with each other*

No. of Add. Capits.	750–900	900–1100	1100–	Totals
1	20 (52.6%)	7 (33.3%)	6 (60.0%)	33 (47.8%)
2	13 (34.2%)	8 (38.1%)	1 (10.0%)	22 (31.9%)
3	1 (2.6%)	4 (19.0%)	3 (33.3%)	8
4	2 (5.3%)	2 (9.5%)	0	4
5	1 (2.6%)	0	0	1
6	1 (2.6%)	0	0	1
	38	21	10	69

So the transmission of popular capitularies is really quite diverse: each has its own associations and peculiarities. This makes the association between additional capitularies and *leges* more meaningful, and further emphasises how careful we need to be when studying capitulary transmission. A recent study by Davis pointed out differences between the capitularies of Charlemagne, Louis the Pious, and Charles the Bald in terms of a contraction in the variety of the transmission.[171] But, taken on a capitulary-by-capitulary basis, the distinction between the transmission of Charlemagne's and Louis's capitularies looks less extreme. The case of Charles the Bald may be different, considering the importance to the tradition of manuscripts linked with Hincmarian Rheims.[172] But the content of the texts seems very important, and there is a case for emphasising the active choices of scribes above the requirements of kings when explaining the features of the manuscripts.

Association of additional capitularies with each other

Are the additional capitularies associated with *each other* in the manuscripts? Do they form a meaningful group? Table 3.14 shows the full range of manuscripts, with each capitulary labelled, and a count of how many additional capitularies can be found in that manuscript. Table 3.15 summarises the statistics. The first result is that nos. 41, 134, 135, and 142 *never* appear without at least one other additional capitulary. Of those with a smaller distribution, only no. 68 ever appears on its own. Still, in the summary figures, we see that in around half of all manuscripts considered, only a single additional capitulary is to be found. There is no sense in the figures that additional capitularies were transmitted together, as a group.

171 J. R. Davis, 'The king and his Law: Carolingian rulers through the lens of the Capitulary Manuscripts' (2005), Paper delivered at the International Medieval Congress, Leeds, July 2005.
172 See above Nelson (1983), 'Legislation and consensus', pp. 202–22.

3.4.2 Particular groups of manuscripts

So far we have seen that the additional capitularies are very well associated with the *leges* in their manuscripts, but that there is no evidence that they were transmitted as a group. The aim here is to use two groups of manuscripts to investigate their transmission further, and ask whether our patterns might be related to the direct or indirect influence of any particular group of manuscripts.

The view from the *leges*-scriptorium

The *leges*-scriptorium manuscripts were identified as a group by Bischoff, dated to the 820s–30s, and associated with Louis the Pious's court. They are considered in detail in Chapter 5, and the question of whether they had some kind of offical status, as Bischoff and later McKitterick suggested, is given particular weight. If we assume for now that they were official in some sense, then their contents are surprising.

Only three *leges*-scriptorium manuscripts, out of fourteen or so, contain additional capitularies: BN nouv. acq. Lat. 204 and BN Lat. 2718 contain no. 139, and Vat. Reg. Lat. 991 contains no. 68.[173] The two Paris manuscripts are somewhat eccentric in form and content, so their intended purpose and use is difficult to ascertain, as discussed in detail later.[174] Of particular interest for the transmission of no. 139 is the difference between the prologues transmitted in the two manuscripts.[175] These manuscripts are the sole witnesses to Capitulary no. 144, which concerns the provision of justice by counts, and is given the title *Capitula legi salicae addenda*.[176] Of the *leges*-scriptorium manuscripts, these give the only hints that any of the additional capitularies might possibly have been transmitted in some official capacity.

Vat. Reg. Lat. 991 is a typical large *leges* manuscript of the kind identified by McKitterick as a 'lawbook'.[177] It contains *Lex Ribuaria*, *Salica*, *Alemannorum*, *Baiuwariorum*, and *Epitome Aegidii*. One would have thought that it would be the ideal vehicle for producing texts updated with the newest relevant additions, but only the Bavarian additional capitulary is present, and is also in a different, later hand from that of the rest of the manuscript.[178]

As we see later, the *leges*-scriptorium manuscripts are very problematic in many ways. For now all we can say is that the bringing of additional

[173] See Mordek's comments on these Codices 'mit ihrem minimalen Kapitularienangebot' in Mordek (2000), 'Kapitularien und Schriftlichkeit', pp. 336–8.
[174] See Chapter 5, sections 5.1.5 and 5.2.1 below.
[175] See section 3.3.2 above.
[176] For titles in the editions see section 3.2.2 above.
[177] McKitterick (1989), *Written word*, pp. 45–60.
[178] Mordek (1995), *Bibliotheca*, p. 840.

capitularies into the same manuscripts as *leges* can scarcely be attributed to the influence of manuscripts associated with the *leges*-scriptorium.

The Rheims group: modification in manuscripts

This is the second-largest group of early medieval legal manuscripts with clear common features, but unlike the *leges*-scriptorium group, it is characterised by similarity of content rather than by palaeography. An awareness of links between some of the manuscripts and Hincmarian Rheims goes at least as far back as Devisse's work in the 1960s, and since then Mordek has described the similarities in most detail, outlining the features of the 'Ansegis-Worms Corpus' with distinctive additions.[179] BN Lat. 10758 is linked palaeographically with Rheims and Schmitz has demonstrated from Hincmar's citations of Ansegis that he used a manuscript probably identical with Berlin Phil. 1762.[180]

Here are the manuscripts of the group:

Berlin Phil. 1762	ix$^{med.}$ (before 860)	Used by Hincmar	*B7*
Sélestat 14 (104)	ix$^{3/3}$	W. France	*Sel*
BN Lat. 10758	ix$^{4/4}$	Rheims	*Par/P2*
Bamberg Can. 12	x$^{1/4}$	Germany?	*Bav*
BN Lat. 4628A	x/xi	France	*P3*
BN Lat. 4638	xi	France	*P6*
Avranches 145	xii$^{2/2}$	Mont-Saint-Michel	*Av*
Berlin Lat. Fol. 626	xii$^{1/2}$	Diocese of Liège	*B*
BN Lat. 4631	xv	France	*P47*

The ninth-century representatives of the group each display a particular interest in the additional capitularies, or in the text found also in Benedictus Levita quoted above, which refers to them.[181] The most spectacular example is the Sélestat manuscript's presentation of Capitulary no. 142 in a *libellus*.[182] This manuscript included additional Capitularies nos. 39, 134, 139, so more additional capitularies than other members of the group, even though it did not contain a *lex*.

The other examples relate to the incorporation of the distinctive additions into the Ansegis text, the most relevant of which is in this case the insertion of the *Capitula a Benedicto Levita singillatim tradita*, text **H** above, which refers the reader to the *statuta priorum capitulorum quae legi Salicae sunt addita* in cases concerning homicide or injury of

179 Devisse (1962), *Hincmar et la loi*, pp. 64–72. See especially Mordek (2000), 'Recht im Kloster Weißenburg', pp. 261–79 as well as individual entries for the manuscripts in Mordek (1995), *Bibliotheca*.

180 *Ansegis* pp. 320–30.

181 Section 3.2.3 above.

182 See section 3.3.6 above.

clerics.[183] Berlin Phil. 1762 interestingly suggests that the addition of this text was not without its problems for compilers or readers. At exactly the point at which the text is found, after Ansegis IV,14, the chapter numberings have been altered by a second hand, both in the chapter index and in the text.[184] The implication can only be that at some point in the compilation or use of the manuscript the difference between this manuscript's arrangement and that of a 'normal' Ansegis manuscript was noted. However, it does not necessarily point to any particular reference to this passage.

In BN Lat. 10758, presentation of the additions is still more singular. The main text jumps on pp. 199–200 from *Ans* II, 32 to II, 35, but a small strip of parchment, 'p. 200bis' is stuck in to provide the additions '*Ans* II, 33' and 'II, 34', which consist of Capitulary no. 167 (which Boretius called *Capitula Francica*) c.2 and 3, very generic pronouncements on the need for doing *iustitia*, especially to widows and orphans. These chapters are found only in the Rheims group manuscripts. The additions are still more interesting because in the Sélestat manuscript the rubrics and title numberings of the additions, but not their texts, are found in place in the Ansegis text on fol. 88r, whereas the text of the two chapters is found out of place on fol. 138r. On 138r the numberings link c.2 of *Capitula Francica* with the previous short capitulary collection, in which texts of four capitularies (as edited) are numbered through: so c.2 (of *Capitula Francica*) appears in sequence as *XXV cap.*[185] C.3, however, jumps to a title number of XXXIV, which betrays its intended place within the Ansegis corpus. In BN Lat. 4628A, the fairly direct copy of BN Lat. 10758, the titles alone are similarly presented in sequence in the Ansegis text (fol. 103ra), and the texts themselves are also presented independently, numbered XXXIII and XXXIV, but placed this time before Ansegis, on 78ra-b.

It is puzzling though that the strips, and evidence for contact with the strips, is in the *later* two of the ninth-century codices, while Berlin Phil. 1762 incorporates the extra texts without issue. But this fact might help us get somewhere with how and when the additions were made into the distinctive Rheims text.

Schmitz showed that the Ansegis texts of the three ninth-century manuscripts were not direct or indirect copies of each other, but of a common manuscript or family.[186] His findings are given in a stemma, shown in Figure 3.3. So the additions were possibly in their first or

[183] See section 3.2.3 above.
[184] Mordek (1995), *Bibliotheca*, pp. 61–2. I have seen the manuscript, but sadly did not take pictures.
[185] A clear list is provided in Mordek (1995), *Bibliotheca*, p. 712.
[186] Summarised at *Ansegis* pp. 278–9.

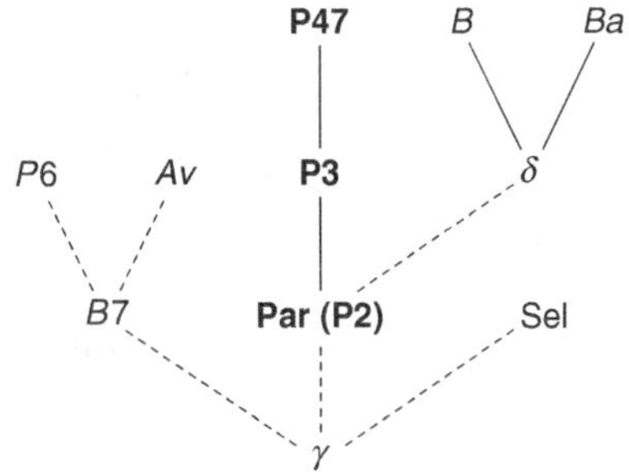

Fig. 3.3 Stemma of Ansegis text in Rheims group manuscripts

second generation in our extant manuscripts: their common exemplar or exemplar family did not have them, or at least not all of them.

All of this gives the impression that various instructions on the construction of the manuscripts were given, but only partially, confusedly, followed, so that the results needed to be corrected. It seems that there may have been a system for correcting these manuscripts over distance, and that the difference between the 'Rheims' Ansegis and the 'normal' Ansegis was sometimes noted and did provoke a sense of unrest. Indeed, one Ansegis manuscript linked palaeographically with Hincmarian Rheims is quite 'normal', with no additions.[187] This is a clear sign that the manuscripts were read, and that references by book and chapter were used. So a tradition of interpretation focused on ninth-century Rheims valued precise citation by number quite strongly, and aimed for consistency. Incidentally, this aim is also attested in the tenth century: the earlier tenth-century Rheims codex Vat. Reg. Lat. 417, carried a 'normal' Ansegis redaction, but a second scribe, very slightly later than the main scribe, added the Rheims group insertions.[188] All of this certainly fits well with what we know about how carefully Hincmar cited Ansegis, and demonstrates that, while in many ways the structural similarities of legal manuscripts show a broadly comparable legal culture across the Carolingian empire, local control could be tight and peculiarities deliberately preserved.

The relevance to additional capitularies in all of this is, in a sense, partial: the passage of Benedictus was just one of the additions. However, in the Sélestat manuscript and BN Lat. 10758, but not Berlin Phil. 1762, Capitulary no. 39 is present, with rubrics specifically relating the text to the *Lex Salica*.[189] The addition therefore directed a reader

[187] St Gallen 727. Mordek (1995), *Bibliotheca*, pp. 664–5.
[188] Mordek (1995), *Bibliotheca*, pp. 823–5.
[189] Sélestat 14 (104) preserves *capitula que in lege salica mittenda sunt*, and BN Lat. 10758 *incipiunt capitula que in lege Salica domnus Augustus Karolus ann ab incarnatione domini hostri Iesu Christi*

to another part of the manuscripts. The most important point about the Rheims group manuscripts is that they show individual scribes grappling with the problems of consistency, and choosing to incorporate texts that provided cross-references into manuscripts in which they also copied additional capitularies. The compilers of the manuscripts can be seen actively collecting texts, and making their manuscripts usable in somewhat individual ways, rather than simply passively receiving centrally disseminated material.

3.4.3 Summary: the contribution of the survey of manuscripts

So in the Carolingian period, the transmission of the capitularies is various, and this is a variety which cuts across rulers. The 'additional capitularies', whether or not we see them as comprising a distinct group, were copied unusually frequently into manuscripts containing the *leges*, and this is not something we can attribute to patterns of official dissemination. It seems that each capitulary's transmission relates at least in part to its perceived nature, and that decisions about groupings were made by individual scribes.

3.5 SUMMARY

While others have stressed the inadequacy of the additional capitularies as elements of an imperially inspired programme of reform of the *leges*, I have interpreted them more as quite diverse expressions of a broad movement of engagement with the texts, which certainly involved kings and emperors, but also involved independent, local initiatives. It may be a mistake to make too strong a distinction between the private and the public-royal-imperial. Private and public work are perhaps best viewed as part of the same programme: one was not straightforwardly a response to the other.

This interpretation has involved opening texts edited as capitularies wider even than some of the most recent work. Christina Pössel recently emphasised how diverse the processes and discussions that resulted in the drawing up of capitularies were, and showed that by no means all capitularies were the products of assemblies. But she still argued, in line with a general assumption running through the historiography from Boretius onwards, that there was a 'lowest common denominator' among texts that qualifies them to be numbered among the capitularies, that there was some kind of more or less standardised

DCCCIII. imperii vero sui anno tertio praeponendo addere iussit. See my discussion of the titles and the importance of Rheims in section 3.3.1 above.

'Capitulary treatment'. Pössel also emphasised the capitularies' status as strong expressions of a royal will.

But there is no strong, positive evidence for such a 'capitulary treatment'. We are still very much in the dark about how capitularies were disseminated, so we cannot posit a standardised mechanism of distribution without further evidence, and the stylistic variation between texts is surely too great to propose the existence of a finishing office that standardised the form of raw records of discussion or reports of proclamation.[190] The additional capitularies, the texts we might expect to be the most explicitly phrased as royal will, are in general the *least* explicitly phrased as such. At the same time it is very striking how much variety there is in the length, scope, rhetoric, and nature of the additions they made. The longest, and most clearly expressed as royal will is Louis's no. 139. This, and the equivalent text no. 39 from Charlemagne's reign may well have been distributed energetically, perhaps involving the *leges*-scriptorium in the case of no. 139, and may have had explicit ideological underpinnings of some sort. A few of their additions responded to obvious, jarring omissions in the *Lex Salica* itself, and appear to assume that the *leges* would be practical reference works. But the sense in which they added to the *lex* was also very general: they were to be added into books of law, in much the same way as the Merovingian capitularies seem to have been before them. The greatest symbolic weight is to be associated with Charlemagne's Bavarian capitulary, which directly wrote the Carolingians into the Bavarian order, and it may be that there was some resistance to this view.

The other texts we have seen, especially nos. 41 and 142, take us far deeper into the world of application, and may well give a unique insight into the way in which *leges* were interpreted on a day-to-day basis, independently of the workings of royal capitulary processes. I have suggested that their origins can be traced further from a court context than previously imagined, and that they were explicitly framed as imperial legislation only in the decades after their construction. Understood in this way, they show how *lex* could be an important point of reference in particular disputes. While consensus was central to dispute settlement, the construction of consensus might regularly involve reference to texts of *lex*. The *leges* could be used to frame an argument, and that argument could carry some weight, but it could bend the *lex* in all sorts of ways. Importantly, *lex* was not the only kind of authority, and could be flatly ignored.

So we need to take some of these texts seriously as relating to the problems encountered relating the *leges* to realities on the ground. We

[190] Cf. F. L. Ganshof, *Was waren die Kapitularien?* (Darmstadt, 1961), pp. 70f.

may also need to pay more attention to the changing perceptions of scribes, most of whom were working some time after the production of our texts, and their capacity to reframe capitularies in new contexts. We also need to take seriously their efforts to group relevant material together, not as a response to a royal programme or a particular 'official' channel of transmission, but possibly as a response to the requirements of readers. I shall now try to identify some contexts in which readers found use for the *leges* and the additional capitularies.

Chapter 4

THE READING OF NORMATIVE TEXTS: BENEDICTUS LEVITA AND REGINO

In the first two chapters I suggested, using the *leges* themselves and their manuscripts, as well as charters and hagiography, that *leges* might be read, and indeed compiled, when trying to understand social rank, traditions of landholding, and service obligations, for the purposes of making land transactions. In the third chapter I suggested that certain texts edited as capitularies preserved evidence that *leges* might be read by those involved in settling disputes for their material on quite a wide range of subjects, such as marriage, the responsibility of children, homicide, and theft. We turn in this chapter to consider the use of *leges* in practice from another angle. The approach is not to search for needles suggestive of reference to *leges* in the haystack of all extant Carolingian charters, but rather to follow a small number of leads suggestive of resonance with and reference to legal texts. These cases involve the only instances in which material from *leges* is incorporated into collections considered and edited as discrete texts: that is, where the *Lex Ribuaria* was used in Regino of Prüm's *Libri Duo* in the context of manumission, and where the *Lex Baiuwariorum* was used in Benedictus Levita's collection in the context of compensations for homicide and injury of clerics. We are able in these two cases to situate the quotation of *lex* in a context of the use of other texts, and identify some possible underlying pressures leading to a particular kind of interpretation. We can see something of how the *leges* sat alongside other normative texts, notably capitularies and canons, as possible sources of material for use in arguments at very major fault lines in Carolingian thought: the distinction between clerical and lay status, and between servile and free.

4.1 CLERICAL COMPENSATIONS

4.1.1 Texts and problems

While the earliest redactions of the *Lex Salica* famously do not cover situations involving clerics at all, the question of how to compensate injuries and homicides of churchmen was treated with some variety and detail in the following centuries. A number of normative statements about clerical compensations can be found in the Frankish and sub-Frankish *leges* from the seventh and eighth centuries: *leges Baiuwariorum, Alemannorum,* and *Ribuaria.*[1] In the ninth century normative statements were made about the problems, some of them relatively general, some adding explicitly to *Lex Salica.* The first chapter of Capitulary no. 39, whose most common title is *capitula que in lege salica mittenda sunt* reads[2]:

1. About homicide of clerics. If someone kills a subdeacon, he is to pay 300 *solidi,* a deacon, 400, a priest 600, a bishop 900, a monk 400.[3]

Capitulary no. 139 went on to set levels of fines for injuries of clerics.[4] References outside the texts themselves also mention 'additional capitularies' in the context of just this problem. These are in the letter from Charlemagne to Pippin of Italy edited by Boretius as Capitulary no. 103, and in a passage of the partially forged capitularies of Benedictus Levita, also found excerpted in the 'Rheims group' of Ansegis manuscripts.[5] The Carolingian E and K texts of *Lex Salica* also inserted clerical *wergelds,* in one of the few cases where substantially new material was added in the process of revision.[6]

So normative texts, particularly from the earlier Carolingian period, show a great interest in how clerics are to be compensated. Each text had different answers.[7] Indeed, the penalties not only disagree with each other from text to text, but also, in the case of *Lex Salica* and *Ribuaria,* from redaction to redaction. Strikingly, they vary in these *leges* even from manuscript to manuscript. While there is a certain, minor, fluidity in the exact figures in all subjects covered in the *leges,* this particular subject provoked the most energetic individual modifications of all. Here the texts of the *leges* are far from fossilised.[8]

This modification is very clear in the case of the *Lex Ribuaria* and of the *Lex Alemannorum,* but not in the *Baiuwariorum.* It is difficult to comment in the case of the *Lex Salica* because of the state of its edition. The differences may in part relate to the chronology of the traditions

1 *Leges Alamannorum* ed. K. Lehmann 2nd edition (Hannover, 1966), MGH Leges nationum Germanicarum V, 1, pp. 76–8 XI-XV; *Lex Ribuaria* pp. 93–4 c.40,5–9. *Lex Bav* I, 8–10 pp. 278–83.

2 On this capitulary and its titles see Chapter 3, section 3.3.1 above.

3 MGH Capit. I no. 39 p. 113 c.1: *De homicidii clericorum. Si quis subdiaconum occiderit, CCC solidos conponat; qui diaconum, CCCC; qui presbiterum, DC; qui episcopum DCCCC solidos componat; qui monachum, CCCC solidis culpabilis iudicetur.*

4 MGH Capit. I p. 281 no. 139 p. 281 c.2.

5 Texts B and H in Chapter 3, section 3.2.3 above.

6 *Lex Salica* Vol. 1 p. 209 K LVIII, 2–4.

7 Patzold discusses some of the differences in Patzold (2005), 'Veränderung', pp. 79–80.

8 See the apparatus in each of the texts. References as for note 1.

of each text: we have seen that the Bavarian *lex* has an unusually late transmission, and the Ribuarian and Alemannic *leges* unusually early transmissions. Indeed we can provisionally date the bulk of the modifications to the earlier ninth century or before. In *Lex Ribuaria*, a greater variety is found in the A tradition than the B, and a greater proportion of A texts than B are extant from the early ninth century. Indeed, the tradition of *Lex Ribuaria* as a whole is also weighted slightly towards the first half of the ninth century, with sixteen (43 per cent) earlier ninth century against fourteen later (37 per cent).[9] The early ninth-century manuscript Vat. Reg. Lat. 991, described in more detail below, shows in a different way very clear signs of having been read for what it says about clerical compensations.[10] It contains many *Nota* monograms in the margins, the bulk of them in the *Epitome Aegidii*, but a number next to the barbarian *leges*, and most of them for passages concerning the injury or homicide of clerics, or homicide conducted within churches.[11] The monograms are, of course, not easy to date, especially from microfilm, but are possibly ninth-century. Despite some uncertainties and exceptions, then, the pattern, both in compilation of new texts and in the modification of older *leges*, is that the later eighth and earlier ninth centuries saw a particularly energetic engagement with the problem of how to compensate for injuries and homicides of churchmen.

There are differences between the texts' approaches, and between the kinds of modification made to existing texts. On close reading, the texts that refer to additional capitularies are initially puzzling. The MGH editors attributed Charlemagne's reference to *capitula quae in lege scribi iussimus* in his letter to Pippin to just that passage of Capitulary no. 39 quoted above.[12] But the content of the letter actually shows a very different approach to the problem. Capitulary no. 39 defines compensations for the homicide of each grade of cleric according to the grade: a bishop has a different compensation from a subdeacon, and so on. The letter, on the other hand, imagines that compensation would

9 Very early A manuscripts include München Lat. 4115, BN Lat. 4404, and BN Lat. 4629 from close to the turn of the century.

10 Chapter 5, section 5.1.5 below.

11 The Notas in the *Epitome* are extremely interesting but must be considered in future work. Notas next to *Lex Salica*: 25r: does not concern the subject in question, but does mark a passage of the K text not found in earlier redactions: *Hanc quoque legem et de uitibus furatis obseruari iussimus*..., see *Lex Salica* Vol. 1 p. 43; 46v is also not directly related to theme: *Si quis corpus hominis mortui...expoliauerit*...; 47r: *Si quis ecclesiam incenderit... Si quis diaconem interfecerit...Si quis presbyterum interfecerit*; *Lex Al*: 56r: *Si quis liber liberum infra ianuas ecclesiae occiderit*...; 58r X2: *Si quis episcopo aliquam iniuriam fecerit*..., *Si quis presbyterum parrochianum iniurauerit*...; *Lex Bav*: 75v X2: *Diaconum uero cum cc solid. soluat*..., *Si quis episcopum quem constituit rex uel populus elegit sibi pontificem occiderit*...

12 Text B, Chapter 3, section 3.2.3 above.

be some multiple of what it would have been had the cleric been a layman, determined by his social status from birth:

So concerning priests it seems to us that if one was born free, he is to be compensated with a triple compensation according to his *lex*; and if he is wounded, according to the nature and extent of the wounds or disciplinings[13] he is to be given a triple compensation by him who committed the deed. If however he was born a *servus*, he is to be given a triple compensation according to his *nativitas* in wounds and disciplinings. And concerning deacons may it be the same.[14]

Perhaps the letter was referring to a lost text, but the essential point is that Charlemagne's letter and his Capitulary no. 39 have very distinct ways of approaching the relationship between clerical and social status for the purpose of calculating compensations.

The two approaches could, however, be combined within individual texts and manuscripts, and there were various attempts in the ninth century to find new solutions, and ways of reconciling the variety. The *Lex Baiuwariorum* uses a mixture of the two approaches, as does the collection of Benedictus Levita, examined in more detail below. Indeed, Benedictus uses the *Lex Baiuwariorum* heavily, even though he altered almost all of the figures set out in it. Similarly in the *Lex Ribuaria*, the approach is basically that of 'fixed grade penalties', even though the manuscripts offer little agreement as to what those penalties are. But a major alternative reading can be found in c.40,5 in the revised Carolingian B text: for the low status *clericus*, a payment simply according to status by birth is supplied.[15] In one manuscript, the earliest *Lex Ribuaria* codex, München Lat. 4115, a correcting hand from the beginning of the ninth century has scrubbed out the A reading of c.40,5 and replaced it with the B, having to spill into the margins to do so.[16]

So the production of new texts, the revision of old texts, and the recombination of texts in collections and manuscripts all show a

[13] To what *disciplina* refers in this context is obscure.

[14] MGH Capit. I no. 103 p. 212: *Verumtamen de presbiteris videtur nobis, si liber natus est, per triplam compositionem secundum suam legem fiat compositus; et si plagatus fuerit, secundum qualitatem vel quantitatem plagarum vel disciplinae tripla compositione emendetur ab eo qui hoc perpetraverit. Si autem presbiter servus natus fuit, secundum illius nativitatem tripla compositione solvatur in plagis et disciplinis. Et de diaconibus similiter fiat.* Admittedly the wording is open to interpretation. It seems to me that the half sentence before *et si plagatus fuerit* does refer to homicide: it is not clear to what else it could refer, but it does not mention homicide directly.

[15] It is not quite clear what a *clericus* was here. The best guide to clerical status seems to be Hrabanus Maurus, *De institutione clericorum libri tres* ed. D. Zimpel (Frankfurt am Main, 1996), Freiburger Beiträge zur Mittelalterlichen Geschichte 7. There is a certain flexibility in many descriptions of status at a higher level: Hincmar and Ebbo are frequently referred to as bishop or archbishop interchangeably in the sources for periods when they were both archbishop. On deacons, see R. Reynolds, 'An early medieval tract on the diaconate' *Harvard Theological Review*, 72 (1979), pp. 97–100. And in general R. Reynolds, *Clerical orders in the early Middle Ages: duties and ordination* (Aldershot, 1999).

[16] R. Buchner, *Textkritische Untersuchungen zur Lex Ribuaria* (Stuttgart, 1952), p. 226.

significant and varied interest in and response to the question of how injuries and homicides of clerics should be compensated.

4.1.2 *Homicide of clerics in descriptive sources*

How then does this activity in the normative texts relate to our descriptive evidence for compensations for clerics? Unfortunately, homicide of clerics and the procedures for punishing them have proved extremely difficult to find in descriptive sources of the Carolingian period. Only one royal charter mentions the compensation due from the homicide of a cleric.[17] It is a grant by Lothar to Prüm from 854, waiving the *leudes* incurred from the homicide of a certain Gozelmus in the *villa* of Awans, which he had granted to Prüm the same year.[18] This *leudes* was due to be paid by the *homines nostri fisci* in that *villa*, and it seems that ensuring the payment of the fine would, after the grant, have been the responsibility of Eigil, abbot of Prüm.[19] The charter provides significant evidence on the ways in which Lothar might have gone about extracting fines, and what fines he felt entitled to, something we can so rarely see in descriptive sources. It also shows how crippling the burden of a homicide fine could be on a whole community. But above all it shows again how common problems only impinge on our documents when they happened to have a bearing on cases in which a church won or gained confirmation of lands or rights. Here we are unusually lucky that an outstanding debt was repackaged in a way that made it into an object of a grant. It should not necessarily surprise us that we do not have better descriptive evidence here, but it is, yet again, somewhat frustrating.

4.1.3 *Anxiety over status at low social levels*

However, a context for the interest in our normative texts and manuscripts in how to compensate for clerics can be traced, because other Carolingian texts show anxiety over the conflict between clerical status and social status. In the capitularies and canons, we can see a clear concern with the status of *servi* who were made clerics. The central text is Capitulary no. 138 c.6 from 818–19, which refers to the *canones* to argue that a *vilis persona* should not be engaged in sacerdotal office, and that *servi* should be freed, if it was necessary to make them clerics.[20] This

17 *Die Urkunden Lothars I und Lothars II* ed. T. Schieffer (Berlin, 1966), MGH Diplomatum Karolinorum III, p. 295 no. 132.

18 Ibid., p. 293 no. 131.

19 On this notion of collective action on a village level, see Wickham (2005), *Framing*, p. 396.

20 MGH Capit. I no. 138 c.6 pp. 276–7: *quia iuxta sacros canones vilis persona manens sacerdotii dignitate fundi non potest.* For the canon referred to, see section 4.2.2 below. The essential article is Schmitz (1990), 'Capitulary legislation', pp. 425–36.

chapter sometimes circulated independently of the rest of the capitulary, attached to Capitulary no. 140. It is also discussed in a letter from Louis the Pious to archbishop Hetti of Trier, which is also extant in a version for Adalramm of Salzburg, and one for Bernowin of Besançon.[21] Various other canonical texts and excerpts show an interest in the problem.[22]

The reason given in Louis the Pious's letter was that not just *servi* but other *viles* individuals had entered sacred orders, explicitly 'desiring to abolish them'. The practice of allowing them to do this was a *prava et valde reprehensibilis consuetudo.*[23] Schmitz argued that underlying this was a conflict of interest between the bishop and the landowner in appointments of clerics in 'proprietary churches', and certainly the relative social statuses of the proprietor, his clergy, the congregation, and the relationships between them could have a great impact on the work of the church and on local power dynamics in a wider sense.[24] I suggest in the next case study that competition over social control of priests was actually not restricted to one side of the free-servile divide, and that the precise circumstances of manumission could affect the continued relationships and duties of the manumitted. But the immediate point is that the position of servile priests was a subject of some interest.

Some of the adjustments in the legal texts, therefore, might be seen as attempts to uphold particular understandings of what happened when individuals of low status entered clerical ranks. An example is the peculiar pattern in the *Lex Ribuaria* B text, where there is a movement

21 See MGH Capit. I p. 286. Louis's letter to bishop Hetti of Trier is edited as Capit. no. 173 pp. 355–6, and that to Adalramm of Salzburg in MGH Epp. V pp. 311–12. These letters have a remarkable, early transmission. The letter to Bernowin of Besançon is lost. See T. Sickel, *Acta regum et imperatorum Karolinorum, 2. Teil: Regesten der Urkunden der ersten Karolinger (751–840)* (Vienna, 1867), pp. 321–2.

22 So *Statuta Rhispacensia, Frisingensia, Salisburgensia* (799–800), MGH Conc. II, 1 pp. 205–13, p. 211 c.31: *Ut nemo presumat servum alterius ministrum ecclesiae constituere vel benedicere, antequam a domino suo tradatur in manus pontificis in libertate integra persistendum omnibus diebus; et sciat dominus eius post illum diem nullo dominationis iure in eum exercere. Et tunc, si dignum est, ad sacrum ordinem accedat.* The anxiety is that a master should not have control over the priest, also displayed in MGH Capit. I p. 55 no. 22 c.23: *ut nec monachus nec clericus in secularia negotia transeat. Et ut servum alterius nullus sollicitet ad clericalem vel monachicum ordinem sine voluntate et licentia domini sui.* See also the passage of *Epitome Iuliani* incorporated into the Rheims group Ansegis manuscripts: *Epit. Iul.* CXV, 454, cited in *Ansegis* pp. 269 and 444: *Si seruus sciente et non contradicente domino in clero sortitus sit, ex hoc ipso liber et ingenuus fiat. Si enim ignorante domino consecratio facta fuerit, liceat domino intra annum tantum condicionem probare, et proprium seruum recipere. Sin autem seruus sciente uel ignorante domino secundum ea, quae diximus, ex ipso honore clericatus libertatem meritus, postea ecclesiasticum ministerium reliquerit, et ad laicorum uitam transierit, domino suo in seruitio tradatur.*

23 MGH Capit. I no. 173 p. 356: *consuetudinem pravam et valde reprehensibilem qua usque in praesens viles quaeque et servili condicione obligate personae ad presbyteratus ordinem passim admittebantur abolere cupientes...*

24 Schmitz (1990), 'Capitulary legislation', pp. 429–30. On all aspects of the history of the proprietary church see S. Wood, *The proprietary Church in the Medieval West* (Oxford, 2006).

away from compensations based solely on the clerical rank, but only for those of lowest status. The first rung of ecclesiastical status, and the first rung only, was to have no increased *wergeld* from that of the birth status of the cleric: a *servus* who became a *clericus* would keep his *wergeld* of 36 *solidi*, not triple it to 100. This would clearly have lessened the effect of ordination on the status of a *servus*.

The complexities of adjustment might, however, have been related to other, locally specific understandings of clerical status. It is not easy to penetrate conceptions of status of the lower clerical orders, but Carine van Rhijn's recent reading of the *Capitula Episcoporum* has presented intriguing possibilities. She suggested that priests could be quite wealthy, and could behave much as we might expect from a social elite, and even that they sometimes acted together to protect their interests as a group against, for example, the demands of a bishop.[25] Priests are by no means of the lowest status in the compensation lists, so perhaps some of the variation might even be explained by priests acting together to protect their own interests by keeping low the status of those newly ordained.

It is not possible to demonstrate links any more specifically than this, nor can a specific link be proposed between the reading of a text and the application of a penalty. The most important point is simply that those caught up in trying to understand social and clerical status at a fairly local level may well have turned to texts of the *leges* in search of answers. In a certain sense, then, we can see that the *leges* were important here less for their bearing on ethnic identity than problems associated with other kinds of status.

4.1.4 Ebbo and anxiety over status at high social levels

We can also detect an anxiety in ninth-century texts about a clash between ecclesiastical and social status at higher levels, and can tentatively map this side of the clash more specifically to legal texts.

The key source is Thegan's *Gesta Hludovici*, one of the two biographies of emperor Louis the Pious to have survived, compiled probably in the period 835–8, so when the emperor was still alive.[26] In Thegan's analysis, the disturbances and rebellions of Louis the Pious's reign all stemmed from the evil influence of Ebbo, Archbishop of Rheims, who was of unfree birth. Although apparently loyal in the 830 rebellion, Ebbo was involved in some way with the 833–4 rebellion against Louis the Pious,

[25] van Rhijn (2006), 'Priests', pp. 219–38. For the view that priests were generally poorer, see for example J. L. Nelson, 'Making ends meet: wealth and poverty in the Carolingian church' in: Nelson (1996), *The Frankish World*, pp. 145–53.

[26] On dating see *Thegan, Astronomus* p. 6.

and in his public penance.[27] While other texts, such as the annals of St Bertin, shared Thegan's view that Ebbo was the evil genius behind the whole affair, Thegan's diatribe against Ebbo was by far the most bitter to have survived, and it centred on his social status.[28] He famously claimed that Louis had made Ebbo free, 'but not noble, since that is impossible', and, more importantly here, blamed his poor moral character entirely on the fact that he had a clerical status vastly higher than his social status.[29] Thus the central political crisis of the 830s is blamed entirely on a failure to understand and respect social structure.

There is evidence for an alternative, more positive way of remembering Ebbo, although the relevant texts do not directly mention his canonical or social status. The Astronomer notes that he was rebellious, but with far less vitriol than Thegan.[30] More important still is the mention in the Annals of Xanten and the revised *ARF* of Ebbo's earlier career in the 820s as a missionary in the North.[31] And there was certainly very good reason in the 840s and in fact into the 860s to remember Ebbo and his role in the politics of the 830s, which could have kept these differing views relevant. The context is Ebbo's continued claim that his deposition had been uncanonical, and Lothar's support for it until 846, followed by the continuing controversy over the status of the priests Ebbo had ordained during his brief restoration to the archbishopric of Rheims in 840–1. Hincmar, archbishop of Rheims from 845, had deposed them, but the canonical validity of this action was contested over the next two decades. The problem of Ebbo and his *canonical* status, then, did not go away.

The case of Ebbo has been central to wider discussions of social mobility in the Carolingian period, because there are really no other surviving records of social journeys as spectacular as his. Arguments about the extent of social mobility at high levels in Carolingian society are therefore necessarily indirect, and have led to widely varying conclusions.[32] Stuart Airlie has shown, however, that there was at least a

27 This account is largely based on that in P. McKeon, 'Archbishop Ebbo of Rheims (816–835)' *Church History*, *43* (1974), pp. 437–47 and S. Airlie, 'Bonds of power and bonds of association in the court circle of Louis the Pious' in: Godman and Collins (1990), *Charlemagne's heir*, pp. 191–204. On the public penance see M. de Jong, 'Power and humility in Carolingian society: the public penance of Louis the Pious' *EME*, *1* (1992), pp. 29–52.

28 For example *Annales Bertiniani* pp. 7–11.

29 *Thegan* pp. 232–8 c.44: *fecit te liberum, non nobilem, quod impossibile est.* Translated in P. E. Dutton (ed.), *Carolingian civilization: a reader* (Peterborough, 1993), pp. 170–2.

30 *Astronomus* p. 500f. c.54. Trans. in *Son of Charlemagne; a contemporary life of Louis the Pious* trans. A. Cabaniss (Syracuse, 1961), p. 106.

31 *ARF* p. 163 for 823; *Annales Xantenses* p. 6 for 823. On Ebbo's mission see also J. Palmer, 'Rimbert's Vita Anskarii and Scandinavian mission in the ninth century' *Journal of Ecclesiastical History*, 55 (2004), pp. 235–56 and his references.

32 So K. F. Werner, 'Important noble families in the Kingdom of Charlemagne' in: T. Reuter (ed.), *The medieval nobility: studies on the ruling classes of France and Germany from the sixth to the*

wide spectrum of opinion about what the case *ought* to be. He pointed to the works of Walahfrid Strabo, including his preface to his revision of Thegan's *Gesta*, and of Agobard of Lyons, where an alternative, more positive view of social mobility is found to that provided by Thegan.

For our purposes, broad arguments over social mobility at higher social levels are certainly relevant as a context for the interest in and manipulation of texts concerning the compensation of different grades of cleric. But the specific case of Ebbo, and the specific intensification of debate concerning his career in the texts of the 830s and 840s, may also be more directly relevant to the treatment of the problem in the work of Benedictus Levita.

4.1.5 Benedictus Levita

The nature of the text

The capitulary collection of Benedictus Levita, which purported to collect secular and ecclesiastical capitularies of Charlemagne and Louis the Pious, as a continuation of the work of Ansegis in the 820s, is generally associated with the forged Pseudo-Isidorian Decretals that appeared in the mid-ninth century. Dating and locating any of the forgeries and attributing them to an author has proved a grisly task, so the relationship between the texts as a cluster and their relative chronology is still unclear.

Uncovering a set of agendas for the Pseudo-Isidorian Decretals is a little easier. They clearly presented a view hostile to those who deposed Ebbo in 835. Everything in the text, from the style of the invocation in the first line, to the views on deposition and chorbishops points to an authorship in the party of opposition to Louis the Pious.[33] Ebbo himself has often been seen as the author of the decretals, but Zechiel-Eckes convincingly argued that it was constructed in the later 830s in Corbie, possibly by Paschasius Radbertus.[34]

twelfth century (Amsterdam, 1979), pp. 137–202 takes a minimal view of the possibility, arguing that opportunities for advancement were even more limited under the Carolingians than the Merovingians: 'In general one may say that the Carolingians, even in the period of their greatest power, were much more closely restricted than the early and powerful Merovingians in the choice of their helpers to men of noble birth, and, as we have seen, to men of suitable grade and rank'. Airlie (1990), 'Bonds of Power', pp. 191–204 is not so convinced.

33 This has certainly been clear since Seckel's work. See for example E. Seckel, 'Pseudo-Isidorian Decretals and other forgeries' in: *The New Schaff-Herzog Encyclopedia of Religious Knowledge* (London, 1911), pp. 343–9; E. Seckel, *Die erste Zeile Pseudoisidors, die Hadriana-Rezension: In nomine domini incipit praefatio libri huius, und die Geschichte der Invokationen in den Rechtsquellen* (Berlin, 1959), Sitzungsberichte der Deutschen Akademie der Wissenschaften zu Berlin, Klasse für Philosophie, Geschichte, Staats-, Rechts- und Wirtschaftswissenschaften 4.

34 H. Fuhrmann, 'The Pseudo-Isidorian Forgeries' in: D. Jasper and H. Fuhrmann (eds.), *Papal letters in the early Middle Ages, History of medieval canon law* (Washington, DC, 2001), pp. 137–95;

Still, Benedictus Levita's relationship with the Pseudo-Isidore material is not easy to characterise. His work cannot have been completed in full before 847 because of its reference to Otgar of Mainz, so it is possibly removed from the Pseudo-Isidore by more than a decade. Even identifying clear agendas from it on the themes of the Pseudo-Isidore is difficult: it is far more internally contradictory on central themes such as the status of metropolitans and chorbishops. Its early reception in the *capitula episcoporum* of Isaac of Langres and Herard of Tours was also in a context far removed from the kinds of dispute that provoked extensive use of Pseudo-Isidore, notably the disputes between the Hincmars.[35] But it still seems perfectly plausible to link the compilation of Benedictus's capitularies with an interest that exonerated Lothar and Ebbo from wrongdoing in 835: this was still very much a theme in the political machinations between the three sons of Louis the Pious in the 840s, and of course Ebbo only seems to have given up his claim to Rheims in 846. Recently McKitterick has noted the inclusion of material at the very beginning of the collection concentrating on the church reform of the mid-eighth century, with collaboration between the Carolingians and the papacy a clear theme.[36] This might even fit into the more immediate context of Lothar's manipulation of relations in the 840s with the new pope Sergius II, elected in 844, and his attempt to have him restore Ebbo. The alignment of this specific interest was, however, broken in 846, after an apparent falling out between Ebbo and Lothar, and Louis the German's grant to Ebbo of the bishopric of Hildesheim in that year.[37] In short then, there is vast scope for the text to represent a particular political viewpoint related to that of the Pseudo-Isidore in the late 830s, but reacting to slightly different conditions, but it is very difficult to be sure of anything. We may not be able to identify the attitude to Ebbo with any precision, but his possible relevance is worth considering as background to the following discussion.

K. Zechiel-Eckes, 'Auf Pseudisidors Spur. Oder: Versuch, einen dichten Schleier zu lüften' in: W. Hartmann and G. Schmitz (eds.), *Fortschritt durch Fälschungen?: Ursprung, Gestalt und Wirkungen der pseudoisidorischen Fälschungen* (Hannover, 2002), MGH Studien und Texte 31, pp. 1–28. Also K. Zechiel-Eckes, 'Ein Blick in Pseudoisidors Werkstatt. Studien zum Entstehungsprozeß der falschen Dekretalen' *Francia, 28* (2001), pp. 37–90 and J. Fried, *Donation of Constantine and Constitutum Constantini: the misinterpretation of a fiction and its original meaning* (Berlin, 2007), Millennium-Studien 3.

35 These points have been made most clearly in G. Schmitz, 'Die allmähliche Verfertigung der Gedanken beim Fälchen. Unausorgenes und Widersprüchliches bei Benedictus Levita' in: Hartmann and Schmitz (2002), *Fortschritt durch Fälschungen?*, pp. 29–60.

36 R. McKitterick, 'History, law and communication with the past in the Carolingian period' *Settimane, 52* (2005), pp. 941–79.

37 See McKeon (1974), 'Archbishop Ebbo', pp. 445–7.

Benedictus and clerical compensations

On the problem of clerical compensations Benedictus repeats additional capitulary texts accurately, adds unique material, and quotes the relevant chapters of the *Lex Baiuwariorum* in heavily modified form. The result seems intended to provide a unified answer to the problem of compensation, both for injury and for homicide, with a more comprehensive scope than any other Frankish legal text. As we can see in Table 4.1, Benedictus's is the only extant text in which every penalty for every grade can be found.

But at this stage, what should we make of the fact that the text was at least partially forged? It is not clear how categories of 'genuine' and 'forged' are directly applicable as opposites in early medieval legal texts.[38] A 'legitimate' text was not necessarily a royal text, even in a collection that purported to collect the capitularies of particular rulers. Ansegis's collection already included excerpts of Roman law as chapters of Louis the Pious's capitularies. Was this material 'genuine'?[39] In general, as we have seen with the additional capitularies, not all texts that made their way into legal manuscripts need be associated with royal promulgation. Bishops issued their own capitularies, the *Capitula Episcoporum*, and we have suggested that some of the minor *leges* might have been produced much further from a court context than often imagined. We have also seen how very many manuscripts of the *leges* modified the penalties for homicide of clerics. Benedictus's treatment of the *Lex Baiuwariorum* does not go beyond such level of manipulation, and Regino's treatment of *Lex Ribuaria* in his *Libri Duo*, not normally considered a work of forgery in quite the same sense as Benedictus's work, shows more extreme selective quotation.[40] In any case, Seckel thought that about 70 per cent of Benedict's texts were genuine, and Mordek has recently argued that some texts Seckel saw as forgeries should be seen as royal capitularies.[41] I shall treat Benedictus's modifications, therefore, as on a spectrum of flexible engagement with *leges*.

Benedictus's sources for these penalties are Capitulary no. 39 and *Lex Baiuwariorum*, and in all cases but one, the compensation for a *subdiaconus*, the contradictions between the two texts have been avoided by selective quotation. This always meant following the text of the capitulary, indeed in accordance with the passages of Benedictus's text already seen, which insist that homicides be settled *iuxta statuta priorum capitulorum quae Legi*

38 In addition to work already cited, see the articles in D. Jasper (ed.), *Fälschungen im Mittelalter* (Hannover, 1988), MGH Schriften.

39 See Schmitz (1990), 'Capitulary legislation', pp. 425f.

40 See section 4.2.2 below.

41 See Mordek (1995), *Bibliotheca*, p. 1023.

Table 4.1 *Summary (and simplification) of penalties for homicide of clerics in various legal texts*

		Sal E/K	*Rib*	*Al*	Capit. 39	Capit. 103	*Bav*	Capit. 139	*Ben Lev*
subdiaconus	hom		200		300		x2		x2 or 300
	inj						x2	x3	x3
diaconus	hom	300	300	300	400	x3	?400		400
	inj			x2		x3	x3	x3	x4
presbyter	hom	600	600	600	600	x3	300		600
	inj			x3		x3	x3	x3	x4
episcopus	hom	900		like *dux*	900		a lot		900
	inj			x3 / like *dux*				(x3)	x4
monachus	hom			300	400		x2		400
	inj			x2			x2		x1
'clericus'	hom		100 or x1	x1$\frac{1}{3}$			x1		x1
	inj			x1 or x2			x1		x1

Note: 'x3' and so on means that the penalties are three times the compensation according to original, pre-clerical, social status. 'hom' and 'inj' refer to penalties for homicide and injury. 'A lot' refers to a complex procedure involving weighing out gold according to the weight of a lead cloak made for the dead bishop. These are figures from the *Urtext* only, so do not take full account of very extensive differences between redactions and manuscripts.

Salicae sunt addita. The *Lex* text here is used when it provides answers not covered by the capitularies.

The use of the Bavarian *Lex* in material probably compiled far outside Bavaria is noteworthy, but need not be a problem unless we stick to legal personality (and its counterpart, territoriality) as determining the sphere of applicability of each *lex*. Benedictus was not alone in using Bavarian material outside a Bavarian context. We have already noted the influence of the text on *Ewa ad Amorem*. Other examples include the tenth-century BN Lat. 4995, which preserves one chapter of each of *Lex Alemannorum* and *Baiuwariorum* numbered through from a collection of capitularies of Louis the Pious. Equally, München Lat. 19416 from late ninth-century South Bavaria preserves a single chapter of *Lex Ribuaria* between two capitularies. Instead of a cynical forgery, or conscious use of inapplicable text to a political end, this could very easily represent a genuine attempt to find and use authoritative material where the Frankish material failed to provide an answer. *Lex Baiuwariorum* simply had the most comprehensive penalty table of any legal text.

The attempt to make Benedictus's use fit with personal law has led to some contortions in the historiography. Benedictus's version of the *Lex Baiuwariorum* presented some divergences from the *Urtext*, so Brunner suggested that he was working from a proto-*Lex Baiuwariorum*, which might be equated with a lost edict of the Merovingian king Dagobert II.[42] Seckel argued instead that this text might be a special ecclesiastical redaction of the *Lex*, a *Lex Baiuwariorum Canonice Compta*.[43] The source Benedictus used is clearly important, because it would affect both our assessment of whether or not he knew that his material was Bavarian in origin, and our confidence in attributing the differences between Benedictus's text and a *Lex Baiuwariorum Urtext* to conscious modifications by Benedictus himself. In 1927, Krusch argued convincingly that there was no reason that the excerpts could not come from a 'real' *Lex Baiuwariorum* text, and pointed out textual similarities with two distinct groups of manuscripts: Lupus of Ferrières's redaction, and a Bavarian group, represented primarily by the earliest surviving manuscript of the *Lex*, München Univ. Bibl. 8 132.[44] The use of two different texts of *Lex Baiuwariorum* greatly increases the likelihood that Benedictus knew the origin of the text. More recently, Schmitz has

[42] H. Brunner, 'Über ein verschollenes merowingisches Königsgesetz des 7. Jahrhunderts' *Sitzungsberichte der Preussischen Akademie der Wissenschaften*, *39* (1901), pp. 932–55.

[43] E. Seckel, 'Studien zu Benedictus Levita II-V' *Neues Archiv*, *29* (1904), pp. 299, 303 and E. Seckel, 'Studien zu Benedictus Levita VI' *Neues Archiv*, *31* (1906), pp. 104f.

[44] Krusch (1927), *Neue Forschungen*, pp. 39f. I was denied access to this manuscript in Munich, but a facsimile is available: *Lex Baiuvariorum. Lichtdruckwiedergabe der Ingolstädter Handschrift des Bayerischen Volksrechts mit Transkription, Textnoten, Übersetzung, Einführung, Literaturübersicht und Glossar* ed. K. Beyerle (Munich, 1926).

readdressed the problem, and concluded from another angle that there was no intermediary collection.[45]

If we accept that Benedictus was using a 'real' *Lex Baiuwariorum*, most of his manipulation is broadly understandable in terms of one of the ends of the Pseudo-Isidore complex, that is, to increase the dignity of all ecclesiastical ranks: the compensations are simply increased. A substantial peculiarity, however, is the lowering of the levels of compensation for injuries of monks. This is puzzling indeed, but could be related to competition over status between episcopal and monastic centres. We might also make something of the fact that the approach grounded in penalities fixed for each clerical rank, regardless of birth, is used whenever it was to be found in a source text: this would, doubtless, have worked to Ebbo's advantage. The 900 *solidus* figure is far in excess of anything a reasonable multiple of the *wergeld* of a freedman would be.

4.1.6 Summary

The central point is that throughout the ninth century, the problem of clerical *wergelds* produced a varied and significant textual response. This often affected the text of *leges* themselves, but also capitularies identified as explicitly 'additional', and private collections. There is little unanimity in the texts on how the problem should be solved, or what the details should be within each form of solution. The *leges* here seem to have been consulted, but always alongside other texts. They did not provide the only answer, and certainly do not seem to have been 'applied' in a straightforward sense.

We can tie this engagment to wider debates and anxieties in Carolingian society over the ordination of unfree people and the promotion of those of low birth to high clerical office. The impression from our collections is that texts of the *leges* were pulled in as resources in discussions concerning these themes, and manipulated heavily, in a way that fits very awkwardly their imagined attachment to particular ethnic groups. The *leges* appear as a mine of material of use in discussion of social status, rather than of ethnic status.

4.2 MANUMISSION *FORMULAE AND REGINO OF PRÜM'S LIBRI DUO*

4.2.1 Preliminaries

While the previous case linked manuscripts and compilations with the concerns of high politics, the evidence in this next study allows a more detailed view of the relationship between normative legal sources and

[45] G. Schmitz, 'Benedictus Levita und die Lex Baiuvariorum' *ZRG KA*, 97 (2011), pp. 20–58.

practice. Although in this case too the charters provide only limited help, we are able to use manumission *formulae*.

Manumission is a prominent subject in the *leges*, especially the *Lex Ribuaria*.[46] The *Lex Ribuaria* describes two procedures for manumission, one *secundum legem Ribuariam*, involving a ritual of the 'penny-throw', in which a coin was knocked out of the hand of the manumittee by the manumittor, in the presence of the king, and the other *secundum legem Romanum*, involving written charters, to be performed in church. Tracing the role the *Lex Ribuaria* might have had on the practice of manumission is not directly possible through surviving charters of manumission or *formulae*, because such sources never directly cite the *lex*, nor refer to it. Frustratingly, it is the *Lex Salica* that is often invoked in such sources, although the text of *Lex Salica* itself refers only very briefly to any process of manumission.[47] All the same, Mordek argued that the continued practice of manumission by *Schatzwurf*, that is penny-throw, as attested in charters and *formulae* through the Merovingian, right into the Ottonian period, was attributable to direct reference to the texts of *leges*, and so is one of the best examples of the practical use of normative texts.[48] His suggestion was that references in manumission charters and *formulae* to *Lex Salica* in fact meant references to the *Lex Ribuaria*, because the two texts were so often transmitted together.[49] This argument is plausible enough, but in this chapter I try to do better, to find more specific links between *formulae*, charters, and normative texts, and to uncover their meaning.

4.2.2 Regino

The only direct evidence for the reading of *Lex Ribuaria* in the context of manumission is found in Regino of Prüm's *Libri Duo de synodalibus causis*. Here we find two manumission *formulae*, surrounded by various normative texts concerning manumission, including a passage from the *Lex Ribuaria*. The collection consists of c.400–419 of book I of Regino's work.

The collection was compiled in the very earliest years of the tenth century, so it is necessary to be careful about projecting back understandings derived from his work into the ninth century. There is, however, a plausibile case that Regino found the relevant passages already arranged in a manuscript associated with mid-ninth-century Metz. Staubach's work has shown that Regino had access to a letter collection compiled by Adventius, bishop of Metz (858–75), concerning Lothar

46 Esp. the detailed *Lex Ribuaria* pp. 107–112 c.60–1.

47 *Pactus Legis Salicae* c.26 pp. 96–7.

48 Mordek (2000), 'Leges und Kapitularien', pp. 348–50.

49 See also Nehlsen (1977), 'Aktualität und Effektivität', pp. 476–7.

II's divorce, now preserved in an early modern partial transcription, and suggested Adventius's nephew Bertulf, archbishop of Trier, as a linking figure.[50] The chapters of Regino's *Libri Duo* relevant here also present a connection with Adventius: the manumission *formula* Regino I, 413 is also extant in a transcription from a mid-ninth-century manuscript from Merseburg, now lost, but in this lost manuscript it was filled in with Adventius of Metz's name.[51] It is theoretically possible that Regino used this very manuscript, which also contains a second *formula* found in Regino's collection.[52] But it is also possible that he used a different manuscript containing a fuller dossier on manumission associated with Adventius.

The only text in the collection from after Adventius's death is the passage from the Council of Tribur from 895, but it falls at the end of the collection and could have been tacked on. Of the other texts of known provenance, the latest is from the council of Meaux-Paris 845–6, so there is no strong case against the existence of a pre-existing dossier on the basis of the dating or nature of the texts used. Still, if Regino was drawing on an earlier compilation, it is clear that he adapted it himself at least superficially. For example, the reference to St Peter in the other manumission *formula* (Regino I, 414) in Regino's collection suggests association with the Cathedral at Trier, where Regino worked.

The origins of the collection matter because the arrangement of the normative texts, and their specific relationships with the *formulae*, turn out to be extremely interesting. I suggest that there are strong hints that one of the *formulae* was adapted, put into its current form, with direct and specific reference to normative texts, and that the collection as we have it reflects, at least indirectly, the process by which the *formula* was adapted.

Preliminary textual work: the capitularies and *Lex Ribuaria* in the *Libri Duo*

The most obvious way to investigate the origins of the collection is meticulous text-critical study to try to determine the likely relationships between texts. Some of the chapters preserve material not found in other places, making comparisons impossible, and the state of the editions of

[50] N. Staubach, *Das Herrscherbild Karls des Kahlen. Formen und Funktionen monarchischer Repräsentationen im früheren Mittelalter* (Münster, 1982), pp. 153–66.

[51] On this manuscript, Merseburg BDS 100, which also contains the *Dacheriana* collection of canons, see L. Kéry, *Canonical collections of the early Middle Ages (ca. 400–1140) : a bibliographical guide to the manuscripts and literature* (Washington, DC, 1999), p. 89. A collation made by W. Holzmann can be found at www.mgh-bibliothek.de/Merseburg/hsc5.htm last viewed 5 August 2014.

[52] MGH Form. p. 563 edited as *Form. Extr.* II, 20.

the pre-Carolingian canons makes comparisons next to impossible for them too.[53] But we can investigate the texts of the capitularies and of the *Lex Ribuaria.*

Schmitz has showed that the text of Ansegis's collection used by Regino was related to the twin manuscripts Vat. Pal. Lat. 582 and BN Lat. 9654.[54] Indeed, we find that the readings in the capitularies used in this part of Regino's collection do sometimes agree with particular readings in these manuscripts. The omission of *vero* in I, 408, and the ordering of *dominis propriis* in I, 409 are examples.[55] The text of the council of Meaux-Paris also corresponds well with the Vatican Paris twins.[56] But Regino's Ansegis text also has a notable number of distinctive readings, unparallelled in other manuscripts, including the Paris and Vatican twins, such as *ignotum sit* for *ignoraverit.* And it also has one very distinctive reading, *abstrahere*, which is found in just three other manuscripts. Two of them are from the twelfth century, and one from the tenth, which has been localised to East France, even possibly to Metz or its surroundings.[57] It seems possible that some of the Ansegis text in this section was derived from manuscripts not normally used by Regino, and possibly one of them was associated with Metz. It could be, then, that the chapters covering manumission in Regino's collection were found by him already collected by a compiler with access to Metz manuscripts.

In the case of the *Lex Ribuaria* there turn out to be too many unknowns to make firm conclusions, but the results for the text are worth relating in any case because of their wider relevance to its textual history.[58] Regino either edited the *Lex Ribuaria* substantially, or he had access to a source already heavily edited, or possibly even an early version of *Lex Ribuaria*, an otherwise lost textual strand, even a *Lex Ribuaria Canonice Compta* of the sort proposed by Seckel in the case of the use of *Lex Baiuwariorum* in Benedictus Levita's collection.[59] Here is the relevant extract of Regino's collection, compared with the *Lex Ribuaria* B text:

53 On the unknown material see W. Hartmann, 'Die Capita incerta im Sendhandbuch Reginos von Prüm' in: O. Münsch and T. Zotz (eds.), *Scientia veritatis: Festschrift für Hubert Mordek zum 65. Geburtstag* (Ostfildern, 2004), pp. 207–26.

54 G. Schmitz, 'Ansegis und Regino. Die Rezeption der Kapitularien in den Libri duo de synodalibus causis' *ZRG KA*, *74* (1988), pp. 95–132.

55 Text in *Ansegis* pp. 483–5 and 480.

56 MGH Conc. III p. 109.

57 *Ansegis* pp. 483–4 and 480. The manuscripts are Berlin Phil. 1737 ($x^{2/2}$, East France, ?Metz) see *Ansegis* pp. 81–2; Bonn S402 (xii, Rhineland); Schaffhausen Min 75 ($xii^{2/2}$, SW Germany).

58 The text was not considered by Buchner in his edition or Buchner (1952), *Textkritische Untersuchungen*.

59 For references and comment see section 4.1.5 above.

Lex Ribuaria B c.61	Regino, *Libri Duo* I, 417
1. *Hoc etiam iubemus, ut qualiscumque francus Ribvarius* seu tabularius *servum suum pro animae suae remedio*[a] seu pro pretio[b] *secundum legem Romanam libertare*[c] *voluerit, ut*[d] *in ecclesia coram presbyteris*[e] *diaconibus seu cuncto clero et plebe in manu episcopi servum*[f] *cum tabulis*[g] *tradat, et episcopus archidiaconum*[h] *iubeat, ut ei tabulas secundum legem Romanam, qua*[i] *ecclesia vivit*[j]*, scribere*[k] *faciat; et tam ipse quam*[l] *omnis procreatio eius liberi permaneant et sub tuitione ecclesiae consistant vel omne*[m] *reditum status* aut servitum tabularii[n] *eorum ecclesiae reddant.*	*Hoc etiam volumus, ut qualiscunque Francus Ripuarius servum suum pro remedio animae suae secundum legem Romanam liberum facere voluerit, ut in ecclesia coram presbyteris, diaconibus seu cuncto clero et plebe in manu episcopi servum cum tabulis tradat, et episcopus archidiacono iubeat, ut ei tabulas secundum legem Romanam, qua ecclesiae vivunt, scribere faciat, et tam ipse, quam et omnis procreatio eius liberi permaneant et sub tuitione ecclesiae consistant et omnem reditum status sui ad ecclesiam persolvant,*
Et nullus tabularium[o] *denariare ante regem praesumat. Quod si fecerit, duccentos sol culp iud et nihilominus ipse tabularius et procreatio eius tabularii persistant, et omnis reditus status eorum ad ecclesiam reddant;*	
et non aliubi quam ad ecclesiam, ubi relaxati sunt, mallum teneant.	*et non aliubi nisi ad ecclesiam, ubi relaxati sunt, mallum teneat.*
4. *Tabularius autem qui absque liberis discesserit, nullum alium quam ecclesiam relinquat heredem.*	*Et si absque liberis discesserint, nullum alium nisi ecclesiam relinquant heredem.*

[a] *remedium* A [b] *pretium* A [c] *liberare* A [d] *eum* add. A [e] *et* add. A [f] *servo* A [g] *tabulas* A [h] *archidiacono* A [i] *quam* A [j] *ecclesiae vivunt* A5 [k] *conscribere* A [l] *et* add. A [m] *omnem* A [n] *aut serv. tab.* om. A except for A8, 9, 11, 12 [o] *aut servum tabularii* add. A4, 9

Regino's text shows some unparalleled readings, such as *volumus* for *iubemus*, and *liberum facere* for *libertare*. It also displays some clear A readings, such as *quam et omnis procreatio*; otherwise, however, it is closer to Buchner's B text, displayed here as the base text for comparison. Buchner's *Ur*-redactions, however, are only even approximately close to a handful of manuscripts.[60] Many of the B readings found in Regino's text are also present in A5, which also has the single closest parallel with the reading *ecclesiae vivunt*. It appears then that Regino's text, or his source's text, was from Buchner's 'mixed class', with some resonances with A5, which is Wien ÖNB 502, ascribed to South Germany, and from the tenth century.[61]

60 This is described in most detail in Chapter 5, section 5.2.3 below, but we have already seen an example of the problem in München Lat. 4115 in section 4.1.1 above.

61 Mordek (1995), *Bibliotheca*, pp. 907–8.

Otherwise of note is Regino's text's coverage of two points of textual stress, that is, moments where there is particularly significant variation between manuscripts, or where something can be noted about the construction of the texts. The first is the omission of *seu tabularius*, which Buchner, employing Beyerle's work, thought a late interpolation, although it was found in all of his manuscripts.[62] The second is the omission of the phrase *aut servitum tabularii* or similar. This phrase is found in two different places across the manuscripts, suggesting it was derived from a marginal note or gloss. Not all manuscripts have it at all, and A9 has it twice. This pattern could have no meaning at all, but it could possibly be attributed to some features of an early redaction of the text, which avoided incorporation of certain additions that made it into the mainstream manuscript tradition.

If this is right, however, we have a clash with the evidence of the B readings, which suggest, if we follow the conventional dating, a *terminus post quem* of the beginning of the ninth century. The way through is to imagine that the process we find in the tradition, and most clearly in the remarkable Munich manuscript of *Lex Ribuaria*, of updating older texts with reference to B texts, took place somewhere in the back-tradition of this text too, but that only grammatical and orthographical readings were filled in, not the new substantial interpolations.[63]

We simply cannot go any further here with this passage with a view to understanding how Regino manipulated his texts, and what features of Regino's presentation were earlier than Regino.

Forgery, manuipulation, and the unknown texts

What about the nature of the use of texts in the collection? This has been the subject of some controversy among the great textual scholars of Pseudo-Isidore, who approached Regino's work with a view to uncovering what was 'genuine' and what was 'forgery'.[64] Schmitz's advance on his use of capitularies involved identifying Vat. Pal. Lat. 582 and BN Lat. 9654 as related to Regino's exemplar, and slightly modifying the terms in which Regino's alteration of his sources should be seen. For Schmitz, Regino saw himself 'not just as a collector and transmitter, but perhaps just as much a reviser of his sources'.[65] His

62 See *Lex Ribuaria* pp. 160–1, and Beyerle (1935), 'Gesetzbuch Ribuariens', pp. 33–9.

63 References on the status of the text as for note 60.

64 See the review of the work of Seckel, Fuhrmann, Krause, Wasserschleben in Schmitz (1988), 'Ansegis und Regino', pp. 97–102.

65 Schmitz (1988), 'Ansegis und Regino', pp. 129–30: 'Regino erweist sich nicht oder doch nicht nur als Sammler und Überliefer, sondern fast in gleichem Maß als Bearbeiter seines Quellenmaterials, der - wiederum mit vielen Zeitgenossen verglichen - die von ihm behandelte Materie in sehr beachtenswerter Weise beherrschte und strukurierte. Dies trägt seinem Werk ingesamt den Rang einer für die ausgehende Karolingerziet ungewöhnlich selbständigen Arbeit ein'. See also K. Ubl, 'Doppelmoral im karolingischen Kirchenrecht? Ehe und Inzest bei Regino

use showed a flexibility, a willingness to paraphrase and modify his texts, which however did not straightforwardly constitute 'forgery'. Such an approach, I have argued, is crucial to understanding the use and interpretation of *leges* texts in general, particularly with reference to Benedictus Levita.

The treatment of texts here is entirely consistent with this view of Regino's working methods, although of course that does not establish that Regino did not find at least some of the texts already edited. In general the texts are reproduced faithfully, but there is some very selective quotation, especially in the *Lex Ribuaria*. The large lacuna in Regino's text is a portion of the *Lex Ribuaria* that refers to the process of *denariare ante regem* – manumission by penny-throw in the presence of the king. Regino's text, therefore, removes all reference to the king, and to an alternative process of manumission not involving the Church. The only significant modification of text is in the capitulary material derived from Ansegis, and pulls in the same direction. The phrase *coram fidelibus laicis* is replaced with *omni clero*: the manumission and ordination of a slave was to be done in church, but in the presence of 'the priests and all the clergy' rather than by 'the priests and the lay *fideles*'.[66] The role of the laity is minimised.

The material without parallel in other texts further develops this marginalisation of the laity and of kings. It is worth translating in full the passages I term 'commentary', found in chapters 414b, 415, 416. They sit between the manumission *formulae* and the *Lex Ribuaria* citation:

414b

The charters of freedom written above ought to contain not just the name of him who asks for them to be made, but also the names of the priests and lay nobles who were present there, arranged in order with signs written with their own hands: for without their confirmation the bare page is to be considered of no authority. It is also fitting that it have the place, day, year and consul, and indiction written at the end or in the margin in this way ... For the Roman authority says: '*leges* are not to be valid if they are proposed without day and consul'.[67]

von Prüm' in: W. Hartmann (ed.), *Recht und Gericht in Kirche und Welt um 1900* (Munich, 2007), pp. 90–124.

[66] Libri Duo p. 186 :*Et quandocunque de familia ecclesiae utilis inventus aliquis ordinandus est, in ambone ipsa auctoritas coram populo legatur, et coram sacerdotibus et omni clero* (***et coram fidelibus laicis*** *Capit.*)*... libertatem consequatur et tun demum ad gradus ecclesiasticos promoveantur.*

[67] *Libri duo* pp. 188f.: *Debent autem suprascriptae ingenuitatis cartae non solum nomen illius, qui has fieri rogat, sed etiam nomina sacerdotum et nobilium laicorum, qui ibi adfuerunt, in ordine digesta cum signis propria manu impressis continere: nam sine horum adstipulatione pagina auctoritate testium nudata pro nihilo deputatur. Oportet etiam, ut locum, diem, annum et consulem, indictionem, in fine vel in margine adnotatam habeat in hunc modum: Actum illa civitate, in domo sancti Petri, Kalendis illis, anno dominicae incarnationis illo, regnante illo rege, et praesidente in cathedra supradictae civitatis episcopo illo, vel in monasterio illo, indictione illa, in Dei nomine feliciter. Amen. Ait enim Romana auctoritas: Quaecunque leges sine die et consule fuerint prolatae, non valeant.* For interest in consular dating in a different context, see M. Handley, 'Inscribing time and identity in the kingdom of Burgandy' in: S.

415
Moreover the laity are to be instructed, so that they understand that in no way are they able to free their own *servi*, which they have decreed to have been attached to the *castris dominicis*, except in a sacred church in the manner described above.[68]

For how can clerics, who are apart from *lex mundana*, and for whom it is forbidden to go to secular judgement, attain their freedom outside the church, how can they be released from the bond of servitude by secular judgement?

But perhaps someone could say: 'he is not permitted to become a cleric unless he obtain the dignity of freedom before taking up the clerical office'.

In fact he is speaking the truth, and therefore, what can be weakened or nullified, should be guarded against.[69]

416
Not only those who are to be advanced to the order of cleric are to be manumitted in church, but also those whom someone wants to free for the good of his soul ought to be absolved in church according to *lex mundana* and be commended to the *patrocinio* of that church. For it is written in the *Pactus Francorum*:[70]

The message here, despite the obscurity of expression in c.415, is quite clear: the procedures described in the canons and the capitularies used by Regino, and enshrined in his manumission *formulae*, are to be followed not only in cases of *servi* of the church freed for the immediate purpose of being ordained, but to *all* manumissions in *all* situations. There is only one way to manumit *servi*, whatever their original status and whatever the purpose of their manumission, and that is in church by the process described.

The collection as a whole, its chain of authority and its patterns

How then, do the texts fit together, and what is the role of the *Lex Ribuaria*? Regino presents two *formulae*, one after another, the first for the manumission of a *servus* about to be promoted to sacred orders, and the second for a manusmission in unspecified circumstances. Both have strong parallels with similar *formulae* found in other manuscripts.

Mitchell and G. Greatrex (eds.), *Ethnicity and culture in late antiquity* (London, 2000), pp. 83–102 and M. Handley, *Death, society, and culture: inscriptions and epitaphs in Gaul and Spain, AD 300–750* (Oxford, 2003), pp. 129–35.

68 Note *castris dominicis* links the passage with the capitulary and canon above. See section 4.2.3 below.

69 *Instruendi sunt praeterea laici, ut sciant, quod nullatenus alio loco manumittere proprios possunt servos, quos dominicis castris aggregari decreverunt, nisi in sacrosancta ecclesia ordine supra notato. Quomodo enim clerici extra ecclesiam libertatem consequi possunt, qui a lege mundana extranei sunt, et, quibus interdicitur, ne ad seculare iudicium procedant, quomodo seculari iudicio a iugo servitutis absolvuntur? Sed fortasse dicit aliquis: clericus fieri non permittitur, nisi ante susceptum clericatus officium ingenuitatis dignitate potiatur. Revera verum dicit, et ideo, quod infirmari vel vituperari potest, praecaveri debet.* The meaning of the last phrases here seems somewhat obscure.

70 *Non solum autem, qui ad clericatus ordinem promovendi sunt, in ecclesia manumittendi sunt, verum etiam hi, quos quisque pro remedio animae suae emancipari vult, secundum legem mundanam in ecclesia absolvi debent, et eiusdem ecclesiae patrocinio commendari. Scriptum quippe est in Pacto Francorum.*

The *formulae* are surrounded on both sides by normative texts about the manumission of those about to be ordained: not only the relevant passage of *Lex Ribuaria*, but also excerpts from canonical texts, from Louis the Pious's Capitulary no. 138, and a law of Constantine.[71] The relevant excerpts are listed, in order, in Table 4.2. Regino linked his texts explicitly in some cases. First and foremost, the *formula* I, 413 is described as *Exemplar libertatis supra notatum*: '*exemplar* for freedom as described above', while its prologue claims that 'ecclesiastical authority clearly urges, and also royal majesty offers its agreement with canonical religion'[72] that slaves should be freed before they are ordained. The material 'above' is taken accordingly from canonical and capitulary texts. The canons covered prohibitions against ordaining certain kinds of *servi*, such as those belonging to someone else, or those from another parish. The major thrust of the capitulary is to take a single principle that *servi* must be freed before they can be ordained, and work out its implications in practice, for example what to do if someone was ordained and did not know about his servile status at the time.[73] Another crucial aim of the capitulary was to establish clarity over the procedure for a moment in which social relations changed. The perception that a correct procedure was followed, and the importance of the public performance of that procedure, were of central importance in ensuring that a transaction was as difficult as possible to dispute at a later stage.[74] In one sense then, the normative material that preceded the *formulae* provided a context for their use by setting out the situations in which the *formluae* might be used, and elaborating on some points of procedure.

But Regino's texts are also linked still more specifically, and we can identify a chain of reference to authorities. First of all he grouped his texts quite clearly by genre: first canonical material **(1)**, then capitulary material **(2)**, likely to be understood here as in some sense connected with royal-imperial authority, then *formulae* **(3)**, then the connective commentary translated above, not found in other sources, and possibly written by Regino himself **(4)**, finally followed by excerpts of *lex mundana* from the *Lex Ribuaria* – given the title *Pactus Francorum* – and from the *Lex Romana* **(5)**. The impression of careful arrangement is strengthened by the fact that Regino follows cross-references in the texts where they occur, and adds them himself when they are not clear. Thus the capitulary material which refers to the *canones* is prefaced with relevant material from the canons: I, 408 refers quite clearly to

71 All of these are in fact possible sources for the *formula* text, as I suggest in section 4.2.3 below.

72 *Auctoritas ecclesiastica patenter admonet, insuper et maiestas regia canonice religioni assensum praebet*…

73 See *Libri Duo* I, 408 p. 183. For the texts on this principle see section 4.1.3 above.

74 Cf. *Form. Arv.* no. 4: the procedure is definitely to be done *in puplico, nam non in secreto.* On publicity, procedure and legitimacy see Davies and Fouracre (1986), *Settlement of disputes*, pp. 214–28, Innes (2000), *State and society*, pp. 94–5 and earlier references.

Table 4.2 *Sources and cross-references in Regino of Prüm's* Libri Duo *I, 400–19*

		Title	Source	Summary		CrossRef
(1)	400	*De examinatione ante ordinationem.* Ex eodem cap. CXXXVI	Council of Chalcedon	Priests must be examined before they are ordained.		
	401	*De eadem re.* Ex Conc. Meld.	Council of Meaux-Paris (845-6)	Elaborates on this.		
	402	*Ut ordinati litteras accipiant a suis ordinatoribus.* Ex Conc. Af.	Africa (?419)	The ordained must obtain a document confirming their ordination.		
	403	*Ut nullus alterius servum ordinare presumat.* Ex Ep. Leo pap.	Letter of Leo I	No one is to ordain the *servus* of another.		
	404	*De eadem re.* Ex Conc. Mog.	'Council of Mainz' (in fact Orléans 511)	Compensation is due to the master if someone else ordains his *servus.*		
	405	*Ut nullus ministrorum alterius parochiae clericum latenter ad ordinationem subintroducat.* Ex Conc. Nan.	'Concilio Nannetensi' (Unknown)	No one is to ordain someone from another parish. Those with no *dignitas natalium* or *morum*, specifically *servi*, are not to be ordained.	⥣	Chalcedon
	406	*Item de servis ordinandis.* Ex Conc. Tol.	Toledo IV	Distinguishes the rights of those manumitted to be admitted to orders on the basis of what rights their *patronus* reserved at the time of manumission.		

(cont.)

Table 4.2 (*cont.*)

		Title	Source	Summary		CrossRef
(2)	407	*De eadem re*. Ex Capitularibus, tit. LXXXIV	*Ans* I, 84, 2	If laymen present a worthy candidate to a bishop for ordination, he is not to reject him.		
	408	*De eadem re*. Ex Capitularibus, tit. LXXXII	*Ans* I, 82	No bishop is to promote someone to sacred orders, unless he has been given freedom by his master.	⇑	'Sacri canones'
	409	*De peculio servorum*	*Ans* I, 82	The *dominus* is to decide whether the manumitted can keep his property.		
	410	*De peculio ordinatorum*	*Ans* I, 82	But the canons that say that consecrated should own nothing are to be upheld.	⇑	'Canones'
	411	*De ecclesiarum servis*	*Ans* I, 82	Procedure for ordaining a slave of the church found 'useful'.		
	412	*De monasteriorum familiis*	*Ans* I, 82	The same procedure is to be used for candidates put forward by members of the church's wider *familia*.		
(3)	413	*Exemplar libertatis supra notatum*		See above.	⇑	
	414a	*Exemplar libertatis de proprio servo*		,,	⇓	

(4)	414b		Unknown	The *carta ingenuitatis* should contain very full witness lists and details of the time and place of transaction.	(⇓)	'Auctoritas Romana' (*CodTh* I,1,1)
	415	*Quod manumissio in ecclesia debet fieri*. Unde supra	Unknown	All *servi* are to be manumitted in church.		
	416	*De eadem re.* Unde supra	Unknown	Not just those who are to be advanced to orders, but also those freed for the good of someone's soul are to be manumitted in church, according to *lex mundana*.	⇓	'Pactus Francorum' (*Lex Rib*)
(5)	417	*De eadem re.* Ex Pacto	*Lex Ribuaria*	Procedure for manumission in a church, including the drawing up of a document.	⇓	'Lex Romana'
	418	*De eadem re.* Ex lege Romana	*CodTh/LRV*	Those freed in church are to be treated as *cives Romani*.		
	419	*Quod carta libertatis in ambone sit legenda*. Ex Conc. Trib.	Council of Tribur (895)	The manumission documents of ordination candidates are to be read in public from the pulpit.		

I, 403. The canon referred to in I, 410 is found earlier in the work, at I, 220. The *formula* is then described specifically as 'according to the above'. Next, Regino's commentary covers good documentary practice, quoting Roman law directly, before turning to the situations in which documents should be drawn up, arguing from the *lex mundana*. Quotations from *lex mundana* follow, starting with the *Pactus Francorum,* then followed by some *Lex Romana,* to which the *Pactus* had already referred. The cross-references are marked with arrows in Table 4.2.

So Regino provides two parallel chains of authority leading towards and away from the *formulae*. The first is based in the *canones* and mediated through the capitularies, the second is based in *lex mundana* mediated through Regino's own, or someone else's, independently constructed interpretative commentary.

1. Councils ⟹ 2. Capits. ⟹ **3. *Formulae*** ⟸ 4. Commentary ⟸ 5. *Lex*

The *Lex Ribuaria* is associated, then, with Roman law, more than with the canons or the capitularies, but integrated into a wide argument using a rather full range of normative texts. It is associated with the Franks in general, not 'Ribuarians'.

4.2.3 Distinctive terminology, and comparisons with other manumission formulae

Related *formulae*

The evidence for careful arrangement of normative texts and the awareness of links between them, combined with the willingness of the compiler to quote selectively and to modify his texts subtly, encourages us to take a closer look at the text of the *formulae* and their relationship with normative texts. There is in fact good reason to believe that the kind of textual subterfuge we see in Regino's use of the *Lex Ribuaria* and of the capitulary also invaded the texts of the *formulae* on a subtle but important level.

As well as making clear the explicit cross-references, Regino also arranged his texts in a way that highlights some very distinctive shared terminology. Firstly, I, 408 and I, 403 share the phrase *castris dominicis*, which is also repeated in the connective commentary translated above. Secondly, the text of the one of the *formulae* shows some manipulation of other distinctive terminology found also in other manumission *formulae*. Both *formulae* in Regino's collection are very closely related to other *formulae* found in Carolingian manuscripts, and the nature of these relationships needs some investigation before the meaning of the manipulation comes into view. The relevant manuscripts used in Zeumer's edition are:[75]

		MS date	Text date
F. Imp. 33	BN Lat. 2718	ix$^{2/4}$	819-
F. Imp. 35	BN Lat. 2718	ix$^{2/4}$	819/821
F. Imp. Add. 2	Leiden Voss. Lat. O. 92	ix	
F. Extr. I, 16	Unknown/lost		
F. Cod. Laud. 14	BN Lat. 11379	903-930	
F. Sal. Merk. 44	Vat. Reg. Lat. 612	ix/x?	890s?
F. Extr. I, 17	Merseburg, BDS 100	ix$^{3/4}$	858-75

Zeumer already noted a relationship between various manumission *formulae*, and more recently Rio has suggested that the relationship was a result of the diffusion of *formulae* edited as part of the *Formulae Imperiales* collection. The *formulae* from that collection seem to have travelled as single texts, rather than as a coherent group, and the most popular independent traveller was *Formula Imperialis* no. 33, a charter of manumission especially interesting for its relationship with written law.[76] This *formula* and Louis the Pious's Capitulary no. 138 share the distinctive phrase *cornu altaris* in their descriptions of the manumission procedure, and the manuscript of the *Formulae Imperiales* juxtaposes the text of no. 33 with the capitulary, with no break. Both texts are about the manumission of a *servus* about to be promoted to ecclesiastical office. The *formula*, and some of those related to it, also show a further textual influence, that of the *Lex Ribuaria*. The most telling phrase linking the two is *portasque apertas,* although the insistence of the texts that the freed *servi* are to be considered *cives Romani* is also relevant.

The textual resonances can be summarised as follows:

Formulae Imperiales no. 33	Capit. no. 138, c.6
Idcirco in Dei nomine ego ille episcopus illius urbis, vel abbas vel abbatissa illius venerabilis monasterii, quendam ecclesie nostre famulum nomine illum, sacris ordinibus dignum, ad ***altaris cornu,*** *nobilium virorum in praesentia,* ***civem Romanum***	*De ecclesiarum vero servis communi sententia decretum est... et coram sacerdotibus vel coram fidelibus laicis* ***ante cornu altaris,*** *sicut in nostra auctoritate continetur, remota qualibet calliditate, libertatem consequatur et tunc demum ad gradus ecclesiasticos promoveatur.*

[75] The source for these dates is Rio (2009), *Frankish Formulae.*

[76] Rio (2009), *Frankish Formulae*, pp. 110–11 and 162–4.

per hoc auctoritatis testamentum statuo, ita ut ab hodierno die et tempore bene ingenuus atque ab omni servitutis vinculo securus permaneat, tamquam si ab ingenuis fuisset parentibus procreatus vel natus. Eam denique pergat partem, quamcunque volens canonice elegerit, habensque ***portas apertas****, ita ut deinceps nec nobis neque successoribus nostris ullum debeat noxie conditionis sevicium neque aliquo libertinatis obsequium, sed omnibus diebus vitae sue sub certa plenissimaque ingenuitate, sicut alii* ***cives Romani****, per hunc manumissionis atque ingenuitatis titulum bene semper ingenuus atque securus existat.*

Lex Ribuaria c.64,1 *Si quis servum suum libertum fecerit et* ***civem Romanum portasque apertas*** *conscriberit, si sine liberis discesserit, non alium quam fiscum habeat heredem.*

LRV CodTh IV, 7, 1 Int. (Const. I) *Qui manumittendi in sacrosancta ecclesia habuerit voluntatem, tantum est, ut sub praesentia sacerdotum servos suos velit absolvere, noverit eos, suscepta libertate* ***cives esse Romanos****: nam si clerici suis mancipiis dare voluerint libertatem, etiamsi extra conspectum fecerint sacerdotum vel sine scriptura verbis fuerint absoluti, manebit,* ***sicut civibus Romanis****, integra et plena libertas.*

The relevant *formulae* are related to *Form. Imp.* no. 33 to varying degrees. They all share the distinctive terminology already highlighted, and seem to be derived from each other or from common sources. They all survive in manuscripts or collections of the ninth or, at the latest, the early tenth centuries, but most are difficult to date precisely. In just three cases have datings, places or names survived. We have Einhard's text (*Form. Imp.* no. 35) from 819 or 821, for Saint Servatius in Maastricht; the *formula* already mentioned found in Merseburg, BDS 100, which refers to bishop Adventius of Metz (858-75); and another (*Form. Sal. Merk.* no. 44), which refers to an Odo, probably the Odo who became king after the deposition of Charles the Fat in 888.[77] We also have some less direct hints at dating and location in other cases. *Form. Imp.* no. 33 itself has a *terminus post quem* of 819, if we accept that its wording is taken from Capitulary no. 138, which is dated to that year. It survives in a manuscript from the 820s–30s linked with Tours, BN Lat. 2718. Regino was based at Trier when he found something very similar to Adventius's charter at the very beginning of the tenth century. A similar *formula* seems to have been present at Laon in the ninth century, judging from the hand in BN Lat. 11379.[78] As far as we can tell, then, the focus of circulation was temporally the ninth century and spatially Lotharingian, with the exception of Laon, and Tours.

The *formulae* are related in different ways and to different extents. It seems clear that *Form. Imp.* no. 33 was used directly, or nearly so, in two later ninth-century derivatives, of Odo and of Adventius. Odo's *formula* in particular is nearly identical with *Form. Imp.* no. 33. The two have only minor differences in orthography, grammar, and word order: Odo's

77 Rio (2009), *Frankish Formulae*, p. 106.
78 Rio (2009), *Frankish Formulae*, p. 211.

for example is pluralised. The relationship between *Form. Imp.* no. 33 and Einhard's contemporary or near-contemporary charter (*Form. Imp.* no. 35) is rather less clear, since both interpolations and abbreviations of existing texts are possible. *Form. Imp.* no. 35, for example, retains the details of the manumittor, Einhard, and the manumittee: it may well be filled in from *Form. Imp.* no. 33, interpolating both these details and some rather florid extra text, elaborating on no. 33's barer wording. Or the opposite could be true: no. 33 could be a simplified and anonymised version of no. 35. Some of the *formulae* have much more distant relationships with each other and with *Form. Imp.* no. 33. Regino I, 414 retains much of its basic structure, but almost the only points of contact in the language are two of the distinctive phrases identified. *Form. Sal. Merk.* no. 44 is much more closely related to *Form. Imp.* no. 33 by language, but has a rather different structure.

So manumission *formulae* were diffused, and routinely adapted, sometimes in minor ways, sometimes major. Below, we see that the prologues of the *formulae* can betray very different emphases, and try to uncover some of the pressures that led to the adaptation. But for now we turn to the *formula* associated with Adventius of Metz and Regino of Prüm, where the adaptation of *Form. Imp.* no. 33 was very limited in scale, but rather striking in character. The most significant adaptations in this case were purely terminological. Regino's or Adventius's *formula* diverges from *Form. Imp.* no. 33 almost only where the distinctive phrases identified above are found: *civem Romanum* is absent, and we do not find *habensque portas apertas.*[79] These are very likely omissions of text present in the exemplar because, without the phrases, the sense of the text is somewhat garbled.

The distinctive linking phrases

We immediately encounter problems understanding these distinctive phrases. Firstly, the meaning and significance of *portas apertas* is unclear. The relevant passage of *Lex Ribuaria* is rather difficult to translate elegantly, but it seems that in some sense 'open doors' were ascribed to the manumittee.[80] One manumission charter from 882 describes a ritual actually involving open doors, but this appears to be isolated, and the phrase seems at other times and places to have been more metaphorical

79 A table, systematically comparing all of the *formulae* discussed in this section, was too large to fit in this book, but can be found in the thesis on which this book is based: T. Faulkner, 'The Frankish leges in the Carolingian period' in: *The Frankish lages* (Cambridge 2009), unpublished PhD dissertation, University of Cambridge, pp. 180–3.

80 Text as in the extract above. The most recent English translation found an elegant translation by glossing over the strange terminology, providing 'If anyone makes his slave a freedman and openly bestows legal status and liberty upon him' (Laws of the Salian and Ripuarian Franks, (1986) p. 194). The alternative might be something like: 'assigns [him the status of] Roman citizen and ascribes open doors [to him]'. Neither seems ideal.

than literal.[81] But it is the status of freed slaves as *cives Romani* that is the most difficult to understand, since one must navigate through complex attitudes to Roman law across time and space. Roman laws preserved in the Breviary of Alaric, most clearly at the beginning of the Institutes of Gaius, provide many methods of manumission, and also many statuses of freedmen.[82] A freedman would by no means always be considered a *cives Romanus*: the distinction consists in the ability of a *cives Romanus* to make a will and pass on his property to heirs.[83] Ian Wood has suggested convincingly that the compiler of *Lex Ribuaria* had access to laws of Constantine from the Theodosian code or Breviary of Alaric on manumission.[84] But the meaning of *cives Romanus* as set out in the Institutes of Gaius was modified in the *Lex Ribuaria*, where the fundamental right to make a will is restricted by the requirement that his property was to go to the fisc if he died without children.[85] One *formula*, however, that indeed shares the phrase *portas apertas* with *Lex Ribuaria*, clearly shows an awareness of Roman legal texts that define the precise status of a *cives Romanus* in this context.[86] So it is quite a complex problem to unravel the various possible meanings of the term here.[87]

A possible way through is to understand the distinctive phrases less as standalone technical terms than as pointers to the normative texts that contain the same terminology. This seems to have been Regino's approach, or his source's, in arranging his texts, when he linked passages with the phrase *castris dominicis*, just as the manuscript of *Form. Imp.* 33 linked the *formula* and preceding capitulary with the term *ad cornu altaris*.[88] In the case of Regino's/Adventius's *formula*, then, what coupling or uncoupling of texts might the removal of distinctive phrases from its exemplar have been intended to achieve? The problem, again, concerns the *cives romanus*. In this case Regino deleted it once in the text, but not when it appears a few lines lower. The decisively deleted phrase was

81 *Urkundenbuch Niederrheins* p. 38 no. 73.

82 *Gaii Institutiones* I–II, e.g. I, 1 *LRV* p. 314: *tria sunt genera libertatum... aut cives Romani sunt, aut Latini, aut dediticii.*

83 *LRV* p. 316: *Sed inter haec tria genera libertorum ideo cives Romani meliorem statum habent, quia et testamenta facere et ex tesamento quibuscunque personis succedere possunt: nam Latini et diditicii nec testamenta condere, nec sibi ex testamento aliorum aliquid dimissum possunt ullatenus vindicare*; A. Nitschke, 'Die Freilassung – Beobachtungen zum Wandel von Rechtsgebärden' *ZRG GA*, *99* (1982), p. 222.

84 Wood (1993), 'Theodosian Code', p. 175. Wood draws the parallel with *Theodosiani libri XVI cum Constitutionibus Sirmondianis: et leges novellae ad Theodosianum pertinentes* ed. T. Mommsen and P. Meyer (Berlin, 1905), pp. 190–1 Vol. 1, 2 4.12.3 and 5 [hereafter *CodTh*].

85 *Lex Ribuaria* 64,1.

86 *Form. Bit.* no. 9, while sharing the *portas apertas* terminology with *Lex Ribuaria*, specifically refers to Roman law on the different forms manumission can take, and explicitly quotes the right of the *cives romanus* to make a will.

87 See Nitschke (1982), 'Freilassung', pp. 220–51. See also A. Harrill, *The manumission of slaves in early Christianity* (Tübingen, 1995), Hermeneutische Untersuchungen zur Theologie 32, pp. 53f.

88 See the extract of *Formulae Imperiales* 33 above.

portas apertas. The key may be that *cives romanus* and *portas apertas* are found together in the *Lex Ribuaria*, and that while the *Lex Ribuaria* used Roman laws in its treatment of manumission, it had a very different understanding from that of the Roman texts of what a *cives romanus* was in this context. The passage of *Lex Ribuaria* (64,1) that used both terms *portas apertas* and *cives romanus* explicitly claimed for the fisc the property of the freedman who died without heirs. This is not exactly the part Regino omitted from the passage he quoted from the *Lex Ribuaria*, but was exactly the kind of passage of *Lex Ribuaria* Regino may have sought to ignore, because it referred to revenues flowing somewhere other than to the church. The impression is that Regino (or the earlier compiler from Metz) had a collection of excerpts from normative texts, and arranged them almost exactly as I have above, perhaps even using parallel columns, with one column containing normative excerpts and the other a *formula* very close to *Form. Imp.* 33. In seeking to remove attention from the parallels with the offending passage of *Lex Ribuaria* he removed the distinctive parallel terminology from the *formula* text, as well as neglecting to include the passage of the *Lex Ribuaria* in the finished collection. What was left was a far more neutral parallel between the *cives romanus* of the *formula* and that of the Roman law.

The authority in the prologues

Regino's and Adventius's *formula* is the only one in the group considered to strip out distinctive phrases in such a way, but it is instructive to compare the differences between members of the rest of the group of related texts. The most significant differences can be found in the prologues. *Form. Imp.* no. 33 stresses that the authority for the transaction was 'ecclesiastical authority' and 'canonical religion', which 'royal majesty' had confirmed. This is echoed in most of our related *formulae*, but with some notable exceptions. Regino, I, 414, in general the least directly related to *Form. Imp.* no. 33, adopts an altogether simpler moralistic view: whoever agrees to free someone 'is not to doubt that he will gain a reward in the future with the Lord'.[89] *Form. Extr.* I, 16 replicates the prologue text of *Form. Imp.* no. 33 almost exactly, but does not include the crucial word *regia,* (assuming, as ever, that Zeumer's edition is accurate here). The meaning of the resulting passage is not quite clear, but the sense of *ecclesiastica* was carried to

89 Regino of Prüm, *Libri duo de synodalibus causis et disciplinis ecclesiasticis.* ed. F. Wasserschleben (Leipzig, 1840), p. 187 [hereafter *Libri duo*]: *praemium in futuro apud dominum sibi provenire non dubitet.* See also *Das Sendhandbuch des Regino von Prüm* ed. and German trans. W. Hartmann (Darmstadt, 2004).

auctoritas, and the effect is to strip the royal conponent out of the passage altogether.[90]

In the prologue of *Form. Imp. Add.* no. 2, considered elsewhere in the context of royal ideology, but is worth quoting again in full: the opposite tendency is displayed from that of *Form. Extr.* I no. 16: 'ecclesiastical authority' is still there, but the history of Roman law and its confirmation by *Hludowicus serenissimus imperator* are much more prominent.[91] The law in question may be apocryphal, but it is quite possible that it was the law of Constantine already quoted, preserved in the Theodosian code.[92] This law did not quite do what the prologue claimed of the law Louis had made *sanctus*, but the passage need not be read as Louis 'confirming' laws enacted by Constantine: he could be establishing new law 'following on from' the *decretum augustorum*. Such an interpretation could very easily fit that implied in Regino's presentation of his related *formulae,* where texts followed on from each other, arranged in a loose chain.

So in the explicit statements of authority we see some variations: the texts in general stress concordance between Roman, royal/imperial, and ecclesiastical authorities, but also reveal something of a tug of war over where the emphasis should lie.

4.2.4 The background of practice

I have argued that Regino's treatment, or his source's treatment, of the normative texts shows intimate and broad knowledge of legal texts, and an acute awareness of the different sources of authority that underlay those texts. Regino presents laws from different authorities as in harmony, but that harmony has a pronounced leaning towards the authority of clergymen and towards the church. Regino's arrangement and manipulation of texts provides a context in which the subtle removals from *formulae* of the distinctive terminology I identified could have a real meaning, could present an argument, that complemented and extended the various kinds of argument found in the prologues to those *formulae.* But what was this argument really about, if it was not just an

90 *Form. Imp.* no. 33: MGH Form. pp. 311–12: *Auctoritas ecclesiastica patenter admonet, insuper et maiestas regia canonice religioni adsensum praebet...*; *Form. Extr.* I, 16: MGH Form. p. 543: *...insuper et maiestas canonicae religioni assensum praebet.*

91 A translation is provided in Chapter 3, section 3.1 above. MGH Form. p. 328: *Auctoritas ecclesiastica confirmatur, dum nostris quoque temporibus maiorum statuta roborantur. Siquidem novimus, domnum Hludowicum serenissimum imperatorem post decretum augustorum Constantini atque Theodosii salubri institutione sanxisse, illos, qui ad sacros promovendi sunt ordines, quovis servitutis vinculo detineantur, a propriis dominis libertatis munus debere promereri, quo eo dignius, immo liberius dovinis famularentur cultibus, quo se meminerint ab humano famulatu esse liberos.*

92 See 'Related formulae' above.

expression of a nebulous sense of propriety and priority? What was really at stake?

The key seems to be the ongoing relationship between the manumittor and the manumittee. It has long been recognised that, although many *formulae* insist that the status of a freedman was to be as if he was born of free parents, freedmen very often owed various kinds of dues.[93] I shall suggest that the sensitivity to terminology and to the particular authority associated with each text was rooted in real arguments over the direction of service and revenues following manumission.

Different views on the flow of revenues associated with manumission can be found in normative texts. In the *Lex Ribuaria*, we have seen how a man manumitted by penny-throw in front of the king was to leave his property to the fisc if he died without heirs, but someone freed in church was to leave it to the church.[94] C.61,1 is difficult to interpret, but in prohibiting someone from manumitting by penny-throw someone who had already been manumitted in church, refers to a conflict over the destination of what the most recent translator interpreted as the 'whole income of their social position'.[95] In the *Lex Alemannorum*, murdered freedmen should be compensated to the church in which they were freed, or their son, but one late ninth-century manuscript changed the destination from the son to the fisc.[96] The additional capitulary to the Bavarian *Lex* is also important, since it aggressively claimed for the king the *wergeld* for any kind of freedman, whether freed by penny-throw, in a church with a charter, or with a charter 'when they chose no *patrocinio* or *defensio*'.[97]

This *patrocinio* may often have involved payment of dues to a church or a lord, as the *formulae* and extant charters suggest. Rio has noted that very many *formulae* from the ninth century, and specifically in eastern Francia, suggest that the grip of specific churches over the manumitted was strong, and strengthening, and identified eleven *formulae* that appear to manumit 'to the church'.[98]

93 See for example the classic account in Brunner (1906), *Deutsche Rechtsgeschichte*, pp. 35f. Material about free parents in the *formulae* was argued as distinctively Frankish in Nitschke (1982), 'Freilassung', pp. 226–7. An attempt to systematise some of the following material can be found in H. Brunner, 'Die Freilassung durch Schatzwurf' in: Brunner (1931), *Abhandlungen*, pp. 240–93.

94 *Lex Ribuaria* pp. 108 and 110 c.60,4 and 61,4.

95 *Laws of the Salian and Ripuarian Franks* trans. T. J. Rivers (New York, 1986), p. 195; *Lex Ribuaria* pp. 108–9: *et omnis redditus status eorum ad ecclesiam reddant.*

96 *Lex Alemannorum* p. 79. The manuscript is BN Lat. 4759B (ix$^{3/4}$, E. France or left Rhein).

97 MGH Capit. no. 68 p. 158 c.4–6: c.6 *Hi vero qui per cartam ingenuitatis dimissi sunt liberi, ubi nullum patrocinium et defensionem non elegerint, similiter regi conponantur quadraginta solidis.*

98 *Form. And.* 20, 23, *Form. Sal. Big.* 2, *Form. Sal. Lind.* 9, 11, *Form. Sal. Merk.* 14, *Form. Arg.* 2, *Form. Aug. Coll. B* 21, 34, *Form. Extr.* I, 19–20. Rio (2009), *Frankish Formulae*, pp. 142–3.

While a good number of manumissions survive in the royal charters edited in the MGH, it is rather difficult to find private manumission charters. But those that do survive tend to specify some kind of a continued render to the church.[99] Interpreting this broad pattern of survival is not straightforward. On the one hand, churches had no incentive to preserve documents of manumission, if manumission had improved the status of their tenants. On the other, a manumission charter 'to the church' gave the church proof of a revenue stream. There was certainly also a motive for churches to preserve manumissions for churchmen, and there are two examples of the preservation of such charters in cartularies.[100] But for those from whose labour the churches might benefit, the preservation of manumissions might be a reasonable function for hypothetical lay archives, which have not survived.[101] And charters would be extremely valuable to the children of the manumitted as a way to prove their status. In one of Louis the German's manumissions, indeed, the phrase *ac natus illorum* has been added into the charter by a different hand to the names of two dependents to be freed.[102]

We can say more with the larger number of extant royal charters, as shown in Table 4.3. These royal charters are nearly all Lotharingian or East Frankish, and they all describe manumission in a way pointedly ignored, if not specifically ruled out, by Regino: they are almost always explicitly by penny-throw, often explicitly according to *Lex Salica,* and two of Louis the German's charters even free priests, those already ordained.

Zwentibold's charters are worthy of particular scrutiny since they are in space and time closest to Regino's work. In one of his charters we

99 So Wampach (1930), *Grundherrschaft Echternach*, p. 71 no. 104 from 789–90 reserves for a church the *mundoburdum vel defensionem* and a yearly render of wax. *Urkundenbuch zur Geschichte der mittelrheinischen Territorien* ed. H. Beyer and L. Eltester and A. Goerz (Aalen, 1974), pp. 85–6 no. 79, however, has no description of the manumission procedure. This is one of the few charters in the Prüm *Liber Aureus* not recording a grant to Prüm. See N. Nösges, 'Die Urkunden Lothars I. für die Abtei Prüm' in: R. Nolden (ed.), *Lothar I.: Kaiser und Mönch in Prüm: zum 1150. Jahr seines Todes* (Prüm, 2005), p. 113. Also a charter from a private individual in 784 *Chartae Latinae antiquiores: facsimile edition of the Latin charters* ed. A. Bruckner and R. Marichal (Olten, 1954), p. 133 no. 106 manumitted a *servus*, with the condition that he continue to pay an annual sum to St Gallen. Thanks to Alice Rio for this reference. Also *Urkundenbuch Niederrheins* p. 38 no. 73 from 882, in which the freedmen were obliged to pay wax to the church at Gerresheim, some 40 km north of Cologne, which retained their *mundbyrd*, and which specified that *post obitum uniuscuisque eorum preter tantum quod obtimum habeant aut in equis siue in bubus seu in porcis aut in ceteris rebus dare festinent.*

100 *Die Urkunden Ludwigs des Deutschen, Karlmanns und Ludwigs des Jüngeren* ed. P. Kehr (Berlin, 1934), MGH Diplomatum Karolinorum I [hereafter *UrkLD*] no. 10 and no. 152 for Passau and St Emmeram.

101 For lay archives see above all Brown (2002), 'When Documents', pp. 337–66. See also Rio (2009), *Frankish Formulae*, p. 9.

102 *UrkLD* p. 180 no. 129.

Table 4.3 *Carolingian royal manumission charters*

Issuer	Charter no.	Place of issue	Date	Penny-throw?	By *Lex Salica?*	Extant form
Louis the German	10	Regensburg	833	Yes		Passau cartulary (xiii).
	121	Regensburg		Yes		Original in St Gallen.
	129	Regensburg	868			Original in Zurich.
	152	Augsburg				St Emmeram cart. (ix^{ex}.)
Lothar I	74	Aachen	843	Yes	Yes	Original in Arezzo.
	113	Aachen	851	Yes	Yes	Liber Aureus of Prüum.
Charles the Fat	4		877	Yes	Yes	Andlau cartulary.
Arnulf	164	Mattighofen	898	Yes	Yes	Passau cartulary (xii).
Zwentibold	10	Nijmegen		Yes	Yes, and by *Lex Francorum*	Utrecht cartulary (xii).
	28	Diest	900	Yes	Yes	Complex late Liège trans.
Louis the Child	45	Rottweil	906	Yes	Yes	Original in Bonn lost.

actually get an indirect hint that the *leges* had been consulted: no. 10 refers both to *Lex Salica* and to *Lex Francorum*:

We also assented to his request, then gave two *mancipia* in exchange, as *Lex Salica* teaches, to the aforementioned church, and then according to *Lex Francorum* we knocked out her penny and thus we freed her from the bonds of servitude and granted her confirmation of her freedom.[103]

This distinction between *Lex Salica* and *Lex Francorum* may be comparable with Regino's description of *Lex Ribuaria* as *Pactus Francorum*, and it is even possible that the provision of *mancipia* in exchange for freeing a *servus* of the church is related to a requirement to do so in the *Lex Ribuaria*.[104] We might also relate the careful specification of the *leges* to the arguments made in Chapter 1 about consensus, choice of law, and reference to multiple *leges* in the Netherlands area: after all Nijmegen was not far from the region in question, and Elst is actually in the Betuwe.[105]

But it is the procedural oddities we find in Zwentibold's charters that might link more interestingly with Regino's work. No. 28 records the *denarius* as being thrown 'from the hand of the bishop' rather than the hand of the manumittor as is conventional.[106] The notary is also recorded as being Franco, plausibly identified as the bishop of Liège, where the charter was preserved. The complex textual history of this charter makes it very possible that this is a corruption of the original text, as Schieffer, the MGH editor thought, but if not, it would sit interestingly in this context, since we have something of a mixture of the two distinct procedures described in the *Lex Ribuaria*, while one of them – *denariare* – was pointedly glossed over, if not explicitly ruled out, by Regino.[107] Both Zwentibold's charters also describe the manumissions as responses to the petitions of others. In no. 28 it is count Angilram; in no. 10, however, it is actually another bishop, 'Egilbaldus', whose identification is problematic.[108] Why would Egilbald need to petition Zwentibold for a manumission of a certain Odburg *e familie iure sancti Martini in Elste*?

103 *Die Urkunden Zwentibolds und Ludwigs des Kindes* ed. T. Schieffer (Berlin, 1960), MGH Diplomatum Karolinorum IV, p. 36: *Nos quoque petitioni eius acquiescentes datis postea in mutationem, ut lex Salica docet, duobus mancipiis prefate ecclesie prius et postea secundum legem Francorum denarium eius excutientes et sic eam servitutis vinculo liberavimus et ingenuitatis ei confirmationem tribuimus.*

104 The latter is suggested in Brunner (1931), 'Freilassung durch Schatzwurf', p. 258, and see also Nehlsen (1977), 'Aktualität und Effektivität', pp. 476–7. *Lex Ribuaria* p. 110 c.61,3: *Nemo servum ecclesiasticum absque vicarium libertum facere presumat.*

105 See Chapter 1, section 1.4.3 above.

106 See Nitschke (1982), 'Freilassung', pp. 244ff. and note the other cases of eccentric procedure he identified.

107 *Urk. Z* pp. 66–8.

108 *Urk. Z* pp. 35–6.

4.2 *Manumission* formulae *and* Regino of Prüm's Libri Duo

A possible explanation for these curiosities is that Lotharingian and East Frankish kings were using manumission as a display of power, often with rituals involving high office holders, counts, and bishops. The charters could be read almost as transcripts of rituals of power, adding a symbolic function to whatever economic function the manumissions may have had. And it is possible that this apparent resurgence of royal manumission was accompanied by arguments from texts. It could have been in some sense inspired by the provisions of the *Lex Ribuaria* about *denariare ante regem*, especially if we read in Zwentibold's charter no. 10 a reference to the same text. It is also tempting to link Louis the German's activity in Bavaria, seen in the charters for Augsburg and Regensburg, with the provisions of Capitulary no. 68, the additional capitulary to the *Lex Baiuwariorum*, on the rights of the king to revenue from the manumitted.[109] Whatever their relationship with written texts, however, the charters make Regino's work comprehensible as a reaction to royal activity, even if he was adapting a pre-existing dossier. Although Regino was close to the power holders of his day, he was openly hostile to Zwentibold in his *Chronicon*, and even claimed that he relied overly on women and the low-born.[110] By restricting control of manumission of the low born, along with its economic and symbolic potential, to the church, the *Libri Duo* might be read as coded criticism of royal activity.

So there does seem to be a good practical context, rooted in competition for control of manumission, for the subtle variations between, and adaptations of, *formulae*. In Regino's work, *formulae* are surrounded in a mesh of normative text, and both are manipulated symbiotically. His work suggests most clearly that an awareness of the conflicting provisions of various normative texts might underly some of the variation between manumission *formulae*, and that at least the *Lex Ribuaria*, with its provisions on manumission in Church and in the presence of the king, had an especially important role to play.

109 On this capitulary see Chapter 3, section 3.3.3 above.

110 Cited and translated in S. MacLean, 'Insinuation, censorship and the struggle for late Carolingian Lotharingia in Regino of Prüm's Chronicle' *EHR*, *124* (2009), p. 8: 'He was running the affairs of the realm with women and the lesser-born, deposing all the more honourable and noble people and stripping them of offices and dignities. For this reason he became hated by everyone'. Regino of Prüm, *Reginonis abbatis Prumiensis Chronicon cum continuatione Treverensi* (Hannover, 1890), MGH SRG 50, p. 148: *Cum mulieribus et ignobilioribus regni negotia disponens honestiores et nobiliores quosque deiciebat et honoribus et dignitatibus expoliabat. Pro huiuscemodi itaque causa omnibus odiosus efficitur.* For kings, magnates, Regino, and his *Chronicon*, see S. Airlie, '"Sad stories of the death of kings": Narrative Patterns and Structures of Authority in Regino of Prüm's Chronicon' in: E. Tyler and Balzaretti R. (eds.), *Narrative and history in the early medieval West* (Turnhout, 2006), pp. 105–31, and MacLean (2009), 'Late Carolingian Lotharingia', pp. 1–28.

4.3 SUMMARY

These two studies have shown how identifiable points of debate and conflict, revolving around social status, could involve a reference back to the texts of the *leges*. The central points are that the texts in these contexts were highly malleable, not fossilised. This should perhaps not be altogether surprising considering the fate of other normative texts at the hands of an Ansegis or a Regino, but it is worth pointing out that the *leges* are not apparently approached any differently, that they certainly do not seem to be approached as hardened repositaries of tradition. They were brought into play apparently because they contained material that was usefully deployable in real arguments, which were bound up in, and might have a real impact on, ecclesiastical politics in our first case, and the economic and symbolic control of manumission in our second. We have seen hints that kings and ecclesiastics might turn to the *leges*, and indeed the capitularies adding to them, to support a particular view of manumission, but our sources have not shown a use of the *leges* that can be characterised as application in an obvious sense. We also see in these studies no hint that ethnic identity was a factor in the use of our texts. The *Lex Baiuwariorum* was used far outside Bavaria, and the *Lex Ribuaria* was referred to as relating to Franks, not Ribuarians, nor Ribuarian Franks. The firm impression from our manuscripts in the first study is that the *leges* were read for their bearing on social and clerical status, rather than ethnic identity. Some of these conclusions are thoroughly familiar from the previous chapters, but derived here from very different kinds of evidence.

Chapter 5

THE MANUSCRIPTS OF THE *LEGES*-SCRIPTORIUM

5.1 PRELIMINARIES

5.1.1 The importance of the material

The *leges*-scriptorium group, identified by Bischoff and later studied in detail by McKitterick, is the largest group of early medieval manuscripts with broadly legal concerns the members of which can be associated with each other on palaeographical grounds.[1] Bischoff and McKitterick attributed them to the 820s–30s, linked them with a style current at Tours, and with the imperial court of Louis the Pious.

At the very least, this group sheds some light on the circulation of legal texts soon after their composition, since those containing Louis's capitularies have contents roughly contemporary with their construction. But McKitterick went further, and argued that they may indeed show something of how legal texts, capitularies as well as up-to-date texts of the *leges*, were disseminated by the imperial court. Otherwise only a very few fragments of what could be early rotula survive to help us establish what capitularies looked like in their original manuscript context, their first written fixing after some kind of promulgation.[2] Establishing the precise status of this scriptorium, then, is a task of the very highest importance in the study of Carolingian legal culture, possibly allowing us a rare direct insight into the tangible, direct contribution of the Carolingian court to the textual history of capitularies and *leges*.

[1] McKitterick (1989), *Written word*, pp. 57–9; R. McKitterick, 'Zur Herstellung von Kapitularien: Die Arbeit des Leges-Skriptoriums' *Mitteilungen des Instituts fur Österreichische Geschichtsforschung*, *101* (1993), pp. 3–16; B. Bischoff, *Latin palaeography: antiquity and the Middle Ages* trans. D. Ganz and D. Ó Cróinín (Cambridge, 1990), p. 205; B. Bischoff, 'Die Hofbibliothek unter Ludwig dem Frommen' in: Bischoff (1981), *Mittelalterliche Studien*, pp. 179f.; B. Bischoff, 'Die Bibliothek im Dienste der Schule' in: Bischoff (1981), *Mittelalterliche Studien*, pp. 231–3.

[2] For the early fragments, see for example Mordek (2000), 'Kapitularien und Kapitulariensammlungen', pp. 1–55. For the most comprehensive recent treatment of the production and early dissemination of capitularies, see Pössel (2006), 'Authors and recipients', pp. 253–74.

A further study of these manuscripts is particularly needed because, as McKitterick herself noted, they display notable eccentricities, if we do imagine that they are products of a scriptorium systematically disseminating correct, 'official' texts for use in courts. Chief among these is the discrepancy between the redactions of the *Lex Salica* the scriptorium produced.[3] While some contain the 'Karolina' (K) text, considered a product of Charlemagne's court, others copied the earlier Carolingian E text.

I start with a survey of the manuscripts and their content, and draw attention to further discrepancies in the texts they reproduced. I then discuss other notable divergences in the form of the manuscripts, their dimensions, use of abbreviations, and use of Tironan notes, which have not been noted explicitly so far. I attempt to relate these curiosities to a more thorough examination of the function of the scriptorium and the nature of the link with the imperial court than has been attempted before. In the next section I plunge into textual criticism, in an attempt to understand the origins of the texts used in the *leges*-scriptorium manuscripts, and to trace their influence on other early medieval manuscripts. First I examine the texts of the capitularies and the barbarian *leges*, then the texts of Roman law, *formulae*, and various miscellaneous material. Finally I examine the relationships between the various texts of Roman law and *formulae* found in the manuscript. I argue that Tours could have been a centre of revision of legal texts, including the *Lex Salica* as well as Roman law and *formulae*.

5.1.2 *The* leges-*scriptorium manuscripts considered*

Tables 5.1 and 5.2 are based on the list given in McKitterick's 1993 article, which is far fuller than Bischoff's limited printed work. Bischoff's most detailed discussion was limited to a single paragraph, where he gave no extended commentary, and refers rather vaguely to five manuscripts 'among others': 'it appears that in a scriptorium writing in a style like that of Tours and affiliated to the palace a considerable number of manuscripts of *leges* and *formulae* was produced, as the public administration of justice required them; their origin may date to the chancellorship of abbot Fridugis of St Martin (819–32)'.[4]

Other accounts of the extent of the group contain various confusing irregularities. The first is that Mordek included more manuscripts than McKitterick or Bischoff. I do not consider as *leges*-scriptorium products Montpellier H 136, or BN Lat. 4827, which Mordek described, and which Wormald included; but they are listed below as possible court

[3] McKitterick (1989), *Written word*, p. 57.

[4] Bischoff (1990), *Latin palaeography*, p. 205.

Table 5.1 *The manuscripts of the* leges-*scriptorium 1: the texts*

	Sal	*Rib*	*Al*	*Bav*	*Burg*	*Vis*	Rom (H no., group)	*Form.*	Capits.	*Isid.*	Other
Group 1											
Warsaw BU 1 (Q. 480)	E13						*LRV* (36, II)	*Tur.*	7	*Isid.*	Canons
Berlin Lat. Q. 150							*LRV* (37, II)				
Vat. Reg. Lat. 846	E11						*EpA* (75, V)		7, 20a	*Isid.*	Patristics parallel with BN Lat. 2718
St Gallen 729	E14		A10				*EpA* (57, IV(A))		7		
Group 2											
BN Lat. 4418	K24	B5			B2	E1	*EpI*, *EpA* (49, IV(A))				
BN nouv. acq. Lat. 204	K27		B37	E6a	B3		*EpA*	[*Imp.*]	139, 141, 143–5		
Vat. Reg. Lat. 857	K70		B21				*LRV* (43, III)	[*Tur.*]			Two prayers in later hands.
Vat. Reg. Lat. 991	K71	B16	B22	E3			*EpA* (55, IV(A))		(68)		Alcuin, prayers.
Group 3											
BN Lat. 4408							*LRV* (29, II)			*Isid.*	
Vat. Reg. Lat. 852							*EpA*	*Marc.*, *Tur.*			
Vat. Reg. Lat. 1431	K(x)										
BN Lat. 10756 (part 2)								*Tur.*			
BN Lat. 2718								*Imp.*	136–41, 143–5		Patristics and misc. material.
BN Lat. 4416							*EpA*(47, IV(A))				

( ) are for later additions. [ ] are for short portions of text.

Table 5.2 *The MS of the* leges-*scriptorium 2: more details*

Name	Dimensions [written] (mm)	No. of fols.	Lines per page	Main text	Annotations	Provenance
Group 1						
Warsaw BU 1 (Q. 480)	235 × 165 [180 × 130]	269	24	Min	Tir	In Langres in s. xi?
Berlin Lat. Q. 150	250 × 185	187	24–8	Min	Tir?	
Vat. Reg. Lat. 846			25	Min, Tir	Tir, Min	Paris in s. xi?
St Gallen 729	230 × 155 [175 × 100]	203	20–5	Min	Min	St Gallen (in ix$^{med.}$ cat.)
Group 2						
BN Lat. 4418	425 × 280 [330 × 215]	292	39	Min		Once Colbert's
BN nouv. acq. Lat. 204	235 × 190 [192 × 140]	95	27	Min		
Vat. Reg. Lat. 857		148	22	Tir, Min	Tir, Min	
Vat. Reg. Lat. 991	255–190 [195 × 130]	171	23	Min	Min	Patau, Christina of Sweden
Group 3						
BN Lat. 4408		217				
Vat. Reg. Lat. 852		99	21	Min, Tir	Tir, Min	
Vat. Reg. Lat. 1431		1	19	Min		
BN Lat. 10756 (part 2)	200 × 140		23–7			
BN Lat. 2718	c.150 × 240 [c.100 × 200]	140	14–29		Tir, Min	St Martin, Tours
BN Lat. 4416			22	Min, Tir	Tir, Min	

'Tir' and 'Min' refer to tironian notes and caroline minuscule.

products.[5] The second irregularity is the confusion between BN Lat. 4416 and BN Lat. 4418, both of which contain Roman law. McKitterick listed as a *leges*-scriptorium product BN Lat. 4416 in 1993, followed by Mordek in 1995.[6] But 4416 contains only an *Epitome Aegidii*, and the contents appear to have been confused in McKitterick's 1989 and 1993 work with those of BN Lat. 4418.[7] Wormald and Mordek both included BN Lat. 4418 in their lists of *leges*-scriptorium manuscripts.[8] Bischoff's published discussion of the script of BN Lat. 4418, on the other hand, linked it to Louis the Pious's court directly, rather than to the *leges*-scriptorium with its Tours style. He compared its hand with that of the Brussels Gospel book.[9] The distinction is important here, and a fresh consideration of the hand of BN Lat. 4418 is needed to resolve the discrepancy in the accounts. My approach here is to leave the palaeography to those better qualified, and to include both BN Lat. 4416 and 4418, while making the arguments transparent enough to unpick my connections easily. In all other cases I have accepted McKitterick's 1993 list as authoritative.[10]

McKitterick identified three groups of *leges*-scriptorium manuscripts. Group 1 manuscripts contain *Lex Salica* E and the *Breviary of Alaric*, or its abbreviated form the *Epitome Aegidii*. Again, there is some confusion in the literature about exactly which of these texts each manuscript contains, but I have listed the texts as I found them in the manuscripts.[11] Group 2 has the K redaction of *Lex Salica*, and Group 3 contains mostly Roman law and formularies. The groups should not be seen as rigid, or as especially meaningful: Berlin Lat. Q. 150 is included in Group 1 because it is the textual sister of Warsaw BU 1,

5 Mordek (1995), *Bibliotheca*, p. 432; Wormald (1999), *The making*, p. 62.

6 McKitterick (1993), 'Zur Herstellung', p. 11; Mordek (1995), *Bibliotheca*, p. 423.

7 McKitterick (1989), *Written word*, p. 58.

8 Mordek (1995), *Bibliotheca*, p. 1031 (but not at p. 423); Wormald (1999), *The making*, p. 62, but elsewhere he refers to it as a pure court product.

9 Bischoff (1981), 'Hofbibliothek', p. 180. So D. Liebs, *Römische Jurisprudenz in Gallien (2. bis 8. Jahrhundert)* (Berlin, 2002), p. 111 attributes BN Lat. 4416 to the *leges*-scriptorium, but not BN Lat. 4418. Wormald includes both. See, however, the comments by K. Ubl, who finds a Tours-related origin for BN Lat. 4416 'nicht plausibel' at www.leges.uni-koeln.de/en/mss/codices/paris-bn-lat-4416/, last viewed 30 August 2014. This work was completed before the recently published third volume of Bischoff's catalogue was accessible. B. Bischoff, *Katalog der festländischen Handschriften des neunten Jahrhunderts. Teil III.* (Wiesbaden, 2014).

10 I have seen all of the manuscripts listed either in person (Paris manuscripts) or on microfilm or digital copy (Vatican manuscripts), or on printout from microfilm (Warsaw) with the exception of Berlin Lat. Q. 150, now in Krakow, of which I have seen only a few pages on microfilm printout kindly lent to me by Prof. McKitterick. Thanks to Alice Rio for lending me Microfilms of BN Lat. 2718 and Vat. Reg. Lat. 852.

11 There are, for example, discrepancies between McKitterick (1993), 'Zur Herstellung', pp. 3–16; McKitterick (1989), *Written word*, pp. 57–8; the relevant entries in Mordek (1995), *Bibliotheca*; Liebs (2002), *Römische Jurisprudenz*, pp. 221–2.

although it contains only the Breviary of Alaric in its current form. Vat. Reg. Lat. 1431 contains only one folio by a *leges*-scriptorium scribe, a fragment of *Lex Salica* K, so is not readily classifiable in its current form. BN Lat. 2718 is a curiosity on very many levels, finding almost no parallel in any other early medieval manuscript.[12] So the groups are really only useful for the purposes of presentation and organisation of commentary.

5.1.3 Other relevant manuscripts associated with Tours

Before going any further, I list some legal manuscripts associated with Tours, which feature below in the discussion:[13]

BN Lat. 4404	ix$^{inc.}$	Capits, *Sal*A1, *Rib*A2, *Al*A9. It has a related redaction of *Lex Al* to that found in the *leges*-scriptorium product St Gallen 729.
BN Lat. 18237	ix$^{2/4}$	Capits, *Ans*34, *Sal*C4, *Al*B35, *Isid.* Mordek suggested that Part 1 of the manuscript was from near Tours. Its *Lex Al* text fits with other Group 2 *leges*-scriptorium texts. It has the richest, but unedited, Isidore excerpts.
BN Lat. 4636	ix$^{med.}$	*Ans*27, *Ben Lev*. Has an Ansegis redaction close to that of BN Lat. 18237. The *Ben Lev* is the oldest example.
Leiden VLQ 119	ix$^{4/4}$	Capits, *Sal*K17, *Rib*B21, *Bav*A2, *Al*B19, *Isid.* 'France' palaeographically, but related to BN Lat. 4404, and its Aquitainian content possibly links it with Tours (on the north border of Aquitaine.) Includes the letter of Chrodebert of Tours.

These contain a variety of *Lex Salica* redactions: A, C, and K are all represented. The redaction in Leiden Voss. Lat. Q. 119 is also remarkable because it includes the full range of Merovingian additions to the *Lex Salica*, not alongside the Merovingian A redaction as they are otherwise transmitted, but alongside the Carolingian K. The implications of this for the textual history of the *Lex Salica* are followed up later.[14]

[12] See section 5.1.5 below, and for a recent summary Rio (2009), *Frankish Formulae* esp. pp. 108–11.
[13] For all of these, see the entries in Mordek (1995), *Bibliotheca*.
[14] See section 5.2.4 below.

5.1.4 *Other legal manuscripts associated with the court*

Other relevant legal manuscripts that have been suggested as court productions, but that were not defined by McKitterick as *leges*-scriptorium products are as follows:[15]

BN Lat. 4627	c. 818	*Lex Salica* D8 and *formulae*. To my eyes this is not a *leges*-scriptorium manuscript, as Mordek suggested.
Leiden BPL 114 and BN Lat. 4629	viii/ix and $ix^{inc.}$	*Lex Salica* E15. The suggestion of the court connection seems to be Mordek's alone, and has been discounted here.
Montpellier H 136	$ix^{1/3}$	Roman law and *Lex Salica* D7, Capitularies. Repeated attempts to obtain a microfilm from Montpellier have failed, so this manuscript must be considered in later work.

If BN Lat. 4627 really were a court product, the problem with the Carolingian revisions of the text of *Lex Salica* would be deeper still: not only would two-thirds of the E redaction manuscripts originate from the *leges*-scriptorium, but two-thirds of the D texts would have some rather different kind of a court connection. The court would therefore be one of the only places which *resisted* producing only K copies. The only manuscripts of the hypothetically early Carolingian redactions D and E not connected with the court would be:

St Gallen 731	793	W. Switzerland	D9
Berlin Phil. 1736	$x^{2/2}$	France	E16
BN Lat. 4409	$ix^{ex.}$	France	E12

Considering also that Berlin Phil. 1736 is a direct or indirect copy of BN Lat. 4629, the E text would, by proportions, be yet more strongly associated with the court. In comparison, the position of the K text as the 'official' redaction would look even weaker.

5.1.5 *Script, physical appearance, the court link*

We are now finally in a position to discuss the *leges*-scriptorium manuscripts. Firstly we investigate the nature of the link with the court, and what we can tell about their intended function from their physical form.

15 Note that Mordek linked Leiden BPL 114 and BN Lat. 4629, but this link has been doubted by Ganz: D. Ganz, 'Some Carolingian questions: a text from Charlemagne's days' in: D. Ganz and P. Fouracre (eds.), *Frankland: the Franks and the world of the early Middle Ages: essays in honour of Dame Jinty Nelson* (Manchester, 2008), p. 90.

Palaeographically, the *leges*-scriptorium manuscripts are best associated with each other, with St Martin's, Tours, and with a date of the 820s–30s. The connection with the court of Louis the Pious has been argued with reference to the role of Fridugis, abbot of St Martin's, Tours, as royal chancellor in the period 819–32, and to the prominent use of Tironian notes in many of the manuscripts, interpreted as a notable feature of chancery production.[16] The manuscript BN Lat. 2718 has more specific features that have been used to argue for a court connection. It included what has been seen as an official imperial collection of *formulae*, the so-called *Formulae Imperiales,* and its hand has also been identified as that of a scribe working in Louis the Pious's chancery. The key role of this manuscript in arguments for an association between the scriptorium and the court, therefore, makes a more thorough discussion worthwhile.

BN Lat. 2718 and the connection with the court

Bischoff compared BN Lat. 2718 to BN nouv. acq. Lat. 1448, a volume of texts of Augustine he thought was compiled at Fridugis's request, from an Italian uncial codex (s. vi or vii), which seems to have travelled through England, before ending up in Lorsch.[17] The obvious linking figure would be Gerward, Louis the Pious's librarian and abbot of Lorsch.

But who was the scribe? Fleckenstein thought he was 'perhaps' one of Fridugis's underlings, and McKitterick suggested that one hand might be Hirminmaris, Fridugis's chief charter scribe.[18] Ganz suggested in addition that Fridugis himself as well as his successor Theoto could be scribes.[19] But the suggestion of Hirminmaris was incorporated into Mordek's *Bibliotheca* as a fairly definite fact.[20]

[16] On the imperial *cancellarius* see J. Fleckenstein, *Die Hofkapelle der deutschen Könige I* (Stuttgart, 1959), Schriften der MGH 16, 1, pp. 79f. On the Tours connections, and the view that Tironian notes link the manuscripts with the court, see McKitterick (1989), *Written word*, pp. 57–8. My understanding of McKitterick's comment on Vat. Reg. Lat. 991 is that the 'palaeographical grounds' for linking the manuscript with the court are *indirect*: it is linked to the court through its palaeographical similarities with BN Lat. 2718. The reference is to McKitterick (1993), 'Zur Herstellung', p. 12: 'Jetzt wissen wir aus paläographischen, Gründen....daß [Vat. Reg. Lat. 991] tatsächich der fränkischen Kanzlei besonders nahestand'.

[17] B. Bischoff, *Die Abtei Lorsch im Spiegel ihrer Handschriften* (Lorsch, 1989), Geschichtsblätter für den Kreis Bergstrasse, Sonderbd. 10, p. 56. See also D. Ganz, 'Paris BN Latin 2718: Theological Texts in the Chapel and the Chancery of Louis the Pious' in: Münsch and Zotz (2004), *Scientia veritatis: Festschrift für Hubert Mordek zum 65. Geburtstag*, pp. 137–52. Bischoff's argument relies on an identification with a codex in the third Lorsch library catalogue.

[18] References as for note 16. On the charters in which Hirminmarus is referred to as *magister*, see O. Dickau, 'Studien zur Kanzlei und zum Urkundenwesen Kaiser Ludwigs des Frommen' *Archiv für Diplomatik*, 34–5 (1988–9), pp. 104f.

[19] Ganz (2004), 'Paris BN Latin 2718', p. 151.

[20] Mordek (1995), *Bibliotheca*, p. 422 writes of the manuscript: 'entstanden wohl unter Mitwirkung des Mönches Hirminmaris von Saint-Martin'.

However, a recent analysis by Mersiowsky of Hirminmaris's tironian note hand as found in charters has suggested that it is not the same as that used in BN Lat. 2718.[21] There are strict limits as to how convincing such an argument can be, since we do not have a large sample of Hirminmaris's handwriting: Bresslau believed that Hirminmarus and Durandus rarely wrote more than the *Rekognition* of charters themselves.[22] Mersiowsky's argument was in any case based on the rate of the note writing, the degree of cursiveness, which would probably vary in different contexts. The tironian notes in the *Rekognition* could even be argued to have been deliberately cursive, as a kind of signature. Perhaps the tironian note hand in BN Lat. 2718 might even be different from the main minuscule hand. This could explain the peculiarity of the repetition of the text of Capitulary no. 143 described below.[23]

One further possible link between Hirminmaris and this manuscript has been suggested, based on the inclusion of a private charter of Einhard in the *formulae* found in the manuscripts. Hirminmaris was involved in the production of at least one of Einhard's charters preserved in the Lorsch cartulary.[24] But this too is only a speculative link.

A problem in assessing the precise significance of BN Lat. 2718, then, is that we cannot identify a scribe with any certainty. Fridugis's position as abbot of St Martin's is all, so far, that links the Tours-style script with Louis the Pious.

The use of tironian notes is also not conclusive proof for chancery involvement, since royal charters are by no means the only or even the major sources employing them. Ganz, for example, has pointed out the extensive evidence for use of tironian notes in both the texts and annotations of manuscripts of patristic and classical texts.[25] His survey emphasised broadness: 'we find them [tironian notes] in use in the royal chancery and in episcopal chanceries for the production and authentication of official documents, in the studies of scholars trained in

[21] M. Mersiowsky, 'Saint-Martin de Tours et les chancelleries carolingiennnes' in: P. Depreux and B. Judic (eds.) *Alcuin de York à Tours: écriture, pouvoir et réseaux dans l'Europe du haut Moyen Age* (Rennes, 2004), pp. 73–90.

[22] H. Bresslau, *Handbuch der Urkundenlehre für Deutschland und Italien* 2nd edition (Leipzig, 1912), pp. 374–6, based on M. Tangl, 'Die Tironischen Noten in den Urkunden der Karolinger' *Archiv für Urkundenforschung, 1* (1907–8), pp. 87–166.

[23] See section 5.2.1 below.

[24] The suggestion is found in Mersiowsky (2004), 'Chancelleries carolingiennnes', pp. 83–4. The charter is translated in Dutton (1998), *Einhard*, pp. 54–5. *Codex Laureshamensis* Vol. 1 pp. 301–2.

[25] D. Ganz, 'On the history of Tironian Notes' in: P. Ganz (ed.), *Tironische Noten* (Wiesbaden, 1990), pp. 35–57 with a list of tironian notes in patristic works. See also M. Hellmann, *Tironische Noten in der Karolingerzeit: am Beispiel eines Persius-Kommentars aus der Schule von Tours* (Hannover, 2000), MGH Studien und Texte 27.

major monasteries or cathedral schools, and in scriptoria'.[26] Indeed the scriptorium of Tours was an especially prominent user of Tironian notes, if not the most prominent.

The extent to which the *formulae* found in BN Lat. 2718, the so-called *Formulae Imperiales*, can be considered an official collection, intended to replace Marculf, has recently been challenged on the basis of the extremely chaotic arrangement of the texts in the manuscript, and their very limited influence beyond that manuscript.[27] Their link with Louis the Pious's court and dating to the 820s is, however, beyond doubt because of definite references made in the texts, so it is clear that the scribes (or perhaps a scribe) of the manuscript had business in the imperial chancery.

But in general there is no convincing evidence that the *leges*-scriptorium was located physically at a royal palace, or associated with the imperial writing office, wherever its personnel were active: our good evidence for the court connection comes entirely from the presence of *formulae* texts in just one manuscript of the group.[28] And this is the most anomalous of the group in terms of the texts copied (indeed it does not include even a single *lex*) and in terms of its unparalleled oblong format, which led Rio to suggest that it was a scribe's scrapbook, containing texts for personal use.[29] Perhaps this scribe was trained in the *leges*-scriptorium and then became active at some point in Louis the Pious's chancery, taking his personal scrapbook with him. Below I suggest that the scribe may have travelled in search of texts, copying them into his book to be brought back to the scriptorium, to serve as exemplars there.

Variation between manuscripts

The format of BN Lat. 2718 is extraordinary, and the format of the other manuscripts is also variable in the dimensions and the number of lines per page. Some are written only in caroline minuscule, some mix tironian notes, and there is a great deal of variation in the extent of annotations, some of which, judging from use of tironian notes, may be attributable to the *leges*-scriptorium scribes themselves.[30] The size of the script relative to the ruling of the page, and its internal proportions, vary too: Vat. Reg. Lat. 991 has a far more spacious feel than the others, and ascenders and descenders are longer than in the other manuscripts. All

26 Ganz (1990), 'Tironian Notes', p. 48.

27 Rio (2009), *Frankish Formulae*, pp. 108–11.

28 The function and status of the palaces, especially Aachen, needs to be considered carefully, as made clear most recently in McKitterick (2008), *Charlemagne*, pp. 137–213 esp. pp. 175–6.

29 Rio (2009), *Frankish Formulae*, p. 37.

30 It has not been possible, unfortunately, to decode the Tironian notes in the margins. Serious study of these marginalia should be a priority for future work.

this suggests that the intended audience and function of the manuscripts were rather different. At one extreme, Vat. Reg. Lat. 991 seems to be of 'export quality', and may be a luxurious display volume, although it certainly displays clear signs of having been used at some stage.[31] At the other extreme, BN Lat. 2718, as already noted, appears to be a kind of personal scrapbook, and many of the smaller volumes may have had a function somewhere in the middle. Certainly the use of tironian notes would have narrowed the potential audience, but in Vat. Reg. Lat. 852 a later hand (s. x?) has expanded the Tironian notes in the first few sides (20r–21r) of the *Epitome Aegidii*, something also to be found occasionally in BN Lat. 4416.

The contents of the manuscripts are also very various, in their choice both of legal texts and of non-legal texts. Some manuscripts contain much patristic material, letters, and devotional material. The redactions of the *leges* are not consistent, as noted above: we find both E and K redactions of the *Lex Salica*, and A and B redactions of the *Lex Alemannorum*. The form in which Roman law is found is still less consistent. We have the full Breviary as well as the *Epitome Aegidii*, and a shortened Breviary form Mommsen referred to as *Breviarium decurtatum*, in which the *Interpretationes* alone are found.[32] I shall argue in the next section that the degree of care the scribes took with the text is related to the care they took over the presentation of the manuscripts.

5.2 THE TEXTS, THEIR SOURCES, AND THEIR INFLUENCE. I. THE CAPITULARIES AND BARBARIAN *LEGES* IN *LEGES*-SCRIPTORIUM MANUSCRIPTS

We have seen how establishing the precise nature of the link between the court and the *leges*-scriptorium on palaeographical grounds is difficult, but it is possible to say more about the manuscripts' associations by looking closely at the texts they reproduced. If it is possible to establish the sources of the texts, and what their further influence was, it might be possible to say something about the links between the scriptorium, the court, Tours and other centres, on the one hand, and with the nature of the reception of the *leges*-scriptorium manuscripts, how and by whom they were read, on the other.

The investigation of textual links is slowed down decisively, however, by the unhelpful state of the editions, which I describe in more detail as

[31] For 'export script', see R. McKitterick, 'Carolingian Bible production: the Tours anomaly' in: R. Gameson, *The early medieval Bible: its production, decoration and use.* (Cambridge, 1994), p. 71. For signs of use see Chapter 4, section 4.1.1 above.

[32] *CodTh* Vol. 1, 1 p. XCV. On the *Interpretationes* see J. Matthews, 'Interpreting the interpretationes of the Breviarium' in: R. Mathisen (ed.), *Law, society, and authority in late antiquity* (Oxford, 2001), pp. 11–32.

I go along. I have been forced to take sample collations from manuscripts where the editions are unsatisfactory, but have not seen everything relevant.[33] Another fundamental difficulty is distinguishing between manuscripts related to sources of *leges*-scriptorium texts, and manuscripts influenced by *leges*-scriptorium texts. Very often it is only possible to place *leges*-scriptorium texts into large families, and stemmata of very complex textual traditions can only be approximate and speculative.[34] The approach here is to go through every relevant text in turn.

5.2.1 *Capitularies*

Capit. no. 143 in BN Lat. 2718

BN Lat. 2718 contains Capitulary no. 143 twice, once on fol. 73 in tironian notes (Boretius's text 1), and once in minuscule on fol. 110 (Boretius's text 2). The textual variations between the two are relatively minor, but are significant enough to suggest that they were derived from different exemplars. Text 1 was the basis for Boretius's *Urtext*, and text 2 omits material found in text 1 needed for the sense of the passage.[35]

This text 1 is very close to that in BN nouv. acq. Lat. 204 (text 4), another *leges*-scriptorium product, suggesting that they used related exemplars, or that one was a copy of the other; and the minuscule text is very closely related to that found in Wolfenbüttel Blank. 130 (text 3), a later Carolingian Italian manuscript. These four are the only extant texts of Capitulary no. 143. The relationship is sketched in Figure 5.1.

The implications of this are not obvious. Considering the hypothetical purpose of BN Lat. 2718 itself, it seems odd that a scribe would bother to copy a capitulary twice, but it would be by no means impossible if the scribe had forgotten he had already copied a text, and perhaps some years later copied it again. Alternatively, we could be dealing with two scribes: BN Lat. 2718 could have been a scrapbook that was passed around between individuals.

The peculiarity does suggest that the texts used by *leges*-scriptorium scribes were not entirely consistent. There was not a single exemplar,

33 Editions of samples can be found in Editions at the back of this book.

34 A clear, recent essay on the methodology of editing is M. Reeve, 'Cuius in Usum? Recent and future editing' *The Journal of Roman Studies*, 90 (2000), pp. 196–206. For an overview of the traditional methodology I have used J. Willis, *Latin textual criticism* (Urbana, IL, 1972), Illinois Studies in Language and Literature 61.

35 MGH Capit. I p. 294 c.1: 1 and 4 give: *Et ubi* ***emptor cuiuslibet utitur*** *herba aut lignis aut aliis villaticis commodis, cum eo cuius sunt quibus utitur agat iuxta aestimationem* ***usus****, et quod iustum est de tali re illi persolvat.* 2 gives: *Et ubi* ***emitur cuiuslibet ut iter agens*** *herba aut lignis aut aliis villaticis commodis, cum eo cuius sunt quibus utitur agat iuxta aestimationem* ***huius****, et quod iustum est de tali re illi persolvat.* 3 gives: *Et ubi* ***emit quislibet iter agens*** *[corrected?] herba aut* ***lignas aut alia villaticas commoda****, cum eo cuius sunt quibus utitur agat iuxta aestimationem* ***huius rei****, et quod iustum est de tali re illi persolvat.*

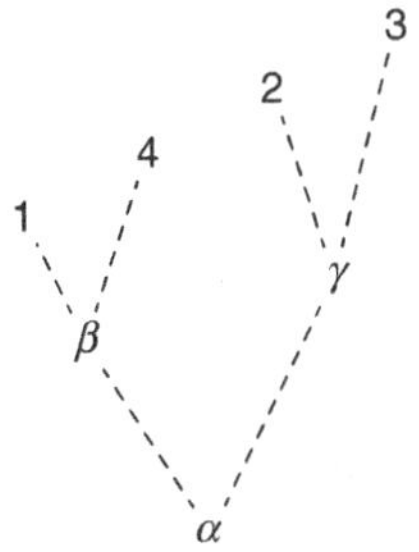

Fig. 5.1 Stemma of Capitulary 143

even for a text that, at least as conventionally imagined, should be as close as it is possible to get to a product of the court. This is particularly striking considering the attempts Louis the Pious made to have capitularies preserved in a public archive.[36] It could be that the public archive never really came together. Equally, if we imagine that the orders were carried through effectively, that the palace archive really did store a single, authoritative copy of the capitularies, it would seem that the *leges*-scriptorium scribes did not use the archive, at least not exclusively. Louis's Worms Capitularies incorporate text from Capit. no. 139, but it is interpolated heavily with material about public penance, so does not allow a firm judgement from textual variants about what kind of text was available to Louis's capitulary authors in 829.[37] It seems at least possible, then, that the scribes of the *leges*-scriptorium physically moved around, or borrowed volumes from diverse centres, even for copying legal texts. This fits with Ganz's arguments about the sources of the patristic texts in BN Lat. 2718. While some were available at Tours, others have strong links with manuscripts from centres such as St Martial, Limoges, and Corbie.[38]

Other capitularies and the wider tradition

Table 5.3 shows a list of all the manuscripts containing capitularies also found in manuscripts of the *leges*-scriptorium with the exception of Capitularies nos. 138 and 20a, which have many manuscripts not shown. In general, if we accept that Boretius's transcriptions were accurate, it is clear that the texts in *leges*-scriptorium manuscripts are generally among

[36] The crucial evidence for this is MGH Capit. I pp. 273–5 no. 137 *Proemium Generale*, whose earliest manuscript is indeed BN Lat. 2718, and is found otherwise only in Kopenhagen Kgl. Saml. 1943. See also MGH Capit. I pp. 303–7 no. 150 *Admonitio ad omnes regni ordines*. A recent consideration of this material is S. Airlie, '"For it is written in the law": Ansegis and the writing of Carolingian royal authority' in: Baxter et al. (2009), *Studies in Memory of Patrick Wormald*, p. 224.

[37] MGH Capit. II no. 193 p. 18.

[38] Ganz (2004), 'Paris BN Latin 2718', pp. 139–42.

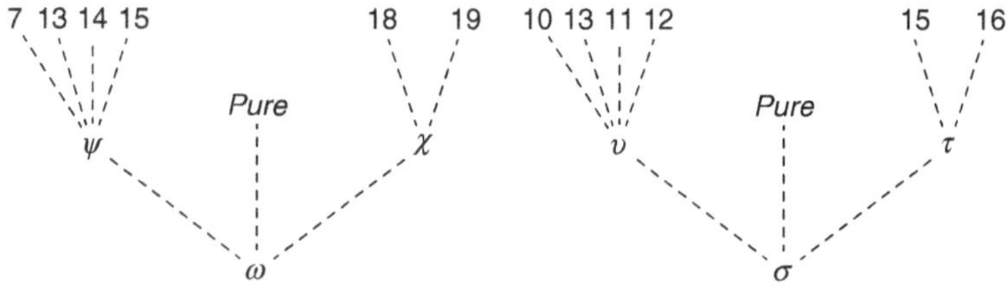

Fig. 5.2 Stemmata of Capitularies nos. 139 (left) and 140 (right)

the closest to his *Urtext*. In the case of Capitulary no. 141, for example, BN Lat. 2718 records one error, while BN nouv. acq. Lat. 204 has a perfect text. Unfortunately no obvious groupings and no stemma can be drawn for this text from Boretius's apparatus.

The clearest groupings are in the tradition of Capitularies nos. 139 and 140, which provide parallel stemmata as shown (no. 139 left, no. 140 right) in Figure 5.2, suggesting that the texts were generally copied together. Specifically, an Italian group from *c.*1000 of Cava dei Tirreni 4 and Vat. Chigi F. IV. 75 emerges (texts 18/15 and 19/16), thoroughly in line with our knowledge of the close relationship between the two codices:[39]

The other group (texts 7/10–15/12) is made up of later ninth-century and early tenth-century codices:

London Eg. 269/2832/BN Lat. 4633	$x^{1/4}$	N. E. France
BN Lat. 4628	$ix^{2/3}$	N. France
BN Lat. 4995	x	France
Wolfenbüttel Blankenburg 130	$ix^{3/4}$	N. Italy/Augsburg

This again leaves the *leges*-scriptorium manuscripts as representatives of a more 'pure' group, which is in fact rather large, too large to allow us to go any further in tracing the specific influence of the *leges*-scriptorium manuscripts. It is rather striking that a tradition with so many manuscripts, thirty-two, does not display *more* variation. Such variation as there is seems related to dating. Nineteen of the thirty-two manuscripts are ninth-century, only two of which fit into a particular variant group (c.10 per cent), but of the thirteen post-Carolingian manuscripts, four are from such groups (c.34 per cent). It is possible that this relative purity early in the tradition relates to the ready availability of close exemplars from the *leges*-scriptorium group, in other words that the group was doing as McKitterick suggested. But the evidence suggests only that this is possible.

39 Mordek (1995), *Bibliotheca*, p. 99.

Table 5.3 *The manuscripts containing capitularies found in* leges-*scriptorium products*

Manuscript	Date	Place	136	137	138	139	140	141	143	144	145
Berlin Phil. 1737	$x^{2/2}$	Metz?			10	X	X	X			
Cava dei Tirreni 4	c.1005	Benevento?				19	16	X			
Gotha Memb. I 84	x/xi	Mainz			8	20	17	13			
Ivrea XXXIII	$ix^{med.}$	N. Italy				17					
Ivrea XXXIV	c.830	Pavia			9	16	14	11			
Kopenh. Gl. Kgl. Saml. 1943	$ix^{ex.}$	E. France		X	X	X	X				
London Eg. 269/2832/BN Lat. 4633	$x^{1/4}$	N.E. France				7	13+				
Montpellier H 136	$ix^{1/2}$ (after 819)	France Hof-nahe			5	8	7	7			
München Lat. 4460	$xi^{2/2}$	S. Germany?				X					
Münster msc. VII 5201	$x^{2/4}$	Corvey				6	6	6			
BN Lat. 10753	$ix^{med.}$	France				23					
BN Lat. 18237	$ix^{2/4}$	Tours?				X					
BN Lat. 18238	$ix^{1/2}$	France?			2	2	2	2			
BN Lat. 2718	c.830	*leges*-scriptorium		1	1	1	1	1	1,2	1	1
BN Lat. 4280 A	$ix^{ex.}$ (and x)	Rheims			3	3	3	3			
BN Lat. 4626	x/xi	France			6	9	8	8			
BN Lat. 4628	$ix^{2/3}$	N. France				14	11+	10			
BN Lat. 4628 A	x/xi	France				11	9	9			

(*cont.*)

Table 5.3 (*cont.*)

Manuscript	Date	Place	136	137	138	139	140	141	143	144	145
BN Lat. 4631	xv	France				X	X	X			
BN Lat. 4632	$ix^{3/4}$	St Stephen, Tem- pleuve				10					
BN Lat. 4760	x	Lyons				X					
BN Lat. 4788	$ix^{2/3}$	France?			4	4	4	4			
BN Lat. 4995	x	France?				13	10+				
BN Lat. 9653	$ix^{1/2}$	Burgundy?				21					
BN nouv. acq. Lat. 204	$ix^{2/4}$	*leges*-scriptorium				12		14	3	2	1
Sélestat 14 (104)	$ix^{3/3}$	W. France				X	X+				
St Paul im Lavanttal 4/1	$ix^{1/4}$ (817–23)	N. Italy/Aquliea				5	5	5			
Stuttgart Jur. Q. 134	x/xi	Alemannia				X	X				
Vatikan Chigi F. IV. 75	x/xi (c.1000)	Central Italy				18	15	12			
Vatikan Reg. Lat. 338	$ix^{med.}$ (also x)	N. France				X					
Wolfenbüttel Aug. 4 50.2	$ix^{1/2}$	N.E. France				22					
Wolfenbüttel Blank. 130	$ix^{3/4}$	N. Italy			7	15	12+		4		
Ansegis						X	X	X	X		

'X' denotes a manuscript in which the text is present but not edited. '+' denotes the presence of the Zusatzkapitel to Capitulary no. 140.

The very late ninth-century South French manuscript Kopenhagen Gl. Kgl. Saml. 1943 was not seen by Boretius, but Mordek suggested that it was derived from a *leges*-scriptorium exemplar on the grounds of its inclusion of the full sequence of Capitularies nos. 137–140, otherwise uniquely attested in BN Lat. 2718, its provision of a collection of model letters to exalted people, and its more general juxtaposition of legal and theological works.[40] The texts in the Kopenhagen manuscript seem very plausibly to be related to those of BN Lat. 2718, but variant readings suggest that it is very unlikely to be a direct copy. In the text of Capitulary no. 138, for example, it shares the variant reading *consecrandis* with BN Lat. 2718 in c.6, but in c.7, it has the mainstream reading *inconsulta*, where BN Lat. 2718 has *inutili*. Equally the texts share the omission of *vel imperiali* in the same c.7, but the Kopenhagen manuscript preserves *illum dignum* in the last chapter, a phrase not found in BN Lat. 2718.[41] The texts in the Kopenhagen manuscript of Capitularies nos. 139 and 140 fit squarely into the large 'pure' group. So the capitularies in this volume are closer to those in BN Lat. 2718 than any edited by Boretius.

The Capitulary of Herstall in Vat. Reg. Lat. 846 is quite rich in unique readings, and it has not been possible to relate the text to any others on the basis of Boretius's edition. Some readings are clearly mistakes, such as the omission of *non* in c.2, and the spelling *pararochia* in c.4. A notable feature is that this capitulary is presented immediately after the *Decretio Childeberti*, with the same layout and similar title, very much anchoring Charlemagne into a line of rulers. A line of rulers is indeed found in the king list in the same manuscript.[42]

5.2.2 Lex Visigothorum *and* Lex Burgundionum

The *Lex Visigothorum* in BN Lat. 4418 was copied, apparently directly, into BN Lat. 4614, a tenth-century North Italian manuscript.[43] 4614's *Lex Alemannorum* and *Lex Baiuwariorum* are also from the same families as in other *leges*-scriptorium texts.[44]

The *leges*-scriptorium texts of *Lex Burgundionum* have been considered part of the B class, which contained material additional to the basic

[40] Mordek (1995), *Bibliotheca*, pp. 192–5. The manuscript can be seen online at www.kb.dk/permalink/2006/manus/84/eng/ last viewed 10 August 2014.

[41] Other variant readings in this manuscript have turned out to be quite significant, but unfortunately cannot be examined here.

[42] See section 5.3.4 below.

[43] *Leges Visigothorum* ed. K. Zeumer (Hannover, 1902), MGH Leges nationum Germanicarum I, p. XIX. See also M. C. Diáz y Diáz, 'La Lex Visigothorum y sus manuscritos. Un enseyo de reinterpretación' *Anuario de historia del derecho español*, 46 (1976), pp. 163–224. For the suggestion that the *Lex Visigothorum* text in BN Lat. 4118 was the result of the influence of Benedict of Aniane see Wormald (1999), *The making*, p. 64.

[44] See sections 5.2.6 and 5.2.7 below for the other texts.

eighty-eight chapter common text, and both contain a *Zusatzkapitel* from the *Lex Romana Burgundionum*, found in only three other manuscripts:[45]

St Paul im Lavanttal 4/1	ix$^{1/4}$	N. Italy
BN Lat. 4633	x$^{1/4}$	N. E. France
BN Lat. 4758	ix$^{1/3}$	Burgundy

The pronounced restriction of manuscripts of this group to the early ninth century suggests that this strain of the tradition lost out in terms of influence thereafter.[46] Although it is just possible that BN Lat. 4758 was influenced by the *leges*-scriptorium manuscripts, the likeliest candidate, on the grounds of dating, is BN Lat. 4633. Equally, the *leges*-scriptorium might have got its text from Italy or Burgundy. There are not enough manuscripts to make a clear case, so the position of the text must remain mysterious.

5.2.3 Lex Ribuaria

Lex Ribuaria and St Gallen Stadtbib. 338

Buchner rated the text of the *Lex Ribuaria* in Vat. Reg. Lat. 991 as the single 'best' of the revised B redaction, and also rated highly that of BN Lat. 4418.[47] He identified the text in St Gallen Stadtbib. 338 (Mainz, ix$^{1/3}$, with later ix additions from St Gallen) as most closely related to Vat. Reg. Lat. 991, suggesting the possibility of some kind of line of transmission. However, the redactions of *Lex Alemannorum* in the same manuscripts, although both B texts, fall into quite different sub-families of B texts, as I describe below. Samples of Vat. Reg. Lat. 991 have been used to say something about its *Lex Salica* K text, but I have not been able to see the unedited St Gallen manuscript, so cannot make a more detailed argument.[48] There is no contradiction here, since there is no reason why more than one text would have been copied from a *leges*-scriptorium product. Indeed, one *leges*-scriptorium manuscript, BN Lat. 4418, contained the *Lex Ribuaria* without the *Lex Alemannorum*. The difference between the *Lex Alemannorum* texts only suggests that no direct contact was made between the two specific manuscripts Vat. Reg. Lat. 991 and St Gallen 338.

45 *Leges Burgundionum* ed. L. R. de Salis (Hannover, 1892), MGH Leges nationum Germanicarum II, 1, p. 16. The origin of the division between redactions and the meaning of the extra material is not clear. See F. Beyerle, 'Zur Textgestalt und Textgeschichte der Lex Burgundionum' *ZRG GA*, *71* (1954), pp. 23–54 and particularly p.27 for conflicting stemmata.

46 Cf. comments on the *Epitome Iuliani* in section 5.3.1 below.

47 Buchner (1952), *Textkritische Untersuchungen*, pp. 88–9 and 80–1. Texts B16 and B5.

48 The Stadbibliothek manuscripts are not yet online.

Buchner's other most 'pure' *Lex Ribuaria* B texts may or may not derive from *leges*-scriptorium exemplars, but are worth listing anyway:

B1	St Gallen Stadtbib. 338	$ix^{1/3}$	Mainz
B11	Hamburg 141a in scrino	$ix^{3/4}$	Fulda Heimat
B12	BN Lat. 4417	$ix^{ex.}$	Burgundy
B18	Vat. Reg. Lat. 338	$ix^{1/2}$	N. France

Lex Ribuaria and BN Lat. 4632 and 4628

But Buchner found that a wholly strict division between revised Carolingian B texts and older A texts of *Lex Ribuaria* cannot be maintained.[49] Many manuscripts are best classified as mixtures, which could be explained if A texts were corrected with 'pure' B texts, and then copied. In the case of München Lat. 4115 (s. viii/ix), we can see that the text has actually been corrected in this way in a hand of the very early ninth century.[50] What were these 'pure' B manuscripts? Is it possible that these were deliberately disseminated by a centre, and intended to circulate? If so, the purity of the *leges*-scriptorium manuscripts is tantalising.

The example of München Lat. 4115 is from the period before the *leges*-scriptorium, but the variety in the tradition of *Lex Ribuaria* may suggest that such a process of correction continued later into the ninth century. We can compare the texts found in Autramnus's manuscript BN Lat. 4632 and BN Lat. 4628. Both are from the later ninth century, and as Charles West has pointed out, the contents are in many respects very similar.[51] The choice of texts is close, with both including a set of *Lex Salica, Ribuaria* and *Alemannorum*, and capitularies. A highly distinctive arrangement of the chapters in Capitulary no. 40 is shared.[52] This is a very strong argument for relationship: apart from these two manuscripts, only BN Lat. 10753 (s. $ix^{med.}$) shares this arrangement, in a remarkably mixed tradition.[53]. Yet 4632 has a *Lex Ribuaria* classified as A11, while 4628 has B13, a B text recognised as very close to the A.[54] Was there, then, a similar kind of correction of an A text using a 'pure' B text in a manuscript that linked the two?

We can only say that this was possible. Other texts in the manuscript seem to have quite different origins. The text of Capitulary no. 139 is rather different in the two manuscripts: BN Lat. 4628, Boretius's text 14, belongs to a variant text family as shown on the stemma, while 4632

49 Buchner (1952), *Textkritische Untersuchungen*, p. 132: 'Eine feste Grenze zwischen A und B besteht nicht'.
50 See discussion in Chapter 4, section 4.1.1.
51 See West (2009), 'Carolingian advocate', pp. 197–8.
52 See Chapter 3, section 3.3.1.
53 I explore this elsewhere. See Chapter 3, section 3.3.1 and section 5.2.7.
54 Buchner (1952), *Textkritische Untersuchungen*, pp. 85–6.

Table 5.4 *Comparison of Manuscripts BN Lat. 4632 and 4628*

BN Lat. 4632		BN Lat. 4628	
Folios	Text	Folios	Text
1r–7r	*Lex Ribuaria* A11		
7r–29v	*Lex Salica* K39	1r–22v	*Lex Salica* K28
29v–31r	Capit. no. 39	22v–24r	Capit. no. 39
31r–32r	Capit. no. 40	24r–25r	Capit. no. 40
32r–v	Capit. no. 104 c. 7	25r–26r	Capit. no. 44
32v–37r	Capit. no. 139 (10)	26v–30v	Capit. no. 139 (14)
37r	Capit. no. 134 c. 2	30v–32r	Capit. no. 140
37r–38v	Capit. no. 142	32r	Capit. no. 156
		32r–v, 41r–v	Capit. no. 141
		33r–40v, 42r–49r	*Lex Ribuaria* B13
39r–59v	*Lex Alemannorum* B	50r–66v	*Lex Alemannorum* B

belongs to the more 'pure' class. This is the opposite result we would expect, if we imagined that the capitulary texts might also have been corrected according to *leges*-scriptorium exemplars: BN Lat. 4628 has a *Lex Ribuaria* closer to the *leges*-scriptorium text than does BN Lat. 4632, but a Capitulary no. 139 further removed from the *leges*-scriptorium text. The *Lex Alemannorum* texts are both in the same group of the B tradition as described below, but it is difficult to go further with textual links from the edition.[55] The manuscripts also contain somewhat different capitularies, although they have almost exactly the same place in the structure of the manuscripts, as illustrated in Table 5.4.

So the two manuscripts exhibit striking similarities, but also substantial differences. It is just possible that some of the differences relate to contact between a manuscript containing an early redaction of *Lex Ribuaria* and a *leges*-scriptorium manuscript with an updated redaction, but only possible.

5.2.4 Lex Salica

The original problem in the argument attributing a straightforwardly 'official' character to the *leges*-scriptorium manuscripts is the mixture of redactions of *Lex Salica* they contain. McKitterick suggested that the period of the *leges*-scriptorium was one in which the K redaction was still gaining acceptance.[56] I explore some alternative possibilities here.

[55] They are B7 and B5 in the edition. See section 5.2.5 below.

[56] McKitterick (1989), *Written word*, p. 57.

The K text

The state of the edition makes a satisfying assessment of the influence and nature of the *leges*-scriptorium K texts a herculean task. According to my count, Eckhardt neglected thirty-one manuscripts entirely, and relied on the work of earlier editors, sometimes only on partial collations, for many of the others.[57] Of the *leges*-scriptorium manuscripts, only BN Lat. 4418 was used in Eckhardt's edition (as K24). When Hartmann tested the accuracy of the most recent editions of the *leges* in 1996, he found Eckhardt's A–E texts generally reliable, but he found some noteworthy errors in some of his K texts.[58] An absolutely full study of the place of the *leges*-scriptorium K texts in the tradition must wait for a comprehensive new edition.

Eckhardt was, however, already able to point to some loose, speculative parallels between some manuscripts.[59] The only result of consequence for these purposes is his link between K24 and K25: that is between BN Lat. 4418 and BN Lat. 4417. The edited texts suggest there is no obviously 'mixed' class of texts such as we can observe with the *Lex Ribuaria*. That is, there is no evidence for a programme of improvement of older texts with reference to new. So far, only a single interpolation of K text into an A has been found, in BN Lat. 9653 (ix$^{1/2}$, Burgundy), text A4 of *Lex Salica*, found at c.1,3.

At least, this lack of mixing holds true in a hypothetical *reception* phase of the tradition, but Eckhardt pointed to some quite significant features of the texts of K24 and K17 that he thought shed important light on the process of construction of the K text itself and that have some affinity with Buchner's theory concerning the mixing of A and B texts of *Lex Ribuaria*.[60] He determined, convincingly, from the K tradition as a whole, that almost every previous redaction was used in the construction, not just A and C, but also E, and the shadowy, only partially and indirectly attested B text. But he argued that traces in the texts of K24 and K17 were shadows of two quite different processes of redaction, carried out only under a common broad plan. Most of his very striking evidence consisted of significant omissions at precisely the point where different redactions were spliced together into

57 The total list of manuscripts Eckhardt used in some form, that is in photocopy, original, or through someone else's edition or collation, in full or in part is K17-21, 24-5, 28-35, 38-9, 41, 46, 49, 51-2, 56, 63-6, 68, 68a, 75, 78-9, 80a. See my partial edition in Editions below for further details.

58 W. Hartmann, 'Brauchen wir neue Editionen der Leges?' in: R. Schieffer (ed.), *Mittelalterliche Texte: Überlieferung, Befunde, Deutungen* (Hannover, 1996), pp. 233–45. His answer was 'Ja, wir brauchen neue Editionen der *Leges*'.

59 These are: K17, K18, which have a relationship with K19; K20–1; K24–5; K31–36; K61–2; K65–7. *Pactus Legis Salicae. I: Einführung und 80 Titel-Text* ed. K. A. Eckhardt (Göttingen, 1954), Germanenrechte neue Folge. Westgermanisches Recht, p. 219.

60 For what follows, see (1954) *Pactus Legis Salicae. I: Einführung und 80 Titel-Text*, pp. 219–28.

the mainstream K tradition, and misplacement of additional vocabulary associated with the mainstream K text. These could derive from the misplacement of marginal additions in an exemplar somewhere earlier in the transmission. The fundamental difference between K24 and K17 was that the former was derived from an exemplar in which a C text was revised, and material and readings incorporated from a B and an E text, whereas the latter was derived from an exemplar in which an E text was reorganised, and material incorporated from the C text. In the case of K17, the unparalleled presence of the Merovingian 'additional capitulary', found otherwise only with A texts, might strengthen such an argument.[61] If Eckhardt was right, all this represents an extremely sophisticated editorial process. This sophistication, he argued, must be evidence of royal or imperial involvement.

Eckhardt's work from the 1950s on the relationship between the court and the K text can now be combined with the palaeographical arguments developed in subsequent decades. Both the key manuscripts Eckhardt identified are now thought to derive in some measure from the court-Tours axis. K24 is indeed the *leges*-scriptorium manuscript (or court product) BN Lat. 4418, and K17 is the extraordinary later ninth-century manuscript Leiden Voss. Lat. Q. 119, which has connections with Tours.[62] As shown in the tables above, we know that both Tours and the court preserved and produced a variety of redactions of the *Lex Salica*, so we have quite a range of evidence that either could have been responsible for the construction of the K text. The variety in Tours's holdings is still deeper than the court's, tantalisingly including an A text, and I argue below that Tours was also a centre of revision of Roman law. It is possible, then, that the K *Lex Salica* was produced at Tours.

The search for textual links has involved constructing an edition of samples of the texts of all the *leges*-scriptorium K manuscripts, as well as a number of other manuscripts not used in the MGH edition. None of the *leges*-scriptorium manuscripts has any of the lacunae Eckhardt found in K24 and K17 (indeed, none of the manuscripts I have seen does), so I have not found any evidence in them for the process of construction of the K text.

Otherwise, nothing in the admittedly small samples I have taken from the *leges*-scriptorium texts rules out a relationship between them, but there are not many conclusive hints at such a relationship either. Strikingly there is a large difference in the care with which the various manuscripts copied the K text, and this mirrors the care taken over their presentation. The text of Vat. Reg. Lat. 991 is

61 See section 5.1.3 above.
62 See the summary of the link with Tours in section 5.1.3 above.

accurate, Carolingian Latin, just like its texts of *Lex Ribuaria* and *Lex Baiuwariorum*.[63] Here again, from a different angle we can see that the *leges*-scriptorium produced quite different products, presumably for quite different audiences. Full details are given in the commentary to the edition.[64]

The only clear case in which a *leges*-scriptorium text may have been copied directly is in Vat. Reg. Lat. 338 (K69), from France, perhaps North France, s. $x^{1/2}$. The text is nearly identical with that of BN Lat. 4418. Its *Lex Ribuaria* (B18) was also rated as one of the 'purer' texts by Buchner. The manuscript is missing two quires from the beginning, and is damaged at the end, but was clearly a handbook of sorts, with dimensions 180 × 150 mm and a written area of 140 × 100 mm, written on only fourteen lines per page. This is a surprising result, because it shows how the texts in a gigantic display volume such as BN Lat. 4418 might be closely related to those in a much more humble working book. The manuscript has later additions, of the *Recapitulatio Solidorum*, as well as Capitulary no. 139, both of them relating in some sense to the *Lex Salica*, showing perhaps that the manuscript continued to be used.

The E text

More can be achieved, less painfully, with the E text because it is well edited. The manuscripts are as follows, in the groups identified by Eckhardt:

E11	Vat. Reg. Lat. 846	$ix^{2/4}$	*Leges*-scriptorium
E12	BN Lat. 4409	$ix^{ex.}$	France
E13	Warsaw BU 1	$ix^{2/4}$	*Leges*-scriptorium
E14	St Gallen 729	$ix^{2/4}$	*Leges*-scriptorium
E15	BN Lat. 4629	$ix^{inc.}$ (c.805)	Bourges
E16	Berlin Phil. 1736	$x^{2/2}$	France

So fully half of the manuscripts of this redaction are *leges*-scriptorium products, a proportion rivalled only by the *Epitome Aegidii*.[65] Eckhardt also determined that the E text used in the K redaction was close to the related manuscripts E13–14, both of which are from the *leges*-scriptorium, further enhancing the argument above that the court-Tours axis was involved in the construction of the K text.[66]

63 McKitterick (1989), *Written word*, p. 58 for this manuscript.

64 See Editions at the back of this book.

65 See section 5.3.1 below.

66 *Lex Salica. 100 Titel-Text* ed. K. A. Eckhardt (Weimar, 1953), Germanenrechte neue Folge. Westgermanisches Recht, pp. 220f.

But only one E text can be shown to have a close relationship with the *leges*-scriptorium text, that is BN Lat. 4409.

5.2.5 *Summary, and alternative channels of dissemination of the* Lex Ribuaria *and* Lex Salica

The codices that most plausibly demonstrate influence from *leges*-scriptorium texts so far are:

Kop. Kgl. Saml. 1943	ix^ex.	S. France	BN Lat. 2718: Capits.
St Gallen SB 338	ix^1/3	Mainz	Vat. Reg. Lat. 991: *Lex Rib.* Its *Lex Sal* has not been seen.
Vat. Reg. Lat. 338	ix^1/2	N. France	BN Lat. 4418: *Lex Sal*, and possibly also its 'pure' *Lex Rib.*
BN Lat. 4417	ix^ex.	Burgundy	BN Lat. 4418: *Lex Sal* (loose), and a speculative *Lex Rib* connection.
BN Lat. 4409	ix^ex.	France	Vat. Reg. Lat. 846: *Lex Sal* E.
BN Lat. 4614	x	N. Italy	BN Lat. 4418: *Lex Vis.*
BN Lat. 4633	x^1/4	N. E. France	BN Lat. 4418 and BN n. a. Lat. 204: *Lex Burg.*

If these manuscripts really are linked, they would show the influence of *leges*-scriptorium texts starting already rather soon after their production, in the first third of the ninth century, and continuing throughout the century and into the tenth. The influenced manuscripts are also in a variety of sizes, suggesting somewhat different uses, and there is a reasonable geographical spread throughout the empire. We do not have good, early, information on provenance for most of our *leges*-scriptorium manuscripts, but it is possible that St Gallen 729 was already in St Gallen in the mid-ninth century, if Mordek's identification of it with an entry in St Gallen's catalogue is correct.[67] Equally, additions made to Vat. Reg. Lat. 991 in a later ninth-century hand influenced by insular forms suggest that this 'export quality' manuscript was indeed exported.[68] So it seems that the manuscripts could be sent quite far, quite soon after they were written.

[67] Mordek (1995), *Bibliotheca*, p. 669. For the catalogue and its entry see Chapter 3, section 3.2.3 above p. 100. On relations between Tours and St Gallen see W. Vogler, 'St. Martin de Tours und St. Gallen. Europäische Beziehungen zwischen zwei karolingischen Klöstern' in: P. Ochsenbein and E. Ziegler (eds.), *Codices sangallenses: Festschrift für Johannes Duft zum 80. Geburtstag* (Thorbecke, 1995), pp. 117–36.

[68] Mordek (1995), *Bibliotheca*, pp. 838–41.

This is all significant, but on the basis of this number of manuscripts, it can hardly be argued that the *leges*-scriptorium had a decisive influence on the tradition of the texts considered. More results may be forthcoming if a new edition of the K *Lex Salica* is ever constructed, but it is also worth considering other possible major channels of transmission, which do not involve *leges*-scriptorium manuscripts at all.

One possibility stems from the transmission of *Lex Salica* K with Capitularies nos. 39 and 40 we have seen in Autramnus's manuscript BN Lat. 4632.[69] This arrangement (*Sal*-39-40) is decisively unlike anything we find in *leges*-scriptorium manuscripts, where those capitularies are not to be found at all.[70] In BN Lat. 4632 the group consisting of *Lex Salica*, Capitularies no. 39 and no. 40 occupy very nearly exactly three quaternio quires, and the same is true in BN Lat. 4628. The two manuscripts, although a different size today, since perhaps having been trimmed, have a very similar written area and number of lines per page. Both also have heightened indentation in the text of Capitulary no. 40. Could it be that the omission of certain chapters in some of the tradition, and then the incorporation, sometimes out of sequence, of the remaining chapters, as I describe Table 3.2, had something to do with a desire to keep the group within a certain number of quires, so it could circulate as *libelli*?[71] The indentation could be seen as another strategy for managing coverage of parchment. If so, this would provide evidence of an independent, distinct phase of circulation of *Lex Salica*, with Capitularies no. 39 and no. 40. The number of manuscripts with the same *Sal*-39-40 is just seven, but they are spread throughout the no. 39–40 tradition groups.

5.2.6 Lex Alemannorum

Group 2 manuscripts contain B texts, as well as revised texts of *Lex Salica*, *Ribuaria*, and *Baiuwariorum*. St Gallen 729 from Group 1, however, contains an A text. Lehmann identified a split in the B tradition, with nine families of B texts distinguished by quite different readings near the beginning of the text.[72] The largest and most broadly different group was B19–37. A simplified picture of the tradition looks something like the stemma shown in Figure 5.3.

69 See the discussion of Capitulary no. 39 in Chapter 3, section 3.3.1 above, and the presentation in Table 3.2 of various arrangements of this text with Capitulary no. 40 and *Lex Salica*.

70 See Table 3.2 on transmission of Capits. nos. 39–40.

71 See Table 3.2.

72 See *Leges Alamannorum* ed. K. Lehmann 2nd edition (Hannover, 1966), MGH Leges nationum Germanicarum V, 1, p. 18.

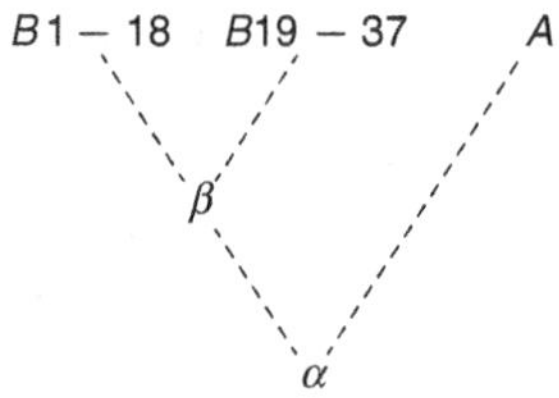

Fig. 5.3 Simplified stemma for *Lex Alemannorum*

The extant manuscripts from the group B19–37, that is the relevant family of *Lex Alemannorum*, are as follows[73]:

St Gallen 732	ix$^{1/4}$ (815-17)	Freising
St Paul im Lavanttal 4/1	ix$^{1/4}$ (817-23)	N. Italy/Aquliea
Vat. Reg. Lat. 857	ix$^{1/4}$	*Leges*-scriptorium
Vat. Reg. Lat. 991	ix$^{2/4}$	*Leges*-scriptorium
BN nouv. acq. Lat. 204	ix$^{2/4}$	*Leges*-scriptorium
Vat. Reg. Lat. 1128	ix$^{1/3}$	France
BN Lat. 4759	ix$^{2/4}$	E. France
BN Lat. 18237	ix$^{2/4}$	Tours in part
Vat. Reg. Lat. 1050	ix$^{\text{med.}}$	France
Wolfenbüttel Blank. 130	ix$^{3/4}$	N. Italy/Augsburg
Leiden Voss. Lat. Q. 119	ix$^{4/4}$	France
BN Lat. 4417	ix$^{\text{ex.}}$	Burgundy
BN Lat. 4614	x	N. Italy
Stuttgart Jur. Q. 134	x/xi	Alemannia
BN Lat. 9654	x/xi	Sens/Metz

So all three of the *leges*-scriptorium B texts are from the same side of the split in the B tradition, which also has early manuscripts from Bavaria, North Italy, and France (including a possible Tours connection). I shall not attempt here to trace directions and currents of influence any more precisely than this.

5.2.7 Lex Baiuwariorum

It has been noted that Vat. Reg. Lat. 991 contains the most accurate Carolingian copy of this *Lex*.[74] But the *Lex Baiuwariorum* is perhaps the single most difficult *lex* to work with for those interested in textual history. Eckhardt's *Lex Salica* edition is certainly confusing in the extreme, and far from comprehensive, but at least the major outlines of the boundaries between redactions are uncontroversial, the cumulative

73 Though relevant texts were also witnessed in two now lost manuscripts from Strasbourg, one used by Sichard (B34) and one by Lindenbrog (B36). See *Lex Alemannorum* pp. 15–17.

74 McKitterick (1989), *Written word*, pp. 58–9, referring to the discussion in Buchner's introduction to *Lex Ribuaria* pp. 37–8.

achievement of generations of editors, and each redaction has been edited independently, as well as synoptically.[75]

The most recent MGH edition of the *Lex Baiuwariorum*, that of de Schwind, on the other hand, explicitly rejected the previous editor Merkel's classification into seven groups.[76] De Schwind abandoned any hope of producing a stemma, limiting his textual commentary to establishing some broad groups of manuscripts which were closer to or further from the *Urtext* he had derived.[77] Soon after its publication, de Schwind's approach was already attacked: for Eckhardt, writing in 1927, the work represented a pronounced 'step backwards', for Krusch, a 'serious derailment'.[78] At the same time however, Eckhardt savaged Krusch's work, based on Merkel's edition, on the place of the Emendata text in the tradition, and proposed a quite distinctive new stemma.[79] The debates surrounding the appearance of de Schwind's edition continued in this vein, and often display a genuinely comic mixture of reverence and disdain for their colleagues, which can make clear judgements very difficult to formulate.[80]

The fundamental issue was the basic order of the redactions, whether what were referred to as *emendata* or *antiqua* redactions might be closer to the *Urtext*. De Schwind's understanding was that the less 'vulgar' E

75 So aside from the two-volume edition *Pactus Legis Salicae, Lex Salica* ed. K. A. Eckhardt (Hannover, 1962–9), MGH Leges nationum Germanicarum IV, 1–2, one can also use the 'Germanenrechte neue Folge' series, which includes *Pactus Legis Salicae. I: Einführung und 80 Titel-Text* ed. K. A. Eckhardt (Göttingen, 1954), Germanenrechte neue Folge. Westgermanisches Recht. The basic grouping of *Lex Salica* manuscripts was certainly already established in the edition *Lex Salica: the ten texts with the glosses, and the Lex Emendata* ed. J. H. Hessels and H. Kern (London, 1880).

76 *Lex Baiuvariorum* ed. E. de Schwind (Hannover, 1926), MGH Leges nationum Germanicarum V, 2; *Leges Alamannorum, Leges Baiuwarioum, Leges Burgundionum, Lex Frisionum* ed. J. Merkel (Hannover, 1863), MGH Leges in folio III.

77 *Lex Baiuvariorum* ed. E. de Schwind (Hannover, 1926), MGH Leges nationum Germanicarum V, 2, pp. 182f.

78 K. A. Eckhardt, *Die Lex Baiuvariorum: eine Textkritische Studie* (Breslau, 1927), p. 9 : 'Rücktritt', and B. Krusch, *Die Lex Bajuvariorum: Textgeschichte, Handschriftenkritik und Entstehung* (Berlin, 1924), p. 252 : 'schwere Entgleisung'.

79 Eckhardt (1927), *Lex Baiuvariorum*, p. 11 praises Krusch's work in general, but states 'Aber mit seiner Einschätzung der Emendata kann ich mich ganz und gar nicht befreunden'. The relevant works are Krusch (1924), *Lex Bajuvariorum* and Krusch (1927), *Neue Forschungen*.

80 See for example the lofty praise of Krusch in W. Stach, 'Geschichtswissenschaft und Rechtsgeschichte im Streit um die Stammesrechte. I. Teil: Probleme der Handschriftlichen Überlieferung der Bayerischen Lex' *Historische Vierteljahrschrift*, *26* (1931), pp. 682–737 at p. 683: in an era of terrible editorial standards, he represents, in a positive sense, a 'lebendige Verkörperung der Traditionen von Pertz und Waitz'. The central message of Krusch's twenty-five page damnation of the views of Heymann, who was at fault apparently because he believed that *some* use could come out of de Schwind's edition, was simply that he should have read and reproduced the conclusions of Krusch (1924), *Lex Bajuvariorum*. See Krusch (1927), *Neue Forschungen*, pp. 14–39 e.g. at p. 16: 'Das quellenmäßige Material für die Textgeschichte war in meinen Buche (d'1) zusammengestellt, so daß man nur aufmerksam zu lesen und richtig zu exzerpieren brauchte'.

text (not that he used the redaction sigle) was close to the *Urtext*, and that the vulgar versions were corruptions of that through bad copying. Krusch's view was the exact opposite: the E text was a conscious revision of the vulgar text, which improved the Latin systematically. Eckhardt was strongly critical of both views and devised what amounted to a middle position: the E text *was* a revised text, but derived from an ancestor of the A-B 'vulgar' text, not from that A-B text itself as Krusch had argued. Siems, some decades later, implied that this would in theory allow readings from the E to be used for an *Urtext*, and argued that a new edition was needed.[81]

The 1920s, then, the time when the most recent edition was produced, was a period of intense strife over the fundamentals of the history of the text. Since then, relatively little has been written on the problem. Kottje's survey of the manuscripts deliberately ignored the problem of the redactions, concentrating on establishing a parallel classification by location and date, and explanation of those patterns.[82] Most other recent discussions focus on the still controversial date and location for the *Urtext*, and on mining it as the fullest source available for the history of pre-788 Bavaria.[83]

It is, therefore, impossible at this stage to get further with the wider status of the *Lex Baiuwariorum* texts in *leges*-scriptorium manuscripts, whether they were revised texts at all, and if so, when and where the revision might have taken place. Also, most existing work has not treated the relationship *between* the emendata texts to any great extent. In this way the *Stand der Forschung* is closer to that for the *Lex Salica* than for the *Ribuaria* or *Alemannorum*, despite the smaller number of manuscripts. The single exception charting this relationship is still Krusch's 1924 work.[84] He distinguished the tradition of E1, 2, and 2a from that of E3-7, 10, 13:

Group 1

St Paul im Lavanttal 4/1	(sP, E1)	ix$^{1/4}$ (817-23)	N. Italy
Wolfenbüttel Blank 130	(E2)	ix$^{3/4}$	N. Italy/Augsburg
Cologny Bodmer 107	E2a	ix$^{ex.}$	N. W. Germany

81 H. Siems, 'Lex Baiuvariorum' in: E. Kaufmann and A. Erier (eds.), *Handwörterbuch zur deutschen Rechtsgeschichte* (Berlin, 1964), p. 1889.

82 Kottje (1986), 'Recht der Bayern', pp. 9–23.

83 Recently P. Landau, *Die Lex Baiuvariorum: Entstehungszeit, Entstehungsort und Charakter von Bayerns ältester Rechts- und Geschichtsquelle* (München, 2004), Bayerische Akademie der Wissenschaften. Philosophisch-Historische Klasse 3. See the comments in Schott (1979), 'Stand der Leges-Forschung', pp. 40–1. H. Siems, 'Das Lebensbild der Lex Baiuvariorum' in: H.-J. Hecker, R. Heydenreuther and H. Schlosser (eds.), *Rechtssetzung und Rechtswirklichkeit in der bayerischen Geschichte* (Munich, 2006), pp. 29–73. See also now, for some stimulating consideration of the text Innes (2011), 'Charlemagne, written law and justice', pp. 180–5.

84 Krusch (1924), *Lex Bajuvariorum*, pp. 139–63.

Group 2

Vat. Reg. Lat. 991	(V, E3)	$ix^{2/4}$	*leges*-scriptorium
BN n. a. Lat. 204	(P5, E6a)	$ix^{2/4}$	*leges*-scriptorium
BN Lat. 4759	(P3, E6)	$ix^{2/4}$	E. France
BN Lat. 4417	(P1, E5)	$ix^{ex.}$	Burgundy
BN Lat. 4614	(P2, E4)	x	N. Italy
BN Lat. 9654	(P4, E10)	x/xi	Sens/Metz
Graz III 37,2	(G, E7)	xii	Fragments
Rome Vallicelliana C 20	(E13)	xvi	

So it is possible, if we accept Krusch's work, to establish the manuscript groups into which the *leges*-scriptorium texts fit for the *Lex Baiuwariorum* as well as the *Lex Alemannorum* in a way that is not quite possible for the *Lex Ribuaria* and the *Lex Salica*. The *Lex Baiuwariorum* group consists of eight manuscripts, the *Alemannorum* of fifteen.

The sharp divergence in the chronological distribution of texts of the families of the *Lex Alemannorum* and the *Lex Baiuwariorum* found in the *leges*-scriptorium reflects the relatively late transmission of the *Lex Baiuwariorum* in general and the unusually early transmission of the *Lex Alemannorum* in general.[85] So the distribution of texts from these families is broadly comparable with that of the textual tradition of the two *leges* in general.

5.2.8 *Summary of connections between texts of* Leges Alemannorum *and* Baiuwarorium

We have found that each text presents particular problems for an investigation of its textual history. The text of the *Lex Salica* is not yet well enough understood for a comprehensive study, and the nature of the transmission of the *Lex Ribuaria* makes connections difficult to establish, despite the unusually good work of editors and commentators. Most of the *leges*-scriptorium texts of the capitularies seem to fit squarely into only rather wide groups, and this is also the case with the *Leges Alemannorum* and *Baiuwariorum*, as far as we can tell from the editions and the limited helpful textual work.

Still, some results are forthcoming:

The manuscripts that share the redactions of *Lex Alemannorum* and *Lex Baiuwariorum* of the *leges*-scriptorium manuscripts are:

BN Lat. 4759	$ix^{2/4}$	E. France	*Sal, Rib, Bav, Al, Isid.*

[85] See Table 1.1.

BN Lat. 4417	ix$^{ex.}$	Burgundy	Capits, *Sal*K25, *Ans, Rib, Bav, Al, Burg*B8, *Epit. Aegid.*
BN Lat. 4614	x	N. Italy	*Bav, Al, Vis* and *Lang.*
BN Lat. 9654	x/xi	Sens/Metz	*Sal*K32 *Rib, Bav, Al,* Capits.
The manuscripts with only a related *Lex Alemannorum:*			
St Gallen 732	815-17	Freising	*Al* only.
Vat. Reg. Lat. 1128	ix$^{1/3}$	France	*Sal*K73 *Rib, Al, Burg*A4 *Vis, LRV*
BN Lat. 18237	ix$^{2/4}$	Tours in part	*Sal*C4, *Al, Ans,* Capits., *Isid.*
Vat. Reg. Lat. 1050	ix$^{med.}$	France	*Sal*K72, *Rib, Al, LRV, Rom. Burg.*, reworked version of some *Form. Tur.*
Stuttgart Jur. Q. 134	x/xi		*Al* and *Ans.*
Manuscripts with a related *Lex Alemannorum*, but an unrelated *Lex Baiuwariorum*:			
St Paul im Lav. 4/1	817-23	N. Italy	*Sal*K19, *Rib, Bav, Al, Burg,* Capits., *Epit. Aegid..*
Wolf. Blank. 130	ix$^{3/4}$	N. Italy/Augsburg	*Sal*K58, *Bav, Al, Burg, Lang* Capits., frag. *Rib.*
Leiden VLQ 119	ix$^{4/4}$	France	Capits., *Isid., Rib*B21, *Sal*K17 *Bav*A2, *Epit. Aegid..*

These results for the *Leges Alemannorum* and *Baiuwariorum* can be compared with those for the capitularies and *Leges Salica* and *Ribuaria* above. Although the parallels for each text considered may be weak, multiple parallels magnify the possibility that there are real connections. It seems that, from this list, BN Lat. 4417 and 4614 are closest to *leges*-scriptorium manuscripts in their other texts. BN Lat. 4759 and BN Lat. 9654 are not especially close to *leges*-scriptorium texts in either *Lex Salica* or in *Lex Ribuaria*, however.[86] Neither are those manuscripts lower on this list related to *leges*-scriptorium products in their other texts.

So in total, we have only a handful of manuscripts of barbarian *leges* with convincing parallels with *leges*-scriptorium texts.

5.3 THE TEXTS, THEIR SOURCES, AND THEIR INFLUENCE. 2. ROMAN LAW, *FORMULAE, INTERPRETATIVE AIDS*

5.3.1 Roman law

Ten of the thirteen *leges*-scriptorium manuscripts contain some kind of Roman law. Two of the three manuscripts without Roman law are fragmentary, giving only a few folios of presumably larger extant

[86] See Buchner (1952), *Textkritische Untersuchungen*, pp. 78–9.

manuscripts, and the third is BN Lat. 2718, with its unique features already discussed. So it is even possible that *all leges*-scriptorium manuscripts were intended to contain some Roman law.

The place of Roman law in the Carolingian period cannot be considered in detail here. Most commonly Roman law is imagined to have fitted into a system of personality and to have found use as the 'law of the church'.[87] We have already noted some of the difficulties with the personality principle, but the law of the church theory is also problematic.[88] When the principle is invoked by historians, evidence tends to be taken out of context. Thus, for Wormald, the invocation of Roman Law at one stage in the Fleury-St Denis case was evidence for the application of a defined principle, even though the resolution of the dispute may well have turned on a capitulary provision.[89] Equally, *Lex Ribuaria*'s incidental remark that a manumission be performed 'according to the *Lex Romana* by which the church lives', is often treated as if it were a normative statement in its own right, binding across all early medieval kingdoms.[90] In any case, what might 'the law of the church' mean? If it meant the personal law of churchmen, that would clash with instances of Italian clerics professing their law as Lombard.[91] Certainly Hincmar of Rheims often cited Roman law in arguments over church property, but he also cited Carolingian capitularies. Charles the Bald's edict of Pîtres, on the other hand, seems to imagine large regions of his kingdom using Roman law.[92] For now, I shall imagine Roman law as being subject to much the same principles as I have argued for the other *leges barbarorum*, as being a possible source of material for disputes and arguments, with

87 Explicitly stated for Frankish Gaul, for example, in I. Wood, 'Roman law in the Barbarian kingdoms' in: A. Ellegård and G. Åkerström-Hougen (eds.), *Rome and the north* (Jonsered, 1996), p. 14. See also in particular Wood (1993), 'Theodosian Code', pp. 159–77.

88 See C. G. Fürst, 'Ecclesia vivit lege Romana?' *ZRG KA*, *92* (1975), pp. 17–36 for further details and references. For the nature of the use of Roman law, for which there is, sadly, no space here to treat in detail despite excellent evidence from Tours, see J. Imbert, 'Les références au droit romain sous les Carolingiens' *Revue Historique de droit français et étranger*, *73* (1995), pp. 163–74; J. Imbert, 'Le droit Romain dans les textes juridiques carolingiens' in: *Studi in onore Pietro de Francisi* Volume III (Milan, 1956), pp. 61–7; J. Gaudemet, 'Survivances Romaines dans le droit de la monarchie Franque du Vème au Xème siécle' *Tijdschrift voor Rechtsgeschiedenis*, *23* (1955), pp. 149–206; J. Gaudemet, 'Le Breviére d'Alaric et les épitomes' *Ius Romanum Medii Aevi I, 2 b aa β* (1965).

89 Wormald (1999), *The making*, p. 64: 'Roman law in the Frankish kingdoms was, as is evident from the Fleury – St Denis case, *par excellence* the law of the Church'.

90 The text of the *Lex Ribuaria*, and variants, are given in Chapter 4, section 4.2.2 above. So for example P. Stein, *Roman law in European history* (Cambridge, 1999), p. 40 provides a straight misquotation: 'In the words of the law of the Ripuarian Franks, "The Church lives by the Roman law"'. The principle, expressed like this, is in fact found first in the eleventh-century *Liber Papiensis*.

91 References in Fürst (1975), 'Ecclesia vivit lege Romana?', pp. 27–30.

92 MGH Capit. II no. 273 pp. 310–28 e.g. at 318–19: *In illis autem regionibus, in quibus secundum legem Romanam iudicantur iudicia...* and see Guterman (1990), *Principle*, pp. 263f.

a 'validity' underpinned in the first instance by consensus, and I shall concentrate on the evidence of the texts in a narrower, technical sense.

There is no clear pattern to the texts of Roman law presented. Haenel considered seven of our manuscripts, and assigned them to four different groups, Groups II, III, IV(A), and V. These are groups for Breviary manuscripts missing many of the *Pauli Sententiae*, for manuscripts of the *Epitome Aegidii*, for manuscripts containing excerpts of the Breviary, and for manuscripts containing fragments of the Breviary.[93] This again shows how many different forms of similar texts are found in *leges*-scriptorium manuscripts, just as in the case of the *leges* described above.

Epitome Iuliani

BN Lat. 4418 is the only manuscript of the group to contain the *Epitome Iuliani*, a late antique educational work based on the Justinianic codification.[94] Kaiser attributed it to group A of the manuscript tradition on the basis of distinctive omissions from its text, even though it broke off before including his 'Appendix A'. The other two members of the group are from North Italy: BN Lat. 4568 (viii/ix) and Milan 668 (viii$^{ex.}$). The *leges*-scriptorium manuscript is thus the youngest of the group, and the only non-Italian example.

The only later example of a manuscript exhibiting contact with an A-group *Epitome Iuliani* text is the so-called *Lex Romana Canonice Compta*, a northern Italian text from the ninth century, which survives in a single manuscript BN Lat. 12448 (N. Italy, $x^{1/4}$).[95] This text was in turn used in the late ninth-century North Italian *Collectio Anselmo dedicata*. It seems more likely on the basis of the manuscript distribution that the *Epitome Iuliani* found its way into the *Lex Romana Canonice Compta* through the use of the North Italian manuscripts than through contact with a *leges*-scriptorium exemplar. However, more time with the manuscript in Paris is needed to establish or rule out a definite link, since, as Kaiser pointed out, Mor's edition of the *Lex Romana Canonice Compta* is too inaccurate to be used for anything other than an assessment of the contents of the manuscript.[96]

There is thus no evidence that the *leges*-scriptorium text of the *Epitome Iuliani* had any influence: it rather seems to represent the dead end of the tradition. A valuable result, however, is that the *leges* scribes seemed to have hunted for this text in northern Italy. The range of texts and of their places of origin is therefore quite wide, especially in BN Lat.

93 *LRV* pp. xl f..

94 Kaiser's weighty study covers this work from every imaginable angle, so is the basis for this section: W. Kaiser, *Die Epitome Iuliani* (Frankfurt am Main, 2004).

95 Kaiser (2004), *Die Epitome Iuliani*, pp. 493f.

96 Kaiser (2004), *Die Epitome Iuliani*, p. 500 referring to *Lex Romana canonice compta* ed. C. G. Mor (Pavia, 1927).

4418, which also included Salic, Ribuarian, Burgundian, and Visigothic material.

Epitome Aegidii

Seven *leges*-scriptorium manuscripts contain the *Epitome Aegidii*, an abbreviated version of the *LRV*, usually considered a product of eighth-century southern France. So more than half of the *leges*-scriptorium manuscripts contain the *Epitome Aegidii*, which is also more than half of all ninth-century manuscripts of the work.[97] The *leges*-scriptorium, then, has a more prominent place in the tradition of this text than of any other, except for the E *Lex Salica*.

Familiar problems with editions plague any attempt to go further with specific textual links to establish the influence of the *leges*-scriptorium texts. The most recent edition is that of Haenel, who appears largely, though not exclusively, to have followed the text produced by Aegidius, its first editor, in 1517.[98] Aegidius's text has no critical apparatus, and the editor does not even mention which manuscripts he used. This problem has not even been mentioned in more recent commentary: discussion in more general works on Roman law in the early Middle Ages has focused on establishing a date, location, and some rudimentary characterisation of the text, while even Lehmann's text-critical work on BN nouv. acq. Lat. 204, a manuscript at that point unedited except for its capitularies, included no text-critical analysis of its *Epitome*, restricting itself to a simple list of which sections of text it included.[99] Surely not only a new edition, but a new comprehensive study along the lines of Kaiser's *Epitome Iuliani* is needed.

I have supplied a partial edition of the prologue and some other excerpts of the text to try to break down this problem.[100] It has not been possible to see all the relevant manuscripts. Haenel's work on the prologue, which is very similar in the *Epitome Aegidii* and the *LRV*, has provided support here, but his text can be exposed as quite inaccurate, or at least as not representative of most of the tradition. His text of the prologue, for example, provided some quite different readings between

97 For a full survey, see Liebs (2002), *Römische Jurisprudenz*, pp. 111f.

98 *Summae sive argumenta legum diversorum Imperatorum, ex corpore Divi Theodosii, ... Novellis Divi Valentiniani Aug., Martiani, Maioriani, Severi, ... nunc primum excusa, etc.* ed. P. Aegidius (Louvain, 1517).

99 For the dating and locating see esp. Liebs (2002), *Römische Jurisprudenz*, pp. 229–30 and Gaudemet (1965), 'Breviére', pp. 42f. K. Lehmann, 'Der Codex Paris lat. nouv. acq. 204' *Neues Archiv*, *12* (1887), pp. 579–85 claims that Hessels used this text in his edition *Lex Salica: the ten texts with the glosses, and the Lex Emendata* ed. J. H. Hessels and H. Kern (London, 1880), but I cannot find anything in Hessels to support this.

100 See Editions at the back of this book.

his *LRV* manuscripts and his *Epitome* manuscripts, which turn out to have no support in the manuscripts I have used. So a major conclusion from the partial edition is that more work needs to be done on the text.

In all this editorial confusion, and lack of detailed study of the texts, it has not been possible to propose definite relationships between *leges*-scriptorium manuscripts and those in the wider tradition. The partial edition presented here by no means rules out a common family for the *leges*-scriptorium *Epitomes*, although it provides little positive support for it either, and we must note how individual the text of BN Lat. 4416 is. One possible link has been found between BN Lat. 4418, BN Lat. 4409, and BN Lat. 4417. But more can be said about the prominence of the *Epitome Aegidii* in the *leges*-scriptorium manuscripts and its implications for the *earlier* history of the texts, and of Tours as a centre of revision and production of legal texts, as I shall explore below.[101]

The *LRV*

The remaining Roman law manuscripts contain the *LRV*, but again in rather different redactions. Vat. Reg. Lat. 857 is from Haenel's Group III (for manuscripts containing excerpts of the *LRV*), and the others, Warsaw BU 1, Berlin Lat. Q. 150, and BN Lat. 4408 from Group II. The general form of these Group II *leges*-scriptorium manuscripts was common enough: they tended to omit the original *Sententiae*.[102] But the Warsaw-Berlin twins also include very rare Novels of Majorian, found in only one other later manuscript of the *LRV*, and in one collection of the Novels of various emperors alone. So the manuscripts containing the Novels are:

Vaticano Ottob./Vat. Lat. 7277	viii/x	Gaul	Novels only
Warsaw BU 1	$ix^{2/4}$	*leges*-scriptorium	*liber decurtatus*
Berlin Lat. Q. 150	$ix^{2/4}$	*leges*-scriptorium	*liber decurtatus*
BN Lat. 9652 / BN Lat. 4406 f.60-7	ix	Beauvais	*liber decurtatus*

[101] See section 5.4 below.

[102] Haenel described them as *codices a quibus verba constitutionum et pauli multae sententiae absunt, et constitutionum quidem verba plerumque aut cum inscriptionibus aut cum subscriptionibus* and listed twenty examples. *LRV* p. xl. For Mommsen they were *libri decurtati*. See *CodTh* Vol. 1, 1 at pp. XCV-VI.

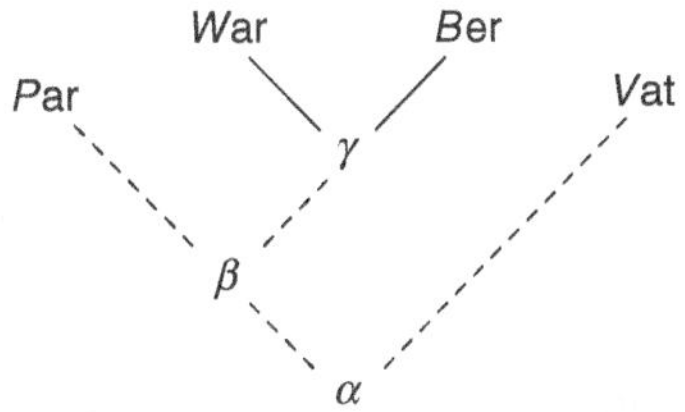

Fig. 5.4 Stemma of Novels of Majorian

We can compare the texts of the Novels from Mommsen's edition, to find that the tenth-century manuscript containing Novels alone, Vatican Ottob./Vat. Lat. 7277, has a quite distinct text.[103] The Berlin and Warsaw manuscripts have almost identical texts, and share a good number of readings with the Paris manuscript.[104] The Warsaw-Berlin and Paris texts do, however, have many divergent readings, suggesting that the relationship is a common source at some point earlier in the tradition: the Paris text is certainly not a direct, or even indirect, copy of the Warsaw-Berlin text. A reasonable stemma might be as shown in Figure 5.4.

It seems unlikely that the Warsaw or Berlin texts had much of an influence. It has not been possible to establish links with BN Lat. 4408 and Vat. Reg. Lat. 857 from the sample of the prologue taken, so we cannot establish that any of the *leges*-scriptorium texts had a wider influence.

5.3.2 Formulae

Five *leges*-scriptorium manuscripts contain *formulae.*

Formulae Imperiales

The *Formulae Imperiales* in BN Lat. 2718 have already been discussed briefly.[105] One of these *formulae* can also be found in BN nouv. acq. Lat. 204. The two manuscripts have parallels with each other also in their capitulary texts and their patristic texts. These parallels between the personal notebook and the 'export' codex, neatly laid out, without tironian notes, indeed make it possible that manuscripts similar to BN

[103] Mommsen and Gaudemet (1965), 'Breviére', p. 33 use Ottob., which has now been replaced by Vat. See G. Dolezalek, *Verzeichnis der Handschriften zum römischen Recht bis 1600* (Frankfurt am Main, 1972) Vol. 2 (unpaginated volume). Here he lists the Novels as s. x, but the *Lex Romana Burgundionum* as s. viii/ix.

[104] This is all based on Mommsen's *CodTh.* Mommsen's ψ and θ are the Warsaw and Berlin texts, and mostly agree. ω is the Paris manuscript, which has a good proportion of readings in common with ψ/θ. γ is the Vaticana, and has mostly independent readings.

[105] See section 5.1.5 above.

Lat. 2718 were used by scribes for collecting useful texts, which would then be copied into more formal manuscripts.[106]

Formulae Turonenses

Three *leges*-scriptorium manuscripts have been identified as containing *formulae* from the collection edited as *Formulae Turonenses*, further reinforcing the impression of a link with Tours.[107] I can now add a fourth manuscript, a fragment in Vat. Reg. Lat. 857, as far as I know not identified to date.[108] Here, however, the texts are not straightforwardly consistent. As Zeumer noted, the text from the Warsaw manuscript, which he used for the most part as his base text for the edition, is in far more accurate Carolingian Latin than BN Lat. 10756. The two do, however, share enough readings for Zeumer to have related the manuscripts more closely to each other than to any others, so it seems possible, though by no means clear, that the 'improvements' seen in the Warsaw manuscript were carried out at Tours, as part of the same programme as the redaction of the K text of the *Lex Salica*.

The text of the fragments of *Formulae Turonenses* in Vat. Reg. Lat. 852 have parallels with two manuscripts: BN Lat. 2123 and BN Lat. 4409. BN Lat. 4409's *Lex Salica* text is E12, which is most closely related in the extant tradition, as we have seen, with E11, Vat. Reg. Lat. 846, another *leges*-scriptorium product. BN Lat. 4409, therefore, shows two independent parallels with different *leges*-scriptorium manuscripts.

It seems again in the case of the *formulae* that the *leges*-scriptorium produced texts of a range of qualities in terms of their Latin, and even that the scribes may have been actively involved in the revision of the Latin. The 'best' text is from the very carefully produced, rather splendid, Warsaw manuscript, whereas Vat. Reg. Lat. 852 is somewhat chaotic, crammed, and full of Tironian notes. BN Lat. 10756 falls somewhere in the middle in terms of presentation: it is cluttered, with much abbreviation, and displays some variation in its hands, but does not mix tironian notes.

5.3.3 The legal compilations extracted from Isidore's Etymologiae

The presence of relevant excerpts from Isidore in legal manuscripts is a significant peculiarity that needs some explaining, and could have some

[106] See section 5.2.1 above.

[107] For what follows, see Rio (2009), *Frankish Formulae*, pp. 91–3.

[108] The most recent survey of the manuscripts is P. Depreux, 'La tradition manuscrite des "Formules de Tours" et la diffusion des modèles d'actes aux VIIIe et IXe siècles' in: Depreux and Judic (2004), *Alcuin à Tours*, pp. 55–71.

significance. It has been seen as marking out a manuscript as a school book, but I prefer to see the text as a practical interpretative aid.[109]

The excerpts were last studied in detail by Tardif in 1895, but his knowledge of the manuscripts was not comprehensive: he did not, for example, consider two manuscripts from our group, Warsaw BU 1 or Vat. Reg. Lat. 846, although he did consider BN Lat. 4408.[110] Tardif grouped the manuscripts by content, by which excerpts of Isidore they took, but did not attempt to establish a more precise link between the texts. He did not consider whether the groups shared a common base text derived from a single exemplar or exemplar family, or whether each group, or even each manuscript, was an independent selection from different manuscripts of Isidore.

Tardif of course did not have access to Lindsay's edition of the *Etymologiae*, which appeared in 1911, so had little firm work on the text to which to relate his manuscripts.[111] In any case the deficiencies of Lindsay's edition, notably his use of only a few manuscripts, still make such an attempt difficult, so it has not been possible to relate the Warsaw or Vatican manuscripts to a text on the basis of Lindsay's edition, or any work discussing it.[112] Porzig in his well-received reassessment of the manuscript groupings did not consider Book V, the relevant book here, nor did he use any of Tardif's excerpts, nor even any manuscripts from Paris.[113]

Study of the texts has only suggested that neither *leges*-scriptorium manuscript is closely related to Berne 263, the only manuscript of the excerpts identified by Tardif to have been edited by Lindsay. It also seems, more surprisingly, that Warsaw BU 1 and Vat. Reg. Lat. 846 are not obviously related to each other. A very small and provisional sample also suggests that BN Lat. 4408, Vat. Reg. Lat. 846, and BN Lat. 18237

109 McKitterick (1989), *Written word*, p. 47.

110 J. Tardif (1985) 'Un abrégé juridique,' pp. 659–81. The question form identified by Tardif is now edited in A. Bühler, 'Capitularia Relecta. Studien zur Entstehung und Überlieferung der Kapitularien Karls des Großen und Ludwigs der Frommen' *Archiv für Diplomatik, 32* (1986), pp. 474f.

111 Isidore of Seville, *Etymologiarum sive Originum Libri XX* ed. W. M. Lindsay (Oxford, 1911).

112 For literature on the problems with Lindsay see J. N. Hillgarth, 'The position of Isidorian studies: a critical review of the literature 1936–1975' *Studi Medievali, 24* (1983), pp. 825f. and his references. The new book-by-book editions of the *Etymologiae* in the *Auteurs latins du Moyen Age* series are not appearing in order of book, and have not yet reached Book V, the most useful for our purposes. The most recent volume in this series is Isidore of Seville, *Etimologías / Isidoro de Sevilla. Libro 19, De naves, edificios y vestidos / introducción, edición crítica, traducción y notas por Miguel Rodríguez-Pantoja* ed. and Spanish trans. M. Rodríguez-Pantoja (Paris, 1995), Auteurs latins du Moyen Age 10. See also B. Bischoff, 'Die Europäische Verbreitung der Werke Isidors' in: *Isidoriana: colección de estudios sobre Isidoro de Sevilla / publicados con la ocasión del XIV centenario de su nacimiento por Manuel C. Díaz y Díaz.* (León, 1961), pp. 339f.

113 W. Porzig, 'Die Rezensionen der Etymologiae des Isidorus von Sevilla' *Hermes*, (1937), pp. 129–70.

(one of whose hands, earlier in the manuscript, is from Tours) might be related, but more work is needed.

In the absence of more evidence from the texts, we might get a little closer to patterns of circulation by examining the wider content of the manuscripts. Vat. Reg. Lat. 1048, Berne 263, and BN Lat. 4409 were suggested as related by Tardif on the grounds of strong parallels between their contents. Certainly all include the rather rare *formula*, which seems to be part of the Tours collection, but was edited by Zeumer as *Formulae Extravagantes* I, 5.[114] All also include the same king list, in a related redaction.[115]

Tardif's manuscripts and groups were as follows:

1.	Extracts of V, 1–27	BN Lat. 4408, BN Lat. 9653, Turin D V 19
2.	Extracts of V and IX 4–6	BN Lat. 4403A, BN Lat. 4409, Vat. Reg. Lat. 1048, Berne 263, Leiden Voss. Lat. Q. 119
3.	Extracts from the above, plus II, 10, and excerpts of XV	BN Lat. 4414, BN Lat. 4415
4.	The above plus XV 16 and 2	BN Lat. 18237

The other two *leges*-scriptorium manuscripts fit loosely into category 1. The texts in both include passages from V, 1–27, in Vat. Reg. Lat. 846's case the whole sequence, and in the Warsaw manuscript's only until c.20.

The title indices, however, complicate matters. Vat. Reg. Lat. 846 lists in its index *De temporibus* as XXVIII, but only goes as far in its text as XXVII. The title refers to Book V, c.28, which is conventionally titled *De chronicae vocabulo*, so the most simple conclusion would be that the scribe of Vat. Reg. Lat. 846 was copying directly from a full manuscript of Isidore's work, rather than an already excerpted text, and copied one title too many from his exemplar.

The titles in the index of the Warsaw manuscript go even further beyond the material actually copied, and the quire structure shows that this is not because of a loss of folios.[116] The title list relates quite clearly to a text of Tardif's group 2, but only V, 1–20 are actually copied. There is, however, a number of differences in the chapter headings from Lindsay's text which are not followed through in the order of the text itself, and

114 Rio (2009), *Frankish Formulae*, p. 93.
115 *Catalogus I*, MGH SRM VII p. 470f.
116 Mordek (1995), *Bibliotheca*, pp. 898–9.

it would be very instructive to see if these peculiarities are replicated in the other manuscripts of this group.

In conclusion, it seems as if the *leges*-scriptorium scribes at least sometimes made independent selections from different manuscripts of Isidore, and it is clear that more work is needed to establish the influence the selections might have had.

5.3.4 *King lists*

The list of Merovingian and Carolingian kings of the Franks, which Krusch edited as *Catalogus* III, is found in Vat. Reg. Lat. 846, and also in a very closely related text in BN Lat. 4409, which also contains *Catalogus* I.[117]

Catalogus III	
C1a	BN Lat. 4409
C1b	**Vat. Reg. Lat. 846**
C2a	Berne 83
C2b	Vat. Pal. Lat. 243
C2b*	München Univ. Bibl. 6

5.3.5 *Summary of links*

The manuscripts with clear links with *leges*-scriptorium texts are:

BN Lat. 4409	King list, *formulae*, *Epit. Aegid.*?
BN Lat. 2123	*Formulae*
BN Lat. 4417	*Epit. Aegid.*?

This is a still more meagre haul than for the barbarian *leges*, although BN Lat. 4409 is looking as if it could have used *only leges*-scriptorium texts. The relationships are far more extensive and interesting *within* the *leges*-scriptorium group, however, and these are analysed next.

5.4 SOURCES OF TEXTS. LEGAL ACTIVITY AT TOURS. THE WARSAW MANUSCRIPT, THE *FORMULAE TURONENSES*, AND THE *EPITOME AEGIDII*

5.4.1 *The use of a 'W-B' Breviary manuscript in the* Epitome Aegidii

Haenel already noted a passage of the *Epitome Aegidii* that hints at its methods of construction and the texts available to its compilers. After

117 See K. Giesriegl, 'Autorität, Chronologie und Gesetzgebung. Königskataloge in fränkischen Leges-Handschriften' in: Corradini et al. (2006), *Texts and identities*, pp. 205–218. *Catalogus IIII*, MGH SRM VII p. 481.

the two Novels of Majorian common to Breviary manuscripts, it lists the titles of a further six novels, but supplies no text, noting:

These six *sententiae* have not been used, because they are found in some books, but not in others.[118]

So the compiler claims access to several Breviary manuscripts with different contents, hinting at the relative sophistication of his efforts.[119] But strikingly, the relevant novels whose titles the *Epitome* took are rare, to be found in only those four extant manuscripts listed above, two of which, the Warsaw and Berlin twin manuscripts, are from the *leges*-scriptorium.[120] So the compiler of the *Epitome* may have had access to a Breviary manuscript closely resembling these two *leges*-scriptorium codices, with their redaction of the *LRV* I shall refer to as the 'W-B' version.

However, we can demonstrate that the compiler of the *Epitome* also used a manuscript with a very different text from this W-B text, because, although he drew primarily on the *Interpretationes*, he also sometimes drew on the original *Sententiae* texts, which are not found in the W-B redaction.[121] We know that Tours did have a full Breviary, with *Sententiae*, at the beginning of the ninth century, because one is extant: BN Lat. 4404, from 804 or so. Although it has quite a distinctive text, which does not seem to be an influence on the Tours formulary, the point is that Tours had a variety of legal manuscripts.[122]

So a first result is summarised:

LRV (W-B) $\Longrightarrow$ *Epit. Aegid.* $\Longleftarrow$ *LRV* (not W-B)

But what is the history of this W-B text itself? The relationship between the text found in Vat. Lat. 7277 and that in the Warsaw-Berlin twins is investigated above, but did not appear distinct enough to allow an argument into how the rare Novels entered this strand of the Breviary

118 *LRV* pp. xxv and 310: *Hae sex sententiae non sunt defloratae, quia in aliquibus libris non inveniuntur, in aliquibus tamen inveniuntur.* See also *Codices Gregorianus, Hermogenianus, Theodosianus: novellae constitutiones imperatorum Theodosii II, Valentiniani III, Maximi, Majoriani, Severi, Anthenii... Quas Iacobus Sirmondus divulgavit.* ed. G. F. Haenel (Bonn, 1842–4), pp. xxxiii and 291–2.

119 For a view that denies such sophistication, see M. Conrat, *Geschichte der Quellen und Literatur des römischen Rechts im früheren Mittelalter* (Leipzig, 1891), pp. 222–8, esp. on the role of *Vorlage*, in utterly impenetrable language, at p. 225: 'Der Versuch, durch Feststellung derjenigen Gesichtspunkte zum Ziele zu gelangen, von welchen aus der Verfasser bei Ausscheidung gewisser Texte der Vorlage von seiner Bearbeitung sich leiten liess, schlägt fehl: es mögen, so scheint mir, zum weitaus grössten Teil die Auslassungen durch die Unvollständigkeit der von Verfasser benutzten Vorlage verschuldet und nur im Gajus und Paulus wirkliche Streichungen, auf welche dann zuweilen ausdrücklich hingeweisen wird, vorgenommen zu sein'.

120 See section 5.3.1 above.

121 For example, *Epit. Aegid.* XI, 1 pp. 168–72.

122 On Roman law in the Tours *formulae* see section 5.4.2 below.

tradition, so we cannot make any further argument about where the *leges*-scriptorium might have found its texts.

5.4.2 *The use of the* LRV *law in the* Formulae Turonenses

It is possible, however, to trace an ancestor of some of the text of the Warsaw/Berlin twins to Tours, by considering the *Formulae Turonenses*. The *Formulae* are deeply infused with Roman law. Ten out of the forty-five in the main collection include verbatim citations of law taken from the *LRV*, the *Epitome Aegidii*, or, as I argue below, some intermediary text. Tables 5.5 and 5.6 list the quotations of Roman law in the *Formulae Turonenses* and examine their likely sources.

A lynch-pin of any argument is of course the association of the *Formulae Turonenses* with Tours and the assumption that it came together as a coherent collection there. In a sense these are big assumptions: it only takes a brief look at the two ninth-century manuscripts in which the Tours corpus is merged with the Marculf corpus to show that *formulae* from different manuscripts were frequently combined in new manuscripts, or split between them.[123] The *formulae* analysed here in the most detail do, however, include specific mention of Tours itself, so the connections hold, but we must be aware that they might not be strictly contemporary with each other.

The argument that links the *Formulae Turonenses* with a Breviary manuscript close to that of the Warsaw-Berlin codices was Zeumer's.[124] In several places where they quote the *LRV* rather than the *Epitome Aegidii*, Zeumer argued that the *Formulae Turonenses* share mistakes with the Warsaw manuscript. He even argued that the Warsaw manuscript, which contains, after all, both the *formulae* and the *LRV*, was a 'fairly direct copy of the *Urcodex*' of the *Formulae*.[125] Zeumer's argument needs renewed attention because it was not able to take account of Mommsen's edition, and because it seems to have been carelessly constructed. His links in the text for the quotation in *formula* no. 16 and the second quotation in *formula* no. 29, as I argue in detail in Table 5.7, simply do not hold up as *exclusive* links, although they by no means rule out his conclusions. But the link in *formula* no. 30 still does convince in a pleasing way.

Again, we can show that the *formulae* also used a different redaction, a 'not' W-B. The Roman law quotation in *formula* no. 19, for example,

123 Rio (2009), *Frankish Formulae*, pp. 91–5.

124 K. Zeumer, 'Über die älteren fränkischen Formelsammlungen' *Neues Archiv*, 6 (1881), p. 59.

125 Zeumer (1881), 'Formelsammlungen', p. 59: 'Nach alle dem ist es durchaus wahrscheinlich, dass wir in dem Cod. Vars. eine ziemlich direkte Copie des Urcodex besitzen'.

used a *Sententia* text. So the next result is:

LRV (W-B) $\Longrightarrow$ *Formulae Turonenses* $\Longleftarrow$ *LRV* (not W-B)

5.4.3 *The use of the* Epitome Aegidii *in the* Formulae Turonenses

The *Epitome Aegidii* was also used in the *Formulae Turonenses.*[126] The use of the text is never utterly exact, but in one case the differences may be instructive. *Formula* no. 11 cites Roman Law directly and explicitly: 'according to that *sententia,* which is given in the fifth book of the Theodosian corpus'.[127] It quotes:

LRV V, 8 Int.	*Epitome Aegidii*	*Formulae Turonenses*
Si quis infantem a sanguine emerit et nutrierit, habendi eum et possidendi liberam habeat potestatem. Sane	*Si quis infantem a sanguine emerit aut nutrierit*	*Si quis infantem a sanguine emerit [aut nutrierit] (BN Lat. 10758 only)*
si nutritum dominus ve pater eum recipere voluerit, aut eiusdem meriti mancipium aut pretium nutritor ***quantum valuerit,*** *qui nutritus est...*	*si nutritum dominus vel pater eum recipere voluerit, aut eiusdem meriti mancipium aut pretium nutritor*	*si nutritum dominus vel pater eum recipere voluerit, aut eiusdem meriti mancipium aut pretium nutritor* ***quantum valuerit***
consequatur.	*consequatur.*	*consequatur.*

The *formulae* then stick to the *Epitome* (as edited) very nearly exactly, with the exception of an inconsequential error (*ve* for *vel*), but also the perhaps more consequential inclusion of *quantum valuerit* from the *LRV.* It seems highly unlikely in this context that the *formulae* would make an independent selection of text from the *LRV* that happened to coincide perfectly with the *Epitome,* nor would the compiler of the *formulae* be likely to use an *Epitome* manuscript and deliberately add such a relatively unimportant reading from the *LRV.* The most likely scenario is that the compiler used an early version of the *Epitome* which, as far as we can tell from the edition and such texts as I have sampled, never made it into the extant manuscripts.

Strikingly, this is also a point at which the *leges*-scriptorium manuscript BN Lat. 4416 provides a wildly different text from that in

[126] For the parallels and texts see Liebs (2002), *Römische Jurisprudenz,* pp. 242f.

[127] MGH Form. p. 141: *secundum sententiam illam, quae data est ex corpore Theodosiani libri quinti, dicens...* For what follows see *LRV* p. 146. The following passage of the *LRV* is translated in *The Theodosian code and novels: and the Sirmondian constitutions* trans. C. Pharr (Princeton, NJ, 1952), p. 110: 'If any person should purchase a newborn child and rear it, he shall have the right to keep and possess it. Certainly, if an owner or father should wish to recover a child that has been so reared, he shall either give to the person who reared it a slave of the same value, or the person who reared the child shall obtain the price which the child that he reared is worth'.

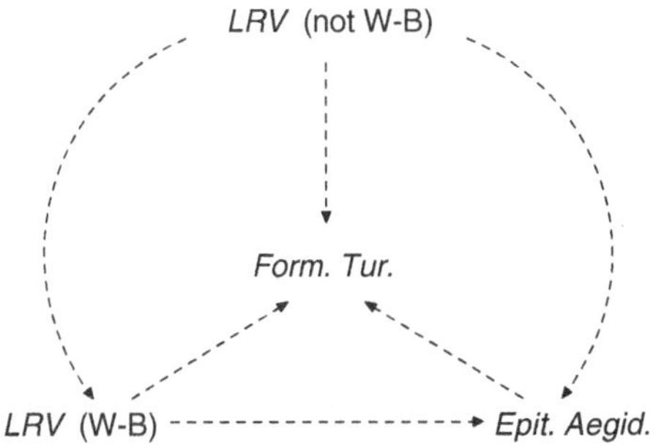

Fig. 5.5 Proposed relationship between the *Formulae Turonenses* and various texts of Roman law

the other *leges*-scriptorium manuscripts or the main tradition, in as far as we know anything about it. The reading in this manuscript is:

Si quis infantem sanguinolentem emerit et nutrierit, si nutritum dominus vel pater recipere noluerit, aut mater eiusdem pretium consequatur. Et si aliquis ex praedictis parentibus taliter recipere distulerit in eius permaneat potestate, qui eum nutrivit.[128]

Although this passage makes an apparent slip in retaining *aut* before *mater*, it generally makes sense, and appears to have taken the subject of *potestas* from the *LRV* itself, rather than any of the other texts of the *Epitome*. BN Lat. 4416, therefore, might preserve an early or alternative version of the *Epitome*, but a different one from that found embedded in the *Formulae Turonenses*. The suggestion is that Tours had access to a very early version of the *Epitome Aegidii*, and I suggest below that Tours might even have been involved in the production of the text. This next result is:

(proto) *Epit. Aegid.* $\Longrightarrow$ *Formulae Turonenses*

So the links between the *Epitome Aegidii*, the *Formulae Turonenses*, and the *LRV* can be summarised as shown in Figure 5.5.

We have clear hints that Tours on the one hand, and the ancestors of the *leges*-scriptorium texts on the other, had some role in the early use and even the construction of the *Epitome Aegidii*. These observations conflict in no way with existing hypotheses that the *Epitome* was constructed in southern France in the eighth century.[129]

128 If someone obtains or raises a newborn child, if his master or father does not want to take the raised child, his mother may pay the price. And if one of those parents puts off taking him as described, he is to remain in the power of him who raised him.

129 See notes in section 5.3.1 above.

Table 5.5 *The quotations from Roman law in the* Formulae Turonenses *1: text as it appears in the* Formulae

11	*LRV* Th V, 8 Int.	*Si quis infantem a sanguine emerit [aut nutrierit], si nutritum dominus vel pater eum recipere voluerit, aut eiusdem meriti mancipium aut pretium nutritor quantum valuerit consequatur*
14	*LRV* Th III, 5, 2 Int.	*Lex et consuetudo exposcit, ut, 'quicquid inter sponsum et sponsam de futuris nuptiis fuerit definitum vel largitum, aut ex consensu parentum aut ipsi, si sui iuris sunt, scripturarum sollemnitate firmetur'.*
16	*LRV* Paul II, 20, 2 Int.	*Viventibus patribus inter filios familias sine voluntate eorum matrimonia non legitime copulantur, sed contracta non solvuntur*
17	*LRV* Paul II, 24, 5 Int.	*si manente coniugio vir uxori vel uxor marito aliquid donaverit, si is cui donatum est prior mortuus fuerit, apud donatorem ea quae donata fuerant remanebunt*
19	*LRV* Th III, 16, 1	*Certis rebus et probatis causis inter maritum et uxorem repudiandi locus patet*
20	*LRV* Th II, 12, 4, Int.	*et lex Romana exposcit, ut, 'quicumque uxoris suae negotium fuerit prosecutus quamvis maritus sit, nihil aliud agat, nisi quod ei agendum per mandatum illa conmiserit'*
21	*LRV* Th II, 24, 1 Int.	*Quicquid pater unumquemque de filiis vel nepotibus habere voluerit, hoc sibi secundum legis ordinem sine consortis repetitione defendat; nec presumat aliquis contra voluntatem patris agere*
29	*LRV* Paul V, 39 Int.	*Si quando cuiuscumque iniusta appellatio conprobatur, sumptus, quos post appellationem adversarium suum accusator conpulit sustinere, non in simplum ei, sed in quadruplum ab accusatore cogatur restitui*
	LRV Th IX, 1, 8 Int.	*Quicumque alium de homicidii crimine periculosa vel capitali obiectione pulsaverit, non prius a iudicibus audiatur, quam se similem poenam, quam reo intendit, conscripserit subiturum. Et si servus alienus accusandus esse crediderit, se simili inscriptione constringat, futurum, ut aut supplicia innocentum servorum aut poenam capitis sui aut facultatum amissione conpenset.*
30	*LRV* Th IX, 11, 2, Int.	*et si quis ad rapinam faciendam adgreditur aut iter agentem insidiaverit aut domum alterius nocturnus spoliaverit, mors anime ipsius ne requiratur.*

Table 5.6 *The quotations from Roman law in the* Formulae Turonenses *2: possible sources of each quotation and notes*

11	L		*Epit. Aegid.*, possibly in an early form	Follows Haenel's *Epit. Aegid.* text closely, but includes the phrase *quantum valuerit* from the *LRV*. The text in BN Lat. 4416 includes an addition, which makes it an unlikely direct source.
14			*LRV*, abridged	Recognisably derived from the *LRV*, but modified along different lines from the *Epit. Aegid.*.
16	L	Z	*LRV* (W-B) or maybe *Epit. Aegid.*	Zeumer pointed out that it has the reading *Sed contracta non solvuntur* rather than the 'normal' *sed* ***coniuncta*** *non solvantur*, and interpreted this as a reading from the Warsaw manuscript. Haenel's edition, however, shows a rather different, though muddy picture: the quotation is in fact identical with Haenel's *Epit. Aegid.* text. For now the differences are listed below from Haenel's edition.
17			*LRV* or maybe *Epit. Aegid.*	Haenel notes no differences between the *LRV* text and the *Epit. Aegid.* here, except for the added words *donata et collecta* between *ea* and *quae*, found in 'some' codices. The Tironian notes in Vat. Reg. Lat. 852 (relevant section p. 88) make it difficult to establish which reading the MS has. BN Lat. 4416 again has a distinctive text, however, so is unlikely to be a related source.
19			*LRV*	Certainly an *LRV* rather than *Epit. Aegid.*, but there is no variation in Haenel's apparatus, nor in Mommsen's, that helps pin down the text any further.

(*cont.*)

Table 5.6 *(cont.)*

20			*LRV*	Again Haenel's work is not helpful. The only difference between this text and Haenel's is that the latter starts *Qui* rather than *Quicunque*. Mommsen notes that BN Lat. 4404 has the reading *uxores*, clearly a mistake, but not one followed here.
21			*LRV*, abridged	Recognisably taken from the *LRV*, but very heavily abridged, though not in the same way as the *Epit. Aegid.*
29	L		*Epit. Aegid.*	Haenel's apparatus does not help to pin this down further.
		Z	*LRV* (W-B) (with proto-*Epit. Aegid.* hints?)	The wording *periculosa vel* links it with the *LRV*, and according to Zeumer, *servus alienus accusandus* links it more specifically with the W-B text. However Mommsen's edition lists many codices with some variant here. The reading *poenam*, although small, possibly links it with a proto-*Epit. Aegid.* text. Again, according to Mommsen, BN Lat. 4404 has some quite different readings.
30	L	Z	Adapted *Epit. Aegid.*, but shows descent from an *LRV* (W-B) text	The words *mors anime ipsius ne requiratur* are a mistake, in the place where the W-B text has the 'correct' reading *mors latronis ipsius a nemine requiratur* through a correction, from the mistake *mors latronis ipsius animnerequiratur.*

Note: 'L' and 'Z' refer to commentary by Liebs and Zeumer.

Table 5.7 *Text of the unedited* formula *in Vat. Reg. Lat. 857, compared with its closest parallels in edited texts*

Vat. Reg. Lat. 857	***Epit. Aegid.* IX, 1, 4**	**Notes**
INTERPRETATIO. tam civile negocium quam criminalem accusationem proferri manu accusatores conscripta procedat	Tam civile negotium quam criminalem accusationem professio accusatoris manu conscripta praecedat *aut vindicta proposita, si vera protulerit, aut supplicum, si fefellerit.*	Haenel's *LRV* Int. text is the same as the *Epit. Aegid.*, without the passage in italics. So the *LRV* itself is a likely source for the fragment.
Paulus sentenciarum Liber V hera XXXVIII de meritis appellatione omni modo puniendum est ut quociens iniusta appellatio pronunciatur. Sumptos post dum sequeretur aduersarius inpendit reddere cogatur. Non symplos sed quadruplos.	***LRV* Paul V, 39** De meritis appellationum Omnimodo ponendum est, ut, quoties iniusta appellatio pronuntiatur, sumtus, quos, dum sequeretur adversarius, impendit, reddere cogatur, non simplos, sed quadruplos.	The fragment has some mistakes and spelling differences, fairly major ones, but otherwise fits the text well.
INTERPRETATIO Si quando cuiuscumque **iniusta appellatio conprobatur** sumptos quos **post appellationem** aduersarium suum conpellit sustinere. Non simplos sed quadruplum ab accusatore cogatur restitui.	***Epit. Aegid.* Paul V, 39 Sententia** Si quando cuiuscunque **iniusta appellatio comprobatur**, sumtus, quos **post appellationem** adversarium suum compulit sustinere, non in simplum ei, sed in quadruplum reformare cogatur.	Here the text in the fragment is closer to the *Epit. Aegid.* than to the *LRV* Sent. or Int. (*comprobatur, post appelationem*). But *symplos* is more resonant with the *LRV* Sent., and *ab accusatore* links it with the form found in the *Formulae Turonenses.*

(*cont.*)

Table 5.7 (*cont.*)

Vat. Reg. Lat. 857	*Epit. Aegid.* IX, 1, 4	Notes
	***LRV* Paul V, 39 Interpretatio** Si quando cuiuscunque **appellatio iniusta pronuntiatur**, sumtus, quos, **dum sequeretur**, adversarium suum compulit sustinere, non in simplum, sed in quadruplum ei reformare cogetur.	So it looks as if the fragment is linking a fairly 'correct' *LRV* Sententia to an Interpretatio which has been modified heavily in the direction of the *Epitome Aegidii* and the form in the *Formulae Turonenses.* This might well provide evidence for a two-stage process for the construction of the *Epitome*: a full Breviary had its Interpretationes modified, before having the Sententiae themselves removed.
EDICTIO LEGIS CONPREHENSA Lex romana pro hutilitate humanu generis exposcit Ut si quando cuiuscumque iniusta appellatio pronunciatur sumptos quos post appellationem aduersarium suum conpellit sustinere.	***Formulae Turonenses* no. 29** Editio legibus conprehensa. Lex Romana pro utilitate humani generis exposcit, ut, 'si quando cuiuscumque iniusta appellatio conprobatur, sumptus, quos post appellationem adversarium suum accusator conpulit sustinere, *non in simplum ei, sed in quadruplum ab accusatore cogatur restitui'*	Here the fragment repeats the same quotation from Roman law, but this time inside a *formula.* But the form of the Roman law quotation is different: *pronunciatur* links it with the Sent. or Int. of the 'pure' *LRV.*
Igitur ego in dei nomen illi Dum cognitum est qualiter apud aliquo homine nomine illo In rationes publicas	Igitur ego in Dei nomine ille. Dum non est incognitum, qualiter apud te nomine illum in rationes publicas ante *inlustri viro illo vel reliquis viris, qui subter tenentur inserti, Turonus civitatem adsteti de aliqua locella nuncupantes illas, sitas in pago illo, quae mihi per legitma successione sunt debita, et tu presenti tempore malo ordine possidere videris;*	How do we explain this lacuna? Could it be an early, rather clumsy attempt to anonymise the *formula* further by removing the reference to Tours? Or is it just a mistake? The sense of the resulting text is not clear.

unde apud me in responsum introire noluisti. Nisi sicut lex edocet tibi inscriptione de sumptus et expensis confirmassem.	unde apud me in responsum introire noluisti, nisi, sicut lex edocet, tibi inscriptionem de sumptis et expensis confirmassem.	
Ideo placuit mihi ut hanc editionem in te adfirmare deberem . quod ita et feci ut si qui me de ipsa causa in rationes uel in iudicium introieris et ipsa causa internos legibus definita fuerit et mea iniusta fuerit accusatio conprobata de eadem accusationem omnique tempore quietus resedeat et sumptas uel expensas superius nominatas quibus pro necessitatibus tuis me compellente uisus est expendisse secundum legibus ordinem transacto tempore partibus tuis cogatur restitui. Et pro regi tocius firmitatis hanc editionem manu propria subter firmaui. Et bonorum uirorum adfirmare decreui.	Ideo placuit mihi, ut hanc editionem in te adfirmare deberem; quod ita et feci: ut, si apud me de ipsis rebus in rationes vel in iudicium introieris, et ipsa causa inter nos legibus definita fuerit, et mea iniusta fuerit accusatio conprobata, de eadem causatione omnique tempore quietus resideas, et sumptus vel expensas superius nominatas, quibus pro necessitatibus tuis, me conpellente, visus es expendisse, secundum legis ordinem, transacto litis tempore, partibus tuis cogar restitui. Et pro rei totius firmitate hanc editionem manu propria subter firmavi et bonorum virorum roborandam decrevi.	The major differences are in spelling and grammar, sometimes quite wild differences.
Ends.	(Adds another quotation from Roman law, to extend the possible uses of the *formula*.)	This could be another indication that the *formula* had not yet reached its final form.

Table 5.8 *Paul V, 39 in various compilations of Roman law*

LRV (Haenel)	De meritis appellationum Omnimodo ponendum est, ut, quoties iniusta appellatio pronuntiatur, sumtus, quos, dum sequeretur adversarius, impendit, reddere cogatur, non simplos, sed quadruplos. INT Si quando cuiuscunque **appellatio iniusta pronuntiatur**, sumtus, quos, **dum sequeretur**, adversarium suum compulit sustinere, non in simplum, sed in quadruplum ei reformare cogetur.[a]
Epit. Aegid. (Haenel)	Si quando cuiuscunque **iniusta appellatio comprobatur**, sumtus, quos **post appellationem** adversarium suum compulit sustinere, non in simplum ei, sed in quadruplum reformare cogatur.[b]
Form. Tur. (Zeumer)	'si quando cuiuscumque iniusta appellatio conprobatur, sumptus, quos post appellationem adversarium suum accusator conpulit sustinere, *non in simplum ei, sed in quadruplum ab accusatore cogatur restitui'*
Fragment A from Vat. Reg. Lat. 846	de meritis appellatione omni modo puniendum est ut quociens iniusta appellatio pronunciatur. Sumptos post dum sequeretur aduersarius inpendit reddere cogatur. Non symplos sed quadruplos. INTERPRETATIO Si quando ciuiscumque **iniusta appellatio conprobatur** sumptos quos **post appellationem** aduersarium suum conpellit sustinere. Non simplos sed quadruplum ab accusatore cogatur restitui.
Fragment B (inside *formula*)	si quando cuiuscumque iniusta appellatio pronunciatur sumptos quos post appellationem aduersarium suum conpellit sustinere

[a] However, the manuscripts of the full *LRV* available to me preserve different readings. Thus the Warsaw manuscript preserves: *de meritis appelationum omnimodo puniendus est ut quotiens iniusta appellatio pronunciatur sumptus quos dum sequeretur adversarius inpendet reddere cogatur non symplos sed quadruplos INT Si quando cuiuscumque iniusta appellatio conprobatur sumptus quos post appellationem adversarium suum conpulit sustinere non in symplum ei sed in quadruplum reformare cogatur.* BN Lat. 4408 preserves something very similar, as does Vat. Reg. Lat. 1128.

[b] Here Haenel's text fits well with the few readings in *Epit. Aegid.* manuscripts available to me. See Editions below.

5.4.4 *A fragment of* Formulae Turonenses *in Vat. Reg. Lat. 857*

As far as I know, this fragment has not been examined in detail before. The text is significant because it prefaces the text of a *formula* with the Roman law it used, showing a rare link between the normative and the practical. The form of the Roman law quotations may also show that the compiler of the fragment was close to a centre of revision of Roman law texts, since some readings seem to fall between the cracks of the *LRV*, the *Epit. Aegid.*, and the text used in the *Formulae Turonenses* as edited, which, as I have argued, might itself fall between the cracks of the former two texts. Each passage of the fragment is compared in detail with its closest parallels in Table 5.7. Also, the form in which the Roman law is quoted above the *formula* is quite different from the form within the *formula*. The forms of the relevant law in the fragment are compared with other sources in Table 5.8. It is possible indeed that the fragment is a remnant of the process of construction of the *formula*, an unfinished draft.

The textual work here, however, must remain strictly provisional, because Haenel's text is so problematic. His readings of the *LRV* simply do not correlate with the few I have seen, which include two *leges*-scriptorium manuscripts. One can only presume for now that Haenel's readings had some basis in manuscripts, and reserve full judgement, again, until a modern edition appears.

5.4.5 *Contexts*

This is not the first time that the sophistication of legal study at Tours has been suggested. Recently Yitzhak Hen has argued that Chrodebert brought a personal archive containing legal material, including an early version of Marculf's formulary, with him when he left Paris to come to Tours in 662.[130] Ian Wood suggested that most Merovingian formularies tended to show a 'secondary development' in the history of the *precarium*, which 'represents the impact of local sensibilities on legal requirements', resulting in the conception of the *precarium* as something firmly embedded in a complex of relationships between two parties.[131] The relevant Tours *formula* on the other hand held out a 'purer' conception of the *precarium*, essentially as a long grant of usufruct. Wood's implication was that Tours resisted the tide of vulgarisation of Roman law longer than other centres.

[130] Y. Hen, 'Changing Places: Chrodobert, Boba, and the Wife of Grimoald' *Revue Belge de Philologie et d'Histoire*, *90* (2012), pp. 225–44.

[131] I. Wood, 'Teutsind, Witlaic and the history of Merovingian precaria' in: Davies and Fouracre (1995), *Property and power in the early Middle Ages*, pp. 43–8. Cf. Levy's language, emphasising 'social and economic rather than legal considerations': Levy (1951), *Vulgar Law*, p. 7 as well as more recent work elaborating the concept of 'autonomy' in legal systems.

It might also be relevant that one of the only Carolingian texts approaching 'political theory' to take a detailed interest in law was Alcuin's *Disputatio de Rhetorica*.[132] There is no firm consensus on the dating of this text, so more work would be needed to relate it to Alcuin's appointment as Abbot of Tours. But Alcuin's knowledge of law has also been suggested in the case of inheritance.[133] And while other centres revised their Latin in the ninth century, Alcuin has played a prominent role in discussions of the 'invention of medieval Latin', providing an intriguing context for the revision of texts in this scriptorium.[134]

Other centres of interest in Roman law have been identified in the Merovingian period, notably Lyons, which is associated with an early manuscript of the Theodosian code, the production of the Sirmondian Constitutions, and an Epitome of the *LRV*. The tradition carried on into the ninth century, when Florus certainly knew some Roman law.[135] Tours, then, can take a place alongside Lyons as an important centre for the study of Roman law, but one that also added barbarian law into the mix with its role in the revision of the *Lex Salica*.

An exactly contemporary context for mass-production of texts can also be found at Tours, in the case of its Bibles, also produced first under Fridugis.[136] And here we also have a parallel in the restricted influence of the text. McKitterick suggested that this was precisely because the Bibles, with their 'export' quality script, were aimed at a tiny elite. With the *leges*-scriptorium group we have more of a mixture of qualities, and where we can trace influence, it comes from texts at various places on the spectrum of grandeur. But the basic activity of mass production and export seems common to both endeavours, and

132 Alcuin, *The rhetoric of Alcuin and Charlemagne: a translation* trans. W. Howell (Princeton, NJ, 1941) and see Chapter 3, section 3.1.1 above.

133 B. Kasten, 'Alkuins erbrechtliche Expertise für Karl den Großen?' in: Depreux and Judic (2004), *Alcuin à Tours*, pp. 301–15.

134 In the sense argued in R. Wright, *Late latin and early Romance in Spain and Carolingian France* (Liverpool, 1982).

135 M. Vessey, 'The origins of the Collectio Sirmondiana: a new look at the evidence' in: Wood and Harries (1993), *Theodosian Code*, pp. 178–99; F. Maasen, 'Ein Commentar des Florus von Lyon zu einigen der sogenannten Sirmond'schen Constitutionen' *Sitzungsberichte Wien, phil.-hist. Classe, 92* (1878), pp. 301–25 and the more recent K. Zechiel-Eckes, 'Florus' Polemik gegen Modoin : Unbekannte Texte zum Konflikt zwischen dem Bischof von Autun und dem Lyoner Klerus in den dreißiger Jahren des 9.Jahrhunderts' *Francia, 25* (1998), pp. 19–38; K. Zechiel-Eckes, *Florus von Lyon als Kirchenpolitiker und Publizist: Studien zur Persönlichkeit eines karolingischen 'Intellektuellen' am Beispiel der Auseinandersetzung mit Amalarius (835–838) und des Prädestinationsstreits (851–855)* (Stuttgart, 1999). P. Ganivet, 'L'"Épitomé de Lyon": un témoin de la réception du bréviaire dans le sud-est de la Gaule au VIe siècle?' in: Rouche and Dumézil (2008), *Bréviaire d'Alaric*, pp. 279–328. The short collection, Florus of Lyon, *Capitula Ex Lege Et Canone Collecta* ed. J.-P. Migne (Paris, 1864), PL Vol. 109 Col. 419–22, cites Roman law.

136 McKitterick (1994), 'Tours anomaly', pp. 53–77; D. Ganz, 'Mass production of early medieval manuscripts: the Carolingian Bibles from Tours' in: Gameson (1994), *Early medieval Bible*, pp. 53–77.

my argument that the texts were not straightforwardly 'official' fits those recently advanced against the older conception of the Tours Bibles as in some way 'official'.[137]

But products of the *leges*-scriptorium are not comparable with the Tours Bibles, in that the scriptorium continued to produce a range of texts, different in structure as well as in language. I have suggested that this might have been related to the active study of texts at Tours, but only sometimes might we imagine that the processes of revision were exactly contemporary with the copying of the texts. Both E and K redactions of *Lex Salica* are known on the basis of manuscript evidence to have been available since around 800 at the latest, a quarter of a century before the activities of the *leges*-scriptorium.

One possibility is that recipient centres demanded different versions quite specifically, either because practitioners had learned or taught from a particular text, or because they were interested in the variations, and wished to study them. The earliest library catalogues from Reichenau show vigorous collection of legal manuscripts. The earliest catalogue, of 821–2, lists seven codices of secular law, and three further ninth-century catalogues record volumes subsequently acquired by a certain Reginbert.[138]

Through Reginbert's efforts, Reichenau's library was augmented by a *further* 'Theodosian code', *Lex Salica*, and *Lex Langobardorum*, as well as *two leges Alemannorum*, two *leges Ribuariae*, and two capitulary collections. There are various obvious explanations for such duplication: the volumes could be unsolicited gifts, or needed for a large volume of simultaneous legal business. The volumes containing capitularies could have filled specific holes in Reichenau's existing capitulary collection.[139] But perhaps the texts themselves were interesting in Reichenau. It seems likely that in the full collection there was a mixture of revised and unrevised texts, although this cannot be demonstrated, and it is possible that the monks realised that the *leges* had been revised, in some cases many times, and actively wanted to know about the complete textual history. The reasons for this could range from the purely practical to the antiquarian. Some could have wanted their texts in a certain style, simply because they believed it more authentic in some sense: we might compare strife over the choice of English translations of the Bible or of the classics. But choice of text genuinely could be related to quite localised considerations about the relationship between the written and the spoken language. It could be possible that there was a continued

137 Esp. McKitterick (1994a), 'Tours anomaly', pp. 63f.

138 Duft (1990), *St. Gallen*, pp. 178–81 at p. 179: Reginbert wrote: *Incipit brevis librorum, quos ego Reginbertus... scripsi aut scribere feci vel donatione amicorum suscepi.*

139 For precise description of the capitularies in the catalogues, see Chapter 3, section 3.2.3 above.

market for various redactions of the *leges* after the construction of the revised texts, and that the *leges*-scriptorium served that market.

5.5 SUMMARY

My argument that the *leges*-scriptorium was not straightforwardly official, based at court, does not in fact clash too strongly with the previous work on the scriptorium by McKitterick and Mordek. That no direct links can be demonstrated between the *production* of the manuscripts and the court only has significance if we maintain an overly narrow conception of what the court was. We should take Stuart Airlie seriously when he pleads for an understanding of the court as a sociological, not just physical entity.[140] Regardless even of Fridugis's status as chancellor, his status and links to the trans-local nobility linked him with the court, and he could use his Tours scriptorium for business connected with the court. This is, I would suggest, also the way that other problematic artefacts of Carolingian legal culture should be seen, notably Ansegis's collection and Lupus's lawbook.[141]

At the same time, this slight recasting of the scriptorium adds some depth to the view that Tours had been a particular centre for interest in and production of legal texts perhaps already in the eighth century, and suggests that this existing interest and activity fed into the Carolingian royal programme. I have argued that Tours might have been the centre at which both the *Lex Salica* K and the *Epitome Aegidii* were produced. The variation in the Latinity of all the texts produced in the scriptorium suggests that the centre was also responsible for more minor revision, and that in some cases this continued right into the 820s and 830s.

I have also argued that the *leges*-scriptorium was quite active in finding texts from distant sources. I have suggested that an *Epitome Iuliani* text was imported from Italy, and that the scribe or scribes of BN Lat. 2718 travelled around, collecting texts for further reproduction. Despite the variation in texts between redactions, the texts within each redaction of the barbarian *leges* seem related, and may derive from related exemplars brought to a single centre.

The *leges*-scriptorium produced manuscripts of varying splendour, and texts of very varying accuracy, suggesting it tailored its products for specific audiences. Vat. Reg. Lat. 991, recognised as having the purest *Lex Ribuaria* text by Buchner, and rated as very close to the

[140] See esp. S. Airlie, 'The palace of memory: The Carolingian Court as political centre' in: S. Jones, R. Marks and A. Minnis (eds.), *Courts and regions in medieval Europe* (York, 2000), pp. 1–20.

[141] Airlie has recently set up Ansegis in a similar way: Airlie (2009), 'Ansegis and royal authority', pp. 219–35 and Airlie (2000), 'Palace of Memory', pp. 6–7.

Lex Baiuwariorum Urtext, however controversially, by de Schwind, does indeed look as if it has the purest K *Lex Salica* as well.

Nevertheless, the influence of the scriptorium remained somewhat restricted. After an exhaustive trawl through the textual traditions of most of the relevant legal works, only a handful of texts in ninth- or tenth-century manuscripts can plausibly be argued to be derived from *leges*-scriptorium exemplars.

CONCLUSION

This study has, quite deliberately, approached the *leges* in the Carolingian period from a variety of angles, using different kinds of source. In some senses, and in some cases, the texts remain as awkward at the end of this study as at the beginning. It may never be possible convincingly to pin down a context for the production and preservation of the minor *leges*, to understand the use of the *Lex Ribuaria*, or why the tradition of the additional capitularies can be so curious. The extrapolation of so much from so few and difficult sources, an unusually elaborate charter here, an interpolated text there, a few possible parallels between manuscript readings, means that a great deal of this work may not convince. Its implications may also not always be clear at this stage of work. Still, setting out the evidence is itself worthwhile, and some patterns do emerge, which might be refined by future work.

In Chapters 1 and 2 I considered the relationship between ethnic identity and *lex* and found it to be very variable. The *Lex Ribuaria* barely corresponded with a Ribuarian *gens*, except in very specific circumstances. In the *Ewa ad Amorem*, *gens* is essentially invisible. The text may have been produced in the context of a reorganisation of landholding in an area of relatively recent Frankish control, in which understanding social status in detail was held to be important. The *Lex Saxonum* may have described the Saxon past, but that past was, apparently, used less for projecting Saxon identity (inwards or outwards) than for arguing about social status within Saxon society, in complex and varied ways.

In these chapters I began to question the role of Frankish kings in the production of written law, which brought into question Wormald's views on the link between legislation and royal-imperial ideology. In Saxony, despite vigorous interest in *lex*, no sources involve Charlemagne in any way with Saxon *lex* until the 880s. I suggested that our sources for Charlemagne's activity in 802 be reinterpreted, that it may not be appropriate to talk of a 'reform' of the *leges* in the years following his imperial coronation.

In Chapter 3, on the 'capitularies adding to the *leges*', I suggested that we go further than abandon our inherited Germanic typology of capitularies, and that we read at least some of the capitularies adding to the *leges* as quite direct reflections of the needs and concerns of those involved in using the *leges*, in what can be described as a practical way. I downplayed their role in an early Carolingian, royally initiated 'reform of the law', the context in which they are most commonly placed, although I noted how their manuscripts might reflect changing views of the relationship between kings and legislation, and the nature of Carolingian authority. Different views of Charlemagne current in Bavaria in the early ninth century, and in the West Frankish kingdom under Charles the Bald, might be reflected in manuscripts of capitularies. I suggested further that the manuscripts demonstrate active and intelligent selection of legal material on the part of scribes.

In Chapter 4 I made some suggestions about the way this legal material was read, using few charters, and instead focusing on compilations, manuscript variations, and resonances with *formulae*. I tried to show how the texts were read for understanding social status, responding to pressures in both high and low politics, and for making arguments about what should happen when social status changed, what manumission and ordination might involve, economically and symbolically. This was, certainly, tied to various conceptions of royal and episcopal authority, but these conceptions become visible only in the context of the application of different texts to particular problems. Different kinds of authority are not visible as somehow self-contained objects of interest for readers of *lex*.

In Chapter 5 I suggested that the *leges*-scriptorium might be seen as a less 'official' project than previously, that it should be placed alongside Ansegis's capitulary collection and Lupus's lawbook, as a kind of public–private enterprise. This had some bearing on our view of the revision of legal texts, including some *leges*, which I further argued might be pinned down to Tours rather than the royal court. I also suggested that this revising activity at Tours was quite eclectic in its choice of texts, encompassing Roman Law, including the *Epitome Aegidii*, as well as *formulae* and barbarian *leges*, and that it went at least as far back as the eighth century.

One conclusion from all this is that uses of the *leges* not involving their specific application to 'practical' problems do not get us far enough to explain the interest displayed in the Carolingian manuscripts. The connection between ethnic identity and *lex* was sometimes important, but was extremely variable, as was that between royal ideology and *lex*.

Wormald's suggestions have enriched our understanding of the texts, but cannot explain the interest in *lex* in their own right. Rather, each use of *lex*, quotation, or reference could encode a particular argument, touching on his themes.

It is also clear that we should expand the kinds of identity we think about beyond the ethnic. We are now accustomed to thinking about some Carolingian capitularies as commentary on relationships, as bound up with a kind of gene therapy, intended to reformulate those relationships in terms of concepts of office. I suggest that the *leges* were at times read in a similar light, but more for their material concerning wider questions of status than questions of office, and at a wide variety of social levels. Indeed, it may be that, for Carolingian scribes, much of the time ethnic identity was hardly relevant at all: scribes copied multiple *leges* in the same manuscript, modified or glossed those we might not expect, or incorporated *leges* from distant parts into collections of excerpts. Some of this evidence gives a sense in the Carolingian period of the *leges*, as a group, acting as a vast repository of material on status, ripe for mining, largely *divorced* from its imagined original contexts.

One consequence of this reading is that it makes the 'deficiencies' of individual *leges* less problematic. It did not matter so much that revised texts of *Lex Salica* provided little help on how to use charters, or on how to treat the church and churchmen, if such material was available for consultation in the same book.

And this is an observation that gets us somewhere with practice too. We have seen examples where the personality principle breaks down, but where territoriality does not fit the evidence either. A way through is to imagine that consensus could underlie the choice of law, and that this could involve recourse to written texts. This view allows for a sense of formality, a sense in which the texts might be taken seriously, and this connects with the kind of formality we can see in extant records of disputes: 'legal' business was not a free-for-all, subject to pure negotiation and status politics.[1] But it also fits with the need to take negotiation seriously in dispute settlements, as in social relations. I am not the first to suggest that law cannot be seen in this period as something externally imposed on to local societies, but I have tried to provide an explanation, rooted in the texts themselves and in their manuscripts, for how legal texts might be used to construct a sense of formality and to act as a focal point for consensus.

So I have tried to move beyond the understanding of written legal texts as tools of an objective state, of a king determined to make his will heard in the provinces. The *leges*-scriptorium seems not to have been an official project, at least not straightforwardly, and a

[1] On formality, publicity, procedure, and legitimacy see references for Chapter 4, note 74.

sense of flexibility can be seen in all the examples of engagement with our *leges*, whether through direct modifications, interpolations, glosses, adaptations in collections, or interpretation by written texts, including additional capitularies and new *leges*. The texts were sometimes interpreted widely, and their provisions were in constant dialogue with other sources of help, whether local practice or custom, other laws, canons, or, especially, moral injunctions, drawn from the Bible through exegesis. Carolingian authors sought to bring legal argument into line with their moral demands, and this could involve a very wide range of attitudes to legal procedures and arguments.

So we need to broaden the effectiveness debate. We can imagine that written law did have a sense of authority, a kind of normative force, but one upheld by the kinds of force serious students of the aristocracy and of local societies have identified, subject to negotiation.

This study has, of course, been limited by time, space, and resources, but has identified some priorities for future work. First and foremost, since much can be made from textual variations, new editions are needed of the *leges*, the capitularies, of Isidore's *Etymologiae*, of *formulae,* of all the compilations in which Roman Law is found in early medieval manuscripts. The *leges*-scriptorium manuscripts require more attention from palaeographers, and from readers of tironian notes. Developments in Italy need to be integrated into the study. But, perhaps above all, the ninth century needs to be linked with the tenth and the eleventh. Post-Carolingian legal manuscripts are numerous and copy, broadly, the same texts as Carolingian manuscripts, although I have pointed to some possible changes in structure, and in differences in emphasis. The relationship between *leges* and capitularies may shift, some texts fall in and out of fashion: Ansegis becomes ever more popular, while *Lex Ribuaria* disappears. There are some extremely rich annotations: in Leiden Voss. Lat. Q. 119, for example, I have identified four annotating hands, the earliest of which may still be from the ninth century, but the others of which are later. Continuities and changes in manuscript structure, choices of texts and the nature of use, in so far as there is evidence for it, need to be combined with the study of charters, especially in connection with changing notions of legal personality, and, crucially, with the study of changing political and social structures. The continuity in manuscripts may fit with the apparent paradox Nelson observed, that across the turn of the tenth century, accounts of royal justice become rare, while accounts of justice at a local and regional level show striking continuity.[2] Further study of the later period might

[2] Nelson (1995), 'Kings with Justice', pp. 797–823 esp. pp. 818–19. The relationship between law and the 'state' in Wickham's post-Carolingian Italy is also, of course, a very pertinent comparison. See C. Wickham, 'Lawyers' time: history and memory in tenth and eleventh-century Italy' in:

well give a rich context for the suggestions I have made about the relationship between kings and the law. With this kind of work, the presence of the *leges* in Carolingian manuscripts may become ever more comprehensible.

H. Mayr-Harting and R. I. Moore (eds.), *Studies presented to R. H. C. Davis* (London, 1985), pp. 53–71.

EDITIONS

CAPITULARY NO. 142

Introduction and manuscripts

This edition is based on that provided by Boretius, but includes a manuscript Boretius missed, Sélestat 14 (104). It compares only the three ninth-century manuscripts, that is BN Lat. 10758, BN Lat. 4632, and Sélestat 14 (104).[1] The other two extant manuscripts are direct copies of BN Lat. 10758. Further, it follows diplomatic, rather than critical principles, presenting the text of the Autramnus manuscript, BN Lat. 4632, the earliest extant, as the base text. Commentary on this edition can be found in the main body of the text, in Chapter 3.

The codices are labelled:

Par:	BN Lat. 10758
Aut:	BN Lat. 4632
Sel:	Sélestat 14 (104)

The text

1. De[b] capitulo primo legis Salicae[a], id est de mannire.[b]

De hoc capitulo iudicatum est, ut ille qui mannitur spatium mannitionis suae per quadraginta[c] noctes habeat.

Et si comes infra supradictarum noctium numerum mallum suum[d] non habuerit, ipsum spatium usque ad mallum comitis extendatur, et deinde detur ci spatium ad respectum ad septem[e] noctes; exinde[f] non noctium spatia, sed proximus mallus[g] comitis ei concedatur.

[1] For fuller details on these manuscripts, see Chapter 3, section 3.3.6 above, and see MGH Capit. I pp. 292–3.

[a] *legis Sal* om. Par [b] *I cap* Sel [c] *xl* Sel [d] *si uero* Sel [e] *vii* Sel [f] *inde* Par, Sel [g] *proximum mallum* Sel

2. De XI[a] capitulo[b] legis Salicae. Si quis servum alienum occiderit vel vendiderit vel ingenuum dimiserit, mille quadringentis[c] denariis, qui faciunt solidos triginta quinque[d], culpabilis iudicetur.[e]

De hoc capitulo iudicatum est ab omnibus, ut, si ille servus qui iniuste venditus vel ingenuus dimissus apparet, non alter pro eo in loco illius restituatur; quia dixerunt aliqui, quod idem[f] servus, qui ingenuus dimissus fuerat, denuo ad servitium redire[g] non debeat: sed pristino domino et servitio restitutus fiat, iudicaverunt.

3. De XIIII capitulo[h] legis Salicae. Si quis ingenuus ancillam alienam in coniugiam acceperit, ipse[i] cum ea in servitio inplicetur.

De hoc capitulo iudicatum est ab omnibus, ut, si ingenua femina quemlibet servum in coniugium sumpserit, non solum cum ipso seruo in servitio permaneat, sed etiam et[j] omnes res quas habet, si eas cum parentibus suis divisas tenet, ad dominium cuius servum in coniugiam accepit perveniat. Et si cum parentibus suis res paternas vel maternas non divisit, nec alicui quaerenti[k] respondere nec cum suis heredibus in rerum paternarum hereditate[l] ultra divisor[m] accedere possit. Similiter et si Francum homo alterius ancillam in coniugium sumpserit,[n] faciendum esse iudicaverunt.

4. Item[o] de eodem capitulo. Si quis uxorem alienam vivo marito tulerit, octo milia[p] denarios qui faciunt solidos CCC[q] culpabilis iudicetur. De hoc capitulo iudicatum est, ut vivo marito cui[r] eadem uxor contra legem subtracta fuerat ab illo qui eam ei iniuste tulerat cum lege suprascripta, id est CCC[s] solidis, reddita fiat.

5. De XXVI[t] capitulo. Si quis puer infra duodecim annos aliquam culpam commiserit, fredus ei non requiratur.

De hoc capitulatio iudicatum est, ut, si infans infra duodecum annos res alterius iniuste sibi usurpaverit, eas, excepto fredo, cum lege sua conponat, [u] et ita maniatur[v], sicut ille maniri[w] cui contra legem fecit, et ita a[x] comite ad mallum suum adducatur, sicut ille[y] adduci potest cui contra legem fecit. De hereditate vero paterna vel materna si aliquis[z] interpellare[a] voluerit[b], usque ad spatium duodecum annorum expectare iudicatum[c] est.

6. Iudicatum est ab omnibus, ut, si Francus homo[d] in servitio sponte sua inplicaverit[e] se, ut, si res suas, dum in libertate sua permanebat, ad ecclesiam Dei aut cuilibet legibus tradidit, ipse cui traditae fuerint,[f] ipsi liberi permaneant.

[a] *XII* Par [b] *de capitulo XII* Sel [c] *I cccc* Sel [d] *xxxv* Sel [e] *excepto capitale et delatura* add. Par, Sel [f] *id est* Sel [g] *reddere* Par, Sel [h] *De capitulo XIIII* Sel [i] *ipso* Sel [j] *et* om. Par [k] *querenti* Sel [l] *haereditate* Sel [m] *divisa* Par, Sel [n] *sic* add. Par, Sel [o] om. *Sel* [p] *VIII* (overlined) Sel [q] *CC* Par, Sel [r] *qui* Sel [s] *CC* Par, Sel [t] *XXXVI* Par, Sel [u] *Reddat* add. Sel [v] *manniatur* Par [w] *manniri* Par [x] *ad* Sel [y] *manniri...sicut ill* om. Par [z] *eum* add. Par [a] *interpellauerit* Sel [b] om. Sel [c] *iudicatus* Par, Sel [d] *vel ingenua femina* add. Par, Sel [e] implicaverit Sel [f] *eas habere et tenere possit; et si filios (filius* Sel) *vel filias, dum in sua fuit libertate, generavit,* add. Par, Sel

7. De XXXVII capitulo. Si quis[a] servus hominem ingenuum occiserit, ipse homicida pro medietate conpositionis parentibus hominis occisi tradatur[b], et aliam medietatem dominus servi[c] se noverit solviturum; aut si legem intellexerit, poterit se obmalare ut leadem[d] non solvat.

Quia nullum[e] de ecclesiatico aut[f] beneficario vel alterius personae[g] discretionem lex facit[h], si ita ecclesiastici aut beneficarii servi sicut liberorum tradi aut dimitti possunt[i], ad interrogationem domni imperatoris reservare voluerunt.[j]

8. De XLVI capitulo, id est qui viduam in coniugium[k] accipere vult, iudicaverunt omnes[l], ut non ita sicut in lege Salica scriptum est eam accipiat, sed cum parentorum consensu et voluntate, velut[m] usque nunc antecessores eorum fecerunt, in coniugium sibi eam sumat.

9. De XLVII capitulo. De eo qui villam alterius occupaverit.

De hoc capitulo iudicaverunt, ut nullus[n] villam aut res alterius migrandi gratia per annos tenere vel possidere possit; sed in quacumque die invasor illarum rerum interpellatus fuerit, aut easdem res quaerenti[o] reddat aut eas, si potest, iuxta legem se defendendo sibi vindicet.

10. De affatomie dixerunt quod traditio[p] fuisset.

De hoc capitulo iudicatum est, ut, sicut per longam consuetudinem antecessores eorum facientes[q] habuerunt, ita et omnes qui lege Salica vivunt inantea habeant et faciant.

11. Et hoc iudicaverunt, ut, si servus cartam ingenuitatis adtulerit, si servus eiusdem cartae auctorem legitimum habere non potuerit, domino servi ipsam cartam falsare liceat.[r]

12. Et hoc iudicaverunt, ut omnis qui alteri aliquid quaerit[s] licentiam habet, prius sua testimonia producere contra eum; et si ille cui quaeritur[t] dixerit, quod legibus teneat ea quae tenet, et talia sunt testimonia qui hoc veraciter adfirmare possint, iudicaverunt, ut huius rei veritas secundum capitula domni imperatoris, quae prius pro lege tenenda constituit, rei veritas conprobetur.

LEX SALICA K

Manuscripts, principles

This is a list of the unedited manuscripts, and whether and how I have used them. The scattering of the manuscripts over Europe has meant that not all of them have been examined. The Vatican manuscripts have

[a]om. Sel [b]*traditur* Sel [c]*servo* Sel [d]*leodem* Par [e]*nulla* Sel [f]om. Sel [g]*persona* Par, Sel; *servo* add. Par, Sel [h]*fecit* Sel [i]*possint* Sel [j]*ad int… voluerunt* om. Par, Sel [k]*congium* Sel [l]*homines* Par, Sel [m]*viro* Par, Sel [n]*qui* add. Sel [o]*quaerendi* Sel [p]*tradicio* Sel [q]*fatientes* Sel [r]This chapter is placed after c.12, although both are labelled correctly Sel [s]*querit* Sel [t]*queritur* Sel

been obtained because they were also interesting as *leges*-scriptorium products. The Paris manuscripts were accessible in Paris. Otherwise the most interesting manuscripts are Wolfenbüttel Blank. 130 and the Copenhagen manuscript, both of them because of their possible relationship with *leges*-scriptorium products. I have not examined any late medieval or early modern codices.

22	Berne 442	$x^{1/4}$	
23	Geneva 50	$ix^{2/4}$	
26	**BN Lat. 4759**	$ix^{2/4}$	Seen.
27	**BN nouv. acq. Lat. 204**	$ix^{2/4}$	Seen.
36	BN Lat. 4631	xv	
37	BN Lat. 4630	xv/xvi	
40	**BN Lat. 3182**	$x^{2/2}$	Seen. Used for XVI and XVII.
42	**BN Lat. 4787**	$ix^{2/3}$	Seen.
43	BN Lat. 4788	$ix^{2/3}$	Seen but scarcely legible so not used.
44	BN Lat. 9656	x/xi	Seen. Used for XVI and XVII.
45	**BN Lat. 10754**	$ix^{2/3}$	Seen.
47	Autun 36	$ix^{2/3}$	
48	Besançon 1348	$ix^{med.}$	
50	Lyons 375(303)	$ix^{1/2}$	
53	**London Add. 22398**	ix/x	Seen.
54	Berlin Phil. 3899	xv	
55	Kopenhagen Gl. Kgl. Saml. 1943	$ix^{ex.}$	Images seen online.
57	Wolfenbüttel Aug. 4 50.2	$ix^{1/2}$	
58	Wolfenbüttel Blank. 130	$ix^{3/4}$	Microfilm used.
59	Wolfenbüttel Gud. Lat. 299	$ix^{3/4}$	
60	Wolfenbüttel Gud. Lat. 327	$ix^{1/4}$	
61	Nürnberg Cent. V, App. 96	$ix^{1/2}$	
62	Cologny Bodmer 107	$ix^{ex.}$	
67	Vatikan Reg. Lat. 1728	xv	
69	**Vatikan Reg. Lat. 338**	$ix^{med.}$	Microfilm used (from Vat.) Ends at c.39
70	**Vatikan Reg. Lat. 857**	$ix^{1/4}$	Microfilm used.
71	**Vatikan Reg. Lat. 991**	$ix^{2/4}$	Microfilm used.
72	**Vatikan Reg. Lat. 1050**	$ix^{med.}$	CD used. Ends at c.38
73	**Vatikan Reg. Lat. 1128**	$ix^{1/3}$	CD used.
74	Rome Ottob. 3081	xv	
76	Florence Laur. 77.1	xvi	

Also used:

K24	BN Lat. 4418	$ix^{2/4}$	In Eckhardt's edition, but resampled.
K(x)	Vat. Reg. Lat. 1431	$ix^{2/4}$	XL and part of XLI only.

Text

The base text is that of K24 as represented in Eckhardt's edition. These passages were selected to give two contrasting portions, from different ends of the text, and so that the fragmentary manuscripts K(x), K72, and K69 could all be used. C.16 and c.17 are also especially rich in variations according to the edition, and *De chrenechruda* has an especially interesting history of transmission across the various redactions.

XVI. *De eo qui villam alienam adsallierit* and XVII *De eo qui mortuum hominem expoliaverit*

XVI[a] De eo qui villam alienam adsallierit[b]

1. Si quis villam alienam adsallierit[c], ipse et omnes qui convicti[d] fuerint, quod in eius[e] contubernio[f] fuissent, MMD denariis qui faciunt solidos LXII semis[g] unusquisque ipsorum[h] culpabilis iudicetur.[i]

2. Si quis villam alienam adsallierit[j] et ibidem[k] ostia[l] fregerit[m], canes occiderit[n] vel homines plagaverit[o][2] aut in carro[p] aliquid[q] inde adduxerit[r], VIIIM denariis qui faciunt solidos CC culpabilis iudicetur[s], et quicquid[t] inde abstulerit in locum restituat.

3. Et quanticunque[u] in eius contubernio fuisse[v] convicti fuerint, unusquisque[w] illorum[x] MMD denariis qui faciunt solidos LXII[y] semis[z] culpabilis iudicetur.[a]

XVII De eo qui hominem mortuum[b] expoliaverit

1. Si quis hominem mortuum antequam in terra mittatur[c] furtu expoliaverit, IVM denariis qui[d] faciunt[e] solidos C culpabilis iudicetur.

2. Si quis hominem mortuum[f] effodierit[g] et expoliaverit, VIIIM denariis qui faciunt[h] solidos CC culpabilis iudicetur. Et postea parentes[i] defuncti iudicem rogare debent, ut inter homines non habitet[j] auctor

[2] The reading *Placaverit* seems to rank as an error as serious as *pactus pro timore pacis* in BN Lat. 18237, as noted in McKitterick (1989), *Written word*, p. 43.

[a]Numbering obscured and confused, not easy to see on microfilm K26; title om. K44 [b]*adsalierit* K72 [c]*adsalierit* K72; *assaluit?* K44 [d]*coniuncti* K42 [e]*ipso* K42 [f]*contubernia* K70 [g]*semis* om. K70 [h]*eorum* K40, K45 [i]*excp* add. K53; *exc cap et d* add. K40; *iudicetur* om. K45 [j]*adsalierit* K70; *assaliert* K44 [k]*ibide* K72, K42; *et* add. K45 [l]*hostia* K53, K27, K45, K44, K58; *hostias* K40 [m]*firgerit?* K44 [n]*hocciderit* K26 [o]*placaverit* K70; *occiderit* K53. [p]*carto* K40 [q]*aliquid* after *inde* K26, K55; *aliquid* before *in carro* K44 [r]*aduxerit* K45 [s]*excepto cpt* add. K53 [t]*quidquid* K73 [u]*quanticumque* K70, K71, K72, K73, K53, K27, K40, K45, K44 [v]*fuisset* K26 [w]*unusquique* K42 [x]*illo cum* K42 [y]*LII et* K72; *LX* K73 [z]*semis* om. K70 [a]*iudicetur* om. K53 [b]*mortuum hominem* K73, K26, K55, K58 (and much of the tradition.) [c]*in* add. K45, K44 [d]*qui* add. K53 [e]*fatiunt* K26 [f]*eum* add. K44 [g]*effoderit* K73, K55, K58; *effodierit* and *expoliaverit* change places K44 [h]*fatiunt* K26; *qui fatiunt* is written twice K26 [i]*ipsi* add. K44, K58

sceleris[a], et qui ei hospitium[b] dederit, antequam[c] parentibus satisfaciat[d], DC denariis qui faciunt[e] solidos XV culpabilis iudicetur.

3. Si quis mortuum hominem[f] aut in noffo[g] aut in petra, quae[h] vasa ex[i] usu[j] sarcofagi[k] dicuntur[l], super[m] alium[n] miserit[o], MMD denariis qui faciunt[p] solidos LXII semis[q] culpabilis iudicetur.[r]

4. Si quis aristatonem[s] super hominem[t] mortuum, capulaverit[u], de unoquoque[v] DC denariis qui faciunt[w] solidos XV culpabilis iudicetur.

LX *De rachinburgiis*, and LXI *De chrenechruda*

LX De rachinburgiis[x], qui secundum legem non iudicant.[y]

1. Si quidem[z] rachinburgii[a] in mallo resedentes, cum[b] causa[c] discussa[d] fuerit[e] inter duos causatores, ammoniti[f] ab[g] eo qui causam requiret[h], ut legem Salicam[i] dicant, et si legem dicere noluerint[j], tunc ab[k] eo qui causam requiret[l] sint interum ammoniti[m] usque[n] tertia[o] vice. Quod si dicere[p] noluerint, tunc dicat ille qui causam requiret[q]:

'Ego vos tangano[r], usquedum vos inter me[s] et contra[t] causatorem meum legem iudicatis[u]'. Et si tunc dicendi se[v] legem distulerint[w], sole[x] culcato[y], septem de illis[z] unusquisque CXX[a] denariis qui faciunt[b] solidos[c] III culpabiles iudicentur.[d]

2. Et si[e] adhuc tunc rachinburgii[f] despexerint[g] nec legem dicere volunt[h] neque[i] de tribus[j] solidis conpositionem[k] facere, tunc[l] unusquisque illorum septem, culcato sole[m], DC denariis qui faciunt[n] solidos XV culpabilis iudicetur[o].

[j] *habitent* K73; *quia* add. K44 [a] *sceleres* K42; *est* add. K44 [b] *ospicium* K69, K73, K42, K26, K44; *ospitium* K72, K45; *hospicium* K27, K40 [c] *a* add. K53 [d] *satisfatiat* K26 [e] *fatiunt* K26 [f] *hominem mortuum* K53, K26 [g] *offo* K40; *toffo* K44 [h] *que* K72, K73, K26 [i] om. K40 [j] *husu* K70; *excusa* K40 [k] glossed with *sepulchra* in the same ink and hand K44 [l] *uel se* add. K44 [m] *per* K53 [n] *alio* K70; *eum* K42 [o] *super alium misit* comes before *quae vasa*... K73, K58 [p] *fatiunt* K26 [q] *semis* om. K70 [r] *iudicetur* om. K53 [s] *aristatorem* K45; *arestationem*, glossed with something illegible - *cauperturo*? K44 [t] *ominem* K72; *mortuum hominem* K26 [u] *capalaverit* K53; *capolaverit* K55 [v] *unoquisque* K42; *ictu* add. K45 [w] *fatiunt* K26 [x] *rachimburburgiis* K45 [y] *De rachineburgiis* K(x); *De Rachinburgiis* K71, K27, K26; *De Rachinburgis* K42; Title om. K73; *De rachimburgiis K53* [z] *Si quis de* K73; *Si quis dem* K45; *Si quis* K53, K58 [a] *racineburgii* K(x); *ragemburgii* K73; *rachinburgiis* K70; *rachimburgiis* K53; *rachinburgis* K42; *rachimburgii* K45 [b] added above K26 [c] *casa* K45 [d] *discausaverit* K53 [e] *fuerit* om. K53 [f] *ammoti* K73; corrected from *ammoti* K58 [g] *hab* K45 [h] *requirit* K73, K53, K58 [i] *saliga* K(x); *saligam* K70, K26, K55 [j] *noluerit* K45 [k] *hab* K45 [l] *requirit* K73, K53 [m] *admoniti* K53; ?*amniti* K45 [n] *a* add. K73; *ad* add. K70 [o] *tercia* K42, K26 [p] *diceret* K58 [q] *requirit* K73, K53 [r] *tangono* K(x), K45 [s] *ne* K42 [t] *cantra* K42 [u] *iudicat* K42 [v] *discendisset* K73 [w] *distulerit* K(x), K73, K70, K42 [x] *solo* K73 [y] *cul cante* K45 [z] *usque* add. K73 [a] *XXX* K53 [b] *fatiunt* K73, K26 [c] *solidus* K73 [d] *iudicentur* om. K53 [e] *sic* K45 [f] *ragemburgii* K73, K26; *rachimburgii* K53, K45 [g] *dispexerint* K73, K27, K42, K45, K55, K58; one or two unclear letters add. K53 [h] *voluerint* K73, K53; *nolunt* K27 [i] *nec* K73 [j] *de tribus* om. K73 [k] *compositionem* K53; *conposicionem* K42, K26 [l] *tunnc* K53 [m] *sole culcato* K53 [n] *fatiunt* K26 [o] *iudicetur* om. K70

3[a]. Similiter si conprobati[b] fuerint legem non iudicasse[c]., septem ex[d] eis[e] unusquisque DC denariis qui faciunt solidos XV culpabiles iudicentur.[f]

4. Si autem rachinburgii[g] legem iudicant, et[h] cui iudicatum[i] fuerit hoc sustinere[j] noluerit[k] et dicit[l] contra legem iudicasse sibi[m] et hoc conprobare non potuerit, contra unumquemque de[n] septem rachinburgiis[o] DC denariis qui faciunt[p] solidos XV culpabilis iudicetur.

LXI De Chrenechruda[q]

Si quis hominem occiderit et in tota[r] facultate sua non habuerit[s] unde[t] legem[u] totam implere valeat, duodecum iuratores donet[v], ut[w] nec super[x] terram nec sub terra[y] amplius de facultate[z] non habeat, nisi quod donatum[a] habet[b].

Postea intrare debet casam[c] suam[d] et de quattuor[e] angulis[f] de[g] terra[h] illa[i] in pugno suo colligat et stare in durbillo[j], hoc est in luminare[k], et intus[l] captare[m] et cum sinistra manu de illa terra ultra suas scapulas[n] iactare super quem[o] proximiorem[p] parentem habet.[q]

Quod si iam pater aut mater vel frater[r] solverunt, tunc super[s] sororem[t] matris[u] aut super suos filios[v] debet illam[w] terram[x] iactare, id est super[y] tres de generatione[z] matris, qui proximiores sunt.

Et postea in camisa[a] distinctus[b] et[c] discalciatus[d], cum palu[e] in[f] manu[g] supra[h] sepem[i] sallire debet, ut pro medietate[j], quantum de conpositione[k] diger est[l], aut[m] quantum lex dicat[n], illi[o] tres solvant[p], id est illi alii[q], qui de paterna generatione veniunt[r], facere debent.

[a]The whole of c.3 om. K26 [b]*comprobati* K53; *cumprobati* K58 [c]*iudicassent* K58 [d]om. K45 [e]*his* K73; *is* K53; *ies* K42 [f]*iudicentur* om. K70 [g]*ragimburgii* K73; *rachimburgii* K53, K45; *rachinburgi* K42 [h]*ille* add. K58 [i]*iudicati* K(x); *dicatum* K42 [j]*sentire* K53 [k]*voluerit* K26; *noluerint* K58 [l]*dicat* K42 [m]*si ibi* K70 [n]om. K58 [o]*racineburgiis* K(x), *ragimburgiis* K73, *rachimburgiis* K53, K45, K55 [p]*fatiunt* K73, K26 [q]*chranechuda* K(x), *chrenecruda* K73, K42, K26, K45 [r]*inota*, apparently corrected to *innota* K27; *toto* K45; *tote* K55 [s]*habuerint* K58 [t]*undo* K55 [u]*lege* K53; *legem* after *totam* K45, K55 [v]*donat* K42 [w]om. K42 [x]*per* add. K(x) [y]*terram* K58; *subtus terram* K53, K26, K45 [z]*sua* add. K45 [a]*datum* K73 [b]*habeat* K73, K58 [c]K70 and K71 both have an erasure in the middle of this word *ca[ ]sam*, so presumably there has been a correction from *causam*; *causam* K45, K55 [d]*in* om. K58 [e]*quatuor* K53 [f]*angulos* K58 [g]*de* om. K(x), K73 [h]*terre* K(x) [i]*illa* om. K53 [j]*durbilo* K70, K71, K(x), K53, K27, K42, K26, K45; *durobolo* K73; *durpilo* K55, K58 [k]*liminare* K70, K71, K27, K42, K26, K45, K55; *limitario* K73; *lumine* K53; *limitare* K58 [l]*nitus* K42 [m]*capta* K53 [n]*scabulas* K27, K26, K45; *scabolas* K55 [o]*quod*K73 [p]*proximioris* K45; *proximorem* K58 [q]*habet* before *parentem* K58 [r]*fratris* K53 [s]*super* om. K73; *semper* K55 [t]*sororis* K45 [u]*matrem* K45 [v]*suus filius* K70, K45; *filios suous* K53 [w]*illa* K45 [x]*terram* om. K53; *terra* K45 [y]*supra* K58 [z]*generacione* K42; *generationem* K45 [a]*cumisa* K55; *camisia* K58 [b]*discinctus* K73, K53, K27, K42, K26, K55, corrected from *discintus* K58 [c]*et* om. K73 [d]*disculciatus* K70, K27, K42, K26 [e]*palo* K73, K26, K58; *palum* K45; *pulu* K55 [f]*im* K53 [g]*manum* K45 [h]*super* K73 [i]*s¿pem* K70; *septem* K27, K55; *VIItem* K45 [j]*midietate* K53 [k]*compositione* K53; *conposicione* K42; *conpositionem* K45 [l]*diriget* K73 [m]om. K42 [n]*iudicat* K26 [o]*ille* K45 [p]*soluantur* K73 [q]*alii* om. K53 [r]*venerunt* K55

Si vero aliquis ex illis pauperior fuerit et non habet, unde ad[a] integrum debitum solvat, quicumque de illis amplius habet,[b] iterum super illum chrenechruda[c] ille qui pauperior est iactet, et[d] ille[e] totam legem[f] conponat.

Quod si[g] nec[h] ipse habuerit, ut totam legem persolvat[i], tunc illum qui homicidium fecit ille qui eum in fide sua habet per quattuor[j] mallos[k] praesentem[l] faciat[m]. Et si eum nullus suorum per conpositionem[n] voluerit redimere, de vita conponat.

Commentary

leges-scriptorium

It is not possible to determine whether the four *leges*-scriptorium texts presented here are related on the basis of this sample. But other important features of the texts do emerge.

K71, that is Vat. Reg. Lat. 991, does indeed seem to be the most 'correct' in the sense of the most classically orthodox. The only clear grammatical mistake is at the very end, where it reads *per conpositione* rather than the more accurate *per conpositionem*. However, K24 also has only one clear error of any consequence, that is *luminare*. At *nullus suorum*... K24 shows an unparalleled word order, but it in no way changes the sense of the text.

The other *leges*-scriptorium manuscripts have clear mistakes, but they share them neither with each other nor with any other manuscripts seen. K70 makes some clear errors of Latin, but does perhaps have the only strictly accurate classical spelling of *disculciatus*. K(x) also makes clear mistakes. It is necessary to disregard the deviations between the spellings of Franco-Latin mixed words, because their spelling in all *leges* texts differs vastly from manuscript to manuscript. We might even note the similar or equivalent reading of *durbilo* and *tangano* as suggesting relationship here. Finally, K70 and K71 apparently both had an exemplar with a mistaken reading *causam*, and both corrected it in exactly the same way.

Others

K73's numerous variant readings in general find no generalisable or noteworthy parallels in other texts. The scribe genuinely does seem to have made a lot of mistakes, or at least changes. One fairly common, though by no means universal, reading is *fatiunt* for *faciunt* and so on,

[a] *an* K42 [b] *unde... habet* om. K53 [c] *crenecrude* K73, *chrenencruda* K53; *crenechruda* K45 [d] *et* om. K73 [e] *illa* K70 [f] *legem* om. K53 [g] *si* om. K73 [h] *nec* added above as a correction K27 [i] corrected from *persolvant* K55 [j] *quatuor* K53, K45 [k] *mallus* K42 [l] *presentem* K26, K70, K73, K53 [m] *fatiat* K73 [n] *nullus suorum* after *per conpositione(m)* K70, K71, K73, K53, K27, K42, K26, K45, K55, K58; *per conpositione* K71; *conposicionem* K42

which could perhaps give a clue to the territorial origin of the scribe. I have not yet found such readings in the *Lex Ribuaria* text in this manuscript, edited as text B8. Buchner rated the *Lex Ribuaria* text as the least pure from his mixed class, and this in some ways fits with the results from this *Lex Salica*. The manuscript displays various lacunae, for example there is a space where the title *De rachinburgiis* ought to be, suggesting that the manuscript was never fully finished.

K69 on the other hand is remarkably close to the K24 text, deviating from it only once, in the spelling *ospicium* rather than K24's *hospitium*.

K72 displays some mistakes, and some minor differences in spelling of Franco-Latin mixed words, but the errors are not disastrous. A noteworthy point is that it often drops the 'h' at the beginning of words.

K53. In c.16 and 17 this text often goes its own way, displaying rather eccentric word order and spelling, and has a habit of missing the final *iudicetur* or similar, or of adding a *excepto capitale et delatura* when it is not present in the mainstream tradition. The latter could plausibly be related in fact to a remnant of the redaction process of the K text, which in general often drops the *capitale et delatura* found in the other redactions. More work would be needed to establish this, however. In c.60 and 61, the eccentricities and mistakes continue, but there are some interesting parallels with K73. Examples are *si quis* at the beginning of c.60, the reading *lumine*, the misreading of *eis*, the spellings *requirit* and *discinctus*. A generalisable pattern is that spellings with *com-* are preferred to *con-*, eg. *comprobati*.

The number of common readings between K73, 53, and 42 might suggest that the manuscripts are from a family. The most notable feature of K42 is that, although the scribe's mistakes are generally in line with those of others, he seems also to have been somewhat dyslexic, sometimes muddling the order of letters in a word in a way not observed in any other manuscripts. Examples are *ies* for *eis*, *nitus* for *intus*.

K26 almost always has *faciunt* at *fatiunt* etc. It also has some readings close to 73 and 53.

K45 has quite bad Latin. In *De chrenechruda* it almost totally loses any sense of inflexion. K44 also has surprisingly bad Latin, considering it is a glossed *Lex Langobardorum* manuscript. See especially the passage in *De chrenecruda*: *Et postea parentes... auctor sceleris*, where it reads *quia auctor sceleris est* in a way that makes no sense of the context.

K55 has a text very close to the base, with occasional readings in common with K26. But in *De chrenechruda* its variations and mistakes become much more pronounced.

K58 shares a number of readings with K73.

EPITOME AEGIDII 1. THE PREFACE

Manuscripts, principles

The base text is taken from Aegidius.[3] Haenel modified Aegidius's text in certain respects, but again provided no details about his sources or methods: his text of the *Epitome Aegidii* is almost wholly devoid of reference to manuscripts in its apparatus.

This work uses manuscripts not edited by Haenel or presumably Aegidius, and resamples those *leges*-scriptorium texts Haenel listed but which are not clearly visible from his edition.

The intention, as with the other samples, is to derive a view of the place of the texts of the *leges*-scriptorium in the wider tradition. Here again, however, the task is vast because of the deficiencies of the editions: in this case, every manuscript of the *Epitome Aegidii*, some twenty-four volumes, would need to be consulted. Concentration on the preface, which did receive some original and detailed treatment by Haenel, should, however, allow something to be said.

The preface as edited by Haenel is very similar in the *Epitome Aegidii* and in the full *LRV*, but with significant enough differences to justify presentation in two columns. But here I shall give a sample of Warsaw BU 1, an *LRV* manuscript, against the same base text as used for the *Epitome*.

The complete list of *Epitome Aegidii* manuscripts according to Liebs is presented here.[4] Those used for the Preface and for the excerpts are marked as such. Some were listed by Haenel, but have been resampled, others were not listed by Haenel:

1. The *leges*-scriptorium group

Vat. Reg. Lat. 846	75		Excpts.	Contains no prologue.
St Gallen 729	57	Pref.		Pref. sample ends at *impugnet obiectio*.
BN Lat. 4416	47	Pref.	Excpts.	Tironian note mixture makes not all variants identifiable.
BN n. a. Lat. 204	P	Pref.	Excpts.	

[3] *Summae sive argumenta legum diversorum Imperatorum, ex corpore Divi Theodosii, … Novellis Divi Valentiniani Aug., Martiani, Maioriani, Severi, … nunc primum excusa, etc.* ed. P. Aegidius (Louvain, 1517).

[4] Liebs (2002), *Römische Jurisprudenz*, pp. 111f.

Vat. Reg. Lat. 852	V	Pref.	Excpts.	Seen in full, but from *impugnet obiectio* the minuscule in the Vatican manuscript becomes heavily infused with Tironian notes, which have not been deciphered, so possibly display further variations.
Vat. Reg. Lat. 991	55	Pref.	Excpts.	Pref. sample ends at *praeceptionem directis.*
2. Other ninth-century manuscripts				
St Paul in Lavanttal 4/1	SP	Pref.	Excpts.	Breaks off before V, 8
Leiden BPL 114				
BN Lat. 4418	49		Excpts.	
Leiden Voss. Lat. Q. 119				
BN Lat. 4409	46	Pref.	Excpts.	
Milan BA A. 46				
BN Lat. 4417	48	Pref.	Excpts.	
BN Lat. 2318				Fragments
3. Later manuscripts				
BN Lat. 4633				
Leiden UB 191				
London Add. 47676	L	Pref.	Excpts.	
BN Lat. 4626				
Stuttgart Würt. LB iur. qu. 134				
4. *LRV leges*-scriptorium manuscripts for comparison				
Warsaw BU 1	W	Pref.		
BN Lat. 4408	29	Pref.		
Vat. Reg. Lat. 857				No prologue text, so not used.

Text

In Christi Nomine incipit praefatio legum romanarum[a] autoritas alarici[b] regis[c]

Utilitates[d] populi nostri propitia[e] diuinitate[f] tractantes, hoc quoque quod in legibus videbatur[g] iniqum[h], meliore[i] deliberatione[j] corrigimus[k],

[a]*romanorum* SP; *[...]nomin incipit liber legum* V; *[..]nomen incipit liber legum* 57, 29; *In Christi nomine incipit liber legum* W; a totally different dedication, not transcribed here, is found in L.; *incipit liber legum auctoritas alarici regis* 46 [b]*salarici* SP [c]*feliciter* add. 55, SP; *Dulcissime ac vere aequitatis, nunc sequitur auctoritas* L [d]*utitlitatis* 57, W, 29, SP [e]*propit[]* W [f]*devitate* 48 [g]corrected from *videatur* SP [h]*iniquum* V, 55, 57, W, L, P, 47, 46, 48, 29; *inicum* SP [i]*meliori* V, 55, 57, W, P, 47, 46, 48, 29 - according to Haenel this is a Breviary reading; *mulieri* SP [j]*deliberationem* SP [k]*corregimus* W, 29, SP

ut omnis[a] legum Romanarum[b] et antiqui[c] iuris[d] obscuritas[e], adhibitis[f] sacerdotibus ac[g] nobilibus[h] in lucem intelligentiae[i] melioris deducta[j] resplendeat[k], et nihil habeatur[l] ambiguum[m], unde se diuturna aut diuersa iurgantium[n] impugnet[o] obiectio.

Quibus omnibus enucleatis atque[p] in[q] unum librum prudentius[r] electione[s] collectis, nec[t] quae[u] excepta[v] sunt, vel clariori[w] interpretatione[x] composita[y], venerabilium[z] episcoporum[a] vel electorum prouincialium[b] nostrorum[c] roborauerit[d] adsensus[e]. Et ideo subscriptum[f] librum qui in thesauris[g] habetur, oblatum[h] Goiarici[i] comiti[j] pro distringendis negociis[k] nostra iussit clementia destinari[l], ut iuxta eius[m] seriem universarum[n] causarum sopiatur[o] intentio.

Nec[p] aliud[q] cuicunque[r] aut de[s] legibus, aut[t] de iure liceat in desceptatione[u] praeponere[v], nisi quod directi[w] libri[x] et infrascripti[y] viri[z] spectabilis[a] Aniani[b] manu[c], (sicut iussimus[d]) ordo complectitur[e]. Prouidere ergo te[f] conuenit[g], ut i(?)[h] foro tuo nulla alia lex neque iuris formula[i] proferri vel recipi presumatur[j].

Quod si factum fortasse[k] constiterit, aut ad[l] periculum capitis[m] tui[n] aut ad dispendium tuarum noueris facultatum, hac[o] vero praeceptionem[p] directis[q] libris iussimus adherere[r], ut[s] uniuersos[t] ordinationis[u] nostrae[v] et disciplina teneat et poena[w] constringat.

[a] *omnes* V, 57, W, 48, 29 [b] *nouellarum* 57, 48; *romanorum* 46, 29, SP [c] *antiqua* SP [d] *iuret* SP [e] corrected from *obscurias* 47 [f] *adhibitur* 29; *?acliitis* SP [g] *hac* V, 57, 46 [h] *nubilibus* SP; *noviles* L; *viris* add. V, 55, 57, W, L, P, 47, 46, 48, 29, SP. This is a Breviary reading according to Haenel [i] *intellegentiae* V, 55, W, 47, 46, 48; *intellegentie* SP [j] *deductec?* 47. Could this be a false reading of a '2 c' a? [k] *?uesplendeat* SP - could this be a scribe with a lisp? [l] *habeat* SP; *abeatur* ?corrected to *habeatur* 47 [m] *ambuguum* SP [n] *iungantium* SP; *iurgantia* V, 57, 46; *iurgantia* corrected from *iugantia* 47 [o] *inpugnet* 57, P; *inpugnat* W, 29 [p] *adque* 55, SP [q] om. 48 [r] *prudentium* 29, ?W [s] *elationem* SP [t] *haec* 55, ?W, L, P, 46, 48, 29; *hec* SP [u] *que* 46, 48, 29; *?qi* SP [v] *excetpta* W; *excerta* 29; *etercita* SP [w] *clariore* SP [x] *interpretationi* L; *interpetratione* SP [y] *conposita* 55, W, P, 46, 48, 29; *conps* with a line on the tp SP [z] *venerauilium* SP [a] corrected from *episcorum* K27; *virorum* with a gloss above it of *episcoporum* 47 [b] *provintialium* 29, SP [c] *nostrarum* L [d] *roburauit* 55; *roboravit* W, P, 46, 48, 29, SP [e] *assensus* L; *absensus* SP [f] *subscribtum* V, *scriptum* L (although Gaudenzi's reading was *suscriptum*) [g] *tabulis* 47 [h] *oblatus* W; *oblatus tibi* 29; *collectus librum* 47; *oblatus librum* 46, 48 [i] *goiarico* 47; *eo arici* SP [j] *comitis* 46; *comite* 48; *Goiarici comiti* om. L, W, 29 [k] *negotiis* L, W, P, 46, 48, 29, SP; *necessariis* 47 [l] *distinari* V, 55, P, 46, 48, 29; *destinare* SP [m] *urdinem longissimum* add. 48 [n] *universarum* om. L; *universa* W, 46, 29 [o] *sopiantur* 47; *sapiatur* SP [p] *ne* SP [q] *aliut* SP [r] *cuicumque* 55, L, W, P, 46, 48, 29; *cuilibet* 47 [s] om. SP [t] *au* SP [u] *disceptatione* V, 55, L, W, P, 46, 48, 29; *disceptationem* 47; *disceptionem* SP [v] *proponere* 29, 48, 46, L, W, 55, 47; *ponere* P, SP [w] *recti* SP [x] *libri* om. L [y] *suprascripti* 55, L, V, P, 46, 48, SP; *subscripti* W, 29; *supscripti* corrected to *supascripti* 47 [z] *libri*47, 48 [a] *expectabilis* 46, 48; *spectauibili* SP [b] *aninani* 47 [c] *Aniani manu* om. L [d] *iussim* SP [e] *conplectitur* 46; *conpleatur* [f] om. SP [g] *uenit* SP [h] *in* 55, L, W, P, 47, 29. SP [i] *formola* V, W, 48, 29 [j] *praesumatur* 55, L, W, P, 29 [k] *forsitanse* 48 [l] *at* SP [m] corrected from *capiti* 46 [n] *tuis* SP [o] *hanc* L, P, 47, 46, 48, 29, SP [p] *praeceptio nec* SP; *praeceptione* W, 29; *preceptionem* 48, V [q] *direptis* K27 [r] om. 48; *adhaerere* L [s] *ad* SP [t] *huniuersos* SP [u] *ordinationes* 48, SP [v] *nostre* 46, SP [w] *pena* SP

Anianus Vir spectabilis[a]

Ex[b] praeceptione[c] gloriosus[d] Alarici regis hunc codicem de Theodosiani[e] legibus, atque[f] specibus[g] iuris vel diuersis libris electum aduris[h] Anno[i] XXII co[j] regnante edidi atque[k] subscripsi[l].

Commentary

By comparing texts of the Breviary and the *Epitome* it has been possible to check Haenel's work. It seems that there is much more fluidity between the two texts in the prologue than Haenel suggested with his double column presentation. Readings such as *iniqum*, *meliore*, *nobilibus* (without *virum*) which Haenel listed as distinctive of the *Epitome* are simply not found in any of the manuscripts surveyed here. Certainly, however, the readings sometimes coincide in the three Breviary manuscripts L, W, and 29, nowhere more clearly than in their common omission of *Goiarici comiti*.

Manuscripts 46 and 48 share some particular readings such as *expectabilis* and *oblatus librum*. More is written about these texts below. Otherwise the prologue sheds little light on manuscript groupings.

EPITOME AEGIDII 2. SELECTED PORTIONS

Manuscripts, principles

The principles of selection of manuscripts are much the same as for the preface. For the texts of V, 8, IX, 11, 2, Paul II, 24, 5, and Paul V, 39, however, Haenel's text has been used as the base for the sake of convenience. The aim of editing these passages in particular, as well as to provide a more even set of samples of the text, is to shed some more light on the relationship between the *LRV*, the *Epit. Aegid.*, and the *Formulae Turonenses* as discussed in the text and set out in the tables. Where the *Epit. Aegid.* text is close to that of the *LRV*, particular *LRV* manuscripts have also been used.

[a] *expectablis* corrected to *ex spectabilis* 47; *Melliflua hic incipitur acumina legum* L, after which L ends; W has something completely different, as does 29, which reads: *In hoc corpore continentur leges sive mores speties iuris de theodoiano vel diversis libris electe vel sicut praeceptum est explanari anno xxi regnante alarico vir inluster gotharico comite feliciter.* [b] om. SP [c] *perceptione* 47; *exceptionem* SP [d] *gloriosi* V, 55, P, 46, SP [e] *theudosiani* SP [f] *adque* 47, SP [g] *species* 55, P, 46, SP; *spetie* 48; *sententiis* 47 [h] *ad uiris* SP [i] om. SP [j] *eo* 55, P, SP [k] *adque* SP [l] *subscribsi* V

Text

Incipiunt tituli legum ex corpore theodosii, liber primus. De constitutionibus principum et edictis.[a]

I Prolatae[b] leges principum[c] sine die et consule, non valebunt.[d] Leges[e] nescire nulli liceat[f], aut qui (q)[g] sunt statuta contemnere[h]. Leges non praeterita[i] damnant[j], sed[k] futura[l] constituunt. Legem quam[m] generaliter omnes tenent, in unius causa[n] eam non posse[o] vacuari[p].

II De diversis rescriptis[q]

Contra leges impetrata[r] non valeant[s].

Quod consors meruit[t], a[u] consorte vindicandum[v].

Induciae[w] q[x] a[y] principe contra leges[z] fuerit[a] impetratae[b], non[c] valeat[d].

Quicquid[e] petitio[f] falsa a principe obtenuerit[g], quia fraus intervenit, non valebit.[h]

Ut damnentur[i] iudices qui data iuxta legem[j] principis praecepta[k] contempserint[l], aut conludio quocunque[m] distulerint.[n]

Ut debitor[o] remoto[p] iudicis patrocinio caustionem[q] suam implere cogatur.

Ne quis possessor principis beneficio[r] soluere tributa recuset.

Actionem[s] quae[t] ab auctore inchoata[u] est, ab haerede[v] peragendam[w]

Et quae[x] ab auctore non fuerit incepta[y], ab haerede[z] minime sit requirenda.

[a]Differs fairly widely by MS, and sadly the variations could not be transcribed here. [b]*prolate* 55, 47, 46, 48, SP [c]*principium* SP [d]sentence om. L [e]*legis* SP [f]corrected from *ceat* 48 [g]*que* L, 49, 47, 46; *quae* V, 55, P, 48 [h]*contempnere* P, 47, SP; corrected to *contempnere* 49, 48 [i]*preterita* L, 47, 46, 48 [j]*dampnant* 47, 48; corrected to *dampnant* 49 [k]*set* SP [l]*futu* 47 [m]*lex qua* L, *quae* V; *que* 47 [n]*causam* SP [o]*potest* L; *possunt* SP [p]*vacari* P [q]*res scriptis* SP [r]*inpetrata* V, 55, 48; [s]*valent* V [t]*meruerit* L, V, 55, 49, P, 46, 48; *meruierunt* SP [u]*ad* SP [v]*vindicare* SP [w]*indutiae* L, 48; *indutie* 47; *indicie* [x]*que* L, 55, P, 47; *quae* 49, 46, 48; *q;* SP [y]om. SP [z]*legem* SP [a]*fuerint* L, 55, P, 47, 46, 48; *fuerunt* SP. [b]*inpetratae* 55, V; *inpetrate* 46, 48, SP; *impetrate* 47 [c]om. SP [d]om. SP; *valeant* V, L, 55, 49, P, 47, 46, 48 [e]*quidquid* SP [f]*petio* SP [g]*obtinuerit* L, 47, 46, 48, SP; corrected to *obtinuerit* 49 [h]*valevit* L; *valebunt* SP [i]*dampnentur* 47; *dampnetur* 48; corrected to *dampnentur* 49; *dannetur* SP [j]*legis* SP [k]*precepta* L, 46, 48, SP [l]*contemserint* L, SP [m]*quocumque* 55, V, 49, 47, 46, 48, SP; *quoque* P [n]*distulerint* SP; *aut… conludio* om. L [o]*debitorem* SP [p]*remuto* L; *e moto* P; *moto* SP [q]*cautionem* V, ?L, 55, 49, P, 47, 46, 48, SP [r]*benefitio* 46 [s]*actio* L [t]*que* 47 [u]*incoata* 46 [v]*herede* L, 55, V, P, 47, 46, 48 [w]*peragenda* L; *peragendam…haerede* om. 46, although a later hand has added the missing text into the margin [x]*que* 47 [y]*incoepta* L, 47 [z]*herede* L, V, 55, 49, P, 47, 48

V, 8 DE HIS, QUI SANGUINOLENTOS EMPTOS VEL NUTRIENDOS ACCEPERINT.[a]

Si quis infantem[b] a[c] sanguine[d] emerit et nutrierit, si nutritum dominus vel pater recipere voluerit,[e] aut[f] eiusdem meriti[g] mancipium[h] aut[i] pretium[j] nutritor consequatur.[k] Poenae[l] vero subiiciendi[m] sunt[n] hi[o] qui contra hanc legem venire tentaverint.[p]

IX, 11, 2

Si quis ad faciendam rapinam aggreditur[q] aut iter agentem in praediis[r] assederit[s] aut domum alterius nocturnus[t] spoliatur intraverit, et occisus fuerit, mors latronis ipsius a nemine requiratur.

Paul Sent. II, 24, 5

Si manente coniugio vir uxori vel uxor marito aliquid donaverit, si is[u], cui donatum est, prior mortuus fuerit, apud donatorem ea, quae donata[v] et collecta[w] fuerant, remanebunt.

Paul Sent V, 39[5]

Commentary

The clearest result is that BN Lat. 4416 (47) has a very distinctive text. This is especially evident in V, 8, where major variations can be found. This passage is discussed above. There is also considerable variation in Paul Sent. II, 24, 5. This is a *leges*-scriptorium manuscript.

In three places a scribe has corrected the readings in BN Lat. 4418 to conform with those in BN Lat. 4416 (*contempnere, dampnentur, dampnant*). They are corrections of different things: *dampnentur* is corrected from *dampnetur*, so pluralises the verb, whereas *contempnere* and *dampnant* involve simple changes in spelling, adding a *p*. It is very puzzling that a corrector would bother to change the spelling in this way. More work would be needed to establish whether BN Lat. 4418 had been corrected systematically according to BN Lat. 4416 or some related text.

Otherwise there is little in these chapters to argue forcefully for groupings. Text 48 certainly continues to preserve many readings in common with 46, as well as with 49: *temptauerint, adgreditur, prediis, adsederit* for example. The conformities here are all in the field of

[5] For this passage, see Table 5.7 above.

[a]inscription om. 47 [b]*infante* P [c]*a* om. 47 [d]*sanguinolentem* 47 [e]*voluerint* 49, P; *noluerit* 47 [f]*mater* add. 47 [g] om. 47 [h] om. 47 [i]corrected in a later hand from *a* 46 [j]*precium* P; *praetium* 48 [k]*Et si aliquis ex praedictis parentibus taliter recipere distulerit in eius permaneat potestate, qui eum nutrivit* add. 47 [l]*Poene* 49; *poena* P, 46; *poenam* 48 [m]*subiacendi* 49, P; *subiaceant* 47; *subiacendos* 46; *subiacendis* 48 [n]om. 46, 48 [o]*hii* 49, P; *hos* 46; *his* 48 [p]*temptauerint* 49, P, 46, 48 [q]*adgreditur* 49, 46, 48 [r]*prediis* 49, 46, 48 [s]*adsederit* 49, 46, 48 [t]*nocturnis* 48 [u]*his* 49, 48; *si is...fuerit* om. 47 [v]*donata et collecta* om. 48 [w]*et collecta* om. 75, 46

spelling, however, which might seem less firm than word order as a critereon for linking. But if these codices were linked, it would place BN Lat. 4409 in a relationship with BN Lat. 4417, and with BN Lat. 4418. This would fit remarkably well with links found in other texts.[6]

The Latin of SP is perhaps the worst of any manuscript seen. Here it genuinely does seem that the scribe did not understand what he was writing.

6 See Chapter 5, sections 5.2.8 and 5.3.5 above.

BIBLIOGRAPHY

Primary sources

Summae sive argumenta legum diversorum Imperatorum, ex corpore Divi Theodosii, ... Novellis Divi Valentiniani Aug., Martiani, Maioriani, Severi, ... nunc primum excusa, etc. ed. P. Aegidius (Louvain, 1517).

Annales Laureshamenses ed. G. Pertz (Hannover, 1826), MGH Scriptores in folio I, pp. 19–39.

Scriptores rerum Sangallensium. Annales, chronica et historiae aevi Carolini ed. G. Pertz (Hannover, 1829), MGH Scriptores in folio II.

Urkundenbuch für die Geschichte des Niederrheins ed. T. J. Lacomblet Volume 1, (Düsseldorf, 1840).

Patrologia cursus completus series Latina ed. J.-P. Migne (Paris, 1841–64).

Codices Gregorianus, Hermogenianus, Theodosianus: novellae constitutiones imperatorum Theodosii II, Valentiniani III, Maximi, Majoriani, Severi, Anthenii... Quas Iacobus Sirmondus divulgavit. ed. G. F. Haenel (Bonn, 1842–4).

Traditiones et antiquitates Fuldenses ed. E. F. J. Dronke (Fulda, 1844).

Brevarium Alarici ed. G. F. Haenel (Leipzig, 1848).

Regesta historiae Westfaliae: accedit codex diplomaticus ed. H. A. Erhard (Münster, 1848).

Leges Alamannorum, Leges Baiuwarioum, Leges Burgundionum, Lex Frisionum ed. J. Merkel (Hannover, 1863), MGH Leges in folio III.

Lex Francorum Chamavorum ed. K. F. von Richthofen (Hannover, 1875), MGH Leges in folio V, pp. 271–6.

Lex Saxonum ed. K. F. von Richthofen (Hannover, 1875), MGH Leges in folio V, pp. 47–84.

Lex Salica: the ten texts with the glosses, and the Lex Emendata ed. J. H. Hessels and H. Kern (London, 1880).

Die vitae sancti Liudgeri ed. W. Diekamp (Münster, 1881).

Annales Bertiniani ed. G. Waitz (Hannover, 1883), MGH SRG V.

Lex Ribuaria et Lex Francorum Chamavorum ed. R. Sohm (Hannover, 1883), MGH Fontes iuris Germanici antiqui in usum scholarum seperatim editi 6.

Capitularia Regum Francorum ed. A. Boretius and V. Krause (Hannover, 1883–97), MGH Legum sectio II, 1–2.

Formulae Merowingici et Karolini Aevi ed. K. Zeumer (Hannover, 1886), MGH Legum sectio V.

Cartulaire générale de Paris ed. R. de Lasteyrie (Paris, 1887).

Textes relatifs aux institutions privées et publiques aux époques mérovingienne et carolingienne ed. M. Thévenin (Paris, 1887).

Leges Burgundionum ed. L. R. de Salis (Hannover, 1892), MGH Leges nationum Germanicarum II, 1.

Constitutiones et Acta Publica Imperatorum et Regum ed. L. Weiland (Hannover, 1893), MGH Legum sectio IV I.

Annales Regni Francorum ed. F. Kurze (Hannover, 1895), MGH SRG VI.

Poeta Saxo ed. P. Winterfeld (Hannover, 1899), MGH Poetae Latini aevi Carolini IV, 1, pp. 1–71.

Leges Visigothorum ed. K. Zeumer (Hannover, 1902), MGH Leges nationum Germanicarum I.

Theodosiani libri XVI cum Constitutionibus Sirmondianis: et leges novellae ad Theodosianum pertinentes ed. T. Mommsen and P. Meyer (Berlin, 1905).

Concilia Aevi Karolini I ed. A. Werminghoff (Hannover, 1906), MGH Concilia, Legum Sectio III II.

Die Urbare der Abtei Werden an der Ruhr ed. R. Kötzschke (Bonn, 1906).

Concilia Aevi Karolini II ed. A. Werminghoff (Hannover, 1908), MGH Concilia, Legum Sectio III.

Annales Xantenses ed. B. von Simson (Hannover, 1909), MGH SRG XII.

Passio Leudegarii Episcopi Augustodunensis I ed. R. Krusch and W. Levison (Hannover, 1910), MGH SRM V, pp. 249–322.

Leges Saxonum et Lex Thuringorum ed. C. von Schwerin (Hannover, 1918), MGH Fontes iuris Germanici antiqui in usum scholarum seperatim editi 3.

Oorkondenboek van het Sticht Utrecht tot 1301 ed. S. Muller and A. C. Bouman Volume 1, (Utrecht, 1920).

Lex Baiuvariorum ed. E. de Schwind (Hannover, 1926), MGH Leges nationum Germanicarum V, 2.

Lex Baiuvariorum. Lichtdruckwiedergabe der Ingolstädter Handschrift des Bayerischen Volksrechts mit Transkription, Textnoten, Übersetzung, Einführung, Literaturübersicht und Glossar ed. K. Beyerle (Munich, 1926).

Vita Lebuini Antiqua ed. A. Hofmeister (Hannover, 1926), MGH Scriptores in folio XXX, 2, pp. 789–95.

Lex Romana canonice compta ed. C. G. Mor (Pavia, 1927).

Die Urkunden Ludwigs des Deutschen, Karlmanns und Ludwigs des Jüngeren ed. P. Kehr (Berlin, 1934), MGH Diplomatum Karolinorum I.

Diplomata Belgica ante annum millesimum centesimum scripta ed. M. Gysseling and A. C. F. Koch, Volume 1, (Brussels, 1950).

Lex Ribuaria ed. F. Beyerle and R. Buchner (Hannover, 1951), MGH Leges nationum Germanicarum III, 2.

The Theodosian code and novels: and the Sirmondian constitutions trans. C. Pharr (Princeton, NJ, 1952).

Lex Salica. 100 Titel-Text ed. K. A. Eckhardt (Weimar, 1953), Germanenrechte neue Folge. Westgermanisches Recht.

Chartae Latinae antiquiores: facsimile edition of the Latin charters ed. A. Bruckner and R. Marichal (Olten, 1954).

Pactus Legis Salicae. I: Einführung und 80 Titel-Text ed. K. A. Eckhardt (Göttingen, 1954), Germanenrechte neue Folge. Westgermanisches Recht.

I placiti del "Regnum Italiae" ed. C. Manaresi Volume 1, (Rome, 1955).

Lex Ribuaria. Austrasisches Recht in 7. Jahrhundert ed. K. A. Eckhardt (Göttingen, 1959), Germanenrechte neue Folge. Westgermanisches Recht I.

De oudste partikuliere Oorkonden van het Klooster Werden ed. D. P. Blok (Assen, 1960).

Die Urkunden Zwentibolds und Ludwigs des Kindes ed. T. Schieffer (Berlin, 1960), MGH Diplomatum Karolinorum IV.

Son of Charlemagne; a contemporary life of Louis the Pious trans. A. Cabaniss (Syracuse, 1961).

Pactus Legis Salicae, Lex Salica ed. K. A. Eckhardt (Hannover, 1962–9), MGH Leges nationum Germanicarum IV, 1–2.

Leges Alamannorum ed. K. Lehmann 2nd edition (Hannover, 1966), MGH Leges nationum Germanicarum V, 1.

Die Urkunden Lothars I und Lothars II ed. T. Schieffer (Berlin, 1966), MGH Diplomatum Karolinorum III.

Charlemagne's cousins: contemporary lives of Adalard and Wala trans. A. Cabaniss (Syracuse, 1967).

Carolingian Chronicles: Royal Frankish Annals and Nithard's Histories trans. B. W. Scholz and B. Rogers (Michigan, 1970).

Oorkondenboek van Holland en Zeeland tot 1299 ed. A. C. F. Koch Volume 1, (La Haye, 1970).

Quellen zur Geschichte der sächsischen Kaiserzeit: Widukinds Sachsengeschichte, Adalberts Fortsetzung der Chronik Reginos, Liudprands Werke ed. and German trans. A. Bauer and R. Rau (Darmstadt, 1971), Ausgewählte Quellen zur deutschen Geschichte des Mittelalters 29.

Codex Laureshamensis ed. K. Glöckner (Darmstadt, 1974).

Urkundenbuch zur Geschichte der mittelrheinischen Territorien ed. H. Beyer and L. Eltester and A. Goerz (Aalen, 1974).

Laws of the Salian and Ripuarian Franks trans. T. J. Rivers (New York, 1986).

The Annals of St Bertin trans. J. L. Nelson (Manchester, 1991).

The Annals of Fulda trans. T. Reuter (Manchester, 1992).

The Breviarium ab urbe condita of Eutropius trans. H. Bird (Liverpool, 1993), Translated texts for historians 14.

Le métier de roi = De institutione regia ed. and French trans. A. Dubreucq (Paris, 1995).

Thegan: Die Taten Kaiser Ludwigs. Astronomus: das Leben Kaiser Ludwigs ed. E. Tremp (Hannover, 1995), MGH SRG 64.

Der Kapitulariensammlung des Ansegis ed. G. Schmitz (Hannover, 1996), MGH Capitularia regum Francorum, Nova series.

Das Sendhandbuch des Regino von Prüm ed. and German trans. W. Hartmann (Darmstadt, 2004).

The Ecclesiastical History of the English People trans. by J. McClure and R. Collins (Oxford, 2008).

Adrevald of Fleury, *Ex miraculis Sancti Benedicti* ed. O. Holder-Egger (Hannover, 1887), MGH Scriptores in folio XV, pp. 474–500.

Alcuin, *Disputatio de rhetorica et de virtutibus* ed. K. Halm (Leipzig, 1863), Rhetores Latini Minores, ex codicibus maximam partem primum adhibitis, pp. 523–50.

Alcuin, *The rhetoric of Alcuin and Charlemagne: a translation* trans. W. Howell (Princeton, NJ, 1941).

Altfrid, *Altfridi Vita Sancti Liudgerii* ed. G. Pertz (Hannover, 1829), MGH Scriptores in folio II, pp. 405–15.

Ammianus Marcellinus, *Rerum gestarum libri* ed. and trans. J. Rolfe (Cambridge, MA, 1963–4), Loeb Classical Library.

Ammiani Marcellini Rerum gestarum libri qui supersunt ed. W. Seyfarth (Leipzig, 1978).

Bede, *Historia ecclesiastica gentis Anglorum* ed. M. Lapidge (Paris, 2005).

Eutropius, *Eutropii Breviarium ab urbe condita* ed. C. Santini (Leipzig, 1979), Bibliotheca scriptorum Graecorum et Romanorum Teubneriana.

Isidore of Seville, *Etymologiarum sive Originum Libri XX* ed. W. M. Lindsay (Oxford, 1911).

Etimologías / Isidoro de Sevilla. Libro 19, De naves, edificios y vestidos / introducción, edición crítica, traducción y notas por Miguel Rodríguez-Pantoja ed. and Spanish trans. M. Rodríguez-Pantoja (Paris, 1995), Auteurs latins du Moyen Age 10.

Jonas of Orléans, *Jonae de Institutione Laicali Libri Tres* ed. J.-P. Migne (Paris, 1864), PL Vol. 106 Col. 121–278.

Nithard, *Historiarum libri IIII* ed. E. Müller (Hannover, 1907), MGH SRG XLIV.

Paschasius Radbertus, 'Radberts Epitaphium Arsenii' ed. E. Dümmler *Abhandlungen der königlichen Akademie der Wissenschaften zu Berlin, phil.-hist. Klasse*, (1900), pp. 1–98.

Regino of Prüm, *Libri duo de synodalibus causis et disciplinis ecclesiasticis.* ed. F. Wasserschleben (Leipzig, 1840).

Reginonis abbatis Prumiensis Chronicon cum continuatione Treverensi (Hannover, 1890), MGH SRG 50.

Sedulius Scottus, *De Rectoribus Christianis* ed. S. Hellmann (Munich, 1906), *Sedulius Scottus*, Quellen und Untersuchungen zur lateinischen Philologie des Mittelalters 1, 1, pp. 19–91.

Smaragdus of St Mihiel, *Smaragdi Abbatis Via Regia* ed. J.-P. Migne (Paris, 1863), PL Vol. 102 Col. 931–970.

Tacitus, *Annales* ed. and trans. J. Jackson (London, 1937), Loeb Classical Library 312.

The annals and the histories ed. A. Church and W. Brodribb (Chicago, IL, 1990).

Secondary works

Airlie, S., 'Bonds of power and bonds of association in the court circle of Louis the Pious' in: Godman and Collins (1990), *Charlemagne's heir*, pp. 191–204.

'Narratives of triumph and rituals of submission: charlemagne's mastering of Bavaria' *TRHS*, 9 (1999), pp. 93–119.

'The palace of memory: The Carolingian Court as political centre' in: Jones, S., Marks, R. and Minnis, A. (eds.), *Courts and regions in medieval Europe* (York, 2000), pp. 1–20.

'Charlemagne and the aristocracy: captains and kings' in: Story (2005), *Charlemagne*, pp. 90–103.

'"Sad stories of the death of kings": Narrative Patterns and Structures of Authority in Regino of Prüm's Chronicon' in: Tyler, E. and Balzaretti R. (eds.), *Narrative and history in the early medieval West* (Turnhout, 2006), pp. 105–31.

'"For it is written in the law": Ansegis and the writing of Carolingian royal authority' in: Baxter et al. (2009), *Studies in memory of Patrick Wormald*, pp. 219–35.

Airlie, S., Reimitz, H., and Pohl, W. (eds.), *Staat im frühen Mittelalter* (Vienna, 2006), Österreichischen Akademie der Wissenschaften Philosophich-Historische Klasse Denkschriften 334.

Amory, P., 'The meaning and purpose of ethnic terminology in the Burgundian laws' *EME*, *2* (1993), pp. 1–28.

Angenendt, A., *Liudger: Missionar, Abt, Bischof im frühen Mittelalter* (Münster, 2005).

Anton, H., *Fürstenspiegel und Herrscherethos in der Karlolingerzeit* (Bonn, 1968).

Bauer, T., 'Die mittelalterlichen Gaue' in: Irsigler, F. (ed.), *Geschichtlicher Atlas der Rheinlande* (Cologne, 1982–).

Baxter, S., Karkov, C. E., Nelson, J. L., and Pelteret, D. A. E. (eds.), *Early medieval studies in memory of Patrick Wormald* (Farnham, 2009).

Becher, M., *Rex, Dux und Gens* (Husum, 1996).

'Non enim habent regem idem Antiqui Saxones... Verfassung und Ethnogenese in Sachsen während des 8. Jahrhunderts' in: Hässler, Jarnut, and Wemhoff (1999), *Sachsen und Franken in Westfalen*, pp. 1–31.

Chlodwig I. Der Aufstieg der Merowinger und das Ende der antiken Welt (Munich, 2011).

Beekman, A., *Geschiedkundige atlas van Nederland* (The Hague, 1913–38).

Bergengrün, A., *Adel und Grundherrschaft im Merowingerreich: siedlungs- und standesgeschichtliche Studie zu den Anfängen des fränkischen Adels in Nordfrankreich und Belgien* (Wiesbaden, 1958), Vierteljahrschrift für Sozial- und Wirtschaftsgeschichte. Beihefte 41.

Bergmann, R. and Stricker, S. (eds.), *Katalog der althochdeutschen und altsächsischen Glossenhandschriften* (Berlin, 2005).

Beumann, H., 'Die Hagiographie "bewältigt": Unterwerfung und Christianisierung der Sachsen durch Karl den Grossen' *Settimane*, *28* (1982), pp. 129–63.

Beyerle, F., 'Das Gesetzbuch Ribuariens. Volksrechtliche Studien III' *ZRG GA*, *55* (1935), pp. 1–80.

'Zur Textgestalt und Textgeschichte der Lex Burgundionum' *ZRG GA*, *71* (1954), pp. 23–54.

'Zum Kleinreich Sigiberts III. und zur Datierung der Lex Ribuaria' *Rheinische Vierteljahrsblätter*, *21* (1956), pp. 357–62.

Bischoff, B., 'Die Europäische Verbreitung der Werke Isidors' in: *Isidoriana: colección de estudios sobre Isidoro de Sevilla / publicados con la ocasión del XIV centenario de su nacimiento por Manuel C. Díaz y Díaz.* (León, 1961), pp. 317–44.

'Die Bibliothek im Dienste der Schule' in: Bischoff (1981), *Mittelalterliche Studien*, pp. 213–33.

'Die Hofbibliothek unter Ludwig dem Frommen' in: Bischoff (1981), *Mittelalterliche Studien*, pp. 170–86.

Mittelalterliche Studien Volume 3, (Stuttgart, 1981).

Bischoff, B., 'Die Schriftheimat der Münchner Heliand-Handschrift' in: Bischoff (1981), *Mittelalterliche Studien*, pp. 112–20.

'Das Thema des Poeta Saxo' in: Bischoff (1981), *Mittelalterliche Studien*, pp. 253–9.

The Épinal, Erfurt, Werden, and Corpus glossaries (Copenhagen, 1988).

Die Abtei Lorsch im Spiegel ihrer Handschriften (Lorsch, 1989), Geschichtsblätter für den Kreis Bergstrasse, Sonderbd. 10.

Latin palaeography: antiquity and the Middle Ages trans. D. Ganz and D. Ó Cróinín (Cambridge, 1990).

Katalog der festländischen Handschriften des neunten Jahrhunderts. Teil I. (Wiesbaden, 1998).

Katalog der festländischen Handschriften des neunten Jahrhunderts. Teil III. (Wiesbaden, 2014).

Blok, D. P., *Teisterband* (Amsterdam, 1963), Mededelingen der Koninklijke Nederlandse Akademie van Wetenschappen 12.

'Holland und Westfriesland' *Frühmittelalterliche Studien, 3* (1969), pp. 347–61.

De Franken in Nederland 3rd edition (Haarlem, 1979).

Boretius, A., *Beiträge zur Capitularienkritik* (Leipzig, 1874).

Boucard, P., 'Indices et sources d'une culture juridique romaine dans l'exégèse biblique carolingienne' in: Rouche and Dumézil (2008), *Bréviaire d'Alaric*, pp. 329–52.

Bougard, F., *La justice dans le royaume d'Italie: de la fin du VIIIe siècle au début du XIe siècle* (Rome, 1995).

Bovendeert, J., 'Royal or monastic identity? Smaragdus' Via Regia and Diadema monachorum reconsidered' in: Corradini et al. (2006), *Texts and identities*, pp. 239–51.

Bresslau, H., *Handbuch der Urkundenlehre für Deutschland und Italien* 2nd edition (Leipzig, 1912).

Brown, W., 'The use of norms in disputes in Early medieval Bavaria' *Viator, 30* (1999), pp. 15–40.

Unjust seizure: conflict, interest, and authority in an early medieval society (Ithaca, NY, 2001).

'When documents are destroyed or lost: lay people and archives in the early Middle Ages' *EME, 11* (2002), pp. 337–66.

(ed.) *Conflict in medieval Europe* (Aldershot, 2003).

'Conflict, letters, and personal relationships in the carolingian formula collections' *Law and History Review, 25* (2007), pp. 323–45.

Brown, W. and Górecki, P., 'What conflict means: the making of medieval conflict studies in the United States, 1970–2000' in: Brown (2003), *Conflict in medieval Europe*, pp. 1–35.

Brunner, H., 'Über ein verschollenes merowingisches Königsgesetz des 7. Jahrhunderts' *Sitzungsberichte der Preussischen Akademie der Wissenschaften, 39* (1901), pp. 932–55.

Deutsche Rechtsgeschichte 2nd edition. (Leipzig, 1906).

Abhandlungen zur Rechtsgeschichte. Gesammelte Aufsätze (Weimar, 1931).

'Die Freilassung durch Schatzwurf' in: Brunner (1931), *Abhandlungen*, pp. 240–61.

'Nobiles und Gemeinfreie der Karolingischen Volksrechte' in: Brunner (1931), *Abhandlungen*, pp. 261–93.

Buc, P., *The dangers of ritual: between early medieval texts and social scientific theory* (Princeton, NJ, 2001).

Buchner, R., *Textkritische Untersuchungen zur Lex Ribuaria* (Stuttgart, 1952).

Die Rechtsquellen (Weimar, 1953), Deutschlands Geschichtsquellen im Mittelalter: Vorzeit und Karolinger.

Bühler, A., 'Capitularia Relecta. Studien zur Entstehung und Überlieferung der Kapitularien Karls des Großen und Ludwigs der Frommen' *Archiv für Diplomatik*, *32* (1986), pp. 305–501.

Carroll, C., 'The archbishops and church provinces of Mainz and Cologne during the Carolingian period, 751–911' (Cambridge, 1999a), Unpublished PhD dissertation, University of Cambridge.

'The bishoprics of Saxony in the first century after Christianization' *EME*, *8* (1999), pp. 219–45.

Cheyette, F., 'Georges Duby's Mâconnais after fifty years: reading it then and now' *Journal of Medieval History*, *28* (2002), pp. 291–317.

Clanchy, M., 'Remembering the past and the Good Old Law' *History*, *55* (1970), pp. 166–72.

Classen, P. (ed.), *Recht und Schrift im Mittelalter* (Sigmaringen, 1977), Vorträge und Forschungen 23.

Clercq, G. de, 'De Capitula adhuc conferenda van Lodewijk de Vrome en de domeinen van de Gentse Sint-Baafsabij in Noord-Frankrijk' in: Duvorsquel, J-M. and Thoen, E. (eds.), *Peasants and townsmen in medieval europe: Studia in honorem Adriaan Verhulst* (Ghent, 1995), pp. 325–45.

Collins, R., *Early medieval Europe (300–1000)* (Basingstoke, 1991).

'Law and ethnic identity in the Western Kingdoms in the fifth and sixth centuries' in: Smyth (1998), *Medieval Europeans*, pp. 1–23.

Conrat, M., *Geschichte der Quellen und Literatur des römischen Rechts im früheren Mittelalter* (Leipzig, 1891).

Cooper, F., 'Beyond Identity' *Theory and Society*, *29* (2000), pp. 1–47.

Corcoran, S., 'Hincmar and his Roman legal sources' in: West, C. and Stone, R. (eds.), *Hincmar of Rheims: life and work* (Manchester, 2015), pp. 129–55.

Corradini, R., Meens, R., and Possel, C. (eds.), *Texts and identities in the early Middle Ages* (Vienna, 2006), Österreichischen Akademie der Wissenschaften Philosophich-Historische Klasse Denkschriften 344.

Coss, P. (ed.), *Moral world of the law* (Cambridge, 2000).

Costambeys, M., 'An aristocratic community on the northern Frankish frontier, 690–726' *EME*, *3* (1994), pp. 39–62.

Coulanges, N. Fustel de, 'Quelques remarques sur la Loi dite des Francs Chamaves' in: *Nouvelles recherches sur quelques problèmes d'histoire* (Paris, 1891), pp. 399–415.

Curta, F. (ed.), *Borders, barriers, and ethnogenesis. Frontiers in late Antiquity and the Middle Ages* (Turnhout, 2006).

Davies, W. and Fouracre, P. (eds.), *The settlement of disputes in early medieval Europe* (Cambridge, 1986).

Property and power in the early Middle Ages (Cambridge, 1995).

Davis, J. R., 'The king and his Law: Carolingian rulers through the lens of the Capitulary Manuscripts' (2005), Paper delivered at the International Medieval Congress, Leeds, July 2005.

Davis, J. R. and McCormick, M. (eds.), *The long morning of medieval Europe* (Aldershot, 2008).

Depreux, P., 'La tradition manuscrite des "Formules de Tours" et la diffusion des modèles d'actes aux VIIIe et IXe siècles' in: Depreux and Judic (2004), *Alcuin à Tours*, pp. 55–71.

Depreux, P. and Judic, B. (eds.), *Alcuin de York à Tours: écriture, pouvoir et réseaux dans l'Europe du haut Moyen Age* (Rennes, 2004).

Devisse, J., *Hincmar et la loi* (Dakar, 1962).

Hincmar, archevêque de Reims, 845–882 (Geneva, 1975).

Devroey, J.-P., 'Les premiers polyptyches rémois VIIe–IXe siècles' in: Verhulst (1985), *Le grand domaine*, pp. 78–97.

Diáz y Diáz, M. C., 'La Lex Visigothorum y sus manuscritos. Un enseyo de reinterpretación' *Anuario de historia del derecho español*, *46* (1976), pp. 163–224.

Dickau, O., 'Studien zur Kanzlei und zum Urkundenwesen Kaiser Ludwigs des Frommen' *Archiv für Diplomatik*, *34–5* (1988–9), pp. 3–156, 1–170.

Dilcher, G. (ed.), *Gewohnheitsrecht und Rechtsgewohnheiten im Mittelalter* (Berlin, 1992), Schriften zur Europäischen Rechts- und Verfassungsgeschichte 6.

Dolezalek, G., *Verzeichnis der Handschriften zum römischen Recht bis 1600* (Frankfurt am Main, 1972).

Droege, G., 'Fränkische Siedlung in Westfalen' *Frühmittelalterliche Studien*, *4* (1970), pp. 271–88.

Duft, J., *Die Abtei St. Gallen Band I: Beiträge zur Erforschung ihrer Manuskripte* (Sigmaringen, 1990).

Dutton, P. E. (ed.), *Carolingian civilization: a reader* (Peterborough, 1993).

Charlemagne's courtier: the complete Einhard (Peterborough, 1998).

Eckhardt, K. A., *Die Lex Baiuvariorum: eine Textkritische Studie* (Breslau, 1927).

Eckhardt, W. A., 'Die Capitularia Missorum Specialia von 802' *DA*, *12* (1956), pp. 498–516.

Eggert, W., 'Rebelliones servorum' *Zeitschrift für Geschichtswissenschaft*, *23* (1975), pp. 1147–64.

Egmond, W. S. van, 'The audience of Early Medieval Hagiographical Texts: Some Questions Revisited' in: Mostert (1999), *Medieval communication*, pp. 41–67.

Eichenberger, T., *Patria. Studien zur Bedeutung des Wortes im Mittelalter (6.–12. Jahrhundert)* (Sigmaringen, 1991), Nationes: historische und philologische Untersuchungen zur Entstehung der europäischen Nationen im Mittelalter 9.

Einhard, *Einhardi Epistolae* ed. K. Hampe (Berlin, 1899), MGH Epistolae V, pp. 105–45.

Vita Karoli Magni ed. O. Holder-Egger 6th edition (Hannover, 1911), MGH SRG 25.

Erhart, P., 'Contentiones inter monachos - Ethnische und politische Identität in monastischen Germeinschaften des Frühmittelalters' in: Corradini et al. (2006), *Texts and identities*, pp. 373–87.

Everett, N., 'Literacy and the law in Lombard government' *EME*, *9* (2000), pp. 93–127.

Literacy in Lombard Italy, c.568–774 (Cambridge, 2003).

'How territorial was Lombard Law?' in: Pohl, W. and Erhart, P. (eds.), *Die Langobarden* (Vienna, 2005), Forschungen zur Geschichte des Mittelalters 9, pp. 345–60.

Ewig, E., 'Das Bild Constantins des Großen in den ersten Jahrhunderten des abendländischen Mittelalters' *Historisches Jahrbuch*, 75 (1956), pp. 1–46.

'Zum christlichen Königsgedanken im Frühmittelalter' *Vorträge und Forschungen*, 3 (1956), pp. 7–73.

'Die Civitas Ubiorum, die Francia Rinensis und das Land Ribuarien' in: Ewig (1976), *Spätantikes und Fränkisches Gallien 1*, pp. 472–503.

Spätantikes und Fränkisches Gallien: gesammelte Schriften 1952–1973 Volume 1, (Munich, 1976).

'Die Stellung Ribuariens in der Verfassungsgeschichte des Merowingerreiches' in: Ewig (1976), *Spätantikes und Fränkisches Gallien 1*, pp. 450–71.

'Volkstum und Volksbewußtsein im Frankenreich des 7. Jahrhunderts' in: Ewig (1976), *Spätantikes und Fränkisches Gallien 1*, pp. 246–55.

Faulkner, T., 'Lex Ribuaria' (2005), unpublished M.phil dissertation, University of Cambridge.

'The Frankish leges in the Carolingian period' (2009), unpublished PhD dissertation, University of Cambridge.

Carolingian kings and the *leges barbarorum*. *Historical Research*, 86 (2013) pp. 443–64.

Fleckenstein, J., *Die Hofkapelle der deutschen Könige I* (Stuttgart, 1959), Schriften der MGH 16, 1.

Florus of Lyon, *Capitula Ex Lege Et Canone Collecta* ed. J.-P. Migne (Paris, 1864), PL Vol. 109 Col. 419–22.

Fouracre, P., 'Eternal light and earthly needs: practical aspects of the development of Frankish immunities' in: Davies and Fouracre (1995), *Property and power in the early Middle Ages*, pp. 53–81.

Freculf of Lisieux, *Historiarum Libri XII* ed. M. Allen (Turnhout, 2002), Frechulfi Lexoviensis episcopi opera omnia. Corpus Christianorum. Series Latina CLXIXA, pp. 9–724.

Freise, E., 'Studien zur Einzugsbereich der Kloster von Fulda' in: Schmid, K. and Althoff, G. (eds.), *Die Klostergemeinschaft von Fulda im früheren Mittelalter* Volume 2,3 (Munich, 1978), pp. 1003–269.

Fried, J., *Donation of Constantine and Constitutum Constantini: the misinterpretation of a fiction and its original meaning* (Berlin, 2007), Millennium-Studien 3.

Froidevaux, H., *Études sur la "Lex dicta Francorum chamavorum" et sur les Francs du pays d'Amor* (Paris, 1891).

Fruin, R., 'Opmerkingen over de Ewa quae se ad Amorem habet' *Verslagen en Mededeelingen van de vereniging tot uitgave der bronnen van het Oude Vaderlandsche Recht*, 7 (1924), pp. 571–96.

Fuhrmann, H., 'The Pseudo-Isidorian Forgeries' in: Jasper, D. and Fuhrmann, H. (eds.), *Papal letters in the early Middle Ages, History of medieval canon law* (Washington, DC, 2001), pp. 137–95.

Fürst, C. G., 'Ecclesia vivit lege Romana?' *ZRG KA*, *92* (1975), pp. 17–36.

Gallée, J. H., *Old-Saxon texts* (Leiden, 1894).

Gameson, R., *The early medieval Bible: its production, decoration and use.* (Cambridge, 1994).

Ganivet, P., 'L'"Épitomé de Lyon": un témoin de la réception du bréviaire dans le sud-est de la Gaule au VIe siècle?' in: Rouche and Dumézil (2008), *Bréviaire d'Alaric*, pp. 279–328.

Ganshof, F. L., *Was waren die Kapitularien?* (Darmstadt, 1961).

Frankish institutions under Charlemagne (Providence, RI, 1968).

Carolingians and the Frankish monarchy trans. J. Sondheimer (London, 1971).

'Charlemagne's programme of imperial government' trans. J. Sondheimer in: Ganshof (1971), *Carolingians and the Frankish monarchy*, pp. 55–86.

Ganz, D., 'The Epitaphium Arsenii and opposition to Louis the Pious' in: Godman and Collins (1990), *Charlemagne's heir*, pp. 537–50.

'On the history of Tironian Notes' in: Ganz, P. (ed.), *Tironische Noten* (Wiesbaden, 1990), pp. 35–57.

'Mass production of early medieval manuscripts: the Carolingian Bibles from Tours' in: Gameson (1994), *Early medieval Bible*, pp. 53–77.

'Paris BN Latin 2718: Theological Texts in the Chapel and the Chancery of Louis the Pious' in: Münsch and Zotz (2004), *Scientia veritatis: Festschrift für Hubert Mordek zum 65. Geburtstag*, pp. 137–52.

'Some Carolingian questions: a text from Charlemagne's days' in: Ganz, D. and Fouracre, P. (eds.), *Frankland: the Franks and the world of the early Middle Ages: essays in honour of Dame Jinty Nelson* (Manchester, 2008), pp. 90–100.

Garrison, M., 'Letters to a king and biblical exempla: the examples of Cathuulf and Clemens Peregrinus' *EME*, *7* (1998), pp. 305–28.

'The Franks as the New Israel? Education for an identity from Pippin to Charlemagne' in: Hen and Innes (2000), *Uses of the past*, pp. 114–61.

Gaudemet, J., 'Survivances Romaines dans le droit de la monarchie Franque du Vème au Xème siécle' *Tijdschrift voor Rechtsgeschiedenis*, *23* (1955), pp. 149–206.

'Le Breviére d'Alaric et les épitomes' *Ius Romanum Medii Aevi I, 2 b aa β* (1965).

Gaupp, E. T., *Lex Francorum Chamavorum oder das vermeintliche Xantener Gaurecht* (Breslau, 1855).

Geary, P., *Phantoms of Remembrance: memory and oblivion at the end of the first millennium* (Princeton, NJ, 1994).

Geary, P. and Garipzanov (eds.), *Franks, Northmen, and Slavs* (Turnhout, 2008).

Giesriegl, K., 'Autorität, Chronologie und Gesetzgebung. Königskataloge in fränkischen Leges-Handschriften' in: Corradini et al. (2006), *Texts and identities*, pp. 205–218.

Gillett, A. (ed.), *On Barbarian Identity: Critical approaches to Ethnicity in the Early Middle Ages* (Turnhout, 2002).

Gluckman, M., 'The peace in the feud' *Past and Present*, *8* (1955), pp. 1–14.

Godman, P. and Collins, R. (eds.), *Charlemagne's heir: new perspectives on the reign of Louis the Pious* (Oxford, 1990).

Goetz, H.-W., 'Herrschaft und Raum in der frühmittelalterlichen Grundherrschaft' *Annalen des historischen Vereins für den Niederrhein*, *190* (1987), pp. 7–33.

'The perception of "Power" and "State" in the Early Middle Ages: the case of the Astronomer's "Life of Louis the Pious"' in: Weiler, B. and MacLean, S. (eds.), *Perceptions of power in medieval Germany 800–1500* (Turnhout, 2006), pp. 15–36.

Goffart, W., *The Le Mans forgeries: a chapter from the history of church property in the ninth century.* (Cambridge, MA, 1966).

Goldberg, E. J., 'Popular revolt, dynastic politics, and aristocratic factionalism in the early middle ages: the Saxon Stellinga reconsidered' *Speculum, 70* (1995), pp. 467–501.

'"More Devoted to the Equipment of Battle than the Splendor of Banquets": frontier kingship, Martial ritual and early Knighthood at the court of Louis the German' *Viator, 30* (1999), pp. 41–78.

Struggle for Empire: Kingship and conflict under Louis the German 817–876 (Ithaca, NY, 2006).

Green, D., *Language and history in the early Germanic world* (Cambridge, 1998).

Green, D., and Siegmund, F. (eds.), *The continental Saxons from the Migration period to the late ninth century* (Woodbridge, 2003), Studies in historical archaeoethnology 6.

Gregory of Tours, *History of the Franks* trans. L. Thorpe (London, 1974).

Grierson, P. and Blackburn, M., *Medieval European coinage* Volume 1 The early Middle Ages (5th–10th centuries) (Cambridge, 1986).

Guterman, S. L., *The principle of the personality of law in the Germanic kingdoms of western Europe from the fifth to the eleventh century* (New York, 1990).

Halsall, G., *Settlement and social organization: the Merovingian region of Metz* (Cambridge, 1995).

'Introductory survey' in: Halsall G. (ed.), *Violence and society in the early medieval West* (Woodbridge, 1998), pp. 1–45.

Hamerow, H., *Early medieval settlements: the archaeology of rural communities in Northwest Europe, 400–900* (Oxford, 2002).

Hammer, C., 'Lex scripta in early medieval Bavaria' in: King, B. and Ridyard, S. (eds.), *Law in mediaeval life and thought* (TN, Sewanee, 1990), Sewanee mediaeval studies 5, pp. 185–95.

'Land sales in eighth- and ninth-century Bavaria: legal, economic and social aspects' *EME, 6* (1997), pp. 47–76.

Handley, M., 'Inscribing time and identity in the kingdom of Burgandy' in: Mitchell, S. and Greatrex, G. (eds.), *Ethnicity and culture in late antiquity* (London, 2000), pp. 83–102.

Death, society, and culture: inscriptions and epitaphs in Gaul and Spain, AD 300–750 (Oxford, 2003).

Harrill, A., *The manumission of slaves in early Christianity* (Tübingen, 1995), Hermeneutische Untersuchungen zur Theologie 32.

Hartmann, W., 'Brauchen wir neue Editionen der Leges?' in: Schieffer, R. (ed.), *Mittelalterliche Texte: Überlieferung, Befunde, Deutungen* (Hannover, 1996), pp. 233–45.

'Karl der Grosse und das Recht' in: Butzer, P. L., Kerner, M. and Oberschelp, W. (eds.), *Charlemagne and his heritage. 1200 Years of civilisation and science in Europe, 1 Scholarship, worldview and understanding* (Turnhout, 1997), pp. 173–92.

Ludwig der Deutscher (Darmstadt, 2002).

'Die Capita incerta im Sendhandbuch Reginos von Prüm' in: Münsch and Zotz (2004), *Scientia veritatis: Festschrift für Hubert Mordek zum 65. Geburtstag*, pp. 207–26.

Hartmann, W. and Schmitz, G. (eds.), *Fortschritt durch Fälschungen?: Ursprung, Gestalt und Wirkungen der pseudoisidorischen Fälschungen* (Hannover, 2002), MGH Studien und Texte 31.

Hartmann, W., Schmitz, G., and Schroder, I. (eds.), *Die Konzilien Der Karolingischen Teilreiche 875–911* (Hannover, 2014), MGH Concilia V.

Hässler, H.-J., Jarnut, J., and Wemhoff, M. (eds.), *Sachsen und Franken in Westfalen: zur Komplexität der ethnischen Deutung und Abgrenzung zweier frühmittelalterlicher Stämme* (Isensee, 1999), Studien zur Sachsenforschung 12.

Heather, P., 'Law and society in the Burgundian Kingdom' in: Rio (2011), *Law, custom and justice in late antiquity and the early Middle Ages*, pp. 115–54.

Heidecker, K., 'Communication by written texts in court cases: some charter evidence (ca. 800–ca. 1100)' in: Mostert (1999), *Medieval communication*, pp. 101–26.

Heidinga, H., *Medieval settlement and economy north of the lower Rhine: archaeology and history of Kootwijk and the Veluwe (the Netherlands)* (Assen, 1987).

'From Kootwijk to Rhenen: in search of the elite in the Central Netherlands in the Early Middle Ages' in: Besteman, J., Bos, J., and Heidinga, H. (eds.), *Medieval archaeology in the Netherlands: studies presented to H. H. van Regteren Altena* (Assen, 1990), pp. 9–40.

Hellmann, M., *Tironische Noten in der Karolingerzeit: am Beispiel eines Persius-Kommentars aus der Schule von Tours* (Hannover, 2000), MGH Studien und Texte 27.

Helvétius, A.-M., 'Les inventions de reliques en Gaule du Nord (IXe-XIIIe siècle)' in: Bozóky, E. and Helvétius, A.-M. (eds.), *Les Reliques. Objets, cultes, symboles. Actes du colloque international de l'Université du Littoral-Côte d'Opale (Boulogne-sur-Mer) 4–6 septembre 1997* (Turnhout, 1999), Hagiologia. Etudes sur la Sainteté en Occident / Studies on Western Sainthood 1, pp. 293–311.

Hen, Y., 'Charlemagne's Jihad' *Viator, 37* (2006), pp. 33–51.

'Changing Places: Chrodobert, Boba, and the Wife of Grimoald' *Revue Belge de Philologie et d'Histoire, 90* (2012), pp. 225–44.

Hen, Y. and Innes, M. (eds.), *The uses of the past in the early Middle Ages* (Cambridge, 2000).

Hillgarth, J. N., 'The position of Isidorian studies: a critical review of the literature 1936–1975' *Studi Medievali, 24* (1983), pp. 817–905.

Hincmar of Rheims, *Ad episcopos regni admonitio altera* ed. J.-P. Migne (Paris, 1879), PL Vol. 125 Col. 1007–18.

De Divortio Lotharii Regi et Theutbergae Reginae ed. L. Böhringer (Hannover, 1992), MGH Concilia IV Suppl. I.

Hofmeister, A., 'Über die älteste Vita Lebuini und die Stammesverfassung der Sachsen' in: Lammers, W. (ed.), *Entstehung und Verfassung des Sachsenstammes* (Darmstadt, 1967), pp. 1–31.

Hoops, J. and Jankuhn, H. (eds.), *Reallexikon der germanischen Altertumskunde* Volume 18, (Berlin, 2001).

Hrabanus Maurus, *Liber de Oblatione Puerorum* ed. J.-P. Migne (Paris, 1864), PL Vol. 107 Col. 419–40.

De institutione clericorum libri tres ed. D. Zimpel (Frankfurt am Main, 1996), Freiburger Beiträge zur Mittelalterlichen Geschichte 7.

Hübner, R., 'Gerichtsurkunden in fränkischer Zeit' *ZRG GA*, *12* (1891), pp. 1–118.

Humfress, C., 'A New Legal Cosmos: late Roman lawyers and the early medieval Church' in: Linehan, P. and Nelson, J. L. (eds.), *The Medieval world* (London, 2001), pp. 557–75.

'Law and legal practice in the age of Justinian' in: Maas, M. (ed.), *The Cambridge companion to the age of Justinian* (Cambridge, 2005), pp. 161–84.

'Cracking the codex: Late roman law in practice' *Bulletin of the Institute of Classical Studies*, *49* (2006), pp. 251–64.

Orthodoxy and the courts in the late antique world (Oxford, 2007).

Imbert, J., 'Le droit Romain dans les textes juridiques carolingiens' in: *Studi in onore Pietro de Francisi* Volume III, (Milan, 1956), pp. 61–7.

'Les références au droit romain sous les Carolingiens' *Revue Historique de droit français et étranger*, *73* (1995), pp. 163–74.

Innes, M., 'Memory, orality and literacy in an early medieval society' *Past and Present*, *158* (1998), pp. 3–36.

State and society in the early Middle Ages: the Middle Rhine Valley, 400–1000 (Cambridge, 2000).

'Charlemagne's government' in: Story (2005), *Charlemagne*, pp. 71–89.

'Land, freedom and the making of the medieval west' *TRHS*, *16* (2006), pp. 37–74.

'Practices of property in the Carolingian Empire' in: Davis and McCormick (2008), *Long Morning*, pp. 247–66.

'Charlemagne, written law and justice' in: Rio (2011), *Law, custom and justice in late antiquity and the early Middle Ages*, pp. 155–204.

Innes, M. and McKitterick, R., 'The writing of history' in: McKitterick, R. (ed.), *Carolingian culture: emulation and innovation* (Cambridge, 1994), pp. 193–220.

Jasper, D. (ed.), *Fälschungen im Mittelalter* (Hannover, 1988), MGH Schriften.

Jong, M. de, 'Power and humility in Carolingian society: the public penance of Louis the Pious' *EME*, *1* (1992), pp. 29–52.

'Old Law and new-found power: Hrabanus Maurus and the Old Testament' in: Drijvers, J. and MacDonald, A. (eds.), *Centres of learning: learning and location in pre-modern Europe and the Near East* (Leiden, 1995), pp. 161–77.

In Samuel's image: child oblation in the early medieval West (Leiden, 1996).

'Charlemagne's Church' in: Story (2005), *Charlemagne*, pp. 103–35.

The penitential state: authority and atonement in the age of Louis the Pious, 814–840 (Cambridge, 2009).

Jong, M. de, M. McKitterick, R., Pohl, W., and Wood, I., 'Introduction' in: Corradini et al. (2006), *Texts and identities*, pp. 11–3.

Kaiser, W., *Die Epitome Iuliani* (Frankfurt am Main, 2004).

Kasten, B., 'Beneficium zwischen Landleihe und Lehen - eine alte Frage, neu gestellt' in: Bauer, D. (ed.), *Mönchtum, Kirche, Herrschaft, 750–1000* (Sigmaringen, 1998), pp. 243–61.

'Alkuins erbrechtliche Expertise für Karl den Großen?' in: Depreux and Judic (2004), *Alcuin à Tours*, pp. 301–15.

Kempshall, M. S., 'The virtues of rhetoric: Alcuin's Disputatio de rhetorica et de uirtutibus' *Anglo-Saxon England*, *37* (2008), pp. 7–30.

Kern, F., *Kingship and law in the Middle Ages* (Oxford, 1948).

Kéry, L., *Canonical collections of the early Middle Ages (ca. 400–1140) : a bibliographical guide to the manuscripts and literature* (Washington, DC, 1999).

King, P. D., *Charlemagne: translated sources* (Kendal, 1987).

Köbler, G., *Das Recht im frühen Mittelalter. Untersuchungen zu Herkunft und Inhalt frühmittelalterlicher Rechtsbegriffe im deutschen Sprachgebiet* (Cologne, 1971), Forschungen zur deutschen Rechtsgeschichte 7.

Kosto, A., 'Hostages in the Carolingian world' *EME, 11* (2002), pp. 123–47.

Kottje, R., *Studien zum Einfluss des Alten Testaments auf Recht und Liturgie des frühen Mittelalters (6.–8. Jahrhundert)* (Bonn, 1964).

'Hrabanus und das Recht' in: Kottje R. and Maurer, H. (eds.), *Hrabanus Maurus: Lehrer, Abt und Bischof* (Wiesbaden, 1982), pp. 118–29.

'Die Lex Baiuvariorum - das Recht der Bayern' in: Mordek (1986), *Überlieferung und Geltung*, pp. 9–23.

Krah, A., 'Zur Kapitulariengesetzgebung in und für Neustrien' in: Atsma, H. (ed.), *La Neustrie. Les pays au nord de la Loire de 650 à 850. Colloque historique internationale 1* (Sigmaringen, 1989), Beihefte der Francia 16/1, pp. 565–81.

Krüger, K., *Studien zur Corveyer Grundungsüberlieferung* (Münster, 2004).

Krüger, S., *Studien zur sächsischen Grafschaftsverfassung im 9. Jahrhundert* (Göttingen, 1950), Studien und Vorarbeiten zum historischen Atlas Niedersachsen 9.

Krusch, B., *Die Lex Bajuvariorum: Textgeschichte, Handschriftenkritik und Entstehung* (Berlin, 1924).

Neue Forschungen über die drei oberdeutschen Leges: Bajuvariorum, Alamannorum, Ribuariorum (Berlin, 1927), Abhandlungen der Akademie der Wissenschaften in Göttingen. Philologisch-Historische Klasse XX, 1.

Landau, P., 'Die Lex Thuringorum – Karls des Großen Gesetz für die Thüringer' *ZRG GA, 118* (2001), pp. 23–57.

Die Lex Baiuvariorum: Entstehungszeit, Entstehungsort und Charakter von Bayerns ältester Rechts- und Geschichtsquelle (München, 2004), Bayerische Akademie der Wissenschaften. Philosophisch-Historische Klasse 3.

'The legislation of Stephan I and Bavarian law', paper delivered at the International Medieval Congress, Leeds, July 2007.

Landwehr, G., 'Die Liten in den altsächsischen Rechtsquellen. Ein Diskussionsbeitrag zur Textgeschichte der Lex Saxonum' in: Landwehr, G. (ed.), *Studien zu den germanischen Volksrechten: Gedächtnisschrift für Wilhelm Ebel* (Frankfurt am Main, 1982), pp. 117–43.

Lehmann, K., 'Der Codex Paris lat. nouv. acq. 204' *Neues Archiv, 12* (1887), pp. 579–85.

Levillain, L., 'Note critique sur la charte du comte Etienne et de la comtesse Amaltrude de 811' *Revue d'Histoire de L'Eglise de France, 116* (1943), pp. 54–74.

'Les comtes de Paris á l'èpoque franque', *Le Moyen Age, 50*, (1941), pp. 137–205.

Levy, E., 'The vulgarisation of Roman law in the early Middle Ages' *Medievalia et Humanistica, 1* (1943), pp. 14–40.

West Roman vulgar law: the law of property (Philadelphia, PA, 1951).

Lewis, A., 'The autonomy of Roman law' in: Coss (2000), *Moral world*, pp. 37–47.

Leyser, K., 'Ottonian government' in: *Medieval Germany and its neighbours 900–1250* (London, 1982), pp. 69–101.

'From Saxon freedoms to the freedom of Saxony: the crisis of the Eleventh century' in: Reuter, T. (ed.), *Communications and power in medieval Europe: the Carolingian and Ottonian centuries* (London, 1994), pp. 51–67.

Liebs, D., *Römische Jurisprudenz in Gallien (2. bis 8. Jahrhundert)* (Berlin, 2002).

Lintzel, M., 'Die Entstehung der Lex Saxonum' *ZRG, 47* (1927), pp. 130–73.

'Die Vita Lebuini Antiqua' *Sachsen und Anhalt, 7* (1931), pp. 76–108.

'Zur altsächsischen Rechtsgeschichte' *ZRG, 52* (1932), pp. 294–321.

Ausgewählte Schriften 2 Volumes (Berlin, 1961).

Lot, F., 'Origine et nature du benefice' in: *Recueil des travaux historiques de Ferdinand Lot* Volume 2, (Geneva, 1970), pp. 331–41.

Louis, R., *De l'histoire à la légende. Girart, comte de Vienne et ses fondations monastiques* (Auxerre, 1946).

Löwe, H., 'Studien zu den Annales Xantenses' *DA, 8* (1950), pp. 59–99.

Lupoi, M., *The origins of the European legal order* trans. A. Belton (Cambridge, 2000).

Maasen, F., 'Ein Commentar des Florus von Lyon zu einigen der sogenannten Sirmond'schen Constitutionen' *Sitzungsberichte Wien, phil.-hist. Classe, 92* (1878), pp. 301–25.

MacLean, S., *Kingship and politics in the late ninth century. Charles the Fat and the end of the Carolingian Empire* (Cambridge, 2003).

'Insinuation, censorship and the struggle for late Carolingian Lotharingia in Regino of Prüm's Chronicle' *EHR, 124* (2009), pp. 1–28.

Matthews, J., 'Interpreting the interpretationes of the Breviarium' in: Mathisen, R. (ed.), *Law, society, and authority in late antiquity* (Oxford, 2001), pp. 11–32.

Mayr-Harting, H., 'Charlemagne, the Saxons and the imperial coronation of 800' *EHR, 111* (1996), pp. 1113–33.

McKeon, P., 'Archbishop Ebbo of Rheims (816–835)' *Church History, 43* (1974), pp. 437–47.

McKitterick, R., *The Frankish church and the Carolingian reforms 789–895* (London, 1977).

The Carolingians and the written word (Cambridge, 1989).

'Zur Herstellung von Kapitularien: Die Arbeit des Leges-Skriptoriums' *Mitteilungen des Instituts fur Österreichische Geschichtsforschung, 101* (1993), pp. 3–16.

'Carolingian Bible production: the Tours anomaly' in: Gameson (1994), *Early medieval Bible*, pp. 53–77.

'Some Carolingian law-books and their function' in: *Books, scribes and learning in the Frankish Kingdoms, 6th–9th centuries* (Aldershot, 1994), pp. 13–27.

'Constructing the past in the early Middle Ages: the case of the Royal Frankish Annals' *TRHS, 7* (1997), pp. 100–30.

'Perceptions of justice in western Europe in the ninth and tenth centuries' in: *La Giustizia nell'Alto Medioevo (secoli IX–XI)* (Spoleto, 1997), Settimane 44, pp. 1075–102.

History and memory in the Carolingian world (Cambridge, 2004).

'The scripts of the Bobbio Missal' in: Hen, Y. and Meens, R. (eds.), *The Bobbio missal: liturgy and religious culture in Merovingian Gaul* (Cambridge, 2004), pp. 19–52.

McKitterick, R., 'History, law and communication with the past in the Carolingian period' *Settimane, 52* (2005), pp. 941–79.

Charlemagne: the formation of a European identity (Cambridge, 2008).

'Charlemagne's missi and their books' in: Baxter et al. (2009), *Studies in memory of Patrick Wormald*, pp. 253–67.

'The uses of literacy in Carolingian and post-Carolingian Europe: literate conventions of memory' in: *Scrivere e leggere nel alto medioevo* (Spoleto, 2012), Settimane, pp. 179–212.

'Werden 8–9 Jht. im Spiegel seiner Handschriften' in: Patzold, S., Rathmann-Lutz, A., and Scior, V. (eds.), *Geschichtsvorstellungen. Bilder, Texte und Begriffe aus dem Mittelalter* (Vienna, Cologne Weimar, 2012), pp. 326–53.

Meens, R., 'The uses of the Old Testament in early medieval canon law' in: Hen and Innes (2000), *Uses of the past*, pp. 67–77.

'Sanctuary, penance, and dispute settlement under Charlemagne: the conflict between Alcuin and Theodulf of Orléans over a sinful cleric' *Speculum, 82* (2007), pp. 277–300.

Mersiowsky, M., 'Saint-Martin de Tours et les chancelleries carolingiennnes' in: Depreux and Judic (2004), *Alcuin à Tours*, pp. 73–90.

Moeller, E. von, 'Der Homo Francus der Ewa Chamavorum' *Mitteilungen des Instituts fur Österreichische Geschichtsforschung, 23* (1902), pp. 217–30.

Moore, S. F., *Social facts and fabrications: 'customary' law on Kilimanjaro 1880–1908* (Cambridge, 1986).

'Certainties undone: fifty turbulent years of legal anthropology 1949–99' *Journal of the Royal Anthropological Institute, 7* (2001), pp. 95–116.

Mordek, H., *Kirchenrecht und Reform in Frankenreich: die collectio vetus Gallica: die älteste systematische Kanonenssammlung des fränkischen Gallien: Studien und Editio* (Berlin, 1975).

Überlieferung und Geltung normativer Texte des frühen und hohen Mittelalters (Sigmaringen, 1986).

'Recently discovered Capitulary texts belonging to the legislation of Louis the Pious' in: Godman and Collins (1990), *Charlemagne's heir*, pp. 437–55.

Bibliotheca capitularium regum Francorum manuscripta: Überlieferung und Traditionszusammenhang der fränkischen Herrschererlasse (Munich, 1995).

'Ein exemplarische Rechtsstreit' in: Mordek (2000), *Studien*, pp. 279–306.

'Fränkische Kapitularien und Kapitulariensammlungen. Eine Einführung' in: Mordek (2000), *Studien*, pp. 1–55.

'Kapitularien und Schriftlichkeit' in: Mordek (2000), *Studien*, pp. 307–39.

'Leges und Kapitularien' in: Mordek (2000), *Studien*, pp. 341–53.

Studien zur fränkischen Herrschergesetzgebung: Aufsätze über Kapitularien und Kapitulariensammlungen ausgewählt zum 60. Geburtstag (Frankfurt, 2000).

'Weltliches Recht im Kloster Weißsenburg/Elsaß. Hinkmar von Rheims und die Kapitulariensammlung des Cod. Sélestat, Bibliothèque Humaniste, 14 (104)' in: Mordek (2000), *Studien*, pp. 261–79.

Mostert, M. (ed.), *New approaches to medieval communication* (Turnhout, 1999).

Müller-Mertens, E., 'Der Stellingaaufstand' *Zeitschrift für Geschichtswissenschaft, 20* (1972), pp. 818–42.

Münsch, O., *Der liber legum des Lupus von Ferrières* Volume 14, Freiburger Beiträge zur Mittelalterlichen Geschichte (Frankfurt am Main, 2001).

Munsch, O. and Zotz, T. (eds.), *Scientia veritatis: Festschrift für Hubert Mordek zum 65. Geburtstag* (Ostfildern, 2004).

Nehlsen, H., 'Aktualität und Effektivität der ältesten germanischen Rechtsaufzeichnungen' in: Classen (1977), *Recht und Schrift*, pp. 449–502.

Nelson, J. L., 'Kingship, law and liturgy in the political thought of Hincmar of Rheims' *EHR*, *92* (1977), pp. 241–79.

'Legislation and consensus in the reign of Charles the Bald' in: Wormald, P., Bullough, D. and Collins, R. (eds.), *Ideal and reality in Frankish and Anglo-Saxon society: studies presented to J. M. Wallace-Hadrill* (Oxford, 1983), pp. 202–22.

'Dispute settlement in Carolingian West Francia' in: Davies and Fouracre (1986), *Settlement of disputes*, pp. 45–65.

'History writing at the courts of Louis the Pious and Charles the Bald' in: Scharer, A. and Scheibelreiter, G. (eds.), *Historiographie im frühen Mittelalter* (Vienna, 1994), Veröffentlichungen des Instituts für Österreichische Geschichtsforschung 32, pp. 435–42.

'Kings with justice, kings without justice: an early medieval paradox' in: *La Giustizia nell'Alto Medioevo (secoli V–VIII)* (Spoleto, 1995), Settimane 42, pp. 797–823.

The Frankish World (London, 1996).

'Literacy in Carolingian Government' in: Nelson (1996), *The Frankish World*, pp. 1–36.

'Making ends meet: wealth and poverty in the Carolingian church' in: Nelson (1996), *The Frankish World*, pp. 145–53.

'Translating images of authority: the Christian Roman emperors in the Carolingian world' in: Nelson (1996), *The Frankish World*, pp. 89–99.

'Peers in the early Middle Ages' in: Stafford, P., Nelson, J. L. and Martindale, J. (eds.), *Law, laity and solidarities* (Manchester, 2001), pp. 27–47.

'Charlemagne and empire' in: Davis and McCormick (2008), *Long Morning*, pp. 223–34.

'Frankish identity in Charlemagne's empire' in: Geary and Garipzanov (2008), *Franks, Northmen, and Slavs*, pp. 71–83.

Niermeyer, J. F., 'Het Midden-Nederlands rivierengebied in de Frankische tijd' *Tijdschrift voor Geschiedenis*, *66* (1953), pp. 145–69.

Nitschke, A., 'Die Freilassung – Beobachtungen zum Wandel von Rechtsgebärden' *ZRG GA*, *99* (1982), pp. 220–51.

Nösges, N., 'Die Urkunden Lothars I. für die Abtei Prüm' in: Nolden, R. (ed.), *Lothar I.: Kaiser und Mönch in Prüm: zum 1150. Jahr seines Todes* (Prüm, 2005), pp. 113–22.

Oliver, L., *The beginnings of English law* (Toronto, 2002).

Palmer, J., 'Rimbert's Vita Anskarii and Scandinavian mission in the ninth century' *Journal of Ecclesiastical History*, 55 (2004), pp. 235–56.

Patzold, S., 'Die Veränderung frühmittelalterlichen Rechts im Spiegel der Leges-Reformen Karls des Großen und Ludwigs des Frommen' in: Esders, S. and Reinle, C. (eds.), *Rechtsveränderung im politischen und sozialen Kontext mittelalterlicher Rechtsvielfalt* (Münster, 2005), pp. 63–99.

Patzold, S., 'Normen im Buch. Überlegungen zu Geltungsansprüchen so genannter "Kapitularien"' *Frühmittelalterliche Studien, 41* (2007), pp. 331–50.

Pertz, G., 'Über das Xantener Recht' *Abhandlungen der Königlichen Akademie der Wissenschaften zu Berlin,* (1846), pp. 411–23.

Pohl, W., 'Telling the difference: signs of ethnic identity' in: Pohl and Reimitz (1998), *Strategies of distinction*, pp. 17–69.

'Zur Bedeutung ethnischer Unterscheidungen in der frühen Karolingerzeit' in: Hässler, Jarnut, and Wemhoff (1999), *Sachsen und Franken in Westfalen,* pp. 193–208.

'Probleme einer Sinngeschichte ethnischer Gemeinschaften. Identität und Tradition' in: Dilcher, G. (ed.), *Leges - Gentes - Regna* (Berlin, 2006), pp. 51–67.

Pohl, W. and Reimitz, H. (eds.), *Strategies of distinction: the construction of ethnic communities, 300–800* (Leiden, 1998), The Transformation of the Roman World 2.

Pohl-Resl, B., 'Ethnische Bezeichnungen und Rechtsbekentisse in langobardischen Urkunden' in: Brunner, K. and Merta, B. (eds.), *Ethnogenese und Überlieferung: angewandte Methoden der Frühmittelalterforschung* (Vienna, 1994), pp. 163–71.

'Legal practice and ethnic identity in Lombard Italy' in: Pohl and Reimitz (1998), *Strategies of distinction*, pp. 205–19.

Pokorny, R., 'Eine Brief-Instruktion aus dem Hofkreis Karls des Großen an einen geistlichen Missus' *DA, 52* (1996), pp. 59–83.

Porzig, W., 'Die Rezensionen der Etymologiae des Isidorus von Sevilla' *Hermes*, (1937), pp. 129–70.

Pössel, C., 'Symbolic communication and the negotiation of power at Carolingian regnal assemblies 814–840' (2004), unpublished PhD dissertation, University of Cambridge.

'Authors and recipients of Carolingian capitularies 779–829' in: Corradini et al. (2006), *Texts and identities*, pp. 253–74.

Prinz, J., 'Das hohe Mittelalter vom Vertrag von Verdun (843) bis zur Schlacht von Worringen (1288)' in: Kohl, W. (ed.), *Westfälische Geschichte* (Düsseldorf, 1983), Veröffentlichungen der Historischen Komission für Westfalen im Provinzialinstitut für westfälische Landes- und Volksforschung des Landschaftsverbandes Westfalen-Lippe 43, pp. 337–401.

Radding, C. M., *The origins of medieval jurisprudence: Pavia and Bologna, 850–1150* (New Haven, CT, 1988).

'Legal theory and practice in eleventh-century Italy', *Law and History Review 21* (2003) available at http://web.archive.org/web/20081016055942/http://www.historycooperative.org/journals/lhr/21.2/comment radding.htm.

Reeve, M., 'Cuius in Usum? Recent and future editing' *The Journal of Roman Studies, 90* (2000), pp. 196–206.

Reimitz, H., 'Omnes Franci: identification and identities of the Early Medieval Franks' in: Geary and Garipzanov (2008), *Franks, Northmen, and Slavs*, pp. 51–68.

Reuter, T., 'Charlemagne and the world beyond the Rhine' in: Story, J. (ed.), *Charlemagne: empire and society* (Manchester, 2005), pp. 183–94.

Medieval polities and modern mentalities ed. J. L. Nelson (Cambridge, 2006).

'The Ottonians and Carolingian tradition' ed. J. L. Nelson in: Reuter (2006), *Medieval polities*, pp. 268–83.

'Regemque, quem in Francia pene perditi, in patria manifice recepit: Ottonian ruler representation in synchronic and diachronic comparison' ed. J. L. Nelson in: Reuter (2006), *Medieval polities*, pp. 127–47.

Reynolds, P. L., *Marriage in the Western Church: the Christianization of marriage during the patristic and early medieval periods* (Leiden, 1994).

Reynolds, R., 'An early medieval tract on the diaconate' *Harvard Theological Review*, *72* (1979), pp. 97–100.

Clerical orders in the early Middle Ages: duties and ordination (Aldershot, 1999).

Reynolds, S., *Kingdoms and communities in Western Europe 900–1300* (Oxford, 1984).

Fiefs and vassals: the medieval evidence reinterpreted (Oxford, 1994).

'Rationality and collective judgement in the law of Western Europe before the twelfth century' *Quaestiones Medii Aevi Novae*, *5* (2000), pp. 3–19.

'The emergence of professional law in the long twelfth century' *Law and History Review*, *21* (2003), pp. 347–66.

Rhijn, C. van, 'Priests and the Carolingian reforms: the bottlenecks of local correctio' in: Corradini et al. (2006), *Texts and identities*, pp. 219–38.

Shepherds of the Lord: priests and episcopal statutes in the Carolingian period (Turnhout, 2007).

Richthofen, K. F. von, *Zur Lex Saxonum* (Berlin, 1868).

Rio, A., 'Freedom and unfreedom in early medieval Francia: the evidence of the legal formulae' *Past and Present*, *193* (2006), pp. 7–40.

'Formulae, legal practice and the settlement of disputes in the Frankish kingdoms: the Formulary of Angers' in: Andersen, P., Münster-Swendsen, M., and Vogt, H. (eds.), *Law before Gratian: law in western Europe c.500–1100 : proceedings of the Third Carlsberg Academy Conference on Medieval Legal History 2006* (Copenhagen, 2007), pp. 21–35.

Legal practice and the written word in the early Middle Ages: Frankish Formulae, c. 500–1000 (Cambridge, 2009).

Law, custom and justice in late antiquity and the early Middle Ages (London, 2011).

Rösener, R., 'Strukturformen der älteren Agrarverfassung in sächsischen Raum' *Niedersächsisches Jahrbuch für Landesgeschichte*, *52* (1980), pp. 107–43.

Rösener, W., 'Zur Struktur und Entwicklung der Grundherrschaft in Sachsen in karolingisher und ottonischer Zeit' in: Verhulst (1985), *Le grand domaine*, pp. 173–207.

Rouche, M. and Dumézil, B. (eds.), *Le Bréviaire d'Alaric. Aux origines du Code Civil.* (Paris, 2008).

Rudolph of Fulda, *Translatio Sancti Alexandri auctoribus Rudolfo et Meginharto* ed. G. Pertz (Hannover, 1829), MGH Scriptores in folio II, pp. 673–81.

Russchen, A., 'De akte van Folker (855)' *It Beaken*, *23* (1961), pp. 91–7.

'Sub lege Francorum. Ein Beitrag zur Abgrenzungen der Frisia Criterior' *It Beaken*, *26* (1964), pp. 251–7.

Scharf, J., 'Studien zu Smaragdus und Jonas' *DA*, *17* (1961), pp. 333–84.

Schmid, K., 'Die Nachfahren Widukinds' *DA*, *20* (1964), pp. 1–47.

Schmidt-Wiegand, R., 'Die kritische Ausgabe der Lex Salica - noch immer ein Problem?' *ZRG GA*, *76* (1959), pp. 301–19.

Schmidt-Wiegand, R., 'Stammesrecht und Volksprache in karolingischer Zeit' in: Beumann, H. and Schröder, W. (eds.), *Aspekte der Nationenbildung im Mittelalter* Volume 1, (Sigmaringen, 1978), pp. 171–203.

'Lex Francorum Chamavorum' in: Hoops and Jankuhn (2001), *Reallexikon der germanischen Altertumskunde*, pp. 317–18.

'Lex Ribuaria' in: Hoops and Jankuhn (2001), *Reallexikon der germanischen Altertumskunde*, pp. 320–2.

Schmitz, G., 'Ansegis und Regino. Die Rezeption der Kapitularien in den Libri duo de synodalibus causis' *ZRG KA*, *74* (1988), pp. 95–132.

'The capitulary legislation of Louis the Pious' in: Godman and Collins (1990), *Charlemagne's heir*, pp. 425–36.

'Die allmähliche Verfertigung der Gedanken beim Fälchen. Unausorgenes und Widersprüchliches bei Benedictus Levita' in: Hartmann and Schmitz (2002), *Fortschritt durch Fälschungen?*, pp. 29–60.

'Benedictus Levita und die Lex Baiuvariorum' *ZRG KA*, *97* (2011), pp. 20–58.

Schneider, R., 'Schriftlichkeit und Mündlichkeit im Bereich der Kapitularien' in: Classen (1977), *Recht und Schrift*, pp. 257–79.

Schott, C., 'Der Stand der Leges-Forschung' *Frühmittelalterliche Studien*, *13* (1979), pp. 29–55.

Schröder, R., 'Die Heimat der Lex Chamavorum' *Monatschrift für die Geschichte Westdeutschlands*, *VI* (1880), pp. 492–502.

Schwerin, C. von, 'Zu den Leges Saxonum' *ZRG GA*, *33* (1912), pp. 390–452.

Seckel, E., 'Studien zu Benedictus Levita II-V' *Neues Archiv*, *29* (1904), pp. 277–331.

'Studien zu Benedictus Levita VI' *Neues Archiv*, *31* (1906), pp. 61–139.

'Pseudo-Isidorian Decretals and other forgeries' in: *The New Schaff-Herzog Encyclopedia of Religious Knowledge* (London, 1911), pp. 343–9.

Die erste Zeile Pseudoisidors, die Hadriana-Rezension: In nomine domini incipit praefatio libri huius, und die Geschichte der Invokationen in den Rechtsquellen (Berlin, 1959), Sitzungsberichte der Deutschen Akademie der Wissenschaften zu Berlin, Klasse für Philosophie, Geschichte, Staats-, Rechts- und Wirtschaftswissenschaften 4.

Seeliger, G., *Die Kapitularien der Karolinger* (Munich, 1893).

'Volksrecht und Königsrecht? Untersuchungen zur fränkischen Verfassungs- und Rechtsgeschichte' *Historische Vierteljahrschrift*, *1* (1898), pp. 1–40.

Sellert, W., 'Aufzeichnung des Rechts und Gesetz' in: Sellert, W. (ed.), *Das Gesetz in Spätantike und frühem Mittelalter* (Göttingen, 1992), pp. 67–102.

Semmler, J., 'Zur Überlieferung der monastischen Gesetzgebung Ludwigs der Frommen' *DA*, *16* (1960), pp. 309–89.

Senger, B. (ed.), *St. Liudger und die Abtei Werden* (Essen, 1962).

Liudger in seinem Zeit (Münster, 1982).

Liudger, Leben und Werk (Münster, 1984).

Sickel, T., *Acta regum et imperatorum Karolinorum, 2. Teil: Regesten der Urkunden der ersten Karolinger (751–840)* (Vienna, 1867).

Siegmund, F., 'Social relations among the Old Saxons' in: Green and Siegmund (2003), *Continental Saxons*, pp. 77–95.

Siems, H., 'Lex Baiuvariorum' in: Kaufmann, E. and Erier, A. (eds.), *Handwörterbuch zur deutschen Rechtsgeschichte* (Berlin, 1964), p. 1889.

Studien zur Lex Frisionum (Ebelsbach, 1980).

'Textbearbeitung und Umgang mit Rechtstexten im Frühmittelalter. Zur Umgestaltung der Leges im Liber legum des Lupus' in: Siems, H. (ed.), *Recht im frühmittelalterlichen Gallien* (Cologne, 1995), pp. 29–72.

'Das Lebensbild der Lex Baiuvariorum' in: Hecker, H.-J., Heydenreuther, R. and Schlosser, H. (eds.), *Rechtssetzung und Rechtswirklichkeit in der bayerischen Geschichte* (Munich, 2006), pp. 29–73.

Smith, J., 'The hagiography of Hucbald of Saint-Amand' *Studi Medievali*, *35* (1994), pp. 517–42.

Smyth, A. (ed.), *Medieval Europeans. Studies in ethnic identity and national perspectives in medieval Europe* (London, 1998).

Sonderegger, S., *Althochdeutsche Sprache und Literatur: eine Einführung in das älteste Deutsch: Darstellung und Grammatik* 3rd edition (Berlin, 2003).

Springer, M., 'Salier und salisches Recht – Beobachtungen zu den Worten Salii und Salicus' in: Wieczorek, A. (ed.), *Die Franken, Wegbereiter Europas. Vor 1500 Jahren, König Chlodwig und seine Erben* (Mainz, 1996), pp. 485–7.

'Gab es ein Volk der Salier?' in: Geuenich, D., Haubrichs, W., and Jarnut, J. (eds.), *Nomen et gens: zur historischen Aussagekraft frümittelalterlicher Personennamen* (Berlin, 1997), pp. 58–83.

'Riparii – Ribuarier – Rheinfranken nebst einigen Bemerkungen zum Geographen von Ravenna' in: *Die Franken und die Alemannen bis zur "Schlacht bei Zülpich"* (Berlin, 1998), pp. 200–69.

'Was Lebuins Lebensbeschreibung über die Verfassung Sachsens wirklich sagt oder warum man sich mit einzelnen Wörtern beschäftigen muß' in: Hässler, Jarnut, and Wemhoff (1999), *Sachsen und Franken in Westfalen*, pp. 223–39.

Staab, F., 'Der Grundbesitz der Abtei Fulda bis zur Mitte des 9. Jahrhundert and seine Stifter' in: Böhne, W. (ed.), *Hrabanus Maurus und seine Schule: Festschrift der Rabanus-Maurus-Schule 1980* (Fulda, 1980), pp. 48–63.

Stach, W., 'Geschichtswissenschaft und Rechtsgeschichte im Streit um die Stammesrechte. I. Teil: Probleme der Handschriftlichen Überlieferung der Bayerischen Lex' *Historische Vierteljahrschrift*, *26* (1931), pp. 682–737.

Staubach, N., *Das Herrscherbild Karls des Kahlen. Formen und Funktionen monarchischer Repräsentationen im früheren Mittelalter* (Münster, 1982).

Rex christianus. Hofkultur und Herrschaftspropaganda im Reich Karls des Kahlen (Cologne, 1993).

Stein, P., *Roman law in European history* (Cambridge, 1999).

Stein, S., 'Lex und Capitula' *Mitteilungen des Instituts für Österreichische Geschichtsforschung*, *41* (1926), pp. 289–301.

Stengel, E. E., 'Über die karolingischen Cartulare des Klosters Fulda' in: *Abhandlungen und Untersuchungen zur Geschichte der Reichsabtei Fulda* (Fulda, 1960), Veröffentlichung des Fuldaer Geschichtsvereins 37, pp. 147–93.

Steuer, H., 'The beginnings of Urban economies among the Saxons' in: Green and Siegmund (2003), *Continental Saxons*, pp. 159–181.

Story, J., 'Cathwulf, kingship and the royal abbey of Saint Denis' *Speculum*, *74* (1999), pp. 1–21.

Charlemagne: empire and society (Manchester, 2005).

Stouff, L., 'Étude sur le principe de la personalité des lois depuis les invasions barbares jusqu'au XIIe siècle' *Revue bourguignonne* (1894), pp. 1–65, 273–310.

Tangl, M., 'Die Tironischen Noten in den Urkunden der Karolinger' *Archiv für Urkundenforschung, 1* (1907–8), pp. 87–166.

Tardif, J., 'Un abrégé juridique des Étymologies d'Isidore de Séville' in: *Mélanges Julien Havet. Receuil de travaux d'érudition dédiés à la mémoire de Julien Havet (1853–1983)* (Paris, 1895), pp. 659–81.

Theuerkauf, G., *Lex, Speculum, Compendium Iuris. Rechtsaufzeichnung und Rechtsbewußtsein in Norddeutschland vom 8. bis zum 16. Jahrhundert* (Cologne, 1968), Forschungen zur deutschen Rechtsgeschichte 6.

Theuws, F., 'Landed property and manorial organisation in Northern Austrasia: some considerations and a case study' in: Theuws, F. and Roymans, N. (eds.), *Images of the past: studies on ancient societies in Northwestern Europe* (Amsterdam, 1991), pp. 299–397.

Tiefenbach, H., *Studien zu Wörtern volkssprachiger Herkunft in karolingischen Königsurkunden. Ein Beitrag zum Wortschatz der Diplome Lothars I. und Lothars II* (Munich, 1973), Münstersche Mittelalter-Schriften 15.

Ubl, K., 'Doppelmoral im karolingischen Kirchenrecht? Ehe und Inzest bei Regino von Prüm' in: W. Hartmann (ed.), *Recht und Gericht in Kirche und Welt um 1900* (Munich, 2007), pp. 90–124.

Usinger, R., *Forschungen zur Lex Saxonum* (Berlin, 1867).

Verhulst, A. (ed.), *Le grand domaine aux époques mérovingienne et carolingienne* (Ghent, 1985).

Vessey, M., 'The origins of the Collectio Sirmondiana: a new look at the evidence' in: Wood and Harries (1993), *Theodosian Code*, pp. 178–99.

Vogler, W., 'St. Martin de Tours und St. Gallen. Europäische Beziehungen zwischen zwei karolingischen Klöstern' in: Ochsenbein, P. and Ziegler, E. (eds.), *Codices sangallenses: Festschrift für Johannes Duft zum 80. Geburtstag* (Thorbecke, 1995), pp. 117–36.

Wallace-Hadrill, J. M., 'The bloodfeud of the Franks' in: *The Long-Haired Kings* (London, 1962), pp. 121–47.

'The Via Regia of the Carolingian age' in: Smalley, B. (ed.), *Trends in medieval political thought* (Oxford, 1965), pp. 22–41.

The barbarian West, 400–1000 revised edition (Oxford, 1996).

Wallach, L., *Alcuin and Charlemagne: studies in Carolingian history and literature* (New York, 1959).

Wampach, C., *Geschichte der Grundherrschaft Echternach im Frühmittelalter* Volume I, Textband (Luxemboug, 1930).

Weitzel, J., *Dinggenossenschaft und Recht: Untersuchungen zum Rechtsverständnis im fränkisch-deutschen Mittelalter* (Cologne, 1985), Quellen und Forschungen zur höchsten Gerichtsbarkeit im Alten Reich 15.

'Gewohnheitsrecht und fränkisch-deutsches Gerichtsverfahren' in: Dilcher (1992), *Gewohnheitsrecht*, pp. 67–87.

Wenskus, R., *Sächsischer Stammesadel und fränkischer Reichsadel* (Göttingen, 1976), Abhandlungen der Akademie der Wissenschaften in Göttingen. Philologisch-Historische Klasse.

'Die ständische Entwicklung in Sachsen im Gefolge der fränkischen Eroberung' *Settimane, 32* (1986), pp. 587–616.

Werner, K. F., 'Important noble families in the Kingdom of Charlemagne' in: Reuter, T. (ed.), *The medieval nobility: studies on the ruling classes of France and Germany from the sixth to the twelfth century* (Amsterdam, 1979), pp. 137–202.

Werner, K.-F., 'Missus-marchio-comes: entre l'administration centrale et l'administration locale de l'empire carolingien' in: Paravicini, W. and Werner, K.-F. (eds.), *Histoire comparée de l'administration (IVe–XVIIIe siècles)* (Munich, 1980), pp. 191–239.

West, C., 'Upper Lotharingia and Champagne c. 850–c. 1100' (2007), unpublished PhD dissertation, University of Cambridge.

'The significance of the Carolingian advocate' *EME*, *17* (2009), pp. 186–206.

Reframing the feudal revolution. Political and social transformation between Marne and Moselle, c.800 to c.1100 (Cambridge, 2013).

White, S. D., 'Tenth-century courts at Mâcon and the perils of structuralist history: re-reading Burgundian judicial institutions' in: Brown (2003), *Conflict in medieval Europe*, pp. 37–68.

Wickham, C., 'Lawyers' time: history and memory in tenth and eleventh-century Italy' in: Mayr-Harting, H. and Moore, R. I. (eds.), *Studies presented to R. H. C. Davis* (London, 1985), pp. 53–71.

Framing the early Middle Ages: Europe and the Mediterranean 400–800 (Oxford, 2005).

Willis, J., *Latin textual criticism* (Urbana, IL, 1972), Illinois Studies in Language and Literature 61.

Wirtz, A., 'Die Geschichte des Hamalandes' *Annalen des Historischen Vereins für den Niederrhein*, *173* (1971), pp. 7–84.

Wolfram, H., 'Ethnogenesen im frühmittelalterlichen Donau- und Ostalpenraum (6.-10. Jahrhundert)' in: Beaumann, H. and Schröder, W. (eds.), *Frühmittelalterliche Ethnogenesen im Alpenraum* (Sigmaringen, 1985), Nationes: historische und philologische Untersuchungen zur Entstehung der europäischen Nationen im Mittelalter 5, pp. 97–151.

Wolfram, H. and Pohl, W. (eds.), *Typen der Ethnogenese unter besonderer Berücksichtigung der Bayern* (Vienna, 1990).

Wood, I., 'Administration, law and culture in Merovingian Gaul' in: McKitterick, R. (ed.), *The uses of literacy in early medieval Europe* (Cambridge, 1992), pp. 63–81.

'The Code in Merovingian Gaul' in: Wood and Harries (1993), *Theodosian Code*, pp. 159–77.

The Merovingian Kingdoms 450–751 (Harlow, 1994).

'Defining the Franks' in: Forde, S., Johnson, L. and Murray, A. (eds.), *Concepts of nationality and national identity in the Middle Ages* (Leeds, 1995), pp. 47–57.

'Teutsind, Witlaic and the history of Merovingian precaria' in: Davies and Fouracre (1995), *Property and power in the early Middle Ages*, pp. 31–52.

'Roman law in the Barbarian kingdoms' in: Ellegård, A. and Åkerström-Hougen, G. (eds.), *Rome and the north* (Jonsered, 1996), pp. 5–14.

'Before or after mission. Social relations across the middle and lower Rhine in the seventh and eighth centuries' in: Hansen, I. L. and Wickham, C. (eds.), *The long eighth century* (Leiden, 2000), pp. 149–66.

'Missionaries and the Christian frontier' in: Pohl, W., Wood, I. and Reimitz, H. (eds.), *The transformation of frontiers: from late antiquity to the Carolingians* (Leiden, 2001), The transformation of the Roman world 10, pp. 209–18.

Wood, I., *The missionary life: saints and the evangelisation of Europe, 400–1050* (Harlow, 2001).

'Beyond satraps and ostriches: political and social structures of the Saxons in the early Carolingian period' in: Green and Siegmund (2003), *Continental Saxons*, pp. 271–97.

Wood, I. and Harries, J. (eds.), *The Theodosian Code: studies in the imperial law of late antiquity* (London, 1993).

Wood, S., *The proprietary Church in the Medieval West* (Oxford, 2006).

Wormald, P., 'Lex Scripta and Verbum Regis: legislation and Germanic kingship from Euric to Cnut' in: Sawyer, P. and Wood, I. (eds.), *Early Medieval kingship* (Leeds, 1977), pp. 105–38.

The making of English law: King Alfred to the twelfth century. Vol. 1, Legislation and its limits (Oxford, 1999).

'The Leges Barbarorum: law and ethnicity in the post-Roman West' in: Goetz, H.-W., Jarnut, J. and Pohl, W. (eds.), *Regna and gentes: the relationship between late antique and early medieval peoples and kingdoms in the transformation of the Roman world* (Leiden, 2003), The transformation of the Roman world 13, pp. 21–55.

Wright, R., *Late latin and early Romance in Spain and Carolingian France* (Liverpool, 1982).

Zechiel-Eckes, K., 'Florus' Polemik gegen Modoin : Unbekannte Texte zum Konflikt zwischen dem Bischof von Autun und dem Lyoner Klerus in den dreißiger Jahren des 9.Jahrhunderts' *Francia, 25* (1998), pp. 19–38.

Florus von Lyon als Kirchenpolitiker und Publizist: Studien zur Persönlichkeit eines karolingischen 'Intellektuellen' am Beispiel der Auseinandersetzung mit Amalarius (835–838) und des Prädestinationsstreits (851–855) (Stuttgart, 1999).

'Ein Blick in Pseudoisidors Werkstatt. Studien zum Entstehungsprozeß der falschen Dekretalen' *Francia, 28* (2001), pp. 37–90.

'Auf Pseudisidors Spur. Oder: Versuch, einen dichten Schleier zu lüften' in: Hartmann and Schmitz (2002), *Fortschritt durch Fälschungen?*, pp. 1–28.

Zeumer, K., 'Über die älteren fränkischen Formelsammlungen' *Neues Archiv, 6* (1881), pp. 9–115.

Zöllner, W., *Karl oder Widukind? Martin Lintzel und die NS- "Geschichtsdeutung" in den Anfangsjahren der faschistischen Diktatur* (Halle, 1975), Wissenschaftliche Beiträge der Martin-Luther-Universität Halle-Wittenberg 10/T9.

GENERAL INDEX

Abd ar-Rahman II, emir of Cordoba, 50
Adalhard of Fleury, *Ex Miraculis Sancti Benedicti*, 86, 92, 105
Adventius, bishop of Metz, 169, 170, 182–5
advocates, 142, *see also* Autramnus
affatomie, 128
Agilolfingdukes, 118
Agobard of Lyons, 163
Adversum Gundobardum, 13
Alcuin, 94–5, 106
Disputatio de Rhetorica, 94, 244
alienation of land, 39
to the Church, 116
Altfrid, *Vita Liudgerii*, 53, 55, 57, 60, 77
Annales Bertiniani, 48–50
Annales Fuldenses, 58
Annales Laureshamenses, 24, 25
Annales Regni Francorum, ARF, 66, 76, 102, 162
Annales Xantenses, 19, 20, 22, 29, 162
Astronomer, 104, 162
Autramnus, lay advocate, 132, 217

bannum, 31, 33, 115, 119, 135
Bede, *Ecclesiastical History*, 54
Betuwe, 37, 40, 190
bipartite estate, 41

Capitula Episcoporum, 161, 165
of Issac of Langres and Herard of Tours, 164
capitularies
capitularies adding to the *leges*, 97–154
'capitulary treatment', 153
monastic, 137
typology, 97–9
Chamavian Franks, 30
Charlemagne
and Bavaria, 118–20, 135
and codification of Saxon law, 61–2
and reform of the laws, 85
imperial coronation, 23–5, 106, 119
Charles the Bald, King, 90, 96, 86, 96, 100, 109, 115, 147
lawmaking, 87, 88
Charles the Fat, Emperor, 182
charters, in Saxony, 63
Christian Roman emperors, as a model for the Carolingians, 84, 87, 88, 91, 96
Chrodebert of Tours, 243
Clovis, king, 3, 13
Cobbo, count, 53, 60
Cologne, 18–20, 22, 134, 188
consensus, 6, 13, 36, 51, 92, 97, 98, 115, 123, 129, 130, 153, 190, 224, 250
consuetudo, 49
Corvey, 42, 61–3, 72, 73, 81
Council of Tribur, 66–8, 179

death penalty, 58, 62, 74, 78–81

Ebbo of Rheims, 161–4, 168
Echternach, monastery, 37
edhilingui, 50
Einhard, 50, 134, 182, 183, 201
Vita Karoli, 24, 25, 61, 66, 102
ethnic identity, 9, 13–23, 32–45, 59–62, 64–8, 83
Eutropius, *Breviarium*, 90
ewa, 30, 69

fiscalinus, 121, 142
Florus of Lyons, 244
forgery
and Regino, 173–5
of capitularies, 165
Franci homines, 32–5
Franco of Liège, 190
Frankish identity, 9, 34, *see also* Salian Franks; Ripuarian Franks
the term 'Frank', 10
Freculf of Lisieux, *Chronicon*, 51, 88
fredus, 31, 33, 78

Fridugis, chancellor, 194, 200, 201, 244, 246
Fulda, 37, 58
Annals, *see Annales Fuldenses*

Gerward, librarian, 200
Gottschalk of Orbais, 64–7, 93

hagiography, *vitae* of missionaries, 52, 62
Hamaland, 30, 40
Heliand, 57
Hildesheim, 164
Hincmar of Rheims, 79–81, 95, 104, 142, 149, 162, 223
attitude to capitularies, 95, 105
Hirminmaris, scribe, 200, 201
Historische Rechtsschule, 1, 11, 23
homicide, 43, 122, 159
in a church, 157
of clerics, 156–68
homo regius, 121
Hrabanus Maurus, 64–6, 73, 93, 145
De oblatione puerorum, 64

Indiculus obsidum saxonum mogentium deducendorum, 76
inheritance, 32, 35, 39, 40, 74, 81, 93, 122, 244
Isidore of Seville, *Etymologiae*, 114, 195, 198, 228–31, 251

Jonas of Orléans, 67, 91–4
De Institutione Regia, 91–4

Königsrecht, 2, 16, 30, 33, 97, 98
king list, Frankish, 231

Laon, 182
Le Mans forgeries, 17
leges-scriptorium, 85, 117, 148, 149, 193–247
legislator, 24, 60–2
leodis, leudes, 130, 159
lex
choice of, 50–2
semantic field, 49
litus, 42, 43, 74, 75, 121
Liudger, missionary, 53
Vita Gregorii, 55
Lorsch, 37
cartulary, 201
Lothar I, Emperor, 20, 47, 48, 159, 164
Lothar II, King, 20, 47, 170
Louis the German, King, 20, 47, 48, 96, 164, 188, 191
Louis the Pious, Emperor, 90, 104
833-4 rebellion against, 161
chancery, 200–2
letter to Hetti of Trier, 160
Lupus of Ferrières, 92, 93
Liber Legum, 86, 107, 167, 246, 249
Lyons, 244

mallum (publicum), 113, 122
manumission, 31, 32, 168–92
by penny-throw, 169
by charter, 32
charters of, 188–91
hantrada, 32
in *Lex Ribuaria*, 169
in Roman law, 184
of priests, 188
of those about to be ordained, 174–9
'to the church', 188
marriage, 66–8, 127
McKitterick, Rosamond, historian, 4, 87, 91, 103, 148, 164, 193, 194, 197, 199, 200, 206, 212, 244, 246
Metz, 131, 169
minor *leges*, 11, 23
missi, 30, 33, 52, 142
monasticisation, 35, 45

Nithard, 48–50

oaths, 48, 116, 121, 122
Odo, king, 182
Old Testament kings, as models for the Carolingians, 86, 87, 90, 115
Oosterbeek, 39
ordo, 25, 91, 115, 120
Otgar of Mainz, 164
Ottonian government, 47

Paschasius Radbertus, 163
Epitaphium Arsenii, 93
Paul the Deacon, *Historia Romana*, 90
perjury, 70, 116, 142
personality principle, 11–13, 66, 68, 69, 223
Poeta Saxo, 61–2
Prüm, 159
precarium, 243
professio iuris, 12
proprietary church, 160
Prudentius of Troyes, 49
Pseudo-Isidorian Decretals, 163–5, 168, 173

Regino of Prüm, *Chronicon*, 191
Reichenau, library catalogue, 101, 245
Rheims, 28, 131, 132, 147, 149, 151, 162, 164
'Rheims group' of legal manuscripts, 105, 131, 132, 142, 149–52, 156, 160
Ripuarian Franks, Ribuarian Franks, Rheinfranken, 16–23

Roman law, 87
  in the capitularies, 165
  'law of the Church', 223
Rudolph of Fulda, *Translatio Alexandri*, 53, 57–62

Salian Franks, 13–15
Satraps, 54, 55
scabini, 113, 142
Sedulius Scottus, 90
Sens, 131
servi
  beneficarii, 129–30
  dominici, 135
  ecclesiastici, 129–30
  promotion to sacred orders, 159
slaves, *see servi*
Smaragdus, *Via Regia*, 90
St Bavo, Ghent, 134
St Gallen, library catalogue, 102
St Servatius, Maastricht, 182
Stammesrecht, *see Volksrecht*
Stellinga, 47–50, 75
Stephen, Count, 109–15
Stephen, King of Hungary, 140

tabularius, 171, 173
terra salica, 14
Thegan, *Gesta Hludovici*, 161–3
Theodosius I, Emperor, 88
Theodosius II, Emperor, 88
Theodulf of Orléans, 106
Theoto, chancellor, 200
tironian notes, 201–2
Tours, 182
  bibles, 244
  legal activity in, 231–45
  manuscripts associated with, 198
  relationship with the *leges*-scriptorium, 199–202
Toxandria, 34
Trier, 182

Utrecht, 37

Vergangenheitsbewältigung, 52, 60, 66
Vita Lebuini Antiqua, 53–8
Volksrecht, 2, 13, 16, 29–30, 33, 97–8, 129

Walahfrid Strabo, 163
Werden, 19, 58
  polyptych, 40
wergeld
  of clerics, 166
wergeld, 106, 116, 121, 156, 161, 168
  of clerics, 156–9, 161
widows, 116, 127
Widukind of Corvey, 72
Widukind, Saxon leader, 39, 58
Wormald, Patrick, historian, 3–5, 9, 10, 32, 34, 84, 85, 87, 97, 103, 120, 137, 197, 223, 248, 250

Xanten, 29
  Annals of, *see Annales Xantenses*

Zwentibold, King, 188, 190, 191

INDEX OF LEGAL TEXTS

Capitularies
- Ansegis, *collectio capitularium*, 39, 69, 72, 95, 104, 149–51, 156, 160, 163, 165, 171, 174, 178, 192, 198, 208, 222, 246, 249, 251
- Benedictus Levita, *collectio capitularium*, 104, 105, 113, 122, 155, 163–8, 198
- Capit. I no. 20, 209
- Capit. I no. 20a, 141
- Capit. I no. 22 *Admonitio Generalis*, 87, 115, 141
- Capit. I no. 26 *Capitulatio de partibus Saxoniae*, 49
- Capit. I no. 27, *Capitulare Saxonicum*, 49, 51–2, 76
- Capit. I no. 34, 114
- Capit. I no. 39 *Capitulare Legibus Additum*, 70, 71, 99, 106, 126, 141, 143–6, 166, 217
- Capit. I no. 40, 69, 100, 108–12, 126, 141, 142, 181, 217
- Capit. I no. 41 *Capitulare Legi Ribuariae Additum*, 71, 99, 121–7, 136, 141, 143–6, 153
- Capit. I no. 44, 141, 142
- Capit. I no. 49, 69
- Capit. I no. 56, 124
- Capit. I no. 68 *Capitula ad Legem Baiuwariorum Addita*, 99, 118–21, 126, 135, 141, 143–6, 191
- Capit. I no. 103, 100, 156, 166
- Capit. I no. 134 *Capitula Legi Addita*, 70, 99, 141, 133–49
- Capit. I no. 135 *Item Capitula Legi Addita*, 70, 99, 133, 134, 141, 143–6
- Capit. I no. 136, 208
- Capit. I no. 137, 208, 209
- Capit. I no. 138, 159, 176, 181, 208, 209
- Capit. I no. 139 *Capitula Legibus Addenda*, 99, 101, 105, 115–17, 128, 141, 143–6, 149, 153, 156, 166, 205–12
- Capit. I no. 139 *Capitula Legibus Addenda*, Old High German translation, 105
- Capit. I no. 140, 160, 206–8
- Capit. I no. 141, 206, 208
- Capit. I no. 142 *Capitula Legi Salicae Addita*, 99, 101, 105, 121, 127–33, 135, 141, 143–6, 149, 153, 253–5
- Capit. I no. 143, 101, 117, 204–5, 208
- Capit. I no. 144, 148, 208
- Capit. I no. 145, 208
- Capit. I no. 167, 150
- Capit. I no. 170, 137, 141, 142
- Capit. I no. 191, 141, 142
- Capit. I no. 192, 141, 142
- Capit. I no. 193, 141, 142
- Capit. II no. 273 *Edictum Pitense*, 88
- *Capitula adhuc Conferenda*, 103, 134–5, 223

Formulae
- *Formulae Arvernenses*, 176
- *Formulae Codicis Laudunensis*, 181
- *Formulae Extravagantes*, 181, 185
- *Formulae Imperiales*, 181–6, 200, 202, 227
- *Formulae Marculfi*, 127, 202, 233, 243, 195
- *Formulae Salicae Merkelianae*, 181, 182
- *Formulae Turonenses*, 195, 222, 228, 231, 246

Leges
- *Ewa ad Amorem*, 13, 26, 29–45, 53, 56, 83
- *Lex Alemannorum*, 73, 156, 166, 167, 187, 195, 198, 203, 210–12, 221, 245
  - influence on *Lex Frisionum*, 26
  - textual groups, 217–18
- *Lex Baiuwariorum*, 43, 118–19, 126, 155, 165, 166, 167, 192, 195, 198, 247
  - influence on *Ewa ad Amorem*, 27, 28
  - *Lex Baiuwariorum Canonice Compta*, 167
  - textual groups, 218–22
- *Lex Burgundionum*, 209, 216, 222
- *Lex Frisionum*, 13, 26

Lex Ribuaria, 13, 26, 27, 45, 73, 77, 83, 116, 121–7, 134, 135, 148, 155, 156, 166, 167, 170–212, 216, 221, 245
  A text, 157, 211
  B text, 157, 158, 160, 211
  influence on later *leges*, 26, 27, 68
  manumission, 169
  origins, applicability, ethnicity, 16–23
Lex Salica, 3, 13, 70, 73, 126, 127–33, 148, 151, 155, 166, 190, 195, 198, 199, 203, 211, 221, 245
  and ethnicity, 13–15
  E text, 156, 194, 197, 215–16, 245
  K text, 156, 194, 197, 199, 212–17, 245, 246, 255–61
  prologues, 15
  Recapitulatio solidorum, 124, 215
Lex Saxonum, 11, 13, 26, 49, 50, 61, 63, 67, 69, 70, 83
  dating, 71, 76
Lex Thuringorum, 13, 26
Lex Visigothorum, 195

Roman law
  Codex Theodosianus, 179, 184
  Epitome Aegidii, 81, 148, 195, 197, 203, 224–6, 231–68
  Epitome Iuliani, 224–5, 246
  Lex Romana Burgundionum, 222
  Lex Romana Canonice Compta, 224
  Lex Romana Visigothorum, 179, 182, 184, 195, 197, 203, 222, 224, 226–7, 231, 246

Other
  Regino of Prüm, *Libri Duo de Synodalibus Causis*, 155, 156, 169–92

INDEX OF MANUSCRIPTS

Autun 36, 256
Avranches 145, 143, 149

Bamberg Can. 12, 149
Berlin Lat. Fol. 626, 143, 149
Berlin Lat. Q. 150, 195–7, 226
Berlin Phil. 1736, 111, 122, 143, 199, 215
Berlin Phil. 1737, 143, 171, 207
Berlin Phil. 1762, 149–51
Berlin Phil. 3899, 256
Berne 83, 231
Berne 263, 229, 230
Berne 256
Besançon 1348, 256

Cambrai 625, 109, 110, 143
Cava dei Tirreni 4, 112, 133, 143, 206, 207
Cologny Bodmer 107, 112, 143, 220, 256

Florence Laur. 77.1, 256

Geneva 50, 256
Gotha Memb. I 84, 107, 110, 133, 143, 207
Graz III 37,2, 221

Hamburg 141a in scrino, 72, 211
Heligenkreuz 217, 143

Ivrea XXXIII, 110, 133, 143, 207
Ivrea XXXIV, 110, 133, 143, 207

Kopenhagen Gl. Kgl. Saml. 1943, 115, 143, 205, 207, 209, 216, 256

Leiden BPL 114, 199, 263
Leiden UB 191, 263
Leiden Voss. Lat. O. 92, 181
Leiden Voss. Lat. Q. 119, 111, 143, 198, 214, 218, 222, 230, 251, 263
London Add. 22398, 110, 143, 256
London Add. 47676, 263
London Cotton Tiberius c.xi, 19
London Egerton 269, 26, 72, 76, 78, 133, 139, 143, 206, 207
London Egerton 2832, 111, 133, 139, 143, 206, 207
Lyons 375(303), 256

Merseburg, BDS 100, 181
Milan 668, 224
Milan BA A. 46, 263
Modena O. I. 2, 110, 144
Montpellier H 136, 107, 111, 144, 194, 199, 207
München Lat. 3519, 118, 119, 144
München Lat. 3853, 112, 119, 144
München Lat. 4115, 157, 158, 172, 211
München Lat. 4460, 119, 133, 144, 207
München Lat. 4639, 118
München Lat. 5260, 118, 144
München Lat. 19415, 110, 118, 119, 144
München Lat. 19416, 110, 144
München Univ. Bibl. 6, 231
München Univ. Bibl. 8 132, 167
Münster msc. VII 5201, 26, 72, 81, 144, 207

Nürnberg 110 447b/47, 144
Nürnberg Cent. V, App. 96, 110, 144, 256

Paris, Bibliothèque Nationale
  BN Baluze 94, 144
  BN Lat. 2123, 228, 231
  BN Lat. 2318, 263

BN Lat. 2718, 115, 117, 144, 148, 181, 182, 195–8, 200–7, 209, 223, 227, 246
BN Lat. 3182, 109, 110, 144, 256
BN Lat. 3851, 110, 144
BN Lat. 4280A, 144, 207
BN Lat. 4403A, 230
BN Lat. 4404, 108, 110, 145, 198, 232, 238
BN Lat. 4406, 226
BN Lat. 4408, 195, 196, 226, 227, 229, 230, 242, 263
BN Lat. 4409, 199, 215, 216, 226, 228, 230, 231, 263, 268
BN Lat. 4414, 230
BN Lat. 4415, 230
BN Lat. 4416, 195–7, 226, 234, 235, 237, 262, 267
BN Lat. 4417, 145, 211, 213, 216, 218, 221, 222, 226, 231, 263, 268
BN Lat. 4418, 195–7, 209, 210, 213–16, 224–6, 256, 263, 267, 268
BN Lat. 4568, 224
BN Lat. 4613, 107, 112, 145
BN Lat. 4614, 209, 216, 218, 221, 222
BN Lat. 4626, 109, 112, 114, 145, 207, 263
BN Lat. 4627, 199
BN Lat. 4628, 111, 114, 145, 206, 207, 211, 212, 217
BN Lat. 4628A, 26, 29, 109, 110, 131–3, 145, 149, 150, 207
BN Lat. 4629, 108, 111, 122, 123, 145, 199, 215
BN Lat. 4630, 256
BN Lat. 4631, 26, 114, 131–3, 145, 149, 208, 256
BN Lat. 4632, 111, 131–3, 145, 208, 211, 217, 253
BN Lat. 4633, 133, 206, 207, 210, 216, 263
BN Lat. 4636, 198
BN Lat. 4638, 149
BN Lat. 4758, 110, 145, 210
BN Lat. 4759, 218, 221, 222, 256
BN Lat. 4759B, 187
BN Lat. 4760, 109, 112, 114, 145, 208
BN Lat. 4787, 256
BN Lat. 4788, 111, 145, 208, 256
BN Lat. 4827, 194
BN Lat. 4995, 107, 111, 113, 114, 145, 167, 206, 208
BN Lat. 9652, 226
BN Lat. 9653, 145, 208, 213, 230
BN Lat. 9654, 26, 29, 30, 32, 111, 124, 131, 145, 171, 173, 218, 221, 222
BN Lat. 9656, 256
BN Lat. 10753, 111, 145, 207, 211
BN Lat. 10754, 109, 110, 145, 256
BN Lat. 10756, 195, 196
BN Lat. 10758, 109, 112, 114, 131–3, 145, 149–51, 234, 253
BN Lat. 10765, 228
BN Lat. 11379, 181, 182
BN Lat. 12448, 224
BN Lat. 18237, 145, 198, 207, 218, 222, 229, 230, 257
BN Lat. 18238, 146, 207
BN nouv. acq. Lat. 200, 204, 116, 117, 146, 148, 195, 196, 204, 206, 208, 216, 218, 221, 225, 227, 256, 262

Rome Ottob. 3081, 256
Rome Vallicelliana C 20, 221

Sélestat 14 (104), 111, 131–3, 146, 149, 151, 208, 253
St Gallen 727, 151
St Gallen 728, 109, 110, 146
St Gallen 729, 195, 196, 198, 215–17, 262
St Gallen 731, 199
St Gallen 732, 218, 222
St Gallen Stadtbib. 338, 210, 211, 216
St Paul im Lavanttal 4/1, 110, 125, 133, 146, 208, 210, 218, 220, 222, 263
St Petersburg Q. v. II. 11, 112, 146
Stuttgart Jur. Q. 134, 146, 208, 218, 222
Stuttgart Württ. LB iur. qu. 134, 263

Turin D V 19, 230

Vatican, Biblioteca apostolica
Vat. Chigi F. IV. 75, 133, 146, 206, 208
Vat. Ottob./Vat. Lat. 7277, 226, 227, 232
Vat. Ottob. 313 f. 111, 114
Vat. Pal. Lat. 243, 231
Vat. Reg. Lat. 263, 142
Vat. Reg. Lat. 338, 146, 208, 211, 215, 216, 256
Vat. Reg. Lat. 417, 151
Vat. Pal. Lat. 582, 124, 146, 171, 173
Vat. Reg. Lat. 612, 181
Vat. Pal. Lat. 773, 71, 111, 126, 146
Vat. Reg. Lat. 846, 195, 196, 209, 215, 216, 228–31, 242, 262
Vat. Reg. Lat. 852, 195–7, 203, 228, 237, 263
Vat. Reg. Lat. 857, 195, 196, 218, 226–8, 239, 240, 243, 256, 263
Vat. Reg. Lat. 991, 118, 146, 148, 157, 195, 196, 200, 202, 203, 210, 214, 216, 218, 221, 246, 256, 260, 263
Vat. Reg. Lat. 1036, 146
Vat. Reg. Lat. 1048, 230
Vat. Reg. Lat. 1050, 111, 146, 218, 222, 256

Vatican, Biblioteca apostolica (*cont.*)
Vat. Reg. Lat. 1128, 218, 222, 242, 256
Vat. Reg. Lat. 1431, 195, 196, 198, 256
Vat. Reg. Lat. 1728, 146, 256

Warsaw BU 1 (Q. 480), 195–7, 215, 226–30, 232, 233, 237, 242, 262, 263
Wien ÖNB 406, 146
Wien ÖNB 502, 126
Wolfenbüttel Aug. 4 50.2, 109, 110, 146, 208, 256
Wolfenbüttel Blank. 130, 112, 117, 126, 146, 204, 206, 208, 218, 220, 222, 256
Wolfenbüttel Gud. Lat. 299, 109, 133, 146, 256
Wolfenbüttel Gud. Lat. 327, 256
Wolfenbüttel Helmst. 532, 119